THE CHURCHES AND THE CHURCH

A Study of Ecumenism

THE CHURCHES
AND THE CHURCH

A Study of Ecumenism

developed from

THE LAURISTON LECTURES FOR 1957

by

BERNARD LEEMING, S. J.

Professor of Dogmatic Theology at Heythrop College

LONDON
DARTON, LONGMAN & TODD

WESTMINSTER, MD
THE NEWMAN PRESS

DARTON, LONGMAN & TODD LTD
29A GLOUCESTER ROAD
LONDON SW7

THE NEWMAN PRESS
WESTMINSTER, MD

First published 1960

The Lauriston Lectures, under the patronage of His Grace the Archbishop of St Andrews and Edinburgh, are delivered annually at the Lauriston Hall, Edinburgh, on a subject of religious interest.

Printed in Great Britain by William Clowes and Sons, Ltd, London and Beccles. De licentia superiorum ordinis: John Coventry, S.J., Praep. Prov. Angl. Soc. Jesu, 11 Novembris 1959. Gulielmus F. Maloney, S.J., Praep. Prov. Marylandiae, datum Baltimorensi, 16 Junii 1958. Nihil obstat: Carolus Davis, S.T.L. Imprimatur: E. Morrogh Bernard. Vic. Gen. Westmonasterii, die 28 Decembris, 1959. The nihil obstat and imprimatur are a declaration that a book or pamphlet is considered to be free from doctrinal or moral error. It is not implied that those who have granted the nihil obstat and imprimatur agree with the contents, opinions or statements expressed.

CONTENTS

INTRODUCTION

The last fifty years have seen an almost revolutionary change in the non-Catholic religious world. An intense realization has grown up that the existing disunity among Christians is contrary to Christ's will and is a serious impediment to the spread of Christianity. There are now over 300 'Churches' and in Africa there are some 1,300 Christian 'sects': such a number of differing presentations of Christianity inevitably confuses non-Christians, frustrates many efforts to maintain and spread the Christian faith, and is manifestly contrary to the will of Christ.[1]

'All Christians must unite. No longer must there be "Churches", but only one universal Church.' Such declarations have become frequent among all varieties of Christian affiliation. The effort to overcome divisions and to bring unity may be spoken of as 'the ecumenical movement', which has brought changes in religious thinking comparable to the changes caused by the 'Reformation' of the sixteenth century.

This book tries to give an account of this movement towards unity. The task, however, is difficult for many reasons. First, there is the complexity of the movement, which has occasioned, as Iremonger says, 'almost countless organizations, societies and conferences', making it hard 'even for those most familiar with the ramifications to avoid being lost in a tangle of parallel organizations' which seem almost like a forest primeval.[2] The formation of the World Council of Churches in 1948 to some extent simplifies the task, but the ecumenical movement is by no means identified with the World Council and considerable difficulty remains. Secondly, there is the development which has taken place in the movement, which renders judgement about it based upon the situation in 1927 or 1937 completely out of date. Thirdly, the movement is literally such: it is not

[1] Cf. *Relations between Anglican and Presbyterian Churches, Being a Joint Report presented by Representatives of The Church of England, The Church of Scotland, The Episcopal Church in Scotland, The Presbyterian Church of England*, January, 1957, p. 13.
[2] F. A. Iremonger, *William Temple, Archbishop of Canterbury, His Life and Letters* London, 1948, p. 389.

a fixed and stable profession of faith or programme of action, but a moving tide of enquiry and search with cross-currents in it, backwaters, ebbing waters and sometimes whirlpools. Fourthly, it is not easy to know to what extent the leaders represent the people, and the theologians the man in the pew; it would be unrealistic to deny that sometimes at least the thought of the leaders is in advance of that of the mass of the ordinary people, as seems to be the case of the theologians who drew up the *Report on Relations between Anglican and Presbyterian Churches*. At the same time it would be equally unrealistic to judge the movement merely by its theology or to underestimate the spirit which the movement fosters and which may slowly be permeating the mass.

Lastly there are different judgements about the movement as a whole, and about particular manifestations of it, such as the Church of South India and the proposed 'integration' of the World Council of Churches with the International Missionary Council.

The literature is enormous and increases almost daily. Books and articles pour out from the presses and to keep abreast of them all would be a life's work.

A friend, hearing that I was writing about the subject, said to me: 'You will do no good. The Catholic faithful have no need to know about the opinions of non-Catholics: let them say their prayers and lead a holy life. This is their best contribution towards Christian unity. Nor will you do any good with non-Catholics. You will be either conciliatory and mislead them or you will be blunt and offend them. In any case they will think that you are in some way "proselytizing", that is, trying to make Roman Catholics of them and they will resent it. Better leave the whole matter alone.'

But in fact Catholics hear a good deal about the ecumenical movement. University students have asked about it and some have not understood the attitude of the Church towards it. Newspapers, periodicals, the radio and television bring the subject to notice, and fragmentary or confused knowledge can lead to mistaken judgements or attitudes. I have heard expressed what I think are mistaken opinions about the World Council of Churches and about the Roman Catholic outlook

towards it. It is certain that many non-Catholics do not understand the attitude of the Church, and it is almost equally
certain that many do not understand the real nature and aims
of the Council itself.

Père Boyer speaks soberly when he says: 'There may be
different opinions about the excellence of the World Council;
but it must be recognized and all Catholics ought to realize
that with it a new force has arisen and it would be unwise not
to take account of it.'[1]

This book accepts as the correct attitude for a Catholic that
of the Roman Unitas Association, which 'across the imperfections of men, tries to make evident that spirit of fraternal
affection and faithfulness to the teachings of Christ which is at
the very heart of the Church's life and the manifestation of
the Holy Spirit at work in her. *Unitas* keeps in close touch with
the Ecumenical Movement and endeavours to aid it in its
quest for unity.' That aim is hard to fulfil, for it is hard to
combine fraternal affection with expression of different religious convictions. It is easy to fail to affirm what ought to be
affirmed and easy to give offence without intending it. My
aim, writing as a convinced Roman Catholic, has been to give
the facts as far as is possible and let them speak for themselves.
For this reason many citations are given and in the Appendices
are printed several documents not easily available: the declaration of the aims of the Roman Unitas Association, the
Instruction of the Holy Office in 1949, the Pastoral Letter of
the Dutch Bishops in 1948, and the *Statement* of the Central
Committee of the World Council of Churches made at Toronto
in 1950, which is perhaps the most fundamental of all the
documents issued under the auspices of the World Council.

A search for unity is surely preferable to hopeless acceptance
of existing divisions among Christians, even though that search
does not immediately discover where alone true unity exists
and where alone it can be found. This book does not disguise
the ambiguities and the prejudices which surround the ecumenical movement; but neither does it disguise my belief that

[1] 'On peut différer d'opinion sur l'excellence du Conseil oecuménique; mais
on doit reconnaître et tous le catholiques devraient savoir qu'avec lui a surgi une
force nouvelle dont il serait peu sage de ne pas tenir compte.' 'Sur la théologie du
conseil oecuménique', *Gregorianum*, xxxv, 1954, p. 593.

very, very many among our separated brethren are guided by the most disinterested motives and that their search has lessened many prejudices and opened many eyes to a new vision of Christ's Church. If this book succeeds in helping even a little it will have fulfilled its purpose.

I have to thank the Rev. James Christie, S.J., and the Catholic Truth Society of the Archdiocese of St Andrews and Edinburgh for inviting me to give the Lauriston Lectures for 1957, and the Edinburgh audience whose sympathetic interest was an encouragement to develop the lectures.

I owe a deep debt of gratefulness to the Rt Rev. George P. Dwyer, Bishop of Leeds, to the Rev. Douglas Carter, of Coventry, to the Rev. Dr J. Robert Nelson, Dean of Vanderbilt Divinity School and former Secretary of the Commission on Faith and Order of the World Council of Churches, and to several of my Jesuit colleagues, all of whom read the manuscript and gave me invaluable advice. They are, of course, in no way responsible for anything said in the book. I am very grateful also to Dr Norman Goodall, for invaluable information about the complex organization of the International Missionary Council.

My very sincere thanks are due to my Publishers, to their readers, and to their editorial staff, who have spared no trouble to ensure the satisfactory production of the book.

ACKNOWLEDGMENTS

Grateful acknowledgment of permission to quote extracts of copyright material is made to the following:

The Very Rev. Charles Boyer, editor: *Unitas*. Burns Oates & Washbourne Ltd: 'Faith and Dissident Christians' by Rev. Charles Davis (*Clergy Review*, Apr. 1959). James Clarke & Co. Ltd: *The Story of Church Union in Scotland* by J. R. Fleming. Faber & Faber Ltd: *Congregationalism* by D. Jenkins; *Revelation* ed. J. Baillie and H. Martin. Miss Margaret Sinclair, editor: *International Review of Missions*. The S.C.M. Press Ltd: *The Nature of the Church* ed. R. N. Flew; *Intercommunion* ed. D. M. Baillie and J. Marsh; *The Reunion of the Church* by Lesslie Newbigin; *Ways of Worship* ed. P. Edwall and others; *The Second World Conference on Faith and Order* ed. L. Hodgson, 'Report on Amsterdam' and 'Evanston Speaks'. The S.C.M. Press Ltd. and The United States Conference for the World Council of Churches: 'The Church'; 'Report on the Lund Faith and Order Conference'. The S.C.M. Press Ltd. and The Friendship Press Inc: *The Household of God* by Lesslie Newbigin. The Managers of the *Tablet*: the *Instruction* of the Holy Office. The Rev. Professor Thomas F. Torrance, editor: *Scottish Journal of Theology*. The Rt Rev. and Rt Hon. J. W. C. Wand, editor: *Church Quarterly Review*. Dr W. A. Visser 't Hooft, General Secretary of The World Council of Churches: 'Many Images of the One Church' by R. R. Nelson (*Ecumenical Review*, Jan. 1957); and for various publications of the World Council. The Independent Press Ltd: *Free Churchmanship in England 1870–1940 with special reference to Congregationalism* by J. W. Grant.

Chapter One

THE ECUMENICAL MOVEMENT

1. Unification of Various Religious Organizations

Speaking very broadly, the ecumenical movement is an effort to unite all Christians both in belief and in organization. The principal leaders in the movement have been members of the Anglican and the 'Protestant' communions, although the Eastern and Slav Orthodox have taken part in discussions, and many Roman Catholics have followed the movement with interest and sympathy. The word 'ecumenical' has come to have a slightly new meaning: of old it meant simply 'universal' and the Roman Empire was called 'ecumenical', signifying that it was universal. The expression 'Ecumenical Council' is familiar, meaning a Council of the universal Church. But latterly the word has come to have an overtone of 'unity', of a tendency to accord and agreement; and the 'ecumenical movement' means the impulse and the effort to promote agreement and unity among all Christians.[1] An 'ecumenical outlook' seems to carry with it the suggestion not only of regard to what is universal but also of a conciliatory and friendly attitude.

Although, of course, Christian history shows that there have always been those who laboured to heal schisms and heresies, nevertheless this movement is comparatively new—new, at least, in its extent and in its results. But it is a 'movement' and ought not to be exclusively identified with the World Council of Churches, which is, indeed, one of its most conspicuous results, but which is rather the effect of the movement than its essence; the movement extends outside the World Council of Churches, and this latter was produced by the same causes

[1] Cf. the admirable note on the use of the word by Dr William Adolf Visser 't Hooft, in *A History of the Ecumenical Movement*, edited by Ruth Rouse and Stephen Charles Neill, London, 1954, pp. 735–41.

which worked towards unification of Churches.[1] For instance, the negotiations which went on from 1900 or so in Scotland towards the unification of Presbyterians and issued in the union of the United Free Church with the Church of Scotland may truly be called 'ecumenical', although quite outside the machinery of what is now the World Council; and the same is true of several unions among Churches of similar traditions, for instance, the union of the American Northern Baptist Convention with the Free Baptist Churches, in 1911, and of the English Methodists in 1931. But the 'ecumenical movement' may in some sense be called a spirit, an atmosphere, even an effort, rather than a definable and definite entity.

What Has the Movement Done?

It is not a movement confined only to the Churches, for it has succeeded in uniting, in various degrees, not only churches but also a whole complexity of organizations of a religious nature. One may divide these organizations into three main classes:

(*a*) Different organizations, not Churches, engaged in practical applications of Christianity.

(*b*) Churches as such, united in the World Council of Churches.

(*c*) Federations or 'alliances' of Churches, not formally represented, save by their constituent member Churches, in the World Council of Churches.

A word about the first two.

(*a*) Organizations under a Christian influence whose aim is mainly social welfare or the practical application of Christianity. These would include The Young Men's Christian Association, the Young Women's Christian Association, and the World Alliance of these, the World Student Christian Federation, and the Student Christian Movement.

Somewhat similar to these, in that they are not strictly 'Churches', are organizations like the International Missionary Council, the Student Volunteer Movement, the Society for the Propagation of the Gospel in Foreign Parts, the International

[1] On the use of the word 'Churches' and the words 'Catholic', and 'Roman Catholic', cf. Appendix I, pp. 278-81.

Council of Religious Education, the United Bible Societies and various 'Councils', 'Commissions', 'Fellowships', or 'Federations' for purposes in which people from various denominations desire to co-operate.

All these—again speaking very broadly—coalesced in the general movement called Life and Work, which was an association of very many such organizations to co-ordinate their work and efforts.

At Edinburgh in 1910 was held The World Missionary Conference, at which a large number of representatives were present both from Churches and from organizations interested in fostering missions. Out of the associations there formed grew the International Missionary Council, the Conference at Geneva in 1920, the Conference for Life and Work at Stockholm in 1925, and at Oxford in 1937, at which latter were present some 300 delegates appointed by the Churches of 120 communions, and an equal number of observers and unofficial representatives. In 1938 the Universal Christian Council for Life and Work transferred its responsibilities and functions to the 'World Council of Churches in Process of Formation'.

This Life and Work movement was primarily interested not in doctrine but in practical work—in international relations and the attitude of Christians to war, to industrial conditions, to racial relations, to the alleviation of distress and similar practical matters. As the 'Message' issued at Stockholm put it, there is an obligation resting on the Churches 'to apply the Gospel in all realms of human life—industrial, social, political and international'.[1]

---

[1] *History of the Ecumenical Movement*, p. 547. Cf., also, William Richey Hogg, *Ecumenical Foundations, A History of the International Missionary Council and Its Nineteenth-Century Background*, New York, 1952. It is of interest to notice that the Executive Committee of the Ecumenical Missionary Conference decided in 1908 that 'only societies sending missionaries among non-Christian peoples' would be eligible for membership in the Edinburgh Conference of 1910. Hogg, p. 120, and cf. E. Stock, *The History of the Church Missionary Society*, London, 1916, iv, pp. 560–2. Professor K. S. Latourette in 'Ecumenical Bearings of the Missionary Movement and the International Missionary Council', R. Rouse and S. C. Neill, *A History of the Ecumenical Movement*, London, 1954, pp. 357, 396, called attention to the fact that: 'Efforts to win Christians from one form of Faith to another—as by some American denominations in the Continent of Europe, or among the ancient Churches in the Near East, or among the Roman Catholics of Latin America—were not in the purview of the Edinburgh World Mission Conference of 1910', from which the International Missionary Council originated.

(*b*) The Churches, as such, have arranged definite and settled co-operation among themselves in the World Council of Churches. This grew partly out of the contacts made in the Life and Work meetings, partly out of meetings of those interested in missions, and partly out of the Faith and Order Conferences. These last were assemblies of representatives from different Churches to discuss their doctrinal position and their manner of worship and government. The most famous of these meetings were: Lausanne, 1927; Edinburgh, 1937; Geneva, 1946; Amsterdam, 1948, at which was formed the World Council of Churches; and, after that, the meetings of Faith and Order at Lund in 1952; and the meeting of the World Council of Churches at Evanston, Illinois, U.S.A., in 1954. The Faith and Order meetings consider doctrine, although naturally not excluding some practical applications, especially in forms and ways of worship. In 1958, it was proposed that Faith and Order should be raised to the standing of a 'Division', which would increase its importance and its influence.

'The Death of our Denominations'

The World Council of Churches now includes in its membership some 170 Churches existing in 43 different nations and may be said to represent a major part of the non-Catholic Christianity of the world. It should be noted that the World Council of Churches embraces in its organization all the organizations which formed the Universal Christian Council for Life and Work.[1] The World Council, therefore, is not a 'super-Church'; it is an organization designed to foster consultation between Churches and other organizations which exist to promote the study of questions relating both to 're-union' and to the impact of Christianity on the world. At Amsterdam in 1948 Dr W. A. Visser 't Hooft, General Secretary of the World Council of Churches, said of the Council:

[1] Cf. the Amsterdam Report of 1948 concerning the exact relations between the World Council of Churches and the International Missionary Council, the World Confessional Councils, the World's Y.M.C.A., Y.W.C.A., the World Student Christian Federation and the United Bible Societies. Their relations are friendly and close, but the exact relation of the very important International Missionary Council to the World Council of Churches was not finally settled at Amsterdam, but since 1957 arrangements have been maturing for closer co-operation and even integration.

'What then is the true function of our Council? Our name gives us the clue to the answer. We are a Council of Churches, not *the* Council of one undivided Church. Our name indicates our weakness and our shame before God, for there can be and there *is* only one Church of Christ on earth. Our plurality is a deep anomaly. . . . Our Council represents therefore an emergency solution—a stage on the road.'[1] Indeed, the Secretary of the Lund Conference on Faith and Order, Dr O. S. Tomkins (subsequently Warden of the Bishop's Hostel, Lincoln, and now Bishop of Bristol), declared that the World Council exists in order to bring about its own dissolution. His words are these:

> By entering into this relationship with each other we have already willed the death of our denominations. That is what I meant by saying earlier that although the World Council is a Council of Denominations, because there are no other units with which it could work, it has already destroyed the justification of our denominations. The essence of denominationalism is to suppose the sufficiency of denominations: the essence of our covenant with each other is to deny that our denominations are enough. The peril of the World Council is that it might encourage the permanency of the units upon which it rests, and it is the peculiar vocation of Faith and Order to bear witness in every part of the Council's life that it has come into being only in order to die as a 'Council of Denominations'.[2]

Dr Tomkins, of course, does not mean to suggest a sudden abolition of denominations; but he does mean that the aim of the World Council is to help to the formation of one sole Church, in which there would be no need of a Council for meetings of representatives of different 'Churches'. Bishop S. C. Neill makes the same assertion even more forcibly: 'The final and terrible difficulty is that the Churches cannot unite, unless they are willing to die. In a truly united Church there would be no more Anglicans or Lutherans or Presbyterians or Methodists.'[3] The same conviction had been

[1] *The First Assembly of the World Council of Churches, the Official Report*, ed. W. A. Visser 't Hooft, London, 1949, p. 28.

[2] *The Third World Conference on Faith and Order, held at Lund, August 15 to 28, 1952*, ed. Oliver S. Tomkins, London, 1953, p. 167.

[3] *History of the Ecumenical Movement*, 'Plans of Union and Reunion, 1910–1948', p. 495. Bishop Neill refers, indeed, to 'these great and honoured names', and faces the difficulties involved.

expressed by the Rev. Peter Ainslie, a Disciple of Christ, at Lausanne in 1927: 'My denomination must grow less in my eyes if I am to grow more towards Christ. I am willing that my denomination shall be forgotten if thereby may be hastened the unity of the Church of Christ.'[1]

2. THE WORLD COUNCIL OF CHURCHES

The World Council has taken more than fifty years to form, and is the result of long experience and many consultations and much prayer. It has close relations with different organs of the United Nations, such as UNESCO (United Nations Educational, Scientific and Cultural Organization), and especially with the Refugee Office of the United Nations. In a sense, the World Council of Churches might be conceived as a kind of ecclesiastical United Nations, except that its aim, at least in the conviction of many prominent members, is to foster such union among denominations that there may ultimately be only one Christian Church. It has its headquarters at Geneva, with a permanent Secretariate, and various sub-divisions for different purposes, not least to study matters of doctrine, liturgy, Church history, method of evangelization, and diverse projects for reunions of Churches. The accompanying plan, p. 10, will indicate the outline of its organization.

The Nature of the World Council

The *Basis* of the World Council of Churches is acceptance 'of our Lord Jesus Christ as God and Saviour'. This acceptance of our Lord Jesus Christ as God and Saviour is not a mere formality, as appeared in a very interesting correspondence in *The Friend*, *The Quaker Weekly Journal*, continuing from March 6th to May 15, 1959, when the editor closed the correspondence. What emerged was that, though some Friends were favourable to closer association with the World Council, the balance of opinion was that the formula 'God and Saviour' was designed to exclude Socinians and Unitarians and various 'Free Christian Churches'. The membership is by 'Churches', which are judged to be such by evidence of 'autonomy',

---

[1] *Faith and Order, Proceedings of the World Conference, Lausanne*, 1927, p. 343.

'stability', reasonable size and proper relationship to other Christian bodies. This last might perhaps exclude some varieties of 'enthusiasts' who fail to observe due politeness or perhaps engage in acrimonious disagreement with other Churches.[1]

The *functions* of the World Council are as follows:

(i) To carry on the work of the two world movements of Faith and Order and Life and Work.

(ii) To facilitate common action by Churches.

(iii) To promote common action in study.

(iv) To promote the growth of ecumenical consciousness in the members of all Churches. (Therefore not exclusively in Churches which are members of the World Council.)

(v) To establish relations with denominational federations of world-wide scope and with other ecumenical movements.

(vi) To call world conferences on specific subjects as occasion may require, such conferences being empowered to publish their own findings.

(vii) To support the Churches in their task of evangelization.

The *spokesmen* of the World Council are:

(*a*) Ultimately the Assembly of all the member Churches, which drew up the Constitution and the Rules. It meets ordinarily every five years.

(*b*) The Central Committee, which numbers about one hundred members of the Assembly chosen by the Assembly. It meets once a year.

(*c*) The Executive Committee of the Central Committee, which numbers thirteen or fourteen. It meets ordinarily twice a year.

(*d*) The General Secretariate (General Secretary, Associate General Secretaries and Assistant General Secretaries) is a permanent body and its officials are permanent.

(*e*) The 'Staff' includes the General Secretariate and the Heads of Departments, such as those of Inter-Church Aid, the

---

[1] The Evangelical Church in Germany and the Swiss Protestant Church Federation are members, in spite of the fact that question might be raised about the 'autonomy' of these bodies with regard to their constituent members.

Ecumenical Institute at Château de Bossey, near Geneva, the missionary department, etc.

A sharp distinction must be made between the World Council of Churches and earlier 'Conferences', such as those at Lausanne in 1927 and at Edinburgh in 1937. In these Conferences 'agreed statements' were made by the participating representatives of the Churches; but the World Council of Churches beyond agreement upon its constitution, its basis and upon the 'staying together' and working for unity, does not make 'agreed statements' about doctrine. Most, if not all, pronouncements of the World Council take the form of Reports from a Committee which are 'received' by the Central Committee or by a subordinate Committee, and are 'commended for study and comment in the Churches'. The remark has been made by the General Secretary on Faith and Order that the member Churches, or many of them, do not send in any comment, though this does not necessarily indicate that the *Reports* or *Messages* have not in fact been studied by the Churches.[1] It would be a serious mistake to take the *Reports* as if they represented the judgements or opinions of the member Churches; they may, indeed, indicate trends of thought and perhaps convictions widely held, but they represent no more, except as they are approved by the member Churches.[2]

In 1950 the Central Committee meeting in Toronto made a most important statement about the implications of membership in the World Council. This is given in Appendix IV; the most significant declaration being that member Churches need not 'recognize other member Churches as Churches in

---

[1] *Commission on Faith and Order of the World Council of Churches, Minutes*, Evanston and Chicago, 1954, paper no. 21, p. 11.

[2] In 1950 the Central Committee of the World Council approved the action of the United Nations in 'meeting aggression and in authorizing a police measure' in Korea, but this approval by the Central Committee did not bind the member Churches. In November 1956 the Officers of the World Council, that is, the Chairman and Vice-Chairman and the General Secretary, issued statements calling attention to what the Churches 'had said together' about the use of force against the territorial integrity of any state, with clear reference to events in Egypt, and to what the Churches had said at Evanston about 'powerful nations removing the yoke which now prevents free determination of other nations' government and form of society', with reference to Hungary. Cf. *Ecumenical Review*, ix, no. 2, January, 1957, pp. 162–3. In 1955 and 1959 the Central Committee 'urged' and 'pleaded' for cessation of atomic tests, unilaterally if necessary, cf. *Ecumenical Review*, viii, October, 1955, pp. 66–8 and xi, April, 1959, pp. 308–9.

the true and full sense of the word'. Nevertheless, member Churches 'recognize in other Churches elements of the true Church. They consider that this mutual recognition obliges them to enter into serious conversation with each other in the hope that these elements of truth will lead to the recognition of the full truth and to unity based upon the full truth.'

Officially, then, the World Council of Churches is an organization for consultation and mutual enlightenment.

The World Council has met some opposition among non-Catholics, perhaps most conspicuously from the so-called International Council of Christian Churches, whose influence, however, is difficult to estimate. This 'Council' has voiced the following objections: that the World Council covers great doctrinal confusion under a façade of unity, denies the independence of the local Churches, seeks a unity 'modelled on that of the Roman Catholic Church which leads to clericalism, ritualism and intolerance', while at the same time the World Council is said to favour Communism and Modernism. Some of these objections are felt by other Protestant bodies, such as the Southern Baptist Convention of the United States, which have not joined the World Council.[1]

3. DIFFERENT 'UNIONS' AND 'FEDERATIONS' OF CHURCHES

Quite independently of the World Council of Churches, reunions, federations, alliances, and amalgamations have been formed between various Churches which had been completely autonomous and independent, if not self-sufficient. These form a somewhat complex pattern, but may be described as falling into three general classifications:

First, there are various 'organic unions' which have been formed by denominations of the same tradition, that is, by groups of Baptists, or of Congregationalists, or Lutherans, or Methodists, or Presbyterians, etc., Churches of the same

[1] Professor James Hastings Nichols, in *Evanston, An Interpretation*, New York, 1955, suggests that the International Council of Christian Churches is largely, if not solely, the work of one man, 'a deposed Presbyterian minister', p. 27. Chanoine G. Thils, *Histoire doctrinale du mouvement œcuménique*, Louvain, 1955, pp. 21–6, takes this International Council more seriously and seems justified by what Dr Norman Goodall says of its influence in Scandinavia, cf. 'Evangelicals and WCC-IMC', *International Review of Missions*, xlvii, April, 1958, pp. 210–15.

STRUCTURE OF THE WORLD COUNCIL OF CHURCHES

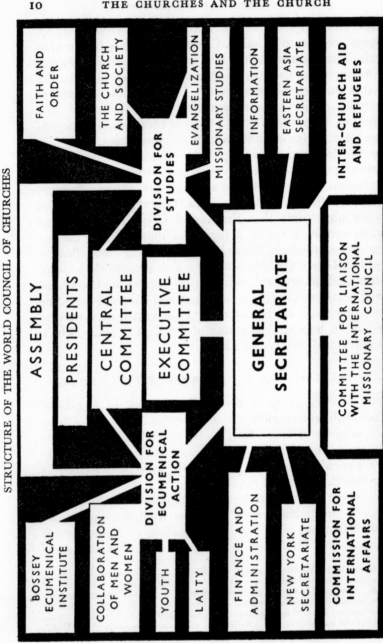

There are four 'Divisions', Ecumenical Action, Studies, International Affairs and Inter-Church Aid and Refugees. It has been suggested that Faith and Order be reconstituted as a distinct 'Division' and have a more important place in the structure of the World Council. The proposals, however, for changes in the organizational structure consequent upon the 'integration' of the World Council with the

general tradition, which differed from one another in some point or points of doctrine and in organization, came together to form only one 'Church', with one structure of 'Church order' and constitutional administration. Since 1911 there have been no less than fourteen of these organic unions formed, as, for instance, the union of the Church of Scotland and the United Free Church of Scotland in 1929; and they have taken place in England, the United States, Central Africa, Korea, Mexico, Holland, Brazil, Madagascar and Switzerland. The American Lutheran Church, which claims a membership of 900,000, in its autumn convention of 1956, voted to unite with the Evangelical Lutheran Church (1,000,000 members) and the United Evangelical Lutheran Church (55,000 adherents), though an absolutely final settlement of all questions of administration is not expected until 1960.

Secondly, there have been 'federal unions less than full organic union.'[1] The nature of these federations varies somewhat, but they generally involve arrangements in such matters as appointment of ministers, collaboration in training ministers, division of territories and common publications.

Thirdly, there have been what is called 'trans-confessional organic unions', that is, different denominations of different traditions coming together to form one organic Church. In 1925 in Canada the Presbyterians, Methodists and Congregationalists united to form the United Church of Canada; in India in 1924 the United Church of North India was formed, mainly from Churches and Missions of a Presbyterian tradition. Other such have been formed in the Philippine Islands, Puerto Rico, Thailand (Siam), Guatemala, France, Japan and in South India; up to 1948 about sixteen such complete unions have been achieved.

4. The Church of South India

The Church of South India is perhaps the most interesting of these, because it involves the union of an episcopal Church

[1] Bishop S. C. Neill lists all these up to 1948 in ch. 10 of *A History of the Ecumenical Movement*, entitled 'Plans of Union and Reunion 1910–1948', pp. 496–506. Dr J. R. Nelson completes the account down to 1956 in articles 'Survey of Church Union Negotiations', *Ecumenical Review*, viii, no. 1, October, 1955, pp. 76–93; and ix, no. 3, April, 1957.

with others whose tradition was against episcopacy. Anglicans, Congregationalists, Methodists and Presbyterians have formed one single Church. This union has caused great discussion, and is sometimes held up as a possible model for other unions. The *Report on Relations between Anglican and Presbyterian Churches*, of 1956, says: 'Even when full account is taken of the great difference between conditions in South India and in Britain, the achievement of Church Union in South India constitutes a challenge which cannot be ignored.' So some consideration of it is justified here.

The Constitution of the Church of South India, published by the Christian Literature Society for India, Madras, 1952, shows the following:

1. The doctrinal basis is simple: acceptance of the Holy Scriptures as containing all things necessary to salvation and as the supreme and decisive standard of faith; and of the Apostles' Creed and the Creed commonly called the Nicene, as witnessing to and safeguarding that faith. Two sacraments, Baptism and the Supper of the Lord, are 'means of grace through which God works in us'.[1] The Constitution does not assert that there are only two Sacraments, or even only two 'sacraments of the Gospel'. Provisions exist for ceremonies or 'ordinances' or procedures not unlike what Catholics and Orthodox call the sacraments of confirmation, penance, orders and marriage; but I have found no reference to the anointing of the sick. The bishop has authority to pronounce sentences of suspension from Holy Communion and to restore the penitent to the fellowship of the Church.

2. As regards the ordained ministry, 'the Church of South India accepts and will maintain the historic episcopate in a constitutional form. But this acceptance does not commit it to any particular interpretation of episcopacy or to any particular view or belief concerning orders of the ministry, and it will not require the acceptance of any such particular interpretation or view as a necessary qualification for its ministry.'[2]

3. As regards ministers not episcopally ordained, they remain in their status and can minister in any of the congregations of the Church, with the proviso, however, that 'neither

---

[1] *Constitution cit.* pp. 4–5.   [2] *Constitution cit.* p. 9.

forms of worship nor ritual, nor a ministry, to which they have not been accustomed, or to which they conscientiously object, will be imposed upon any congregation'. This seems to mean that a congregation which was Anglican will not be compelled to accept a minister not episcopally ordained, and that Congregationalists, Methodists and Presbyterians will not be obliged to accept a minister who was an Anglican at the time of the union.

But all ordinations after the union are to be by an imposition of hands by bishops, with presbyters also laying on hands. Thus in the course of time, all the ministers will be episcopally ordained. Meantime, there are ministers episcopally ordained before the union, those never episcopally ordained, and those episcopally ordained after the union. The difference between the two classes of episcopally ordained ministers is that no Anglican would doubt the orders conferred before the union, whereas some have questioned the orders conferred after the union, on grounds of ambiguity of faith and 'intention'.[1]

4. Those who were elected to be bishops at the time of the union were all 'ordained and consecrated'; but the Anglican bishops received no new consecration. It is provided that the 'ordination and consecration' of a presbyter to the episcopate shall take place by the laying on of hands of three bishops, in which presbyters may also join, unless the Diocesan Council determines that only bishops shall lay on hands.

5. Congregational and presbyterian forms, however, of Church order are maintained by a share given to each congregation in appointing its pastor and in selecting candidates for ordination; and a share given to ministers and lay members in the councils of the Church and the administration of its discipline.[2]

---

[1] In fact, it seems rare for ex-Anglican congregations to accept the Eucharist of non-episcopally ordained ministers, and practically everywhere episcopally ordained presbyters minister only to ex-Anglican congregations and non-episcopally ordained ministers to congregations of other traditions. The old ways of worship are still to a large extent maintained, and in some respects South India is said to be a collection of dioceses and not a Church. Cf. *The South India Churchman*, September, 1957, article 'These Ten Years', by R. D. Paul, p. 5. Theological Colleges are still supported from abroad. But exact and complete information is not readily available, even in South India, and various 'growing pains' are to be expected in an enterprise of this nature.

[2] *Constitution, cit.* pp. 8–9.

6. As regards relations with other Churches, the union, according to the desires of its framers, is to make no change as to communion—that is, the members, ministers and bishops of the new Church keep all the rights which they had before in their old allegiance.[1] The Church of South India, as far as it is concerned, desires to retain full communion with the Anglican, Congregational, Methodist and Presbyterian Churches with which the component parts were previously in communion.

The Church of South India 'claims the right to be free in all spiritual matters from the direction or interposition of any civil government', in which it differs from the Churches of England and of Sweden; and it declares that 'it is an autonomous Church, and free from any control legal or otherwise, of any Church or society external to itself,' though it desires to remember its origin from the Churches of the West and to maintain fellowship with them.[2]

One other provision of the Constitution of the Church of South India deserves mention; it reads as follows:

> For the avoidance of misunderstanding, it is here stated that when nothing is said in the Constitution about any doctrine which has been taught or any practice which has customarily been followed in any of the Churches from which the united Church has been formed, it must not be inferred either that that doctrine or practice is forbidden, or that it is considered to be of no importance. Specific mention of a doctrine or practice has in some cases been regarded as unnecessary, since it was a matter of well-known common agreement among the uniting Churches; in other cases there has been disagreement among those Churches on matters which were of importance yet not such that agreement on them was regarded as a necessary condition of union in one Church, and it was believed that a united Church would in due time be able to come to agreement on them.[3] [What these 'matters of importance' are, is not specified.]

South India and Anglicans

Difficulty arose in the Church of England about admitting the Church of South India into communion. Attention dwelt upon the question of the validity of South India ordinations,

---

[1] *Constitution cit.* p. 13.   [2] *Constitution*, p. 15.   [3] *Constitution*, p. 16.

when neither ordainer nor ordained nor, in fact, the whole body of the 'Church', might have right faith about the Eucharist and episcopacy; upon the communion which the Church of South India maintains with non-episcopal Churches; and upon the possibility of ministers not episcopally ordained functioning in Churches of the Anglican communion. For these reasons the Convocations of 1950 postponed decision about these matters for five years. In 1955 the Convocations of Canterbury and York admitted the validity in the Church of England of South India ordinations, and, though the provisions were a little complicated, agreed to such intercommunion as would exclude non-episcopally ordained ministers from normal functioning in Anglican Churches and implied that members of the Church of South India who wished regularly to attend in the Church of England should be confirmed.

This Church of South India is, in a real sense, a test case. On the one hand it shows that Congregationalists, Methodists and Presbyterians can accept a form of episcopacy without thinking that their principles are compromised. Bishop Lesslie Newbigin was in full communion and good standing in the Church of Scotland, as are the three ex-Methodist and the three ex-Congregationalist bishops (if it is right to say 'ex' of them) in their own communion. On the other hand, it shows that the concept of episcopacy held by the Church of England and some other Episcopalian Churches can stand with different beliefs about its exact nature, provided it is accepted in practice.

Thus it happens that the Church of South India is in communion with Churches which are not in communion with one another. In this sense it is certainly a 'bridge Church'.

Roman Catholic Opinions

Opinions about the Church of South India have differed, both among non-Catholics and Catholics. It may be of interest to refer briefly to three Catholic expressions of opinion. The first is that of Père L. Bouyer, of the French Oratory, in *Istina* (April–June, 1955), translated and published in *Theology* for January, 1956, pp. 3–11, entitled 'A Roman Catholic View of South India', in which he manifested considerable approval for several features which he judged favourable to the Orthodox-Catholic tradition, especially the *Order for the Lord's Supper or the Eucharist*.[1] Father Francis Clark, reviewing in *Unitas*, Winter, 1956, the Rev. Mr Donald Rea's *The Church of South India and the Church*, Oxford, 1956, gave on the whole a favourable judgement, granted the circumstances in South India. The Rev. Robert Murray, writing in *Bellarmine Commentary*,[2] gives the judgement of one who himself was a Congregationalist; he writes:

> It is a striking fact that many members of the C.S.I. of Presbyterian and Free Church origin have already come to value episcopacy of the Anglican type, and that this principle is proving to be one of inner cohesiveness and of firmness towards other bodies. For example, though the C.S.I. is committed to retain communion with all its 'parent churches', talks with the Lutherans in April, 1956 broke down precisely because the C.S.I. would not compromise on the principle of episcopacy. Catholics who see mainly the deficiencies of Anglican episcopal theology cannot easily appreciate what a revolutionary change it is for, say, a Congregationalist to move from his atomic, independent and democratic Church theory and discover the problems which

[1] Père Bouyer's article gave offence to some Anglo-Catholics, notably Mr W. Grisbrooke, cf. *Eastern Churches Quarterly*, Spring, 1956. In one respect the South India Liturgy seems less in the Orthodox-Catholic tradition than the Anglican. There is a rubric which reads: 'If the bread and wine set apart and blessed is insufficient, more may be taken for the purpose of the sacrament. The presbyter may say: "Obeying the command of our Lord Jesus Christ, we take this bread (wine) to be set apart for this holy use, in the name of the Father and of the Son and of the Holy Spirit. Amen." Or the Words of the Institution may be repeated.' *The Service of the Lord's Supper or the Holy Eucharist, authorized by the Synod in January, 1950*, Oxford, 1950, reprint, 1952. The *Book of Common Prayer* has the rubric: 'If the consecrated Bread and Wine be all spent before all have communicated, the Priest is to consecrate more according to the form before prescribed; beginning at *Our Saviour Christ in the same night*, etc., for the blessing of the bread; and at *Likewise after Supper*, etc., for the blessing of the Cup.' In this, at least, the South Indian is more suggestive of a 'receptionist' view of the Eucharist than is the Anglican. A Presbyterian friend who has had much experience in South India writes to me: 'From my experience of the Presbyterian and Methodist Churches prior to Union, I would say that in the great majority of cases the words of institution would be repeated.' But that they should ever be omitted is, in the Orthodox-Catholic faith, an objection raising wide issues. Reservations must also be made because of the reported normal use of unfermented grape juice in many churches. It has been asserted that many communicants are unbaptized; but this has been most categorically denied by a Presbyter of South India and it is difficult to know upon what evidence the statement was ever made. The Church of South India requires Baptism for membership.

[2] Privately printed by the College of St Robert Bellarmine, Heythrop, Oxon., vol. 1, no. 4, October, 1957.

arise as soon as 'the Church' means a unity bigger than he has known. He is brought face to face with the juridical order, and begins to realize that some long-abhorred features of the Roman Church were there not because it is evil but because it is a world unity. Such a man coming back to England may find a local 'church' here unbearably stuffy and petty, because his vision has been so much enlarged.

Most hostile comment on the Constitution has concluded that the articles on creeds and faith are too vague and non-committal to offer any hope of doctrinal cohesiveness. Yet spokesmen of the C.S.I. have insisted that in practice their Church stands by the creeds: 'The liberty of interpretation which we desire to safeguard is not intended to extend to any denial of the substance of the historic faith of the Church.' This may not seem satisfactory to a Catholic, but for people of whom many were brought up in the atmosphere of liberal modernism it is a most impressive return towards dogmatic faith. The present position shows a widespread mood of theological re-appraisal and willingness to learn, in which former Anglicans are not diluting their faith, while former non-Anglicans are moving, some of them fast and far, in the direction of real, if truncated, credal orthodoxy.

Naturally these writers, holding an unequivocally Roman Catholic point of view, cannot approve a Church whose faith is still undefined on many important matters, which to a Catholic are essential, whose orders are derived from a source which Catholics believe to be defective, and which repudiates the authority of the Holy See; nevertheless all three are in substantial agreement that the Church of South India, taking into account the actual circumstances, marks a distinct advance. Its Constitution compared with some of the Reformation formularies of faith is like a breath of fresh air. How the C.S.I. will develop remains to be seen; admittedly it is an experiment and does not claim complete finality.

The approval by the Convocations of the Church of South India, though not complete, caused a minor crisis among Anglo-Catholics and was the occasion on which some of them saw that the Church of England does not really hold the doctrine which they had thought it did. Criticisms by other Anglo-Catholics were, at least in some cases, based upon fear that the Church of England was abandoning its 'Catholic character' and encouraging 'an extreme and unbalanced movement of the Church of England to the Protestant bodies', which seems to be Dr Mascall's view.[1] Is it unfair to suggest that he seems to say: 'Well, it's all right this time, but don't do it again'? In the background lies the proposal of the Archbishop of Canterbury that the Church of England and the Free Churches in England should agree to some ceremony of mutual conferring of ministries, that the Free Churches should accept episcopacy into their existing systems and so have complete intercommunion, without any 'constitutional' or organic union.[2] It is an indication of the somewhat surprising changes that the ecumenical movement has occasioned that Bishop Newbigin speaks favourably of the resistance of 'Catholics' to this type of suggestion. He wants complete unity, as his words make clear, cited further p. 66.

The projected union in Ceylon between Anglicans, Baptists, Congregationalists, Methodists and Presbyterians follows to a considerable extent the South India plan; but there are proposals to avoid the differences which at present exist in the Church of South India between ministers who are episcopally ordained and those who are not. This would take the form of a laying on of hands by bishops with the words: 'Forasmuch as you were called and ordained to the ministry of the Church of God in the . . . Church, and are now called to the ministry of the Church of God as Presbyter within this Church of Lanka (Ceylon); receive from God the power and grace of the Holy Spirit to exercise the wider ministry of this office.'

The Preface to this 'Order of Commissioning' states clearly that, 'the use of this rite does not imply a denial of the reality of any commission previously received by those now seeking to become Presbyters in this United Church; nor is it presumed to bestow again or renew any grace, gifts, character or

---

[1] *The Convocations and South India*, London, 1955.

[2] Cf. *Church Relations in England, Being the Report of Conversations between Representatives of the Archbishop of Canterbury and Representatives of the Evangelical Free Churches of England*, London, 1950. The latter came from Baptists, Congregationalists, Methodists, Moravians, Presbyterians of England, Wesleyan Reformed, Independent Methodists, the Churches of Christ and the Countess of Huntingdon's Connection. On balance, the Report was not enthusiastic; and the Interim Statement, published in 1958, about Anglican-Methodist relations does not seem hopeful of spectacular results in the near future, though it closes no doors.

authority that have already been bestowed upon them by God through whatever means'; but it also declares that,' In so doing, it is the intention of this Church to continue and reverently to use and esteem the threefold ministry of Bishop, Presbyter and Deacon which existed in the undivided Church.'[1]

Besides these federations and organic unions other conversations or negotiations looking toward full union, or at least better understanding, are in progress in many parts of the world; perhaps some twenty series of such discussions are in progress, in England, Scotland, South Africa, Iran, the United States, India, Australia, Nigeria, Madagascar and Pakistan. They envisage unions, for instance, between Anglicans and Presbyterians, between Anglicans and Methodists, between Congregationalists and Presbyterians, between varieties of Lutherans, between Anglicans in Iran and Presbyterians, between Baptists and the Disciples of Christ, between Anglicans, Methodists, Congregationalists and Baptists, and so on. In the Summer of 1957 an organic union was formed in the United States between the Evangelical and Reformed Church, the

[1] A *History of the Ecumenical Movement*, ch. 10 *iam cit.* p. 478, quoted from *Proposed Scheme of Church Union in Ceylon*, Madras, 1949, pp. 13 ff. The language of the proposed Preface seems sounder than that of the Lausanne statement accepted by the authors of the *Report* on Anglican-Presbyterian Relations, cf. below, pp. 114 ff. The Ceylon Preface avoids judgement on the past but declares the mind of the Church of Lanka for the future, whereas the Lausanne statement is as indeterminate about the future as about the past. Yet in the plan for the Church of Lanka, the phraseology proposed for the laying-on of hands, 'the wider ministry of this office', is not perfect. Previously it has been said that those on whom hands are being laid are 'now called to the ministry of the Church of God as Presbyter in this Church of Lanka'; and as the Church of Lanka, *as such*, did not previously exist, the ministry to be received is not 'wider' but is purely and simply ministry in the Church of Lanka and so is to be different from the previous ministry in *exactly* the same manner in which the Church of Lanka is to be different from the disunited Churches. The ministry and the Church go together and the nature of the one corresponds to the nature of the other. The new Church in Ceylon is to be 'wider' than any of the Churches from which it originates, or of which it is formed; nevertheless presumably its doctrine is not to be 'wider' in the sense of being more 'latitudinarian' but in the sense of being more universal. The word 'wider', then, introduces needless complications and it would be more satisfactory, and not, I conjecture, less acceptable, to say 'this ministry committed to thee' instead of the ambiguous 'the wider ministry of this office'. Clergy who would conscientiously accept the Church of Lanka and the proposed Preface could surely accept the ministry of that Church. It may be added that the title 'Order of Commissioning' sounds theological overtones and might well be changed to 'Order of Laying on of Hands'. What has been said of the proposed Church of Lanka applies in the main to the Plan of Church Union in North India and Pakistan, Third ed. 1957. If the process of unification continues, things may look different to the next generation and there is no need to lock any doors which they may wish to open.

Congregational Christian Churches, having between them some 2,000,000 members, and the Disciples of Christ, who have a membership of over 2,000,000. These now form 'the United Church of Christ'.

5. THE SPIRIT OF THE MOVEMENT

In general it can and should be said that the spirit of all these meetings and negotiations has been one of cordiality, of sympathy, of a desire to understand others, in spite of the fact that many Churches are convinced that other Churches are in serious and dangerous error. A very weighty measure of humility has been notable, and a deep sense of the religious issues involved. Again and again the words of Christ have been cited from the seventeenth chapter of St. John, 'that they may all be one'; men and women of different nations, of different cultural and religious backgrounds and traditions, of different strong convictions, have met one another with courtesy, charity and respect for their differing convictions. Very many have expressed the feeling that the actual personal contact with those of other faiths has been a revelation to them of the width of Christian charity, and has made them sad and grieved that they are in any way divided. Again and again there have been expressions of the need of repentance for the prejudices, the ignorances, the narrowness and even the sinfulness which are associated with the divisions between the Churches: and again and again has been expressed the resolve 'to stay together' and to do everything possible to attain to full union.

Miss Ruth Rouse, writing in 1954, says that in the ecumenical movement we see:

A movement which cannot be suppressed, making for Christian unity, with sufficient force to rise above exclusive confessional loyalties; with sufficient dynamic to counteract the inherent tendency of human nature—even redeemed human nature— to schism and division; with sufficient power to overcome in tens of thousands of Christians their inherent prejudice and inertia and to command in them the devotion of their best powers of thought and will to the cause of unity.

A movement showing itself everywhere. No continent or country, no Church or Church party, no religious group or society remains wholly unaffected. It appears amongst youth, in journalism, in the ecclesiastical assemblies of the Churches, and at the grass roots of local church life; in unitive movements of each great confession, including the Roman Catholic and the Orthodox; in impulses to prayer; in emphasis now on the Kingdom and now on the Church, now on Faith and Order and now on Life and Work.

A movement beset with difficulties. Within this movement for unity there are contradictions and tensions between the lay and the ecclesiastical groups, between movements from the top downwards and from the bottom upwards, between 'catholic' and 'protestant' tendencies, between confessional and non-Church trends. The mixture in the bowl of the Church's life is bubbling, churning, changing—what will emerge?[1]

This is well said, and should be kept in mind by all who have an interest in the movement. In the World Council of Churches some 170 Churches are represented and these Churches all have different doctrines and convictions about the nature of the Christian religion, varying from the dogmatic intransigence of the Eastern Orthodox to the aversion to any dogmatism of the Disciples of Christ, whose tradition is against any doctrinal statements other than those of the Scriptures.[2] To imagine any fixity in the movement, beyond the determination to work towards unity, would be unwise. The Amsterdam Report of 1948 said: 'We acknowledge that God is powerfully at work amongst us, to lead us to goals which we but dimly discern. We do not fully understand some of the things He has already done amongst us, or their implications on our familiar ways.'[3]

[1] *A History of the Ecumenical Movement, 1517–1948*, edited by Ruth Rouse and Stephen Charles Neill, London, 1954, p. 640.
[2] Cf. the official answer of the Disciples of Christ to the Lund Report of 1952, *Ecumenical Review*, vi, January, 1954, pp. 169–72.
[3] *Report*, Section I, paragraph VI. It is a pleasure here to refer to *Christian Baptism*, edited by A. Gilmore, a series of essays by Baptist scholars which is a notable contribution to ecumenical discourse.

Chapter Two

THE RISE OF THE IMPULSE TO UNITY

1. THE EVILS OF DIVISION

'The disunion of Christendom is a scandal to the world.'

'By our divisions we are impeding the progress of the Kingdom of God.'

'There is a strong non-Church movement in Japan today, largely because people are tired of the scandal of our divisions.'

'It is useless to preach the charity of Christ while we are divided.'

'Christ willed us to be one and our sins make us not one.'

'Inasmuch as we are far from one another we are far from Christ.'

'The central problem of all religion is the problem of Christian unity.'

'All questions of theology end in the question of the nature of the Church.'

Such, or similar, statements are incessant among those interested in the ecumenical movement. Not, indeed, that everybody would accept each of these statements without qualification; but it is true that there has been a growth of the passionate conviction that existing divisions are contrary to God's will, and that Christians must labour and pray that they may be healed.

The influences behind the growth of this conviction are many and complex, and may be listed roughly—though very inadequately—as follows:

1. Missionary effort among non-Christian populations is impeded by the existing divisions among Christians.

2. There has been and is danger from growing secularism and irreligion. World 'ideologies' are a threat to Christianity as such.

22

3. Co-ordinated action is obviously more effective; and modern life shows a general tendency to centralization in governmental, economic, professional and even social spheres.

4. There has been a 'new look' in much Biblical and theological writing.

5. The prayers of the faithful and the inspiration of the Holy Ghost have helped this impulse to unity among all Christians.

These reasons behind the impulse to unity overlap and interact; and the following amplification of them cannot be strictly systematic.

2. DIVIDED CHRISTIANS CONFRONTING NON-CHRISTIANS

The beginnings of the ecumenical movement of modern times has been placed in the World Missionary Conference which took place at Edinburgh in 1910. Dr K. S. Latourette, of Yale, in his *History of the Expansion of Christianity*,[1] vol. 7, published in 1945, says of the Edinburgh Missionary Conference:

The World Conference on Faith and Order arose in part from this World Missionary Conference at Edinburgh in 1910. It became clear that at this gathering the basic questions of faith and order which had historically separated the Churches were not being faced. With the purpose of obtaining the fullest possible co-operation those concerned with the expansion of Christianity were consciously avoiding the issues which had been traditional sources of division and were seeking to rise above them in meeting together the tasks which all had in common. *Yet these issues remained and prevented the achievement of a united front.* (Italics mine.) Questions of fundamental beliefs concerning the Christian faith, the ordination of the ministry, and the organization of the Church *would not down.* (Italics mine.) It was felt that representatives of the Churches should frankly face them together. If for the moment no way appeared of reconciling the historic differences, sympathetic understanding might be achieved by each of the communions of the reasons why members of other communions believed as they did. It might be that through this understanding

---

[1] Dr Latourette gives an account of all agencies engaged in missionary activities and pays many notable tributes to Catholics; here and there he uses an expression which reveals that he is not a Roman Catholic but on the whole he maintains an admirable impartiality and his book should be read by every student of missiology.

the desire for comprehensive union would be awakened and strengthened and a way, as yet unforeseeable, would be found for attaining the apparently impossible.'[1]

Since the time of that Edinburgh Missionary Conference the conviction has grown that the Christian witness to non-Christians is seriously weakened by the divisions among Christian Churches. Indeed, not a few have said that the scandal is so clear that it is astonishing that more is not done about it. Divided Christendom remains still a most conspicuous and most damaging reproach to Christianity.

These divisions between Churches arose in Europe in circumstances and over issues which seem quite pointless to people in China, Africa, India, Japan, the islands of Australasia and elsewhere. Many illustrations are given of this. One of the most striking is that of the then 'Depressed-class' community in India (now the Scheduled Castes), which under Dr Ambedkar announced its intention of renouncing Hinduism and seeking another faith. Dr Ambedkar said to the late Bishop Azariah of Dornakal, as more than once has been narrated in Missionary Conferences, 'At present we are one community all over India and our strength is in our unity. Can you in any Christian Church offer us any unity comparable to that? Have you one body which we can join as one people?' Dr Ambedkar refused to join the Christians because there was no unity among them.[2] A learned Indian once said to a friend:

[1] P. 30. The decisive influence of this Edinburgh Conference is stressed in many passages in the *History of the Ecumenical Movement*, ed. Rouse and Neill, cf. the index under the heading 'Edinburgh, World Missionary Conference', p. 803. It is significant that many who became prominent in the ecumenical movement began with interest in missionary activities, generally through the Student Christian Movement: Dr John R. Mott, whose influence was deep and far-reaching, Bishop Charles H. Brent of the Philippines, Archbishop Nathan Söderblom of Upsala, Archbishop Germanos of Thyateira, Archbishop William Temple of York and then Canterbury, Bishop V. S. Azariah of Dornakal, India, Dr Joseph Houldsworth Oldham, Professor Julius Ritter, Dr Robert C. Machie, Pastor Henri-Louis Henriod, Dr W. A. Visser 't Hooft and others. Cf. *History, iam cit. passim*; Basil Matthews, *John R. Mott, World Citizen*, London, 1934, pp. 228–74 and 335–381; F. A. Iremonger, *William Temple, Archbishop of Canterbury, His Life and Letters*, London, 1948, pp. 128, 390–404; Edward Duff, *The Social Thought of the World Council of Churches*, London, 1956, pp. 19–24.

[2] The date given is 1935, cf. John W. Sadiq, in his communication on 'Intercommunion and Church Unity', *Intercommunion, The Report of the Theological Commission*, etc., ed. Donald Baillie and John Marsh, London, 1952, p. 290; but cf. the Rev. Farid Auden at Lund, in 1952, *Report*, p. 219. The latter relates the incident as having happened before 1910, the former assigns it to 1935.

'I believe in Jesus Christ as the Way, the Truth and the Life.' His friend answered: 'Then why do you not join the Christian Church?' 'Which Church, please?' was the ironic answer.[1]

Attempts to win non-Christians to the faith certainly meet many difficulties. Often enough the Christian missionary is accused of being a propagandist of a European culture and way of life.[2] Belloc's 'The faith is Europe and Europe is the faith' is periodically headlined, without regard to its context. But when to this is added the spectacle of hundreds of different varieties of Christianity, to some extent competing for conversions, especially in the cities, the local population readily becomes confused, if not sceptical of the worth of a religion which preaches brotherly love yet practises so much separation and manifests if not uncharity, at least lack of that family or caste cohesion to which the East is accustomed. In India there are some 200 Christian denominations: since the last war over 55 different Christian sects or agencies have entered Japan to bring Christianity to the Japanese.

Dr Jorge Cesar Mota, General Sceretary of the Student Christian movement in Brazil, says this:

Protestantism has really made marvellous progress since the American missionaries began to preach in this country (Brazil), but at the same time, in establishing the work of their denominations, they created an unhappy spiritual situation which was later to prove an obstacle to ecumenical understanding within the Christian Church. The Presbyterians arrived in 1859, the Methodists in 1870, the Baptists in 1881 and the Episcopalians in 1890. The 'national' churches arrived with the immigrants —the Church of England, the Reformed Church of Hungary

[1] Told by Rajah B. Manikan, then East Asia Secretary of the World Council of Churches and the International Missionary Council, in his address at Lund in 1952, *Report*, pp. 212–13.

[2] I can say from personal experience that this is most unjustified in the case of the Belgian, Italian and Spanish Catholic missionaries whom I knew in Ceylon and Bombay. Sometimes they were more Sinhalese and Indian than the inhabitants themselves, both Christian and non-Christian, who attended their Colleges; and there is a great desire to learn the techniques of European agriculture, industry and science. The better-bred pigs introduced from Europe at Kandy were certainly welcome guests and their European origin was not held against them. I cherish very warm memories of Kandy and of Bombay.

and the Lutherans from Germany. Some others are still coming like the Free Methodists, the Lutherans from Missouri, the Baptists from the North, the Holiness Church from Japan, and so forth. The Pentecostals are numerically the most important group. One of their churches in S. Paolo has room for six thousand people.

In some of the churches divisions have also been caused by many and various motives, some of them unfortunately by personal interest.

The argument most commonly found on the lips of anyone in the interior or in the capitals of this immense country, when the Gospel is presented, is this: 'But there are so many sects . . . and each says that the other is wrong. . . .' The Catholics say this in one way, the materialists in another, but they all say the same thing. It is true that the Protestants have good arguments that explain the situation or 'excuse' it. Some arrive at the point of rationalizing this phenomenon of the divisions in Protestantism and even give thanks for it. But in reality no sincere believer is satisfied in his heart of hearts.

The 'disgrace' and the gravity of the situation often assume alarming proportions and aspects.[1]

In Africa the problem is equally grave, if not graver. Dr W. A. Visser 't Hooft, who visited South Africa in 1952, stresses this. Among other things he says: 'South Africa has many of the same sects which one finds in other countries. But it has, in addition, the special problem of the Bantu sects which are the produce of the psychological and sociological conditions of Bantu society. The Department of Native Affairs has listed (not recognized) no fewer than 1350 names of such sects. . . . This tremendous growth of the sects is a matter which demands the most serious attention.'[2]

---

[1] 'Evangelicalism and Unity in Brazil', *Ecumenical Review*, vol., 2, January, 1953, pp. 155–58. I am sorry that Dr Mota speaks in less kindly fashion of my own communion. I cite him and other witnesses, not in any way to make capital out of the troubles of our separated brethren—the situation is far too tragic for that, even on a merely human level—but simply that the reasons which make unity imperative may be understood.

[2] 'A visit to South African Churches in April and May, 1952', *Ecumenical Review*, v, 2, January, 1953, p. 194. The same problems exist in Sierra Leone, as Mr S. A. J. Pratt shows in an article entitled 'Spiritual Conflicts in a Changing African Society', *Ecumenical Review*, viii, 2, January, 1956, pp. 154–63. The *International Review of Missions* makes frequent references to this problem.

Neither 'Comity' nor 'Federation' the Answer

Dr J. E. L. Newbigin, a Presbyterian, then Bishop of the South India Church, has stated most powerfully the missionary case for organic reunion (and nothing less) in his *The Reunion of the Churches, A Defence of the South India Scheme*, London, 1948, and in his *The Household of God*, London, 1953 (reprinted 1954 and 1955). These are books which many critics of the Scheme do not appear to have read; but they are books which deserve the attention of everyone interested either in missions or in the ecumenical movement. Speaking of the impatience of the 'younger' Churches, that is, Churches in lands which are mainly non-Christian, he says:

> It might be argued that since the Christians of the Younger Churches certainly do not fully understand the importance of the principles for which Christendom has split into so many fragments, their impatience with these divisions can in reality teach us nothing about how we are to heal them. It is easy for a Churchman of the older Churches thus to dismiss the attitude of the Younger Churches as simply the natural result of a different point of view, but it would be unfortunate if the matter were left there. What is much more difficult is for the younger Churches to understand the astounding complacency of the Churches of the West regarding a situation which so plainly and ostentatiously flouts the declared will of the Church's Lord. That Christians should desire to be united ought not to cause surprise. What requires explanation is that they should be content to be divided. There is certainly a difference of view-point. What has to be challenged is the tacit assumption that the view-point of the older Churches is the true one.[1]

Speaking of the missions, he says: 'The New Testament knows of only one missionary society—the Church. The eighteenth century knew Churches which had totally ceased to be missionary societies and they saw the birth of missionary societies which made no claim to be Churches.'[2] And a little further on:

'*It is not possible to account for the contentment with the divisions*

[1] *The Reunion of the Churches*, p. 9.
[2] P. 10.

of the Church, except upon the basis of a loss of conviction that the Church exists to bring all men to Christ.[1] (Italics mine.)

Bishop Newbigin puts the matter concretely. In mission countries the denominations usually exercise 'comity', that is they divide districts or areas between denominations so as to obviate dissipation of effort and to avoid the scandal of two Christian 'Churches' competing for converts in one small part of the country. But this 'comity' does not help greatly when people travel; an Anglican baptized in infancy is not admitted to Baptist communion, nor are Nonconformists admitted to communion in Anglican Churches. 'There may be in a large town congregation in South India', says Bishop Newbigin, 'men and women whose original affiliation has been Syrian, Lutheran, Anglican, Methodist, Presbyterian, Congregational, Baptist.'[2] In consequence, the Indian Christian, when he settles in a new locality, has to choose between being outside the Church or accepting another denomination. Moreover, how could people so far from Europe, so unfamiliar with its history, be expected to understand the issues, for example, between Episcopalian and Presbyterian theology? Inevitably the Indian Christian would be apt to picture the dispute in terms of a dispute between a pastor and village elders or in terms of some quarrel which he has experienced. Thus the divisions between the Churches leads to real scandal and to very practical difficulties.

Two Temperance Societies in one town is not a scandal. But a Temperance Society whose members are habitually drunk is scandalous. Now the existence of a plurality of 'Churches' (in the modern sense of the word) is scandalous in the same sense, for the Church's unity in Christ is of its very essence.[3] Moreover this unity is both spiritual and corporeal[4] and hence reunion ideas inevitably come as the fruit of the commission to preach the Gospel—'the fruit of an act of obedience to the Gospel'.[5]

'Comity', contends Bishop Newbigin, is not the solution. Comity itself inevitably led on further, and the difficulties 'forced the Church to consider what is the real basis of its

---

[1] P. 11.   [2] *The Reunion of the Churches*, p. 12.
[3] *Ibid.* pp. 23–4.   [4] *Ibid.* pp. 52–3.   [5] *Ibid.* p. 20.

unity and what it is that cuts it off from the pagan world'.[1] 'Comity' itself involves some mutual agreement, an admission that the differences are not 'fundamental', since otherwise each denomination would have to attempt everywhere to erect mission stations. Federation of some kind does not meet the logic of the situation, which pushes on and can stop at nothing less than complete reunion in doctrine and in organization.

Most pertinently Bishop Newbigin asks for alternatives to the South India Scheme; and, to those who do not accept the Roman Catholic position, a workable alternative is hard indeed to discover, for in fact the European representatives of the uniting Churches have not considered that the union involved any breach of their principles.[2]

Bishop Newbigin argues that there is a dynamic in missionary Church relations which proceeds as follows:

Hostility—tolerance—comity—co-operation—federation—organic unity.

The argument seems to be based not merely upon unanswerable logical and theological principles, but likewise upon experience. Hostility is clearly recognized as unchristian; tolerance inevitably leads on to refusal to compete and so to 'comity'; 'comity' is effective only in a rural area with a stable population; co-operation likewise fails to meet the needs in cities and when people travel; federation makes difficult or

---

[1] *Ibid.* p.15.

[2] Father Francis Clark, reviewing in *Unitas*, Winter, 1956, the Rev. Donald Rea's *The Church of South India and the Church*, says: 'A Catholic priest from South India is quoted as saying of C.S.I. "They all love one another and the union is a very good thing for the country. We all think so. The C.S.I. is not working against us, and it is good that the Protestants should be one. We think that God is at work." In the same spirit, we need have no hesitation in agreeing with much that Mr Rea says (in approval of C.S.I.). But there is between us a basic difference of outlook. However much Catholics might rejoice in the good being done through a dissident church (with or without valid orders), they could never approve communion with it, as long as its orthodoxy remained defective and it maintained communion with non-Catholic sects. It is one thing to approve the good results that providence draws from causes which cannot be approved in themselves; another, and a very different thing, to co-operate in maintaining those causes in being for the sake of the resulting good.' This judgement I heartily endorse—(and Father Clark gives his judgement because Mr Rea has appealed to catholic principles)—that is, I wish that all who formed the C.S.I. had become Catholics, but think it better for them to be united among themselves than to remain divided as Anglicans, Congregationalists, Methodists, and Presbyterians, in spite of my deep sympathy with the agonizing problem which the C.S.I. set and still sets before Anglo-Catholics who believe that the Church of England has orders which meet all Catholic requirements.

impossible the enforcement of Christian discipline (which,
Bishop Newbigin knows from experience, is necessary in missionary lands)[1] and is alien to the thought-forms of peoples
whose society is closer to the family. Thus complete organic
union is the only possible answer; and complete organic union
in one country both logically and practically raises the question
of organic unity in other countries, and so throughout the
world. The union of Anglicans, Congregationalists, Methodists
and Presbyterians in South India at once causes discussion
about 'communion' between the one Church in South India
and the divided Churches in other parts of the world. If these
bodies are united in South India, why are they divided elsewhere?

The Church, Bishop Newbigin rightly affirms, is essentially
a missionary society; but without unity the Church cannot
be a missionary society and so missions and unity essentially
imply each other. Bishop Newbigin's arguments are certainly
very powerful against Christians who have missions but not
unity.

3. The Danger of Secularism and Irreligion

Towards the end of the last century and the beginning of
this there were signs in all countries that new forces of secularism and irreligion were arising. Fears were expressed
that the Churches were either not holding their people or were
not keeping pace with the increase of population. This fear
was general and certainly was shared by Roman Catholics,
who have long been worried about the 'leakage'. A definite
instance, however, of this leading to thoughts of new methods
and to a more united effort is given by Dr John W. Grant,
in his *Free Churchmanship in England 1870–1940 with special
Reference to Congregationalism*, a most illuminating book and
excellently documented.[2] He notes that Congregationalism
in England declined in numbers between 1870 and 1923 and

---

[1] The *Report* of the Delegation sent to the Church of South India by the General
Convention of the American Episcopal Church in 1956 speaks of general confidence in the bishops of C.S.I. and in the pastoral value of episcopacy, of firm
rulings on marriage and the requirements of Church membership, of disciplinary
suspension, excommunication and public penance.

[2] I am informed, however, that not all Congregationalists would endorse every
single statement of Dr Grant, though they warmly approve his book in general.

assigns this as one of the reasons for a somewhat changed attitude both toward centralization (for the Congregationalists traditionally held as strongly as the Baptists to the autonomy of the local congregation) and towards an approach to other Churches. The emphasis tended no longer to fall upon 'Congregationalist Principles', but rather upon 'the essential witness of Congregationalism', indicating a turning of thought towards the elements of Congregationalism which were regarded as fundamental in plans for reunion.[1]

Dr Grant also cities J. H. Shakespeare, for long Secretary of the Baptist Union and most influential in bringing about a degree of centralization among Baptists, as startling Nonconformity by his book published in 1918 *The Churches at the Crossroads*. He declared bluntly: 'our modern world will not even listen to a divided Church', stated that there was no middle way between the present separation and corporate reunion and even caused consternation among his Nonconformist brethren by arguing in favour of the acceptance of episcopacy in such reunion.[2] Shakespeare was perhaps in advance of his time; perhaps he was mistaken. Nevertheless he gives one indication that the feeling was growing that only in greater union could the influence of secularism be resisted.

Reunion in Scotland

Similar considerations played their part in helping on the union in 1929 of the Church of Scotland and the United Free Church. In 1911, the joint Committee of the two Churches issued a Report on the religious condition of the country, and the following is an account given of it by Dr J. R. Fleming, *The Story of Church Union in Scotland, its Origins and Progress, 1560–1929*, London, 1929:

> A considerable section of the Report had a practical and a non-controversial interest. It took the form of a 'statement on the ecclesiastical situation', apart from theological or political problems behind the existing divisions. . . . The total population of Scotland was about 4,800,000, as compared with a little over

[1] P. 267.
[2] Pp. 263–4. Shakespeare is still appreciatively remembered by many Baptists, cf. M. S. Aubry, 'John Howard Shakespeare 1857–1928'. *Baptist Quarterly*, July, 1957.

half that number in 1843. Notwithstanding the increase of from 1,000 to more than 3,000 Presbyterian congregations during nearly seventy years, and the organization of a vast system of new agencies in the home field, there had been a distinct failure to overtake the annual increment. The members and adherents of the two leading Churches together did not include one-half of the people of the country. There was also great inequality of distribution. Many of the additional congregations had been planted, not so much to supply the wants of a growing population as to meet denominational requirements. Rivalry of an unseemly kind was most obvious in thinly populated districts, though the evil was apparent in the cities, and it could not well be cured as long as the Churches remained apart.[1]

While up to the end of the nineteenth century it appeared that the Churches had held their own notwithstanding adverse circumstances, later statistics told a different tale. The decline in Sunday scholars, the indifference of multitudes to the claims of religion, the falling off in Church attendance, and the increasing desecration of the Lord's Day, once the characteristic institution of Scottish piety, were other sinister features in the situation. It may be added that while such signs were manifest enough in 1911, the publication of more elaborate figures by the Scottish Churches' Council in 1927 only intensified the force of the argument.[2]

In another account of this union between the Church of Scotland and the United Free Church, that of Dr G. D. Henderson given in his *The Claims of the Church of Scotland*, London, 1951, similar considerations are advanced:

It may above all be maintained that the Churches had gradually been becoming more Christian. The hatreds of the seventeenth century and the bitterness of the Disruption period were now unthinkable. Enlightened study of the Bible, intelligent interest in social problems, and other advances had really brought men to have a much more adequate conception of the Deity, and a much more realistic understanding of Christian principles. The Christians were becoming more Christian. A more adequate doctrine of the Church was emerging. While there was no slighting of the loyalty to Christ of those who at various times had separated from one another, there was growing appreciation of the value of visible unity, and a sense that even our differences are different if we look at them with Christ as background. . .

[1] P. 69.   [2] Pp. 69–70.

The Christians were perhaps more Christian; but there were fewer of them. The first world war made a change in this respect; the second has produced a still greater transformation. Fewer people were going to Church, or reading the Bible; more people were using Sunday for recreation. Opposition to Christianity by celebrated writers was having more influence. Multitudes seemed to be taking their standards from newspapers. It became clear that there were too many Churches. They were getting in one another's way. To outsiders, the distinctions amongst the denominations appeared ludicrous, and Christians were affected by this judgement, asking in their own words like Erasmus: 'Why do we make so strait and narrow Christ's religion which he would have so large?' To those on the foreign field and to those engaged in evangelistic or apologetic work at home the differences were only a grave embarrassment. Everything pointed in the same direction.

Fewer supporters, relatively less money, more opposition, and much more indifference clamoured for the Christians and most obviously the Presbyterians to pool their resources, abandon much of their introversion, and together face the facts of a world situation.[1]

Dr Henderson wrote, of course, thinking mainly of the union of the Scottish Presbyterian Churches; but one need not agree absolutely with all he says in order to see that his words apply, with due limitation, to the position of all denominations. Similar considerations may have their part in suggesting thoughts of church reunion in other countries and denominations.

DOUBTS ABOUT LIBERALISM

In the period between 1920 and 1930 or thereabouts, a reaction began in Free Church circles against 'liberalism'. 'It was becoming evident, moreover', says Dr Grant, 'that the restatement of the Christian faith in a form calculated to appeal to the modern mind had not succeeded in retaining modern men. In *The Free Church Tradition in the Life of England*, published in 1944, Dr E. A. Payne has described graphically the decline in political power and spiritual effectiveness of the Free Churches. Statistics tell the same story. A committee of the

[1] Pp. 117–18. Published by Hodder & Stoughton Ltd.

Congregational Union reported in 1926 that Church Extension had practically ceased, while Church membership was practically stationary. Fear of alienating modern men and women seemed to be proven to be no valid reason for hesitating to declare where the Churches stood.'[1] Such frank and open self-criticism—and similar self-criticism could be quoted in many other Churches,—was a sign of health and of the beginnings of renewal. But it was also one influence which helped to turn minds towards concentrating forces and uniting witness to Christ.

I have given these quotations, not in the least to suggest a decline of non-Catholic Churches, but merely to indicate considerations which were, and still are, in the minds of some who think about the union of the Churches. Certain Protestant denominations, if not all, have increased in numbers of members or adherents. Thus the 'World Alliance of Reformed Churches Holding the Presbyterian System' is said to have almost doubled its communicant membership between 1888 and 1917, and to have increased by two millions in the twelve years before 1925. Dr R. Newton Flew and Dr Davies say that the Baptist numbers have been steadily rising in the present century. Between 1911 and 1928 the Congregationalist Churches increased in membership from 1,376,424 to over 2,000,000. The Methodists likewise seem to have increased.[2]

But statistics about religious 'membership' or 'adherence' are not easy to obtain and are, at best, approximate. Many a man entering the Services will put himself down as C of E, or RC, or C of S, when he has not darkened a Church door for years and knows as much about religion as he does about nuclear fission. Many a man may count himself a Mohammedan, though he never visits a mosque, never prostrates himself in prayer, drinks strong drink and thinks that the fast has nothing to do with him. All the same, this 'nominal'

[1] *Free Churchmanship in England, 1870–1940*, p. 329. Independent Press Ltd.
[2] Cf. R. Newton Flew and Rupert E. Davies, *The Catholicity of Protestantism* London, 1950, pp. 17–18. An increase in Congregationalism, during this period however, did not take place in England. Dr Grant, *op. cit.* p. 328, note 4, quotes the Congregationalist Year Book as giving 459,147 members in 1908 and 453,814 in 1928. But one may doubt the possibility of obtaining accurate figures. Churches may have different standards in reckoning their membership; and these standards raise the theological question of the nature of the Church itself.

membership may mean a latent loyalty which would show itself in a crisis.

The far more important question is this: is the number of Christians increasing in proportion to the increase in world population? It is a question hard, if not impossible, to answer. How obtain statistics from behind the iron curtain? Canon J. E. Fison says boldly: 'The increase in nearly every country in the world is greater than the relative increase in the number of Christians. Relatively to world population, we are a dwindling minority.'[1] The practical conclusion is put by Dr Flew and Dr Davies: 'All the figures of communicant membership put together constitute a minority which seems to shrink to insignificance in face of the total population of the world. No one who reads the reports of ecumenical organizations will easily detect the note of complacency, in view of the task in the world today.'[2] Materialist 'ideologies' like the Fascist, Nazist and Communist, which had a world influence, as Communism still has, played their part in turning thought to Christian co-operation. Yet because these 'ideologies' were to a considerable extent identified in the public mind with nations, comment about them in ecumenical circles gives the impression of being restrained, probably in order to give not the slightest ground for the charge, made in Russia, that the Ecumenical Movement is an instrument of Western 'power-politics'.

However, the absence of any note of complacency, of which Dr Flew and Dr Davies speak, is abundantly justified. In the year in which they wrote, 1950, Whitaker's Almanac gave the following figures.:

Christians:		
Roman Catholics	331,500,000	
Orthodox	144,000,000	
Protestants	206,900,000	
Copts	10,000,000	
	Total	692,400,000
Non-Christians		
Jews	15,980,000	
Moslems	209,000,000	

[1] *The Blessing of the Holy Spirit*, London, 1950, p. 26.   [2] *Op. cit.* p. 19.

Buddhists	150,000,000
Hindus	230,000,000
Confucianists, Taoists	350,000,000
Animists	135,000,000
Unclassified	50,000,000

Total 1,167,450,000

Thus Christians—and many included in these figures must be merely nominal Christians—were about one third of the population of the world, but in Asia they were 34,000,000 as against 978,800,000; in Africa 18,000,000 as against 135,100,000. Only in Europe and North and South America did Christians outnumber non-Christians. It is indeed true that no Christian can sound any note of complacency in view of the apostolic duty of all Christians. Numbers, of course, are not everything, and it would be a mistake to depict the religious situation and hope merely in terms of numbers. But every true Christian must think with deep distress of the vast multitudes of men and women for whom Christ died who do not know or love Him.

4. THE GENERAL TENDENCY TOWARDS CENTRALIZATION

The general tendency towards centralization in government, in business and in international relations has been based upon causes which could not leave the Churches unaffected: rapidity of communications, the spread of ideas by the increase of reading and by radio and television, the interchange of goods, the internationalism of scholarship, the formation of Trade Unions and of various professional associations—these are only hasty indications that the world has in a real sense become smaller and that ecclesiastical methods cannot be based upon conditions of things as they were a hundred or fifty or even ten years ago. The Baptists and the Congregationalists, for instance, hold that the local congregation is autonomous, manifesting in itself the whole of the Catholic Church, and so theoretically no congregation need concern itself with other congregations, save to exercise charity and comity towards them. In fact, however, Baptists and Congregationalists have formed national and international unions, and have felt that this is not really contrary to the spirit of 'a gathered

Church', since the local congregation remains the source of whatever co-ordinating function any central body exercises. Similarly, the 'Free Churches' have formed Councils and various standing Committees for permanent consultation among themselves. What was called 'comity', that is, friendly agreement not to compete in such things as the building of churches, about which I have spoken as it applied in the missions, had a tendency to develop into closer union. The National Council of Free Churches and the Federal Council of Evangelical Free Churches amalgamated in 1941 in the Free Church Federal Council; and a Declaratory Statement was reaffirmed in 1941 as a doctrinal basis.[1] The spread of ritualism and a desire for corporate expression of views about the schools question and some other issues had originally given an impulse towards some form of united action; later came an inclination towards more centralized co-operation, to some extent at least under the influence of men like J. D. Jones (1865–1942), for many years Secretary of the Congregational Union, and the Presbyterian John Wood Oman (1860–1939), Principal, 1922–35, of Westminster College, Cambridge.[2] Dealing with the period between 1909 and 1918, Dr Grant says of this centralizing tendency, in his *Free Churchmanship in England 1870–1940*:

It is unnecessary to seek far to discover reasons for the centralization of authority. Extreme Independency was proving unworkable in an industrial society. Nonconformists flocked to middle-class suburbs and left many poorer districts churchless and many rural districts devoid of support. Despite his opposition to Shakespeare's schemes, Carlile[3] admitted: 'Independency is a fine theory for the strong and the successful; it is a ghastly tragedy for the average man. Congregational and Baptist Churches were paying their ministers less money than a docker earned or a Town Council paid scavengers and dustmen. In a few wealthy Churches men received stipends calculated in four

[1] R. Newton Flew and Rupert E. Davies, *The Catholicity of Protestantism*, London, 1950, p. 30.
[2] It is interesting that Bishop Lesslie Newbigin was at Westminster College, Cambridge, in Professor Oman's time, and in his first book *Christian Freedom in the Modern World*, London, 1937, he expresses gracefully his indebtedness to Professor Oman. Bishop Newbigin's *The Household of God* shows a notable advance on Oman's *The Church and the Divine Order* published in 1919, but Oman himself almost certainly developed his thought in the years after 1919.
[3] 1862–1941, a leading Baptist.

figures, but in a great number of the poorer Churches the salary was less than a hundred pounds a year.'

D. Macfadyen[1] gave as one of his reasons for the advocacy of a stronger central authority the fact that Congregationalists were maintaining such a poor level of village ministry that most Nonconformists were lost when they moved far from the cities. Horton[2] expressed a common opinion when he thus lamented the weakness of an individualistic Independency: 'We should not like to say that we (Congregationalists) desire Episcopacy, or Presbyterianism, or even Methodism; but no one can study the schemes which have been before us without seeing that we covet the substance of these systems, the connection, the unity, the power of concerted action, the ability to occupy the central slums of the city and the sparsely populated districts of the country, the proper guardianship of the entrance to the ministry, and the equalised sustenance of ministers who are permitted to enter.'

Another motive that led men to seek to strengthen the Union was a desire to retain control of many Christian activities for the Church. The colleges, although responsible for the training of ministers, were independent of the authority of either Union, in many cases antedating both. The missionary societies founded under the impulse of the Evangelical Revival were in a similar position. The same applied to many charities and funds intended for the denominations. Churchmanship was the motive that led Williams[3] and Glover[4] to seek to bring admission to the Baptist ministry under direct denominational control. It was beginning to seem intolerable that, through jealousy of external authority, Churches were actually left without control over many aspects of their denominational life.[5]

These new centralizing impulses caused problems touching on doctrine. Many Free Churchmen had tended to think of the ministry as essentially involving care of a congregation, the actual ministration of the Word and the sacraments; a minister was pictured as one who has pastoral charge. The position of ministers who were College Principals, Professors, Denominational Secretaries or Secretaries of interdenomin-

[1] 1867–1936, a prominent Congregationalist.
[2] R. F. Horton, 1855–1934, for many years minister of a Congregationalist Church in Hampstead.
[3] Charles Williams, of Accrington, a Baptist, 1827–1907.
[4] Richard Glover, of Bristol, a Baptist, 1837–1919.
[5] Pp. 190–1.

ational bodies led to a realization that a minister is not merely the pastor of a local congregation, but the minister of the wider community; and this in turn raised questions about the nature of this wider community. One engaged in interdenominational interests owed his loyalty not merely to his own denomination but to the wider body: what then was the ultimate loyalty? And this really asks: What is the Church?

The development of the Baptist Union and of the Congregationalist Conference indicates a new orientation of the older theory of the absolute autonomy of the local congregation.[1]

Various Centralizations

The period after the 1914 war saw an increase in world meetings of denominations, for instance, among Baptists, Congregationalists, Methodists, Presbyterians. The Lambeth Conferences of Anglican bishops from all parts of the world assumed greater importance and their pronouncements in the period between the wars attracted greater attention. The formation of the Church Assembly by the Enabling Act of 1919, though it disappointed the hopes of many in the Life and Liberty movement[2] did give the Church of England greater control of its own affairs, though the Enabling Act kept the ultimate power in Parliament. The Assembly afforded a place to the laity and in some degree approached the Presbyterian Church Order, though Archdeacon Mayfield points out that the members of the Church Assembly can hardly claim to be representative of the Anglican laity.

World associations somewhat similar to the Lambeth Conferences exist among Baptists, Congregationalists, Disciples of Christ, Lutherans, Methodists, Pentecostalists, and Presbyterians.[3]

There had, too, been a growth of common theological writing, that is, groups of theologians of the same general outlook had produced 'symposia' or essays published together

[1] Cf. *The Congregational Quarterly*, xxxi, 1953, p. 179 and in *The Baptist Quarterly*, for April, 1959, the remarks of the editor, W. M. S. West, in his review of Dr Ernest Payne's *A Short History of the Baptist Union*, London, 1959.

[2] An association formed in order to free the Church of England from what many considered excessive control and interference by the State in Church affairs.

[3] Cf. Mudge, L. C., 'World Confessionalism and Ecumenical Strategy', *Ecumenical Review* xi, July, 1959; du Plessis, D. J., 'Golden Jubilee of twentieth-century Pentecostal Movements', *International Review of Missions*, xlviii, July, 1959.

in a single volume. The best-known of these were the Anglican: *Essays Catholic and Critical*, edited in 1926 by Dr F. G. Selwyn, *Essays on the Trinity and the Incarnation*, edited in 1928 by Dr A. E. J. Rawlinson, then Bishop of Derby, and *The Apostolic Ministry*, edited in 1946 by Dr K. E. Kirk, late Bishop of Oxford. The Presbyterians and Nonconformists likewise published similar 'symposia', such as those under the title *Essays Congregational and Catholic* edited in 1931, by A. Peel, for long editor of the *Congregationalist Quarterly*, and the more striking *Evangelical Christianity: its History and Worship* by a group which included various Free Churchmen, John Oman representing the Presbyterians, F. J. Powicke the Congregationalists and N. H. Marshall the Baptists.[1] In 1936 Dr W. R. Matthews, Dean of St Paul's, edited a volume entitled *The Christian Faith*, in which Anglicans, Baptists, Congregationalists and Presbyterians explained their understanding of the essence of the faith, with emphasis upon agreements.

Common statements of the belief existing in Churches involved the combined work of various groups. As many as twenty-five theologians co-operated in producing *Doctrine in the Church of England* in 1938, fourteen in producing *Catholicity*, a statement by the Anglo-Catholic wing of the Church of England, in 1947, and at least fourteen Free Churchmen co-operated in the answer to *Catholicity*, entitled *The Catholicity of Protestantism*, published in 1950. These, and many other publications by different groups at various times, gave experience in a kind of conciliar handling of difficult theological problems, and indirectly prepared for the wider co-operation which takes place in the meetings of the commissions of the World Council of Churches.

These centralizing tendencies, of course, could not fail to meet opposition on diverse grounds, sometimes because the organization was accused of being bureaucratic, sometimes because the central group was felt not to be adequately representative. Nevertheless the evidence points to multiple and strong forces tending to 'combined operations' and to thinking in common. That element in the Protestant tradition which

[1] A number of such books are listed by Dr Grant, *Free Churchmanship in England*, pp. 414–15.

is associated with 'private judgement', 'sturdy independence' and 'liberty of conscience' certainly remains strong; but among the more thoughtful it has been, if not weakened, at least modified, and religious problems tend to be seen as problems of the group rather than of the individual. One may wonder if the reported increase of sects outside the larger denominations may not be a reaction in the opposite direction.

5. THE 'NEW LOOK' IN BIBLICAL AND THEOLOGICAL STUDIES

Theological interest and emphasis have gradually changed between 1925 or thereabouts and the present time. But the change is not easy to describe, and the following brief account must be taken as very much of a bird's-eye view, and as perhaps over-simplified. Every one of the 'tendencies' mentioned may be found resisted by individual theologians and even by groups: and, besides, each 'tendency' itself runs off in different directions and assumes different forms as it is presented by different theologians. The tendencies are by no means all really new; yet there has been a change in the theological climate and the change is still going on.

The new outlook, then, tends:

(1) To esteem 'orthodoxy' and 'dogma' far more than was the case at the end of the last century and the beginning of this. What was called 'Liberalism' inclined to think that Christianity consists in recognizing 'the Fatherhood of God and the brotherhood of man'; the new currents regard such 'liberalism' as shallow and without a future.

(2) To a 'kerygmatic' approach, which means a confident announcement of the good news of the Gospel, rather than a justification of it to 'modern thought'.

(3) To an 'eschatological' view of Christianity, which involves more emphasis upon Christ's second coming and the world to come than upon Christianity as the fulfilment of human aspirations and as a means of happiness upon earth. The *eschata* are the Last Things, the ending of this present historical order and the beginning of 'the world to come'; there are various interpretations of the relation of this present world, or the present historical order of things, to the second coming of Christ and to the future world. One tendency is

so to stress the importance of the world to come that efforts to improve human society and institutions seem of little importance; the other is to insist that Christ has already introduced the kingdom of God into the world and so to lay stress upon efforts at betterment in our present order. In general, an 'eschatological' outlook rejects the older 'liberal' hopes of a Utopia upon earth and magnifies the importance of the world to come compared with the present world.

(4) To emphasize 'revelation', that is, to regard the Bible as God speaking to us, rather than to discuss how God inspired it or how it is to be reconciled with 'modern scientific discoveries'. Theorizing about the 'inerrancy' of the Bible and especially about 'verbal inspiration' are regarded as a misunderstanding of 'revelation', which is made not in 'propositions' but in the whole impact of the 'saving acts' of God in Christ. This tendency is strongly resisted by those who are called 'fundamentalists', who are accused of using Scripture as a collection of 'texts' which they can use to 'prove' preconceived doctrines.

(5) To 'form-criticism', which considers the Gospels, especially those of Mark, Matthew and Luke, as derived in large part from the prayers, hymns and various collections of 'sayings' of Christ, which existed in the Christian community before the Gospels were written. 'Form-criticism' thus goes behind the accepted text of the written documents and finds the origins of the New Testament in the Christian community, and so approaches somewhat to the Orthodox-Catholic concept of 'Tradition'. But some 'form-critics', by examination of ways and manner of speaking, judge some things in the Gospels to be more 'original' and authentic than others, and in doing so tend to lessen the authority of the Gospels.

(6) To lay stress rather upon God's difference from man than upon man's likeness to God. God is often said to be 'wholly other' and therefore human reason cannot establish that there is a God, but must accept God because he speaks to us. This unduly depreciates the power of reason, though it is true that man needs God's help in order to use his reason rightly in establishing the fact of God.

(7) To attend more to Christ's message and to regard him

as the Revealer, rather than to dwell on problems or theories of Christology, that is, the problems raised by the union of Christ's divinity and humanity. There is less interest in discussions about the Virgin Birth, the miracles of Christ (except the Resurrection), the 'Christ of history and the Christ of faith', to which so much attention was paid fifty years ago.

(8) To dwell upon the fall of man and his sinfulness rather than upon man's natural capacities for good. There is a strong reaction against the old 'liberal' idea of an evolutionary force inevitably making things better.

(9) To think of men more as forming a community than as single individuals. Individual 'religious experience' is less emphasized than the 'experience of the Christian community'. There is less attention to the 'psychology of religion', to comparative religion and to the history of religion, or at least these are not considered such important theological subjects as they used to be. The Christian faith tends rather to be taken as 'given' by God, and the emphasis falls rather upon God's choice of the ancient Israel and upon the Church as the new Israel (a community) than upon the processes in human development which lead to religion and to God.

(10) To connect God's 'Word' with Sacraments; and so there has been and is much discussion of baptism, confirmation and the Eucharist.

(11) To examine again the views of the 'Reformers', Luther, Calvin, Zwingli, Bucer, Cranmer, John Knox and others, and not necessarily to understand them as they were understood between the years 1650 and 1900.[1]

(12) To 'demythologize' the Bible. This, put at its best, is an attempt to express what the Bible says in language which the ordinary modern man can understand and which he can feel has a bearing upon the conditions of his own life; put at

---

[1] Very tentatively I venture the opinion that this reassessment is in the direction of emphasis upon salvation by *grace* alone rather than by *faith* alone, or perhaps upon faith as involving, in the concrete, more than subjective assurance of acceptance by God. Yet Professor Ernst Bizer gives the classical interpretation of Luther in his 'The Problem of Intercommunion in the Reformation', cf. *Intercommunion, Report* etc. London, 1952, pp. 58–83. Professor Bizer judges that Melanchthon, though giving away 'nothing that was of importance to Luther', still differs from Luther on the manner of Christ's presence in the Eucharist and approaches nearer to the Reformed view of an 'event-presence'. cf. pp. 74–7.

its worst, it looks like a declaration that the Bible is made up of myths, or even fairy stories, to convey the meaning of God's work of Salvation. It may score against a wooden literalism of interpretation and against a failure to recognize that words change in meaning and connotation, but it verges upon a denial that there is any final truth, with the implication that all formulations of doctrine become meaningless after a time and may be rejected without loss. This ends in theological pragmatism and leads logically to scepticism.

The Doctrine of the Church

Besides these there have been other tendencies, such as an interest in mysticism and a growing interest in liturgy; Neo-Thomism, which has profoundly influenced Catholics, has been studied sympathetically by a number of Anglican and Presbyterian theologians, who show its influence and even make their own contribution.[1] There were and are many diverse currents and cross-currents. The late and lamented Dr John Kenneth Mozley in his *Some Tendencies in British Theology, from the publication of Lux Mundi (1890) till the present day (1949)*, London, 1951, remarks upon the following as characteristic: a desire for theological synthesis; great interest in Biblical theology; renewal of the ancient doctrines of sin, atonement and redemption; a less anxious attitude toward critical problems; greater attention to the doctrine of the Church and the sacraments, especially the Eucharist; interest in apostolic succession, and in the ministry, with an 'eirenic tendency', which is, however, not to be exaggerated.[2] The influence of Sir Edwyn Hoskyns was far-reaching, and modern English biblical scholarship, Nonconformist as well as Anglican (and one may include Roman Catholics, too), owes an immense debt to him. Dr Mozley said:

> It would hardly be going too far to say that the opening words of Sir Edwyn Hoskyns' article, 'The Christ of the Synoptic Gospels', in *Essays Catholic and Critical* (1926) would meet now (1949) with a large measure of agreement from many theologians who are not Anglicans and differ from Anglo-Catholics on not a

[1] For example Professor A. E. Taylor, of Edinburgh, and Canon Demant and Dr E. L. Mascall of Christ Church, Oxford.   [2] *Op. cit.* pp. 57–80.

few doctrinal and practical issues. Hoskyns wrote, 'For the Catholic Christian *Quid vobis videtur de Ecclesia, What think ye of the Church?* is not merely as pertinent a question as *Quid vobis videtur de Christo, What think ye of Christ?:* it is but the same question differently formulated.' It is the approach to a common mind in respect of the identification which Hoskyns declared to exist which is of so great importance. Christians, whether they be scholars or not, are still a long way from agreement as to what is or should be the true doctrine of the Church. It is the sense of necessity for a doctrine of the Church, or, if that be too definitely stated, of due attention to the clauses in the Creeds which express the Christian's belief in the Holy Catholic Church, that has been rediscovered.[1]

The 'Great Church'

These new tendencies gave greater confidence, a sense of a more positive task and responsibility, and, especially as regards the new emphasis upon the Church, led to a feeling that the task was a common one. Anglican and Free Church students often attended the same lectures in Universities and read the same books. There was action and reaction. Dr Grant cites Daniel Jenkins, a Congregationalist, as saying in 1942:

It is undeniable that much of our present interest in the doctrine of the Church is due to the witness of the Church of England.

The Reformed Churches of the Anglo-Saxon world owe a debt of gratitude to the Church of England for her constant witness in recent generations to the unity of the Body of Christ when many of them regarded the Church as little more than a convenient form of religious association, and for her preservation and restoration of much of the rich content of the life and worship of the Great Church throughout the ages when many of them were busy light-heartedly casting away their heritage through ignorance of its true values.[2]

The expression 'the Great Church' was also used by Dr Nathaniel Micklem in his *What is the Faith?* 1936. Dr Micklem compares the relation of the differing Protestant denominations

---

[1] *Op. cit.* p. 62. Space does not allow due tribute to English and Scottish theologians. In general they are less theoretical than their continental brethren, have greater respect for sober reasoning, express themselves more moderately, change their views more slowly, and have greater regard for tradition.

[2] *Free Churchmanship in England 1870–1940*, p. 377, and cf. the whole section entitled 'The Reversal of the Liberal Trend', pp. 374–85.

to the 'Great Church' with the relation of religious orders to the Church.

Let me make quite clear what I conceive to be the truth in the witness of that section of Christendom through which I belong to the Great Church.

It was, I believe, at the call of God and under the guidance of His Spirit that in earlier days men retired from 'the world' into monastic life. In evil days the monasteries may have been the glowing centres of the Church's life, but they were not co-extensive with the Church. Similarly the Congregational Church (or a Methodist denomination) is a close fellowship or religious order of those who are separated by God for the disciplined life of a fellowship at a higher level than the whole Church has attained. These fellowships are not co-extensive with the whole Church, but they are a part of it that is of inestimable spiritual importance. That, unlike the monasteries, the Protestant denominations should be out of fellowship and communion with some part of the Church is tragic. If little or no blame attaches for this to those who went out or were forced out for conscience' sake, great blame would attach to those who should remain out in a satisfied isolation. There is schism in the Body; all sections are to blame for this, and repentance is required of all. A Congregational Church (or Methodist denomination) is now at this moment, like the Church of England, a fellowship within the Great Church. The Church is one, but her unity, which is created by the Word, lacks appropriate expression in outward form and common life.[1]

Anglicans in turn grew more kindly in their references to the Free Churches and read and quoted Nonconformist and Presbyterian writers. An attitude of sympathy and understanding grew, in spite of the negative results, at least as regards 'reunion', following the 'Appeal to all Christian Peoples' made by the Lambeth Conference of 1920 and the overtures made by the Lambeth Conference in 1930 and by the Archbishop of Canterbury in 1946.[2]

[1] *What Is the Faith?* Hodder & Stoughton Ltd, 1936, pp. 216–17. Cf. also, Daniel Jenkins, *Congregationalism, A Restatement,* who also uses the expression 'the Great Church', pp. 77–81.
[2] Cf. G. K. A. Bell, *Documents on Christian Unity,* vol. I, London, 1924, the Lambeth Appeal pp. 1–5; the close of the conversations with the English Free Churches in 1925, *ibid.* vol 2, London, 1930, pp. 98–117, and G. K. A. Bell, *Christian Unity: the Anglican Position,* London, 1948, pp. 108–15; the close of conversations with

6. RECOURSE TO PRAYER FOR THE HEALING OF DIVISIONS

In the Roman Missal one of the prayers before Holy Communion reads as follows: 'O Lord Jesus Christ, who didst say to thy Apostles, I leave peace with you, it is my own peace that I give you; look not upon my sins, but upon the Church's faith, and deign to give her peace and unity in accordance with thy will, thou who art God living and reigning for ever and ever. Amen.[1]

The origins of this prayer are obscure; it seems to be of ninth century Gallican origin and was introduced into the Roman liturgy by St Pius V in 1570. The 'kiss of peace' with which the prayer is associated, is an outward sign emphasizing the significance of the Eucharist. It is the prayer usually said in England when Roman Catholics and members of other religious allegiances meet together to encourage prayer for unity during the 'Week of Prayer', or 'Octave of Prayer', in January.

Agreement about the Need of Prayer

There are many things about which Christians are divided; but about the need of prayer that God may heal divisions not a single voice has ever raised the slightest doubt. Difficulties, however, have unhappily risen about the form that the prayer should take and the precise object of the prayer, that is, whether it should specify, implicitly or explicitly, the manner in which divisions are to be healed.

the Church of Scotland in 1934, Bell, *ibid.* p. 119, and *Documents* III, London, 1948, pp. 122–3. After the issue in 1938 of the 'Outline of a Reunion Scheme for the Church of England and the Free Churches of England' the Free Church Federal Council indicated that many members of their Churches thought that differences so essential had been revealed that 'any reunion would involve illegitimate compromise, a sacrifice of convictions and would rest on too precarious a basis for the reality of unity'. Cf. Bell *Documents*, vol. IV, London, 1947, p. 105. The issues turned mainly upon episcopal ordination, occasional lay administration of the Lord's Supper, communion with non-episcopal Churches, and the admission of women to the ministry. In 1946 the Archbishop of Canterbury, Dr Fisher, suggested intercommunion following some mutual act of commission for the Ministry. The Interim Statement about the Conversations between the Church of England and the Methodist Church, 1958, reveals how 'hard and tortuous is the road towards fuller unity'.

[1] O'Connell's version of the Latin: Domine Iesu Christe, qui dixisti Apostolis tuis: pacem relinquo vobis, pacem meam do vobis: ne respicias peccata mea, sed fidem Ecclesiae tuae: eamque secundum voluntatem tuam pacificare et coadunare digneris: Qui vivis et regnas Deus per omnia saecula saeculorum, Amen.

As to the form of the prayer, the British and Foreign Bible Society, founded in 1804, did not until 1859 have prayer at its committee meetings or at its annual meetings, because the Society wished to have Quakers on its committees and Quakers regarded prearranged prayer as dishonour to the Holy Spirit. The Evangelical Alliance, founded in 1846, mainly for the purpose of promoting Christian unity (though also for the purpose of combating 'popery and Puseyism', which, as Ruth Rouse says, was trying 'to pursue incompatible objectives'), refused to alter its Basis so as to admit Quakers, because its members wished to have 'social' prayer, which Quakers reject.[1]

Even when prayers are composed for a good object, it is possible that they may be expressed in a form which does violence to conscientious convictions. A prayer may, for example, suggest that members of Christ find their true unity not in the earthly Church but only in the glorified Church of the age to come, or that all Christians really form one Church in spite of their divisions. Apart from the actual wording of a prayer, the circumstances in which it is said, and the mentality of those who hear it, may give a colour and a suggestion; in certain *milieux* a formula of prayer which is framed in general terms might cause either misunderstanding or scandal.

His Lordship, François Charrière, Bishop of Lausanne, Geneva and Fribourg, in July, 1958, called attention to the possibility of prayers causing misconceptions, and to the need of avoiding in the wording of prayers any possibility of misunderstanding. Prayer reflects the mind of those who pray and Bishop Charrière said:

> The purpose of ecumenism, considered from the Catholic point of view, is:
> To make our separated brethren understand how the evangelical truths which they profess are found in their integrity in the ensemble of our doctrines. It can be that certain Catholics insist in too unilateral a manner on this aspect of Revelation; that is why we, too, must make progress in truth. When we speak of growing in the truth, let us always recall, however, that, on the one hand the Church as a society assisted by the Holy Spirit

[1] 'Voluntary Movements and the Changing Ecumenical Climate', by Ruth Rouse in *A History of the Ecumenical Movement*, pp. 315, 321.

could never have betrayed, over the course of the centuries, any part of revealed truth. On the other hand, as a living community, she can progress in the uniform explanation of Revelation; and in order to respect the legitimate tradition of our separated brethren, she could always modify her positive legislation on certain points.

This manner of presenting our stand on the union of Christians is at once sufficiently serene not to offend our separated brethren and sufficiently precise not to trouble the Catholic faithful.[1]

A striking instance is at hand to illustrate how the circumstances in which a prayer is said may suggest what is unacceptable. When, for instance, in 1838, Ambrose Phillipps de Lisle founded the 'Association of Universal Prayer for the Conversion of England', he could scarcely have expected Evangelicals or Nonconformists to join him, since he made it clear that he intended prayer for the corporate reunion of England with Rome. When in 1857 he changed the name of the association to 'The Association for the Promotion of the Unity of Christendom', there was scarcely more attraction for Evangelicals and Nonconformists. In the actual circumstances they would have been asked to pray for the corporate union of the Church of England with Rome, to which their opposition was undisguised and vehement.

This 'Association for the Promotion of the Unity of Christendom' was disapproved by Rome in 1864, and the reasons for this are of interest both in themselves and because they have been misunderstood by two writers in *A History of the Ecumenical Movement*. One reference to the Association reads as follows:

'The Association, although it had received papal blessing at its inception, was condemned by the Pope in 1864, and its Roman Catholic members were forced to withdraw. The papal seal was thus put on the idea that united prayer between Roman Catholics and other Christians was impossible—a strange fate for a union of prayer for unity with no other object.'[2]

Now in fact the purpose of the Association was not unqualified 'prayer for unity', but prayer for a particular kind

[1] Cited in *Unitas*, xi, no. 1, Spring, 1959, p. 49.
[2] 'Voluntary Movements and the Changing Ecumenical Climate', *op. cit.* p. 347.

of unity which many wise and thoughtful men, both Catholic and non-Catholic, judged to involve mistaken theological principles. The preamble to the French version of the articles of association spoke of 'the reunion in one sole Body of the three great Bodies which have preserved the heritage of the priesthood and the name of Catholic', which, as Purcell says in his *Life and Letters of Ambrose Phillipps de Lisle*, 'was begging the whole question from the point of view of those who insist upon the Protestantism of the Reformed Church of England, and deny the sacerdotal character of the New Testament.'[1] Moreover, it cannot be denied that there was a close connection between the Association and the *Union Review*, which de Lisle himself called 'the organ of the Association' and which permitted 'some bad and factious Catholic Priests', who 'were at open war with their Bishops', to advocate the abolition of clerical celibacy and to try 'by means of Reunion to overthrow the Discipline of the Church'.[2] Many members of the Association itself did, indeed, disapprove of the *Union Review* and desired to confine the purposes of the Association to general prayer for unity;[3] nevertheless there was evidence enough for the Roman Congregation to say that 'all members are required to offer prayers and all priests to offer sacrifices according to its intention, namely, that the three abovementioned Christian Communions, which, as is supposed, even now make up together the Catholic Church, may at last at some time or other join together to form one body.'[4] It was not 'prayer for unity' as such that was condemned, but a 'prayer for unity' that in the actual circumstances was made a means of spreading ideas about the kind of unity desired and the way in which it ought to come about.

There is another brief account of the condemnation of the Association for the Promotion of the Unity of Christendom in the *History of the Ecumenical Movement*, which reads as follows:

'The Purpose of the Association, as stated at the meeting at

[1] Vol. I, London, 1900, p. 374: 'La réunion en un seul Corps des trois grands Corps qui ont conservé l'héritage du sacerdoce et le nom de Catholique'.
[2] Letter of de Lisle to Lord John Manners, quoted in Purcell's *Life*, p. 415.
[3] Cf. the Address from Anglican Clergy to Cardinal Patrizi, printed in Purcell's *Life of Cardinal Manning*, vol. II, p. 279.
[4] Purcell's *Life and Letters of Ambrose Phillipps de Lisle*, p. 387.

which it was launched was "for united prayer that visible unity may be restored to Christendom". Prominent Roman Catholics and leaders of the second generation of the Oxford Movement (the older men, on the whole, stood aloof) rapidly showed their sympathy by joining the Association. Cardinal Wiseman had been friendly to the project, but by 1864 he had virtually become incapable of directing affairs, and more and more had passed into the unyielding hands of Dr Manning, a former Anglican, but now a bitter enemy of the Church of England. In April 1864 Manning persuaded the English Roman Catholic Bishops to address a letter to the Holy See on the subject, while at the same time making clear at Rome what the reply should be. It was as he desired. The A.P.U.C. was condemned in principle and Roman Catholics were forbidden to have any part in it.'[1]

It is perhaps unfortunate that Purcell, neither in his *Life of Cardinal Manning* nor in his *Life of Ambrose Phillipps de Lisle*, makes any reference to the fact that Cardinal Wiseman, far from being friendly to the A.P.U.C., had expostulated with Phillipps de Lisle and had sent a Report on the subject to Rome as early as 1857, the year of the foundation of the Association. This Report is published in Wilfrid Ward's *Life and Times of Cardinal Wiseman*, and shows that Wiseman took exactly the same view as did Manning, and as did the Congregation of Propaganda when it condemned the Association in 1864. In this Report, which is detailed and lengthy, Wiseman recounts an interview he had with Phillipps de Lisle, in which, 'I then took him to task for his pamphlet, "On the Future Unity of Christendom", which had caused grave displeasure, not to say scandal, among the Catholics. I had not only read it carefully, but annotated it throughout, finding it full of the grossest errors. One of the greatest of these was the way in which he spoke of "the three great denominations" (the term itself is Protestant) "of Christians", i.e. "Catholics, Greeks and Anglicans", as though they were all equal, and could treat of religious union upon a footing of equality. . . . He elsewhere calls them "these three great Churches" and "*the separated portions of the Church*".'[2]

[1] *Op. cit.* p. 279.
[2] Ward, *Life and Times of Cardinal Wiseman*, vol. II, London, 1897, pp. 485–6. The Report is printed pp. 479–91.

Phillipps de Lisle had a generous and enthusiastic nature and there can be little doubt that he cherished ideas that were illusory; for instance, he told Wiseman that ten Anglican Bishops were ready to make their submission to the Holy See, including even Dr Samuel Wilberforce, then Bishop of Oxford, and the aged Dr Henry Phillpotts, Bishop of Exeter; that the leaders of political parties were favourably disposed towards a national reunion with the See of St. Peter, and that 600 or more Protestant ministers were of the same mind. The A.P.U.C., of course, by no means shared these views or was committed to them; but, as Bishop Clifford of Clifton, a cousin of Phillipps de Lisle, put it:

> When first I heard of the Association through you some years ago I understood its object to be to get people to pray for unity, without any view being expressed by the association as to how this end was to be attained. So that Catholics prayed for unity in the only way in which they could pray, viz: that those who were not united to the centre of unity might become united. Father Ignatius Spencer used to engage all persons, Catholics and Protestants, to pray for a similar object in this manner. But of late it cannot be denied that the theory of there being three Christian communions, the Roman, the Greek, and the Anglican, all three branches of the true church, but all more or less in error, as regards minor points, has become one of the most prominent of the doctrines advocated by the association.[1]

Manning, indeed, had small need to use 'persuasion' to induce the English Catholic Bishops to petition for a winding-up of the A.P.U.C. They already saw, as he did, that the purpose and tendencies of the association had become particularist and divisive.

It should also be remembered that in his Pastoral on the subject, written in 1865, Manning called attention to the fact that any plans for reunion must take account of the Free Churches:

> From circumstances of birth and education, from historical contacts, and approximations of opinion, from social and political neighbourhood, and from manifold bonds of kindred, the

---

[1] Purcell, *Life of Ambrose Phillipps de Lisle*, vol. I, p. 402.

Anglican system is more nearly related to the Catholic Church than the Baptist, Independent, Wesleyan, and other Nonconformist bodies. And yet to the Catholic Church the millions who are in separation from the Established Church are an object of the profoundest sympathy and charity. . . . They are marked by a multitude of high qualities of zeal, devotion to duty, conscientious fidelity to what they believe. If they are rougher in their language against the Catholic Church, they are more generous and candid adversaries; more vehement but less bitter, and altogether free from the littleness of personality and petty faults which sometimes stain the controversy of those who are intellectually nearer the truth. For such men it is our duty to cherish a warm charity and a true respect, and not disproportionately to waste upon those who stand nearer to us the time and the sympathy which is their due. The time is come that the Catholic Church should speak, face to face, calmly and uncontroversially to the millions of the English people who lie on the other side of the Establisment.[1]

Manning may have been 'unyielding' and he certainly cannot be accused of any tendency towards liberalism in theology; yet few have spoken more generously about non-Catholics than he:

My experience among those outside the Church confirms all I have written about the doctrines of grace. I have intimately known souls living by faith, hope, and charity, and the sanctifying Grace with the seven gifts of the Holy Ghost, in humility, absolute purity of life and heart, in constant meditation on Holy Scripture, unceasing prayer, complete self-denial, personal work among the poor; in a word, living lives of visible sanctification, as undoubtedly the work of the Holy Ghost as I have ever seen. I have seen this in whole families, rich and poor, and in all conditions of life. Moreover, I have received into the Church I do not know how many souls in whom I could find no mortal sin. They were evidently in the grace of their Baptism. The same is the testimony of priests whom I have consulted.[2]

In short, the Association for the Promotion of the Unity of Christendom was narrow in its conceptions, unrealistic in its approach and suspect in its theology. It assumed the 'branch

---

[1] Purcell's *Manning*, London, 1895, p. 287.
[2] *Ibid.* pp. 780–1.

theory', which the Eastern Orthodox Church rejects as firmly as the Roman Catholic Church, and as do the majority of other Western Christian bodies. Its condemnation involved no disapproval of prayer for unity, but only disapproval of exhortations to prayer for ill-conceived or false ways and kinds of unity.

Praying for Contrary Things?

The principle underlying the matter is that it is right to pray for what it is right to desire. It is, then, right to pray for that unity of the Church which it is right to desire. Consequently it is fully right to pray that all Christians may be united in the one sole Church of Christ, or that they may be united as Christ wishes them to be united. If that is the main and the overriding desire any Christian can share it and pray accordingly. And here is the answer to those who say that such prayers for unity mean in fact, as one non-Catholic has put it, 'that Nonconformists would pray for the conversion of Roman Catholics to the truth, as they regard Rome as being in error'. Similarly, Catholics in prayer for unity would pray for the conversion of Nonconformists and all non-Catholics, as they regard them as being in error. The fallacy, I think, lies in forgetting that in prayer we must always, though we may not realize it, say 'Thy will be done'. When Christians now pray 'that they may all be one', this deepest and overriding intention should be, and, I am sure, is, that Christ's will may be fulfilled,—and the rest is made subject to that. We must desire the visible unity of God's Kingdom 'in the way Christ wills and by the means he chooses'. That formula cannot fairly be accused of any dangerous ambiguity, since it submits all human desires to Christ, and does not violate the conscientious conviction of anyone who is firmly convinced—as certainly Catholics and many others are convinced—that Christ willed a particular form of unity of the Church and that his will is already fulfilled in this or that 'Church'.

In fact, however, if a Plymouth Brother or a Disciple of Christ or any other Christian prays that I may be converted from my errors, I confess that far from being upset, I am glad and am grateful to him. If he turns to God for my welfare,

even though I disagree with him about the nature of my real
welfare, I have no doubt that God can override any human
errors and that God's Holy Spirit can guide us all to truth,
perhaps in ways that may surprise us. Similarly I am sure
that no member of another religious allegiance would feel
hurt if I prayed that he might share with me what I think is
a blessing even though he does not think it is a blessing, for he
in turn would commit the whole matter to God, whose very
foolishness is wiser than men, as St Paul said to the contentious
Corinthians.

There are, happily, very many prayers which all Christians
can and do say with great sincerity and fervour. In Lyons for
instance, in 1939, a week of prayer for unity was observed, and
all Churches used the same form of litany, in which was said:
'Beyond all our frontiers of language, race and nationality:
Unite us, Jesus! Beyond our ignorances, prejudices, and hostil-
ities: Unite us, Jesus! Beyond our barriers, intellectual or
cultural: Unite us, Jesus!'[1]

Prayers that all Christians may be united have been steadily
encouraged by successive Popes. In an apostolic brief, *Provida
Matris*, in 1895 Leo XIII dedicated a Novena of Prayer—the
nine-days devotion before Pentecost—to prayer for the 'Reunion of our separated brethren', and later to the 'Furthering
of unity in Christendom'. In 1909 St Pius X approved an
Octave of Prayer from January 18 to 25, and Benedict XV
commended it to the whole Church. There was, however,
some confusion about the precise meaning of the 'Octave'.
Originally in 1908 it had been promoted by two Anglicans of
'Roman' tendencies, the Rev. Paul Wattson and the Rev.
Spencer Jones, and its almost exclusive purpose was to pray
for the corporate reunion of the Church of England with
Rome.[2] For this reason some Catholics and some non-Catholics
were hesitant to give it their full support; and some confusion
was caused by the fact that when Father Paul Wattson became
a Catholic in 1909, together with his two communities of the
Friars and Sisters of the Atonement, he continued to promote

[1] Quoted in Olive Wyon's *Praying for Unity*, London, 1955.
[2] For details see David Gannon's *Father Paul of Graymoor*, New York, 1952, pp.
32–158; and Père Boyer's 'Father Paul Wattson's Concept of the Unity Octave',
Unitas, viii, no. 4, Winter, 1956, pp. 199–202.

the Octave of Unity. This may have led some non-Catholics
to think that the main object of the Octave was corporate reunion of Anglicans with Rome, and disavowals of this by
Catholics may in turn have given the impression that to join in
the Octave meant an acceptance of the absolute impossibility
of anything except 'individual submission to Rome', from
which most Anglicans, however 'pro-Roman', recoiled.

Later, however, largely due to the regard which many non-
Catholics felt for the late Abbé Paul Couturier, it became more
generally understood that the object of the Octave is not a
'proselytizing' one, but an effort to encourage all Christian
people humbly to turn to God and to pray for that unity of
Christendom which God wills.

Père Boyer accounts that the Abbé Couturier did much to
solve the difficulty as regards the object of the prayer by suggesting that people of all religious allegiances should pray for
the sanctification of themselves and of all others.[1] 'Instead of
praying, for example, "for the return of the Lutherans to the
faith of Rome" he asked for 'the sanctification of the Lutherans", a prayer that Lutherans themselves would willingly
make. In the same spirit interdenominational meetings have
been held during the Octave, in which Catholics and non-
Catholics listen to irenic discourses, hear or sing the same
hymns, and join together in some prayer. In short, those who
take part in such meetings try to show how, in spite of divisions,
they are still united.'

Père Boyer remarks, however, that:

If the attempt has been made to propose a formula of prayer
acceptable to all Christians, this very effort has not produced
the desired effect because the different non-Catholic groups which
observe the Octave publish different intentions.

It is possible, nevertheless, to obviate the difficulty in another
way without detriment to the desire of having the Octave
accepted universally. All Christians, Catholics or otherwise, can
pray for the unity of the Church, such as Christ instituted it.
Let Catholics, then, in their Churches pray in accordance with
their faith, and let them ask resolutely and perseveringly for
the return of their separated brethren to the true fold, since such

[1] *Art. cit.* p. 201.

is the condition of real unity. This should not offend anyone. The word 'return' does not cast any blame; it simply signifies the adherence of a Christian to the Church of Rome after a state of separation; besides, it is not over words that we should contend.[1] As for non-Catholics, by deciding to pray for unity during the same period with Catholics they thereby manifest their desire for unity. To be sure, they pray according to their idea of unity; but as long as we are disunited our prayer for unity will differ, just as our ideas on the Church and its unity differ.[2]

This point was appreciated by non-Romans and in 1941 the Faith and Order Conference began to suggest that an Octave of Prayer might take place preferably in January. In certain quarters uneasiness has been expressed lest this week of prayer be turned into a means of propagating certain particular ideas about the nature of unity; but the Faith and Order Conference has made no change in encouragement given to the January period of prayer and seems to take more or less the same point of view as Père Boyer.[3] One of the most encouraging signs in ecumenical meetings is the insistence upon prayer. Very often indeed it is said that the reunion of Christendom cannot come by human contrivance, but only by God's action, and prayer is urged upon this ground.

In 1950 the Sacred Congregation of the Holy Office issued an *Instruction* to the Bishops, the import of which has, I think, sometimes been misunderstood. Just as the style of a document like the *Report* issued at Evanston in 1954 strikes a Catholic unfamiliar with what Dr Visser 't Hooft calls 'ecumenical language'[4] as lacking in due firmness, so, too, pronoucements

[1] This seems to me a most pregnant and pertinent observation. Words have emotional associations and the word 'submission' has an unpleasant association. The Catholic concept of the papacy is not a simple concept of superiority over inferiors; it is, rather, the feeling of a family whose head is able to speak with loving understanding for the whole body and to be a focus of the obedience and love which all owe to Christ. Without this presupposition of union in charity, of union in a common understanding and in obedience to our loving Saviour, the Catholic idea of ultimate authority in the Church simply does not make sense.

[2] *Art. cit.* p. 202.

[3] Cf. *Commission on Faith and Order, Paper no. 26, Minutes of the Working Committee* p. 29. The Chairman of the Committee, Dr Oliver Tomkins, said: 'In prayer we inevitably have some preconceived ideas in our minds as to how our prayer would be answered, but if we concentrated on God and on prayer for his will to be done then the Holy Spirit in whom our prayer was made was able to transcend our intention and make it acceptable before God.'

[4] 'Notes on Roman Catholic Writings concerning Ecumenism', *Ecumenical Review*, viii, 2. January, 1956, p. 195, see further pp. 110–11.

from Rome strike a non-Catholic unfamiliar with the *stilus Curiae*, of the Holy Office, especially, as unduly brusque and uncompromising. One style tries to persuade, the other decides.[1] I shall return to this cause of misunderstanding in chapter IV. Meantime it may be noted that Père Boyer, than whom few are in a better position to judge, regards the *Instruction* of 1950 as 'the great charter of work for unity'. In the *Instruction* occurs the following paragraph:

> The present time has witnessed in different parts of the world a growing strong desire amongst many persons outside the Church for the reunion of all who believe in Christ. This may be attributed, under the inspiration of the Holy Ghost, to external factors and the changing attitude of men's minds, but above all to the united prayers of the faithful. To all children of the true Church this is a cause for holy joy in the Lord; it urges them to extend a helping hand to all those sincerely seeking the truth by praying fervently that God will enlighten them and give them strength.[2]

These words were, without doubt, most carefully selected and are worth weighing.

First, the growing desire for unity is attributed to supernatural causes. The Holy Spirit of God is declared to be active (*afflante sancto Spiritu*) in causing it, and in the concrete this cannot but apply to the ecumenical movement, since desire for unity has been manifest principally in connection with this movement.

Secondly, a change of outlook is affirmed on the part of those outside the Church. This, again, though it is not said to be confined to any one in particular, has most obvious application to those in the ecumenical movement.

Thirdly, the words 'those sincerely seeking the truth' should be pondered, for in the context they seem to apply especially,

---

[1] Some Reports issued by the Commissions of the World Council are models of clearness and conciseness. Considering that these Commissions have to take into account the feelings—for often there is no clear doctrine—of over 170 bodies which are in greater or less disagreement, their objectivity and clearness is a notable achievement. In this respect the Report on *Intercommunion*, edited in 1952 by Donald Baillie and John Marsh, is outstanding.

[2] Translation published in *The Tablet*, 195, no. 5728, March 4, 1950, p. 175. As this document has been much discussed, and not always understood, it is printed in full in *Appendix 2*.

though not exclusively, to those in the ecumenical movement.

Lastly, Catholics are exhorted both to rejoice in this desire for unity and to help by prayers. The *Instruction* does not, as appears in further passages, confine to prayers the help which Catholics may give, but it lays great stress on prayer.

In his account of the 'Roman Catholic Church and The Ecumenical Movement', Dr Oliver Tomkins ends as follows: 'Even in the face of the deep divisions here recorded, many Christian hearts find their deepest reassurance that the path towards unity will not be for ever barred in the fact that earnest prayer already unites a growing army in all confessions. Other weapons may grow blunt, but no one will ever doubt, even though we cannot measure, the effectiveness of this weapon of self-negating prayer.'[1]

To this it may be added that on several distinct occasions in January, 1959, Pope John XXIII made reference to the Unity Octave of prayer and commended it to the faithful. The first instance was in a letter to the Cardinal Vicar of Rome in which the Pope told of his intention to go to the Basilica of St Paul on the last day of the Octave for a service of prayer for the Catholics of China. In this letter, the Holy Father calls the Octave a 'precious and providential observance'.

The second time he referred to it was during a visit to one of the noted Roman seminaries, the Ateneo Laterano. There the Pope pointed out that it was not a question of another pious practice but that it was an ardent movement of the spirit and of the heart which seeks to make its own the longing and the supreme aspiration of the divine Master, who a few hours before His immolation on the Cross implored of his Father the unity of all men.

Again in a visit to a rest home for ailing priests, Pope John urged them to pray for a particular intention of his during the Unity Octave. It was also significant that the Holy Father chose the date of January 25 to announce the convocation of a general council, one of whose purposes would be the furtherance of Christian unity.[2]

---

[1] *A History of the Ecumenical Movement*, p. 693.
[2] *Unitas*, xi, no. 1, Spring, 1959, pp. 61–2, *ad litteram*.

Chapter Three

DEVELOPMENT IN ECUMENICAL
THOUGHT

1. FIXED POINTS OF AGREEMENT

'All Christians must unite.' This is the most fundamental conviction, indeed a fundamental article of faith, in the ecumenical movement. In spite of the most profoundly different conceptions about the manner of the unity and the nature of the unity this general conviction remains unchanged. It was the same at Edinburgh in 1910 as it was at Evanston in 1954. The idea of unity is basic. It may be a vague idea, possibly even an ambiguous idea. Yet its very indetermination, its very vagueness, helps to make it dynamic. The ideas 'liberty, equality, fraternity' were likewise vague and indeterminate, yet they changed the world's history. 'Liberalism' was a vague idea, almost a mood and a method, yet its influence was great and powerful.

Part of this general idea is the conviction that all Christians must have towards one another not only tolerance but positive and active charity. Christians must try to understand one another and recognize the good not only in individuals but also in groups and 'Churches'. This is, of course, not a new conviction, but it has received new emphasis and prominence. Of old it was said 'Hate the heresy, but love the heretic'; the new outlook might change the saying to 'Love the heretic and find the element of truth in his heresy'. Indeed, the expression 'ecumenical bigotry' has been used, which is a charge that some ecumenists have dislike and even prejudice against anything or anybody appearing to impede the effort towards unification of Churches. Nevertheless, this conviction of the need of mutual understanding must be taken in the actually existing situation, which involves nearly two hundred different

Churches with the most differing outlooks and with deep-seated traditions of opposition to other Churches and with members who do not always grasp what the need for unity implies.

Secondly there is general agreement that unity among Christians ought to be outward and visible and not merely inward and invisible. Here there is considerable difference of outlook, but in general all would agree that Christians must at least co-operate together in friendly fashion and most would tend to desire an approach, at least, toward unity in doctrine and in administration.

Lastly, there is the conviction that the existing divisions between denominations are contrary to God's will. Here perhaps agreement is not so universal, since voices have been raised to declare that diversity is good and that existing divisions, with charity, may be preferable to any proposed or possible alternative. But the trend is against the divisions, and the World Council aims at dissolving the present diversity and reconstituting a complete unity, and herein lies its great problem.

Within this general body of agreement considerable development has taken place during the last fifty, indeed during the last fifteen, years. There is a mass of evidence about this, found in almost every writer on the subject. As the American Theological Committee said in their *Report*, published in the volume *The Nature of the Church*[1], 'It is clear that the Churches in America have moved far from the traditional positions which have been held in the past.'

What direction is this development taking? Speaking very tentatively—for who would venture anything else, where elements so many, so diverse, and so changing are involved?—the development seems to take the following general directions:

1. A clearer and stronger though not universal recognition that doctrinal matters are of the first importance and that to attempt to gloss over differences by ambiguous formulas is wrong both in theory and in practice.

2. A certain strengthening of denominational loyalties.

3. Recognition of 'non-theological factors' as causes of division.

[1] London, 1952, p. 251.

4. A trend to 'sacramentalism'.

Again, I must insist that to treat of these topics is to run the risk of some misrepresentation; but this risk is almost inherent in any treatment of so large a movement. How diverse were judgements upon the Oxford Movement, yet the 'ecumenical movement' is wider in scope and less clearly defined than the Oxford Movement. Somewhat hesitantly, then, a word on each of these points.

2. INCREASED ATTENTION TO DOCTRINAL ISSUES

At Stockholm in 1925 and even at Lausanne in 1927 the Life and Work groups exercised considerable influence in a 'practical' direction. The slogan 'service unites, but doctrine divides' met with considerable approval and it was thought that the agreements among Christians could be listed in such a form that the disagreements would seem of small consequence, while interest in common good works might gradually lessen the disagreements until perhaps they would vanish. But at Edinburgh in 1937 this tendency had much lessened and the supreme importance of facing doctrinal differences frankly was widely, if not universally, recognized.

Very many, both in the movement and outside it, have commented upon this change.[1] Dr Visser 't Hooft, writing about the 'Genesis of the World Council of Churches', in *The History of the Ecumenical Movement*, speaks as follows:

> During the 1920's the separate existence of a movement concerned with 'practical' Christianity and another movement concerned with doctrine and Church order had not seriously been challenged. In the 1930's it was increasingly felt that this separation could not be justified. The slogan 'Doctrine divides, but service unites', used so often as an argument for the separate existence of Life and Work, seemed misleading and inadequate in the new situation in which it was generally realized that the profoundest differences between the Churches in their attitude to society were in the realm of theological thought. Just as Life and Work, in preparing for the Oxford Conference (1937) was forced to face the doctrinal issues, so Faith and Order had to

[1] For instance, Canon Gustave Thils, of Louvain, in his *Histoire doctrinale du mouvement oecuménique*, Louvain, 1955, especially pp. 98–100; Père Congar, in *Divided Christendom*, published in 1939, made some additions to the original French work *Chrétiens désunis*, pp. 140–3.

consider the 'non-theological' factors, e.g. the sociological realities, which constitute obstacles to unity. It is significant that at the meeting of Faith and Order in 1934 the main subject of discussion was 'The Church and the World'. The old distinctions were breaking down.[1]

Dr Visser 't Hooft repeated much the same at Lund in 1952:

About thirty years ago a Faith and Order approach concerning joint planning for the time and place of the Life and Work and Faith and Order Conferences was answered with the dictum: 'Service unites, but doctrine divides.' In the particular situation of those days the fear of a direct attack upon the fundamental difference between the Churches can perhaps be understood. Today such a fear can only be considered as a pure anachronism.[2]

The Chairman of the Lund Conference, Dr Y. T. Brilioth, Bishop of Upsala (Church of Sweden), said in his presidential address:

Looking back, I seem to discern several stages in the history of our movement. The first stage, represented by the preliminary meeting at Geneva, and to a large extent by the Lausanne Conference (1927), was characterized by a certain minimizing of the differences. . . . A certain tendency to gloss over differences by formulas that could be interpreted differently was perhaps not absent at this stage. During the second stage the real depth of our differences became gradually more and more apparent. That was the result of the answers which came in from the Churches, and the very thorough work done by special commissions. . . . Gradually the tenacity of the confessional tradition, the different background and temper of the different Churches, became realized. It is remarkable that the ecumenical movement has had as a parallel, perhaps partly as a result, a great revival of confessional consciousness. The world organizations of Churches belonging to the same tradition have shown a remarkable activity. This is true of Methodism. It is also true of Lutheranism. . . . The whole development of theology has brought with it on the one hand a discarding of earlier controversies—such as that between an eschatological and an immanentist theology—and on the other a reaffirmation of doctrinal positions which seemed to have lost their actuality.[3]

[1] *Op. cit.* p. 700.   [2] *Report of Lund Conference*, 1953, p. 101.
[3] *Report of Lund Conference*, 1953, p. 101.

Bishop Neill also says the same, when he speaks of the frequently suggested 'federation' of Churches, which, he says 'makes a strong appeal to laymen, who tend to be impatient of the subtleties of theological debate'. But 'an acceptable solution cannot be reached merely by the evasion of difficulties. . . . The slogan "Service unites, doctrine divides" has been seen to represent a superficial understanding of the situation . . . those who have started in the field of common Christian action have found themselves driven back from practical problems to theological foundations.'[1]

Co-operation not enough

Some of the actual difficulties inherent in any policy less than complete organic union have been indicated above, when speaking of the missions. But even in Europe and in America, both 'federation' and co-operation when put into practice raise questions of doctrine. There is a very general agreement that a diluted Christianity will not do; and indeed the question how far the 'dilution' should go, how much water should be admitted into the wine of 'true doctrine', would occasion almost as much difference of judgement as do the existing divisions. Training for the ministry in theological colleges can only with difficulty be conducted on 'federation' lines, since training for the ministry presupposes some concept of what the young men are being trained for, and so demands a doctrine about the ministry, because even to assume that there is no Christian doctrine of the ministry is itself the acceptance of a doctrine about the ministry. Inter-denominational theological Colleges have been said to tend to 'liberalism'. Moreover, co-operation between the ministers and the laity, if it is to be permanent, demands some theory of the mutual relations between the two; and the 'Presbyterian' theory regards the laity as having a definite function—not an unimportant one—in the administrative structure of the Church. No system of 'federation' yet devised seems able to reconcile the desire to maintain the 'distinctive witness' of each federating body with the problems of 'intercommunion' which inevitably raise questions of the meaning of

[1] 'Plans of Union and Reunion', *History of the Ecumenical Movement*, p. 493.

baptism, confirmation and the Eucharist, and so of the meaning of 'the Church'. Besides, again and again it has been
repeated that Christ meant his Church to be really one
in faith, organization, worship and witness; and 'federation',
unless it is accepted as a transitory measure, seems to imply
the admission that the unity which Christ willed is impossible;
yet to admit it even as a transitory measure is dangerous,
since it may develop into a substitute for real union.

For this reason Dr Visser 't Hooft at Lund in 1952 warned
against the danger of thinking that co-operation is enough.

> There are still many [he said] who think of the present relation-
> ship of our Churches in the World Council of Churches as an
> end rather than a beginning, as a solution of the problem of
> unity rather than as the first step on the road to unity. The
> danger of this is that in the words of the present Archbishop of
> Canterbury, the World Council can thus become a narcotic
> rather than a stimulant. We must react against the temptation
> of accepting the present established disorder of our ecclesiastical
> world simply because it has been made to look less shocking as it
> has been provided with an ecumenical varnish.[1]

A Plurality of Churches is Absurd

This danger, that the World Council may come to be re-
garded as an adequate form of union is much stressed by
Bishop Newbigin. He points out that the World Council of
Churches has 'a churchly character', and comments:

> It follows from this that, while we must accept the statements of
> the Toronto document[2] that the World Council is *in intention*
> neutral on the question of the form of the Church's unity, we
> cannot agree that it is neutral *in fact*, for it is itself a form of that
> unity. And if the Council be regarded as anything other than a
> transitory phase of the journey from disunity to unity, it is the
> *wrong* form.

Bishop Newbigin then expands his conviction that a federation is neither the New Testament conception of the Church
nor a real Church unity nor a practical scheme.

---

[1] *Lund Report*, p. 130.
[2] Cf. Appendix IV, containing the main heads of this important document,
which clears up many misunderstandings.

All must be one—and so all conceptions of reunion in terms of federation are vain. They leave the heart of the problem—which is the daily life of men and women in their neighbourhood—untouched. . . .

Such conceptions envisage a sort of unity whose foci are not the word and sacrament in the setting of the local congregation, but the conference table and the committee room. They do not grapple with the fact, which any serious reading of the New Testament must surely make inescapable, that *to speak of a plurality of Churches, is strictly absurd.*[1]

After pointing out that many regard the present level of co-operation as sufficient, Bishop Newbigin records his strong disagreement; and it is significant of the somewhat surprising changes which the ecumenical movement has occasioned that a Bishop of the South India Church who was a Presbyterian exhorts 'Catholics' to intransigence:

There is a real danger that the World Council, while proclaiming itself neutral as regards the form of the Church's unity, should in fact come to be accepted as the organ of a sort of federal union. There can be no doubt that very many Protestants[2] who ardently support the work of the Council do so with this underlying idea; they take seriously the fact that the Churches have, in some sense, accepted one another as Churches, and have covenanted together in the Council; and they are hurt and irritated by the refusal of Catholics to take what seems the next step—complete intercommunion among the Member Churches. There are doubtless many who would regard such intercommunion as a step towards organic unity, but the evidence seems to me clear that a vast number would regard it not as a step towards organic unity, but as a substitute for it. The present position of the English Free Churches is an example of the evidence I refer to. In other words, federation is apparently accepted as an adequate goal. In this situation, I think that Catholics may be provisionally justified in their intransigence, that in refusing intercommunion on these terms they are perhaps, in the only way possible to them at the moment, maintaining their witness to the Scriptural

---

[1] *The Household of God*, London, 1953 (italics mine).

[2] Footnote by Bishop Newbigin: 'It will be obvious that here, as frequently throughout the lecture, I am using the two words "Protestant" and "Catholic" in a very loose sense to describe the two major points of view represented in the present ecumenical conversation, and that the word "Catholic" is not here being used as it is in the Creed.'

truth about the nature of the Church which might otherwise be hopelessly compromised.[1]

These words might be pondered by Presbyterians who felt upset when the 1958 Lambeth Conference insisted upon episcopal ordination before intercommunion.

Doctrinal Relativism Condemned

There has been no lack of affirmations from the leaders of the movement that there is no hope in mere 'formulae' and ambiguous language. Dr Visser 't Hooft, writing under the title 'Various meanings of unity and the unity which the World Council seeks to promote',[2] rebuts what he considers some misrepresentations of the attitude of the World Council towards church unity:

> The first [misrepresentation] pretends that the World Council of Churches makes organic unity an end in itself and stands for unity at any price. It is an astonishing fact that in spite of all that we have said and done in order to show that we do not believe in union *per se*, and that we believe that doctrinal relativism is not an ally but rather a danger for the true ecumenism, we still hear some voices which maintain that the World Council minimizes truth.[3] But then there are people who have such a narrow horizon that to them even the attempt to join with other Christians in the search for unity is already treason to the faith.[4]
> We can only affirm in word and in deed, in our declarations of policy, in serious theological study work and in our relationships with the member Churches that the only unity we are concerned with is unity in obedience to truth. Unity sought because we are called by the one Shepherd to form one flock.[5]

[1] *Ibid.* p. 23.
[2] *Ecumenical Review*, viii, October, 1955—September, 1956, pp. 18–36.
[3] This certainly seems to me a very general impression among Roman Catholics, and it was said by a group of Anglican theologians regarding the Evanston 'Message', cf. further, pp. 111–12.
[4] There are a good number of others besides the Roman Catholics who have not joined the World Council, so I do not think the reference is only to Roman Catholics. The International Council of Christian Churches regards the member churches of the World Council as 'apostate', and is strongly opposed to groups which co-operate with it in any way, as, for instance, to the American National Association of Evangelicals, which allows 'observers' or 'consultants' at meetings directly or indirectly associated with the World Council. Cf. H. Lindsell, 'An Appraisal of Agencies Not Co-operating with the International Missionary Grouping', *International Review of Missions* xlvii, April, 1958, pp. 203–9; and N. Goodall, 'Evangelicals and WCC-IMC', *ibid.* pp. 210–15.
[5] *Art. cit.* p. 22.

In an important statement received by the Central Committee of the World Council of Churches at its meeting in Toronto in July, 1950, and commended for study and comment by the Churches, it is said:

> There are critics, and not infrequently friends, of the ecumenical movement who criticize and praise it for its alleged inherent latitudinarianism. According to them the ecumenical movement stands for the fundamental equality of all Christian doctrines and is, therefore, not concerned with the question of truth. This misunderstanding is due to the fact that ecumenism has in the minds of these persons become identified with certain particular theories about unity which have indeed played a role in ecumenical history, but which do not represent the common view of the movement as a whole and have never been officially endorsed by the World Council.[1]

What kind of Unity?

Dr Visser 't Hooft lists some 'outstanding points' which the representative organs of the World Council have made when speaking about unity and which they admit to need further study and closer examination:[2]

(a) That the unity of the Church is a *given* unity, in that it has its essential reality in Jesus Christ Himself. (*Amsterdam Report*, p. 51; *Evanston Speaks*, S.C.M. Press, p. 18; *Lund Report*, p. 20, etc.)

(b) That this unity must be made manifest to the world. (*Evanston Speaks*, p. 19; Toronto Statement, IV; 2, etc.)

(c) That full Church unity must be based on a large measure of agreement in doctrine. (*Amsterdam, Assembly Report*, p. 55, 'Christ—the Hope of the World', p. 20; Edinburgh Report, p. 253).[3]

(d) That sacramental communion is a necessary part of full Church unity. (*Lund Report*, p. 49.)

(e) That a ministry acknowledged by every part of the Church

---

[1] *The Church, the Churches and the World Council of Churches*, London, no date, p. 4.

[2] Père Boyer commented on these 'points' in 'Dr W. A. Visser 't Hooft's Concept of Unity', *Unitas*, viii, No. 1, Spring, 1956, pp. 3–6.

[3] This underlines the radical problem of ecumenism: who is to decide how 'large' must be the 'measure of agreement in doctrine'?

(*Lund Report*, p. 20) and some permanent organ of conference and counsel (*Edinburgh Report*, p. 253) are required, but that a rigid uniformity of governmental structure (*Lund Report*, p. 34) or a structure dominated by a centralized administrative authority (*Amsterdam Report* p. 127) are to be avoided.

(*f*) That the unity of the Church depends on the renewal of the Church. (*Lund Report*, p. 21; *Evanston Speaks*, p. 23.)

(*g*) That this unity is not to be sought for its own sake only, but for the sake of the world in which the Church performs its mission of evangelism. (*Evanston Speaks*, p. 20; 'Christ—the Hope of the World', p. 20; *The Calling of the Church to Mission and to Unity*, Central Committee Minutes, 1951, p. 66.)

I do not claim that this list of affirmations is complete, but it seems to me that these are the recurrent emphases in World Council statements about unity.[1]

Dr Visser 't Hooft frankly declares that the theologians— and indeed people generally—in the movement 'make certain discoveries about unity', and that 'as we seek to understand together what the Divine Lord says to all the Churches, we have come to understand more and more the meaning of unity in Him.'

In this whole matter we are however faced with the great diffi- culty that the categories of our theological thought as they grow out of our various confessional backgrounds are inadequate to express what we have found. Our theologies and particularly our ecclesiologies have not caught up with the new ecumenical situation. There are too few theologians who have woken up to the fact that new answers must be given to the new questions which have arisen as a result of our ecumenical encounter. And I would like that to be, so far as I have any right to make it, an appeal to the theological faculties in our member Churches to take score of the need for much more serious work on this subject.[2]

---

[1] *Art. cit.* p. 22. In point (*e*), relative to 'a rigid uniformity of governmental structure' and to 'a structure dominated by a centralized administrative authority', I am not sure that Dr Visser 't Hooft distinguishes clearly enough between what the Council says about itself and what it says about the Church. By the Toronto Declaration no belief about the nature of the Church is excluded, and hence a Church could be a member of the Council while firmly believing that the Church itself should have a centralized dominating authority. Doubtless the large majority of member Churches are convinced that the Church ought not to be so governed; but this conviction by no means conditions membership in the Council. Cf. p. 180n.

[2] *Art. cit.* p. 25.

The permanent organization of the World Council cannot speak with a final authority; the statements emanating from various bodies, such as the great assemblies and the more limited conferences of Faith and Order, speak with a somewhat different 'authority'. But, says Dr Visser 't Hooft, 'the real distinction is not whether a larger or a smaller body has spoken, but, in the words of William Temple in 1938: "Any authority that it (the Council) may have will consist in the weight it carries with the Churches by its own wisdom."'[1]

The Council, then, can give information, help, encouragement; can select topics for study and discussion; can indicate the lines which it judges plans for unity between member Churches should follow—but it cannot do more than commend its findings and its proposals to the member Churches. Dr Visser 't Hooft adds: 'We do not believe that every coming together of Churches necessarily advances the wider cause of unity. It is possible to conclude union too hastily or on insufficient grounds. As the Lucknow Central Committee said: "It (unity) may be sought without due regard for truth in doctrine and soundness in order."'[2]

3. A STRENGTHENING OF DENOMINATIONAL LOYALTIES

At first sight it may seem surprising that a movement for unity should occasion a strengthening of 'local loyalties'; but this is only one of the many 'paradoxes' which appear in the movement and surprise will vanish when the matter is considered.

First, there is no doubt of the fact. It was noted by Bishop Brilioth, who is cited above, p. 63. The Commission on Intercommunion said:

Experience of the Ecumenical Movement has itself taught us not to seek easy and shallow ways of reunion through a flabby grasp of doctrine and a glossing over of our differences of belief. The Ecumenical Movement, by deepening the sense of the Church, and bringing members of widely different Churches together in Christian fellowship, has driven many Christians to seek a deeper understanding of the distinctive positions of their own Churches. Thus paradoxically the growth of the ecumenical

[1] *Art. cit.* p. 21.   [2] *Art. cit.* p. 29.

consciousness has led to a widespread revival of 'confessional' or denominational consciousness, and a great many Christians (especially of the younger generation) have at the same time become much more ecumenically-minded and developed a new and lively interest in the question: Why am I an Anglican? or Why am I a Lutheran, or an Orthodox, or a Presbyterian, or a Baptist? The very coming together of the Churches shows them how different they are from each other (as well as how close they are in their fundamental Christian faith). Thus at the same time there has emerged a new desire for intercommunion and a new realization of its difficulties; and so the problem has become acute.[1]

This development was natural. Consideration of union with other Churches led on to consideration of what each Church considered essential in its own position, what was its own 'distinctive witness'; and this in turn led to further examination of the origins of denominations and the correlation of their historical 'traditions' with the 'traditions' and usages of other denominations and, latterly, with the common Christian 'Tradition'. It has often been said that no Church in uniting with others, should lose anything which was fundamental to itself or at least nothing good which was fundamental, but that all should bring their contribution to the one universal Church. Inevitably each denomination began to examine more carefully what was 'fundamental' to itself; and this tended to revive memories of almost forgotten history and to increase a sense of loyalty to the characteristic 'traditions' of each. Not a few books have appeared giving accounts of the origins and doctrine of particular denominations. Often, of course, these books have been written in an 'eirenic' spirit, with a view to possible reunion; not seldom they contained very frank criticisms by members of denominations of themselves and of certain developments in their history, but they are symptomatic of a certain intensified denominational loyalty and of the desire of each to 'make its own contribution', as a corporate entity, to any united body.

These 'denominational loyalties' are a complex of mixed elements, doctrinal, administrative, historical and psychological

[1] *Report of the Commission on Intercommunion*, in the volume *Intercommunion*, London, 1952, p. 22.

which is bewildering. A Roman Catholic, for instance, distinguishes matters of faith from matters of custom; the language of the Liturgy is an example. For practical reasons some would prefer a vernacular liturgy, and others would prefer to maintain the ancient languages, either Latin or other ancient languages customary in different parts of the Church. But he has a clear standard of reference, since there is an authority to decide the practical issue and to judge how far practice may impinge upon doctrine. He will be perplexed by the mixture of doctrine with mere customs or usages or feeling in many non-Catholic denominations, even when he has considerable knowledge of them. He will tend to assume that non-Catholics distinguish, as he himself does, between what they accept as a matter of faith, and what they accept as a matter of usage, forgetting the very different outlook of many of his separated brethren, who, especially during the last hundred years, have grown accustomed to a certain absence of sharply defined doctrine, and yet often cling instinctively to their own ways and usages.

The 'denominational loyalties' involve, to simplify almost to excess, things like the following:

1. Doctrinal standards, like the Thirty-Nine Articles or the Westminster Confession, or even, on the part of some, objection to any doctrinal formulation beyond the words of Scripture, including objection to the creeds. There is an anti-dogmatic denominational loyalty as well as a dogmatic loyalty. The Disciples of Christ provide an example of this.

2. Loyalty to conceptions of 'the ministry', and these include such things as the power of a layman occasionally to celebrate the Lord's Supper; the appointment of women as ministers; the ceremony of 'ordination' of ministers; the relation of ministers to superior authorities, such as bishops or diverse 'Unions' or 'Conferences'; the right of local congregations to 'call' the minister they choose, as against the right of a bishop or a patron or some central body to appoint one; the general attitude of the priest, minister or superintendent or 'messenger' to the other ministers and to the people. 'Free Churches' and many others have rooted objection to the appointment of ecclesiastical authorities by any civil power.

In the background of these 'loyalties' lie doctrinal beliefs, such as those in apostolic succession and the priesthood of all believers.

3. The manner of the Church services, which often reflects doctrinal convictions; for instance, the emphasis on preaching as against ritual; 'free prayer' as against set forms of prayer, or, if these latter are admitted, the form they should take; the frequency of the Eucharist and the requirements in communicants; even the type of building used for a church and its decorations, the 'table' for instance as against the altar, ecclesiastical ornaments and even the dress of the clergy.

In the background of all this lie beliefs about the Eucharist and about general sacramental efficacy.

4. Questions concerning Church membership: infant baptism as against adult baptism ('sponsored' or 'believer's baptism'); admission after baptism in infancy to full membership status, and the way in which this is to be conferred, by confirmation at the hands of a bishop or other minister, or by a solemn profession of faith.

5. Attitude of reverence toward those who initiated the denomination (Luther, Calvin, Cranmer, Knox, Wesley, Alexander Campbell, etc.) and the question of celebrations in their honour on occasions like centenaries etc. Here again, doctrinal considerations are mingled with a kind of personal attachment, and the historical is not easily distinguished from the doctrinal. Names become almost like a flag and have immense emotional associations.

These are the briefest indication of the meaning of 'denominational loyalty'—the merest suggestion to enable a reader to grasp something of the complexity of beliefs, usages, inherited mental attitudes and sometimes prejudices with which the Council of Churches has to deal.

This increase of denominational loyalties has its good side and its bad. On the one hand it tends towards an increased appreciation of firmness in doctrinal matters and against watering down the faith; on the other it may tend also to preservation of what is merely accidental or a matter of pride comparable to national pride—from which, indeed, denominational loyalties are not always completely free.

4. Non-Theological Factors Influencing Divisions

One notable advance in ecumenical thought is the recognition of the influence on religion of social, cultural, political and other so-called 'non-theological factors'. These, say the Lund Report, 'were hardly as much as mentioned at Lausanne in 1927. At Edinburgh in 1937 some attention was paid to them in one section of the Conference. Since then there has been an increasing realization of their importance', and various studies have been made of them under the aegis of the World Council. I list some of them:

1. *Memories of persecution.* What is heard from parents and grandparents and what is read in history books (which too often are far from impartial) has a deep effect upon the mind. Logically the fact that the ancestors of one group of people persecuted the ancestors of another group of people ought not to have much effect on present-day groups. But in fact it has. Whatever may be the rights and wrongs in bitter times now past, the fact remains that memories are very long, and some still feel a psychological barrier between themselves and those bearing a name which is associated with the oppressors of their ancestors.

I deliberately refrain from giving instances; but too much attention can hardly be paid to the historical aspect, with which 'our heritage' and 'our traditional outlook' are intimately connected. In nothing can the World Council of Churches do a better service than by using all its influence to secure the exact and impartial writing of history, for religion and history are closely connected.

2. *Political associations.* These are largely intangibles; but the legal connection between a Church and a State, though it may be fully justifiable in several circumstances, nevertheless occasions an intertwining of nationalism and religion which is sometimes hard to disentangle. Totalitarian systems usually tend to 'nationalize' Churches.

Similarly, ideas of liberty and independence associated with certain political systems have a profound influence upon religious outlooks and convictions, just as these latter may have had an influence upon the former. Dr W. E. Garrison, an

American Disciple of Christ, has said how shocking he found the account given him by some of the ablest minds of the Church of Sweden of that Church's connection with the Swedish State. Dr Garrison speaks frankly of his own feelings:

> I shall doubtless go on to the end being a white American, with a firm attachment to the concept of a great deal of individual liberty in economics, industry, government and religion, an unwavering devotion to the Free Church principles of voluntaryism and the separation of Church and State, a certain suspicion of intricate ecclesiastical systems which seem to me to be constructed according to feudal and monarchical patterns that not only are outmoded but never were relevant to the Christian gospel, and a strong belief that the struggle for any high degree of doctrinal agreement among free minds as a condition of unity is both futile and unnecessary. From this standpoint, which I am not likely to abandon and which I know many other Christians will not abandon, I must do my honest best to view the standpoints that are different from mine and try to see how the situation looks to those who occupy these points of view.[1]

Sometimes members of Churches speak in a very satisfied way about the part that the institutions of their Church have played in developing certain political patterns.

3. *'Cultural' factors*, such as education. The voluntary efforts of many Churches have played a laudable part in fostering education of all types; but the modern tendency towards centralization makes problems for Churches which have schools, and this undoubtedly colours their attitude toward other Churches which do not agree with the effort to maintain schools other than the State schools. This is particularly true of England and the United States (for somewhat different reasons), and there is room here for ecumenical influence.

4. *National feeling, language, finance, philosophical background, social position*—all these tend to intertwine with religion and to make for cohesion of groups and against a universal Church.

To call attention to these 'non-theological factors' does a

---

[1] *Lund Report*, p. 185. Dr Garrison is doubtless representative of many American thinkers, and it is interesting to see how he connects his general outlook with his religion.

service in showing that prejudices must be put aside and the religious problem must not be identified with, or made dependent upon anything other than itself. At the same time there are two dangers in emphasis on these factors. The first danger is that of forgetting that religion inevitably influences the whole of life. Although it is true that Christianity is not identified with 'European civilization', and is compatible with, and possibly even more congenial to, certain culture-patterns of the Far East and other lands, nevertheless Christianity is bound to exert an influence on art, literature, and to some extent on law and government. The problems inherent in the impact of Christianity upon non-Christian peoples are not easy of solution and it would be a mistake to attempt to solve them by some glib formula about the distinction between religion and 'culture', as though religion could be made a water-tight compartment. Christians hold the finality of the revelation given by Jesus Christ; and this inevitably leads to conclusions about the nature of marriage, about education of children and about the part Christians may play in activities where secular culture and religious culture are intermingled, as they are in many non-Christian countries. The problems which arise in the expansion of Christianity cannot be solved merely by insisting upon the distinction between 'non-theological' and 'theological' factors, or between 'religious life' and 'secular life'.

Missiologists all agree that the Church must become indigenous to all lands and that all races and nations must find their fulfilment in the Church of God, which fosters every good gift of whatever kind. Yet the Church must be universal. To reconcile these two: a Church which all races and nations feel to be their own, and a Church which belongs to all men in the world, brings problems which can be solved only by superhuman wisdom and heroic holiness.

The second danger is the possible suggestion that all religious convictions are really due to other influences than honest thought about religion. It is perfectly true that character has its effects upon judgement; as St Thomas says: *Qualis est, talis ei finis apparet*—'as a man is, so does he judge of values'. St Paul says 'Mere man with his natural gifts cannot take in the thoughts of God's spirit; they seem mere folly to him, and he cannot grasp them, because they demand a scrutiny which is spiritual.'[1] Yet, granted the influence of the moral factor, the demands of truth remain firm, and the religious problem ought not to be presented as excessively complicated. A man can and must follow the truth where he sees it, at whatever sacrifice.

5. A Trend Towards 'Sacramentalism'

Interest in Liturgy

At Lausanne in 1927 this trend was noted, as the *Report* said: 'We testify to the fact that the Christian world gives evidence of an increasing sense of the significance and value of Sacraments, and would express our belief that this movement should be fostered and guided as a means of deepening the life and experience of the Churches'.[2] Certainly in the ecumenical movement there is ample evidence of a continuing and intensified interest in sacraments and in liturgy. Apart from sincerely held convictions about the meaning of the sacraments, external reasons have tended to increase this interest. Great assemblies, not only of Faith and Order, of Life and Work and of the World Council, but also of the World Christian Student Federation, brought many into concrete touch with different forms of worship, and so widened horizons. Then, with plans for a corporate 'reunion' of Churches, and with respect for conscientious beliefs, went the practical consideration that it would be easier to go back to earlier forms of liturgies, from which existing forms were in one way or another derived, than to attempt to fit together existing service books. In the Church of South India the form of service commended, though not imposed upon the uniting bodies, must be of interest to all liturgists. In the section of the *Constitution* on Holy Communion it is said:

The following parts, numbered (i) to (ix) were before the union in general included in all the services of Holy Communion in the uniting Churches; and in none of those Churches was there in

[1] I Cor. 2: 14; Knox. [2] *Report*, p. 472.

use a service from which any of the more important of these parts was omitted. The Church of South India desires that all these nine parts shall have a place in every Communion Service; but it is not necessary that the order in which they are here given should be exactly observed; and it may be arranged that one or more of the first three parts shall be included in a separate service which (whether held on the same or on a previous day) forms one whole with the actual Communion Service and which all those who will be communicants are expected to attend.

(i)   *Introductory prayers.*

(ii) *The Ministry of the Word,* including readings from the Scriptures, which may be accompanied by preaching.

(iii) *The Preparation of the Communicants* by confession of their sins, and the declaration of God's mercy to penitent sinners, whether in the form of an absolution or otherwise, and such a prayer as the 'Prayer of Humble Access'.[1]

(iv) *The offering of the gifts of the people.*

(v)   *The thanksgiving* for God's glory and goodness and the redemptive work of Christ in His birth, life, death, resurrection and ascension, leading to a reverence to His institution of the Sacrament, in which His own Words are rehearsed, and to the setting apart of the bread and wine to be used for the purpose of the Sacrament with prayer that we may receive that which our Lord intends to give us in this Sacrament.

Note: It is suggested that this section should begin with the ancient phrases and ascription of praise known as the *Sursum Corda* and the *Sanctus.*

(vi) *An Intercession for the whole Church,* for whom and with whom we ask God's mercy and goodness through the merits of the death of His Son.

(vii) *The Lord's Prayer,* as the central act of prayer, in which we unite with the whole Church of Christ to pray for the fulfilment of God's gracious purposes and to present our needs before the throne of grace.

(viii) *The Administration of the Communion,* with words conformable to Scripture indicating the nature of the action.

---

[1] A prayer which in the Book of Common Prayer comes after the absolution and immediately before the prayer of Consecration, in the 1662 Order, but in the *Alternative Order* of 1928, before the Sanctus.

(ix) *A Thanksgiving for the Grace received in the Communion*, with
which should be joined the offering and dedication of
ourselves to God, unless this has been included earlier in
the service. This thanksgiving may be accompanied by an
appropriate hymn.[1]

In accordance with the recommendation of the Constitution
An Order for the Lord's Supper was drawn up and formally approved for use in 1954, and, it is said, it has been welcomed
and is becoming the regular form of eucharistic service.
Père Bouyer considers this liturgy 'more satisfactory than
any liturgy that emanated from the Reformation'.[2]

Symptomatic of this increased interest in forms of worship
are the two books written by special Commissions at the request
of the permanent Continuation Committee of Faith and Order,
the one entitled *Ways of Worship*, the other *Intercommunion*.
On each of these subjects the special Commissions issued a
Report to the Continuation Committee, which in the meeting
at Lund in 1952 issued its own *Report* for the consideration of
the Churches, published in book form, as is usual with Faith
and Order meetings. Each of these three books contains a
Report, together with a series of essays.

The book on *Ways of Worship* is divided into three sections:
'The Elements of Liturgy', 'The Inner Meanings of Word and
Sacrament' and 'Liturgy and Devotion'. The book on *Intercommunion* is divided into two parts: a series of accounts of the
theories and practices of diverse Churches, and a series of
'denominational statements'.

In the Introduction to *Ways of Worship* we read:

One outstanding fact to which our evidence directs attention is
the widespread growth, however tentative in some parts of the
Church, of a Liturgical return. It should not be overlooked that
the new understanding of liturgical values has been fostered by
exegetical, historical and theological study within the separate
communions, widened after the war by the renewed possibility

[1] *Constitution*, pp. 50–2.
[2] 'A Roman Catholic View of South India', republished in *Theology*, lxix, no.
427, January, 1956, p. 4. Père Bouyer cites many of the prayers. All the same,
reservations must be expressed about the doctrine implied, especially in the
rubric prescribed when the consecrated bread and wine are insufficient and more
has to be used.

of international contacts. The development is further due to the experience of ecumenical thinking and personal contacts during a growing series of ecumenical gatherings, both large and small. We may also feel that the values of the *grande tradition* had worked silently and were now beginning to come into their own in places where such renewal might have seemed least likely, even if long desired. Under these various influences the contrast between Word and Sacrament has become at least a carefully studied comparison, and at best a new realization of a needed integration in our total worship of God in the wholeness of His Church.[1]

'Eucharist-centred Worship'

In the *Report* of the Commission on Ways of Worship occurs the following passage:

(1) *Eucharist-centred worship.* This scriptural synonym for the Lord's Supper is appropriate here because it is as a giving-of-thanks that Orthodoxy is supremely centred upon this Sacrament as the norm and fount of all worship. Whatever the tradition, whether the service be thought of primarily as sacrifice or communion, to be Eucharist-centred is to think of all other worship as preparation for, thanksgiving after or meditation upon this central act. By a natural logic such traditions hold the Eucharist as the central and most attended service of every Sunday (and other great festivals), though many would maintain that there is no necessary connection between centrality and frequency.

(2) *Preaching-centred worship.* Others maintain that the characteristically *Christian* element in worship is that it is the proclamation of the Word of God. Just as a central affirmation of Christianity is that the eternal Word was made flesh, so the central act of Christian worship is to attend upon the proclamation of that Word as witnessed to in Scripture, as it is expounded to the congregation of faithful men by those in whom the Church recognises the right of exposition.

The drawing together of these two emphases is one of the signs of our time in the ways of worship.[2]

Under the heading *Current Developments* the Commission remarks that there is a general feeling that all worship ought to be corporate, and then says:

[1] *Report*, p. 11.
[2] *Ways of Worship Report*, London, 1952, p. 20, (italics mine).

Connected with this is the fact that most of the present efforts at liturgical renewal may be said to have started, more or less consciously, from a rediscovery of the sacramental character of worship. In some cases, though by no means all, this has led to an increasingly frequent celebration of sacraments.

There is a widespread genuine unrest, a very definite feeling that worship ought to regain its central place in life, and that it can only do this if Churches return to the primitive patterns.

Reference is made to liturgical studies both among Catholics and non-Catholics, and 'at long last we are beginning to see that, measured by the standards of the New Testament and the early Church, none of our current ways of worship is fully adequate.'[1] But a certain resistance to the liturgical movement is recorded, especially the rise of 'divisive movements of a pentecostal character'.

Real Presence and Sacrifice

The Report of the Commission remarks upon the change with regard to the real presence, and begins from a principle deeper than any ordinarily invoked:

It is of outstanding importance that throughout Christendom there is a reaction against the persistent error which sets the spiritual and the material in opposition to each other. What is being given up is not only the idealism and modernism which preached retirement into the inner castle of the soul, devaluing all outward acts and exalting 'purely spiritual changes'. . . . It is not that the importance of the inner life is diminished but it is set in the context of the human situation in which nothing can have its full importance which is not human all round, physical as well as spiritual. For God did not create merely souls, He created men. He does not merely regenerate our souls, He regenerates us.

The mode of the Real Presence in eucharistic worship is the main question in debate in those Churches which are striving for a liturgical reformation. To quote Bishop Stählin: 'The Real Presence of Christ is the foundation of all liturgy.' Evidence coming from different parts of Christendom reflects two discoveries: (i) The ministry of the Word is no greater guarantee of spirituality than the ministry of sacraments. Its true character

[1] Pp. 20–1.

is lost sight of whenever 'word' is taken to refer to human efforts on the part of a preacher to offer his own thoughts as a means of edification. In the true administration of the Word God Himself imparts His gifts in a quasi-sacramental way, addressing man as a person, comprising body, soul and spirit. The work of the Holy Ghost, *Creator Spiritus*, is not confined to what we are pleased to call spiritual. (ii) The words 'magic' and 'magical' have in the past been used all too loosely and too irresponsibly as terms of reproach. The sin of magic does not lie in the association of divine power with matter, but in the attempt by man to control that power by material means in an ungodly and quasi-independent way. God the Creator alone in His creative activity calls the things which are not into being through His Spirit and in His redemptive activity, His so-called 'new creation', restores them.[1]

The Report also says:

In many Churches, when for practical reasons the celebration of Holy Communion is omitted, the Sunday morning service is called an Ante-communion service. Dr Reed (American Lutheran) and Dr Micklem (English Congregationalist) both suggest that the use of this word expresses the truth that the service is only a torso and that weekly Communion at the least should be the normative practice.[2]

Different views are, of course, mentioned; but it is significant that no rejection of transubstantiation is recorded (though doubtless many do reject it, perhaps misunderstanding what it really means); on the contrary the 'theology of Maria Laach' is suggested as a 'most promising approach to some understanding between the Roman Catholic and non-Roman Churches. The papal encyclical *Mediator Dei* has at any rate not closed this door from the Roman side.'[3]

As regards *sacrifice*, it is said:

Another live issue is the sense, if any, in which eucharistic worship may rightly be regarded as sacrificial. It is well known that both Luther and Calvin rejected this conception on the ground that the sacrifice of Calvary had been offered once for all and was not to be repeated. But recent studies of both the New Testament and the patristic evidence have led to a re-

[1] P. 29.   [2] P. 32.   [3] P. 33.

opening of the question, and it is asked whether sacrificial language does not appear in a new light when the idea of representation replaces that of repetition, and when communion and offering are seen as two sides of the same thing. The paper contributed by Bishop Hicks of Lincoln to the Edinburgh Conference[1] suggests that one cannot receive the sacrifice of Christ without participating in it by offering oneself. This suggests the further thought that the Church, by offering itself, is offering the Body of Christ. In the Eucharist the celebrant is the risen Lord, uniting the members of His earthly Body to Himself in His offering of Himself to the Father.[2]

The whole section is a far, far cry, from the Westminster Confession's 'the Papist sacrifice of the Mass, as they call it, is most abominably injurious to Christ's one only sacrifice', and even from the Thirty-Nine Articles' 'the sacrifices of masses . . . were blasphemous fables and dangerous deceits.'[3]

The Lund Faith and Order Conference recorded disagreements about the sacrificial aspect of the Eucharist:

Some of us believe that in the Lord's Supper, where they enter into communion with the crucified and risen Lord, they only offer a sacrifice of praise and thanksgiving and obedient service as a response in faith to the benefits the Lord gives us. Others would like to insist, however, that in the Holy Eucharist the Lord Jesus Christ as our Great High Priest unites the oblation made by His body, the Church, with His own sacrifice; and so takes up her own adoration into the *Sanctus* of the company of heaven. Between these two views there are others to which a brief reference would not do full justice.

It is felt, however, that a deeper understanding of the meaning of 'unites' in the above paragraph, particularly in the light of biblical eschatology, might help to resolve real divergence and misunderstanding at this point.

N.B. There are those among us who regret that the discussion of the Eucharist has concentrated on this sacrificial aspect. In their opinion the main question is the real bodily presence of the crucified and risen Lord and our receiving of His body and blood.[4]

---

[1] *The Second World Conference on Faith and Order*, London, 1938, p. 325.

[2] Pp. 33-4.

[3] It is needless to delay over the interpretation of this article given by Newman in Tract 90 and by many others since his time, which is based upon the distinction between the rejection of 'sacrifices' and of 'sacrifice'.

[4] *Lund Report*, p. 43. In *Ways of Worship* there are references to the Eucharistic sacrifice in the account given of the Reformed Churches (of Holland and

6. THE COMMUNION OF SAINTS AND MARIOLOGY

Ways of Worship was unique in this, that it contained for the first time in ecumenical history a definite and detailed consideration of the place of the Mother of God in the economy of salvation. There were four essays, one by Father Conrad Pepler, an English Dominican, one by Professor Vladimir Lossky, the famous Orthodox Professor of Paris, one by the Rev. T. M. Parker, chaplain and fellow of University College, Oxford, and the last by Frère Max Thurian, of the community of Taizé-les-Cluny, within the French Reformed Church. In his review of this section of the book, Professor Cyril C. Richardson, of the Union Theological Seminary, New York, says:

> The section on Mariology is even more unrepresentative, not to say surprising, although the four essays on the topic are the best in the book. There is a very readable one by a Roman Catholic. Two are reprints from E. L. Mascall's Symposium, *The Mother of God* (London, 1949) and present the Eastern and High Anglican views very persuasively. T. M. Parker's contribution is especially notable. It has a marked freshness about it, and stresses the need to praise Our Lady (as does the East), rather than to ask her favours (as does the West). Max Thurian shows how the Virgin can be commemorated in the Reformed Church, without compromising its basic tenets. He warns against the dangers of intercessions of the saints, but he appends an Office of the Virgin used in the Cluniac Reformed Community. The Virgin is only invoked in the verse, 'Blessed art thou among women.'[1]

A little further on in the review Professor Richardson says: 'The absence of a vigorous Protestant article against devotion to the Blessed Virgin is a most serious omission.'

Perhaps here Professor Richardson had not space to speak of the duty laid upon the Commission in the matter. The Second World Conference at Edinburgh in 1937 had said

Switzerland) of Lutheran, Anglican, Old Catholic, Orthodox, Roman Catholic (by Dr F. G. van der Meer of Holland); though sometimes the language used is not always luminously clear nevertheless there is certainly a re-examination of the Reformers' views and a most striking absence of language which might offend a Roman Catholic.

[1] *Ecumenical Review*, iv, no. 3, April, 1952, p. 315.

that the communion of saints 'for the Orthodox and certain other Churches and individual believers means fellowship not only with living and departed Christians but also with the holy angels, and, in a very special sense with the Blessed Virgin Mary. In this connection the way in which we should understand the words "all generations shall call me blessed" was considered. No agreement was reached and the subject requires further study.'[1]

The origin of this insertion into the *Edinburgh Report* is given by Professor Nicholas Zernov, in chapter 14 of the *History of the Ecumenical Movement* entitled 'The Eastern Churches and the Ecumenical Movement in the Twentieth Century':

At the Conference at Lausanne in 1927 Professor Bulgakov (1871–1944) caused the greatest stir at the Conference by introducing into its discussions the question of the significance of the Blessed Virgin Mary in the reunion of Christians. Professor Bulgakov said: 'Holiness is the goal and essence of the Church's life: the holiness of the manhood of Christ, actualized in the communion of saints. But we cannot separate the humanity of our Lord from that of His mother, the unspotted *Theotokos*. She is the head of mankind in the Church; Mother and Bride of the Lamb, she is joined with all saints and angels in the worship and life of the Church. Others may not feel drawn, as I do, to name her name in prayer. Yet, as we draw together towards doctrinal reunion, it may be that we are coming potentially nearer even in her regard.'[2]

The suggestion of devotion in prayer to the Virgin Mary provoked sharp opposition from the Protestant wing of the Conference, and Dr A. E. Garvie (a Congregationalist), the chairman of the meeting, stopped the speaker and called his attention to his departure from the subject of the conference.[3] Professor Bulgakov refused to accept this ruling and renewed his plea for the recognition of Mariology as a doctrinal problem of vital importance to the ecumenical movement. His persistence was crowned with some success, for the Communion of Saints was included in the programme of the Faith and Order Con-

[1] *Edinburgh Report*, ch. iv, p. 236.
[2] *Lausanne Report*, p. 656.
[3] Professor Zernov gives references in which the authenticity of the incident may be verified.

4

ference at Edinburgh. The incident was significant for it showed how wide was the gap separating the leaders of the ecumenical movement at the beginning of their work.[1]

Thus the treatment of Mariology which the Commission on Ways of Worship in 1952 inserted into its book had a considerable history behind it. The Commission in 1948 had agreed that 'the matter was primarily a liturgical question', and considerable discussion of it took place the following year.[2] Presumably the Commission's task was to find out what was the meaning and the background of a liturgical matter which in fact plays so large a part in the devotional life of more than half the Christians in the world, and to lay its findings before the Lund Conference, which was then to report on it and send the Report to the individual Churches, who alone have power of any decision. Surely the idea of a 'vigorous Protestant article against the devotion' carries the suggestion that the Faith and Order Conferences are to become somewhat of a debating society, which is to defeat their very purpose.[3]

The Lund Conference, after considering the Commission's *Report* concluded as follows:

We are agreed in believing in the Communion of saints as the fellowship of the whole company of believers on earth and in heaven. In its worship, the Church on earth joins in prayer and praise with angels and arch-angels and all the company of heaven. While all agree in accepting the communion of saints in this sense there is grave difference of interpretation. Some only use the word 'saints' to mean the whole Christian body in general. Others also use it in a special sense to denote the blessed saints in heaven.

Most people are ready to sing hymns of thanksgiving for the saints, thanking God for His victory in the lives of His people. Some would go further and venerate the saints in heaven to the extent of celebrating their feasts; still others would seek their intercession believing that they can help us who are still engaged

---

[1] *History*, pp. 656–7.
[2] *Ways of Worship*, p. 256.
[3] Nor is Professor Richardson quite exact in his account of Dr Parker's admirable article, but space may not have allowed full explanation. Dr Parker did not say that the East only praised Our Lady rather than prayed to her as does the West; but, agreeing that East and West both praise her and pray to her, said that the emphasis was more on the former in the East and on the latter in the West. He also said that he thought all prayer in the West tended to be a little self-interested.

in the earthly warfare. For many of those who venerate the saints, the Blessed Virgin Mary has a unique place. It is obvious that the status of the Blessed Virgin in Christian worship is a matter on which there is deep divergence. (*Cf.* the relevant essays in the *Ways of Worship* volume.)

We must recognize that for some this aspect of worship is an expression of love flowing through Christ's mystical body. Others believe that such usages would be contrary to their understanding of the whole of the Christian faith, and they neither know nor desire any intercessor other than their Saviour.

It is therefore clear that these issues can be discussed properly only in the context of the doctrine of grace and of the work of Christ and of the Holy Spirit.

Another divergence of view emerges in connection with the practice of prayers for the departed. Some hold that the departed require the help of our prayers, and that we are in charity bound to pray for them that the work of God begun in them may be brought to perfection. Others hold that in committing the beloved dead to the care of the God who gave His only Son to be the Saviour of sinners they may find joy and comfort in His love.

This matter also is one which demands most thorough theological work touching as it does the heart of redeeming love.[1]

[1] *Lund Report*, pp. 43–4.

Chapter Four

ECUMENICAL STRAINS AND STRESSES

1. The Paradoxes of Ecumenism

The World Council of Churches has 'gradually developed into an institution, burdened by a very expensive bureaucratic set-up',[1] and publishes voluminously. Yet it exists for no other purpose than to bring about its own death and the death of all its member-churches.

This is a central paradox, from which many other paradoxes proliferate: 'oneness in Christ, disunity as Churches'; wish to be completely united, resolve to maintain 'distinctive witness'; love of separated brethren, denominational loyalty; wish for church order, fear of 'rigid structure'; respect for others' form of worship, resolve to preserve one's own; ministry in a denomination, ministry in the Church universal; general agreement, particular dissent; agreements in disagreement, disagreements in agreements; urgency for decision and action, need of prolonged re-appraisal; accusations of pan-Protestantism, accusations of 'drawing the Protestant Churches in the direction of Rome'[2]; the World Council of Churches, not the Council of the World Church; Dr W. E. Garrison and Archimandrite Hatzopoulos . . . the list could be continued and each item illustrated. Perhaps the most striking paradox is official clearness and popular misunderstanding.

In this protean creature, so difficult to describe or classify, so different in appearance when viewed from different aspects, there is nevertheless a backbone which remains articulate and strong amid all the variations: the conviction that all Christians must unite. 'That they may all be one': these words are meant not only for people in the ecumenical movement, nor

---

[1] 'An Appraisal of the World Council of Churches', *Ecumenical Review*, vi, no. 4, July, 1954, p. 364. The article is by Marc Boegner, President of the Protestant Federation of France and one of the Presidents of the World Council of Churches.
[2] *Art. cit.* in previous note, p. 368.

for those outside it, but are meant to include the millions and millions of men and women who do not know and love our Lord and Saviour. In the face of them, and of the difficulties confronting Christian missionaries and Christians in many lands, surely impatience with one another must cease and bewilderment seek understanding.

The population of India is about 360,000,000 of whom only 2.3 per cent is Christian, that is, between eight and nine million. The population increases each year by about 6,000,000 and so 5,862,000 are added to the non-Christians each year, as against only 138,000 Christians, apart from Christian conversions. By this calculation, the number of Christians is relatively decreasing.[1] In view of the missionary task it is tragic that Christians are divided; and in all thought about the divisions of Christians this tremendous missionary call ought to be kept clearly before our eyes—not, of course, as an argument for doctrinal liquidity, which would hinder the missionary task, but certainly as an incentive to humility and to a deep desire for unity and for all intelligent ways of fostering it. Here is one real significance of the ecumenical movement: it can help or hinder missionary effort.

The Council and the Members

Although the ecumenical movement is not the World Council of Churches, much less the permanent officials of that body, nevertheless the official publications paint a faithful picture. Yet even these, although sometimes written in a style oddly reminiscent of the Canons of the Council of Trent or of the Vatican Council, are not infallible and do not always represent (how could they?) the feelings of all the members of the Council, still less of those who remain outside the Council.

In all these publications the most scrupulous desire for accuracy is manifest; but the difficulty is the multitudinous variety of beliefs and opinions which defy the wit of man to reduce them to coherence.

[1] These figures I take from the *Report of the Delegation sent to the Church of South India by the General Convention, Episcopal Church*, published by the Joint Commission on Ecumenical Relations, 281 Fourth Avenue, New York, no date, pp. 8, 59. A Commission of the American Episcopal Church visited South India in the summer of 1956.

One of the most interesting developments in the movement is the trend away from the mere recording of agreements and disagreements (now dismissed as an unfruitful practice) and towards positive statements about the nature of the Church. As the movement advances less and less is heard of 'Some think this, and others think that', and far more is heard of the Scriptural affirmations about the Church and her nature, with all which that involves. In fact, there is an effort to write something in the nature of a new *Summa Theologica*, an enterprise which admittedly will take ten years or more.[1] 'The two major emphases in the Lund *Report* are that Faith and Order studies need to be thoroughly Christocentric and that they must be truly ecumenical in the sense of being study-in-common rather than comparative descriptions of traditional differences.' The other emphasis is the demand for intensive study of the social and cultural factors affecting Christian unity; and requests have been made to over one hundred universities asking that advanced students should do research upon matters of social and cultural, racial and political, and psychological influences upon church relations. The response of presidents and deans was encouraging and thus the ecumenical movement is having an influence in the universities which affects the orientation of studies and must surely affect the spirit in which research is undertaken and pursued.[2] In fact, the World Council has developed a kind of Theological Faculty with its own presuppositions or 'slant'.

Inevitably in such an organization stresses and strains arise and the wonder is that their effect has not brought about a premature death of the World Council. These stresses manifest themselves in varying ways: in the differing outlooks of youth and age, of the 'Younger Churches' and the 'Older Churches'; in the relations of the central organizations with the Denominations, since the Council must at once respect the Denominations and try to dissolve them; in the choice of language,

---

[1] Cf. *Minutes of the Commission and Working Committee* of Faith and Order, Evanston and Chicago, 1954, Paper no. 21, Lausanne, p. 18. The Theological Commission on Christ and the Church received 'an initial mandate which indicated that their task might take as long as ten years, being a theological enquiry which would explore in the light of recent scholarship the beginnings within the united Church of thought on the nature and work of Christ and the Holy Spirit.'

[2] Cf. the Secretary's *Report*, p. 10 of the document quoted in the previous note.

which must be conciliatory and yet frank; and in the suggestion, now more widely accepted, that theological conviction can only come as a result of action toward unity, a suggestion particularly manifest in the *Report* on Relations between Anglican and Presbyterian Churches. Lastly, there seems a central and a radical theological tension, between the concepts of the Church as visible and as invisible. Each of these merits some discussion.

2. THE DIFFERING OUTLOOKS OF YOUTH AND AGE

This is observable in the tone and style used in the larger Assemblies and in the smaller, that is, between Amsterdam in 1948 and Evanston in 1954 on the one hand, and the Faith and Order meetings, as at Lund in 1952, on the other. These statements are addressed to different audiences, the one kind mainly to a wider public, the other mainly to the theologians and leaders of the Churches. Further, the tone, indeed almost the whole outlook, of the 'Younger Churches' and the 'Youth Groups' is very different from the tone and outlook of the more mature representatives of the 'Western Churches'. Two citations may illustrate this.

The 'Youth Group' Report at Lund in 1952 contains the following:

We would suggest that there is a form of unity inherent in this situation (the need of evangelizing all countries), a unity of witness. It is basically the same Lord to whom we witness. In England, for instance, when an Anglican and a Baptist find themselves side by side at a factory bench the difference of view on episcopacy tends to recede and the fact of witnessing to one Christ comes to the forefront. In saying this we are not making light of doctrinal differences, nor are we trying to bypass them, nor are we being naive. We agree that the witness would be better if they agreed on church order. We are simply stating a fact of unity of witness which many of us have experienced in practice to a remarkable degree in the past difficult years and which tends sometimes to be forgotten in a conference such as this. In connection with this unity of witness we should like to mention that we, as a Youth Group in the conference, have not always been able to see how the theological discussion has been related to the situation of the people living outside the walls of this University. It seems to us that our unity in witness demands a re-thinking of theology to make it relevant in the context of the world today.[1]

No one could fail to sympathize with this statement. Teachers of theology have been ceaselessly exhorted to try to train future clergy in such a way that they will be able to 'talk the language' of the people, avoid theoretical and abstract doctrinal preaching and 'face life as it actually has to be lived by our people'. Such exhortations are sometimes accompanied by exhortations to give dogmatic sermons. Nevertheless this 'Youth Group' statement made at Lund in 1952 is naive.[2] The differences between an Anglican and a Baptist are not merely a matter of one Church being administered by a 'Bishop' and the other by a 'General Superintendent' or a 'Messenger'. The differences, when examined, especially about 'sponsored baptism' and 'believer's baptism', are found to go back to different conceptions of what makes a Christian, and of what is the fundamental nature of the Christian community. Several groups of Baptists have declined to join the World Council of Churches precisely because they feel that there are deep divergences in fundamental doctrine. Baptists and Congregationalists, who hold so much in common both doctrinally and historically, nevertheless find deep differences in doctrinal norms. Such differences have led many in the ecumenical movement to direct their efforts to a deeper study of the Scriptural evidence about the Church and about the beliefs of the earliest Christians, in order, if possible, to modify existing ideas about baptism and episcopacy and what they involve. The differences may look small to a superficial eye, but in fact they are very large.

Yet it is understandable that on the one hand youth should be impatient with what seem to them to be insignificant theological scruples, and on the other that more thoughtful men should try to meet this impatience, while avoiding facile or superficial arrangements which in the long run must fail.

---

[1] *Lund Report*, p. 307.
[2] Yet it was the Youth Groups, I think, who first called attention to the importance of marriage and all that it involves.

This is one of the 'tensions' inherent in a movement embracing so many differing elements. Dr A. C. Craig, in his Speech to the General Assembly of the Church of Scotland, in May 1957, commending acceptance of the *Report* on relations with the Anglican Churches, quoted one ironic observer as having remarked: 'at least the Movement can claim to be semi-divine in its inspiration, since clearly with it a thousand years are as one day.'[1]

The Ideal Church

Sometimes the complete union which is so ardently desired is expressed less in doctrinal than in moral terms. The Rev. Farid Auden[2] said at Lund:

> My vision of the Church that is to be, the Church of my dreams and your dreams, the coming Church I crave and you crave, will have:
>
> The steadiness and devotion to the Bible and the emphasis on the sovereignty of God of the Presbyterian Church.
>
> The emphasis on justification by faith and careful nurture of the Lutheran Church.
>
> The sense of history and the solidarity of the centuries and good taste of the Episcopal Church.
>
> The democracy and adventurous mood of the Congregational Church.
>
> The enthusiastic zeal, and warm heart, and the world parish of the Methodist Church.
>
> The simplicity and love of freedom of the Baptist Church.
>
> The heroism and steadfastness of the Eastern Orthodox Church.
>
> The efficient organization and spirit of obedience of the Roman Catholic Church.
>
> The evangelistic energy of the Disciples of Christ.
>
> The concern for the unfortunates of the Salvation Army.
>
> The missionary enthusiasm of the Moravian Church.
>
> The conception of the Church of God: that you do not join a church, but that you come into it by new birth.
>
> The quietude of spirit, and the sympathy, and emphasis on the Inner Light and the immediacy of God of the Society of Friends.

[1] *The Lost Treasure of Christian Unity*, Edinburgh, 1957, p. 10.
[2] President of the Supreme Council of the Evangelical Churches in Syria and Lebanon and Chairman of the Near East Christian Council.

The whole Church would be vastly enriched if all these accents were the common property of all the Christian Churches, rather than the trade mark of sectarianism. Most of these denominations grew out of some discovery of neglected truth or neglected emphasis.[1]

This is said with generosity of spirit, but it is a pathetic oversimplification and fails to realize the connection between theory and practice. The 'spirit of obedience', for instance, in the Roman Catholic Church is most intimately bound up with a particular belief in the nature of the Church itself and of Christ's manner of union with it. Destroy that belief, or weaken it, and the basis of obedience is destroyed and weakened. The same is true, I think, of many other good moral qualities which the Rev. Farid Auden praises. The matter is by no means so simple, as thoughtful men in the movement appreciate. Yet zeal must not be extinguished. At Amsterdam the Rev. D. T. Niles 'felt that the Older Churches were discussing the reasons and circumstances which had led to their earlier divorce: the Younger Churches were only just getting married.'[2] No one likes to spoil a honeymoon.

Professor Cyril C. Richardson, of the Union Theological Seminary, New York, in a review of *Ways of Worship*[3] thinks that the essays in this book 'do not fully represent what is going on in the Church at large. The geographical distribution is rather poor. The American scene is inadequately represented, the Younger Churches and the mission field not at all.'

'One has the impression that the Faith and Order aspect of the ecumenical movement moves upon lines which are too narrow, and does not take sufficient pains to recruit the help of a wider community.'[4]

The Rt Rev. Dr. J. W. C. Wand, the editor of *The Church Quarterly Review*, indicates some of the stresses in the World Council in downright fashion: 'at the present time' he declared, 'we suffer from too much American money, too much German theology, and too much Dutch bureaucracy . . . we

[1] *Report*, pp. 221–2.
[2] *Report*, p. 62.
[3] *The Report of a Theological Commission of Faith and Order*, edited by P. Edwall, E. Hayman and W. D. Maxwell, London, 1951.
[4] *Ecumenical Review*, iv, no. 3, April, 1952, pp. 315–16.

should not allow ourselves to be overcome by the tremendous learning of the Germans. In the last resort, Continental theology is not the united building it seems to be. It is a façade, and can be broken.' Dr Wand was speaking at the Church Assembly in June, 1955 and wished by no means to weaken the World Council of Churches, but wanted to call attention to the need of admitting a greater English contribution in its deliberations.[1]

Theologians Wanted!

Here one naturally asks: Is the purpose of the permanent Commissions of the World Council that of merely reporting what is the feeling and convictions of the Churches, or is it to give a lead and guidance to the Churches? Neither purpose, of course, is exclusive of the other, but there may be a difference of opinion as to which needs greater attention. The trend seems definitely to be towards the latter purpose of giving a lead to 'ecumenical' thinking, and in this it does not always seem very easy 'to recruit the help of a wider community'. Able men are often engaged in administration and have not the time needed for research, thinking and writing. In the *Report of the General Secretary*, published in the autumn of 1956, Dr Visser 't Hooft indicates this fairly clearly, in a passage quoted in *Unitas*:

> With regard to the . . . question whether the growth of the World Council is a harmonious growth, it seems to me that the main issue is whether theology and policy, reflection and action are in step or out of step in our life. There are those who feel that the World Council is already too much concerned with theology. Personally I fear that our real weakness is the opposite. We have our important theological commissions of 'Faith and Order'; we have the biblical study on the Lordship of Christ, and these fulfil an important function. But we give little if any time to the serious study of the theological problems arising in the life of the World Council itself. *Now it is increasingly clear that many of our structural and organisational problems are essentially theological.* The relation of the World Council to the missionary movement, the relation between inter-church aid on the one hand and the evangelistic and missionary task on the other, or the task of the

[1] He was cited from the *Church Times*, in *Unitas*, vii, no. 2, Summer, 1955, p. 107.

Church in areas of rapid social change, or the vocation of the laity, or the co-operation of men and women, or the question of our Basis, or the whole problem of the ecclesiological implications of the existence of the World Council, or a host of other seemingly practical issues, cannot be clarified if we do not arrive at a clear theology concerning the nature and mission of the Church.

Who is to produce this theology which is to serve as a basis of our own work? It is unfortunately a fact that there is no one in the full-time service of the World Council who can give a major part of his time to theological study. The staff of our Division of Studies or of our Ecumenical Institute does not consist of men or women who spend their time in quiet scholarly study, but of men who have their hands more than full with the largely administrative tasks of organising and co-ordinating ecumenical study work and who must do most of their reading and thinking in aeroplanes or outside their office hours. So in this matter we have been largely dependent on voluntary help from the theologians in the different churches. Few of them have yet discovered the importance of these questions. In fact it would seem that a good deal of the theological literature about the Council is written by theologians of churches which are not members of the Council. Is the Council in spite of its youth already too much taken for granted by its own member churches, especially its theologians? We must hope that before long the theological faculties will give us the help we need in order to get firm ground under our feet in our further development.[1]

Will all the Churches recognize the need for theological study in order 'to get firm ground under our feet in our future development'? No doubt many will. But probably there will also be further manifestations of impatience and demands for concrete if not spectacular results. For my part, I sincerely hope that the need for scholarly study will be far more widely recognized. There is indeed need for firm ground under many feet. Christ talked about a rock, which is surely firm ground. But as things are, it may be recalled that it took about thirty years of effort to unite two Scots Churches, both Presbyterian. To unite one hundred and seventy of different traditions and

[1] 'Report of the General Secretary', *Ecumenical Review*, ix, no. 1. October, 1956. p. 43; *Unitas*, viii, Winter, 1956, pp. 230–1.

nationalities will surely take far longer—unless, of course, God works a miracle, and we can never rule that out.

3. RESPECT FOR THE DENOMINATIONS AND DESIRE TO DISSOLVE THEM

Tension between Council and Denomination

Here the tension is really a paradox. The Council is a Council of Churches; yet it exists in order to dissolve the 'Churches' and make them rise again into The Church. The Council is supported by the denominations; yet it is designed to lead the denominations to death. In theory all accept this position; and in fact several unions of Churches, like that of South India, have resulted in the 'death' of the uniting denominations, certainly as regards use of the name, and almost certainly as regards many specifically denominational outlooks and customs. But others, especially in Europe, show small practical enthusiasm for their own dissolution.

In practice, therefore, the Council must and does show great respect for each of the member Churches, while at the same time trying to lessen denominationalism. In general the World Council emphasizes the need for universalization and tends to lay less emphasis upon the specific characteristics of each denomination. It does try to kill denominationalism, but it tries likewise to give the patients ease during the last days of their separate existence.[1] Dr Visser 't Hooft spoke plainly, even after the Evanston Assembly: 'Radical changes in thought and structure will have to take place before our churches will again be truly responsive to the divine call.'[2]

The Evanston Assembly in its booklet entitled *Evanston Speaks* put a number of questions designed to arouse thought about the various topics treated in the Sectional discussions. The implications of more than one of the questions tend to

---

[1] There is a mass of evidence to this effect, needless to specify here. The *Lund Report* speaks frequently in this sense, and, though friendly and conciliatory, clearly deprecates too much denominational emphasis. 'Often particular emphases become restrictive bonds from which denominational life is not easily freed', p. 61; and cf. pp. 62–5.

[2] 'Our Ecumenical Task in the Light of History', *Ecumenical Review*, vii, no. 4, July, 1955, p. 320.

weaken denominational fixations. Here are some such questions:

> Section I, Q. 3: What are the doctrines or practices on which your Church or denomination is mostly clearly divided from others? Which are just diversities to be welcomed?
>
> Q. 4. Do you believe that these doctrines and practices, as held by your Church, are indispensable for the Church as a whole? On what ground do you base this belief?
>
> Q. 5. Can you conceive of the ways in which your Church might have to offer up some of its accustomed, inherited forms of life in order to unite with other Churches?[1]
>
> Section III Q. 1. The Report says that 'The Churches have come to realize more fully that they have a duty to society as part of their mission in the world'. In what sense is this true with regard to your Church? At what specific points does this report require your Church to reconsider its approach?[2]
>
> Section III, 2 Q. 3. What reforms are necessary in the life and structure of the Church? What are the values and dangers of agreements between Church and State?[3]

Referring to non-Communist countries:

> Q. 1. What are the special temptations of the Church in a traditionalist 'Christian society'?
>
> Q. 3. What is the content of Christian witness toward the large mass of secularized people? How far is this secularization due to the class nature of the Church and the accommodation of its life and message to bourgeois interest and values? What reforms in the life of the Church are necessary to meet these challenges?
>
> Q. 5. What is the responsibility of the Churches in non-communist lands for the cultivation of traditions of freedom and community over against the growing pressure toward social conformity?[4]

Section on international affairs:

> Q. 9. What part can the Commission of the Churches on International Affairs, as a permanent organ of the World Council of Churches and the International Missionary Council, play in offering a Christian testimony on behalf of peace and justice?

---

[1] *Evanston Speaks, Reports from the Second Assembly of the World Council of Churches,* 1954, p. 15.
[2] *Ibid.* p. 45.   [3] P. 58.   [4] P. 59.

How can Christians in their own parish support the work of the Commission?[1]

Section IV, on the Church and racial and ethnic tensions:

Section on Inter-group relations:

Q. 4. How do you explain the serious gap between what the Churches know to be right and true and what they actually do in situations of conflict and social pressure? (This has reference to the relations between 'coloured' people and white: an unhappy way of expressing it, but the clearest.)[2]

It should be observed that these questions are addressed only to the Churches which are members of the World Council;[3] moreover the *Introduction* to Section I which deals with 'our oneness in Christ and our disunity as Churches', says:

It must be remembered that this report *is not at all an official statement of the World Council* with regard to such questions. The fact that the delegates of the Eastern Orthodox Churches felt obliged to register their partial agreement only with Part I, and their dissent from Parts II and III, is clear indication that the World Council is not yet in a position which permits the official promulgation of such strong statements on unity as this report. But the Council's Assembly now sends the report to its member Churches for study, comment and action as each Church may decide.[4]

Underlying all the problems lies the question of the authority of and in the Church; and it may be asked whether many who were present at Evanston did not tacitly assume that each 'Church' or even each member of each Church may decide what is to be believed, and assume, also, that there is no final

---

[1] P. 66.

[2] P. 88.

[3] At first reading a Catholic might possibly be inclined to imagine such questions being addressed to his own faithful and to consider the proposal unsuitable. But the situation among the non-Catholic bodies is very different from our own; the World Council includes some 163 'Churches' [170 in 1958], and the reasons for their separation into independent bodies shows the most astonishing variety of patterns; there are sometimes merely accidental reasons of location in different countries or among different races, and often the doctrinal reasons for separation seem extemely slight. Perhaps, also, reasons of administration and control of invested funds are not always excluded; legal possession of property may be dependent e.g., upon retention of the confession of faith of the Synod of Dort. There is the general tendency to follow accustomed ways.

[4] P. 15, italics mine.

authority in the Church on earth to decide such matters. The Orthodox, by 'registering dissent', challenged any such assumptions which might have existed.

At the same time it must be recognized that the World Council has to deal with a situation which involves long-standing and deep-rooted prejudices or misunderstandings. 'There are millions of American Protestants,' writes Professor Nichols, 'who suppose they are being ecumenical in desiring a united Protestant church which will be the ecclesiastical expression of the "American way of life". There is doubtless a similar pride of culture in many of the younger churches, in India, China and Japan.' Yet is should be gladly acknowledged that many of the leaders among ecumenists, themselves inheritors of a tradition hostile to the Catholic concept of authority, have fearlessly proclaimed that divisions among Christians are due to human sin, have insisted upon the duty of 'obedience to Christ' and have tried to break down prejudice and establish a consolidation upon a wider and more universal basis. Many have explicitly repudiated the idea of 'a united Protestant Church' and their relations with the Orthodox show that the repudiation is more than merely verbal.

Intercommunion

Great assemblies of Christians of different denominations raise in acute form the question of attendance at the religious services of differing 'Communions' and of reception of the 'Sacrament' at Eucharistic celebrations. It is a question which demands decision at each gathering: 'Here and now can I attend the services of another "Church"? Can I advise members of my Church to receive Communion at the celebration of the Lord's Supper, or at the "Mass", of another Church?' An answer to that question brings to a focus the whole series of problems inherent in the existence of different 'Churches' and puts them into concrete visible form; it involves the question of the relation between faith and its outward manifestation and calls for judgement about 'the real presence', 'Orders' and the ministry, the 'historic episcopate' and its powers, the celebration of the Eucharist by those not in the ordinary sense 'ordained', and consequently about the meaning of membership in a Church, or in *the* Church, and the relationships of 'Churches' to one another.

On this practical point the World Council has shown special respect for the conscientious convictions of its member Churches and the official attitude indicates a considerable advance upon that common during the earlier 'enthusiastic' stage of ecumenism. The Commission appointed to deal with the matter in 1939 did not publish its Report until 1952 and its studies were exhaustive and meticulous. The Report contains historical summaries of the practice of the Church and the Churches in the past, and records the judgements, or opinions, given by some ten or more 'denominations'—but the word 'denomination' scarcely applies here, since the lines of division of opinion on this subject are not drawn on merely 'denominational' agreements.

The Report, published by the Lund Conference as part of its proceedings, revealed a variety of opinion and belief which is bewildering, and the currents and cross-currents of thought and of judgement formed a whirlpool. Dr O. S. Tomkins, in his chapter 'Intercommunion in the Ecumenical Movement' dealing with the matter as it has affected the large assemblies, says: 'So long as the Churches vary so much in their principles and practice, ecumenical gatherings will seem to reflect a variety of situations hard to distinguish from sheer chaos.'[1]

The Report of the Lund Conference on Faith and Order, which had this Report before it, ended on a somewhat indeterminate but very serious note: 'We are agreed that this problem be quite specially laid upon the consciences of the Churches and the leaders of the Ecumenical Movement'. Moreover, the Conference emphasized the responsibilities of the Churches, saying:

To call ecumenical conferences is, at any time, a serious responsibility before God, and not the least serious aspect of them is the acknowledgement of our sacramental divisions. Consequently, a heavy *pastoral* obligation rests upon those who involve others

[1] *Intercommunion, the Report of the Theological Commission appointed by the Continuation Committee of the World Conference on Faith and Order together with a selection from the Material presented to the Commission,* edited by Donald Baillie and John Marsh, London, 1952, p. 136.

in such experiences, and this is especially, though not exclusively, true of conferences for young people or for any not habituated to the tensions of an ecumenical meeting. Preparation for worship, and especially for the eucharistic worship, should therefore be taken fully as seriously by the promoters of a conference as the preparation of any other aspect of the programme. This may involve not only carefully written preparatory literature and forms of service for use at the conference, but also provision for dealing pastorally, theologically and personally with the perplexities caused by the worship during the conference itself.[1]

This is a far cry from Archbishop Söderblom's glowing account of the incident at Stockholm in 1925, when many present at the Conference received Communion at the Lutheran High Mass in the Engelbrekts church, only the Orthodox, the Disciples of Christ, the Waldensians and the Quakers (as corporate bodies), abstaining. Speaking of the Lutherans who received the Sacrament he divides them into two classes, those 'who can only be compared for exclusiveness to Romans and a few Anglo-Catholics, and others *more ecumenically minded*'.[2] Archbishop Söderblom evidently regarded such an act of general intercommunion, at least on that occasion, as a reason for rejoicing and as evidence of being 'ecumenically minded'. It is to be hoped that he represented the early 'enthusiastic' stage of ecumenism which has now passed away.[3]

The Report of the Lund Commission showed appreciation of the gravity of the question of intercommunion; and one sign of this is the invitation to a Roman Catholic to write in the volume. Père Yves M. J. Congar explained the Roman Catholic position in such gentle terms that his intransigence may not be appreciated unless his paper is read with care. He ends: 'The aim of the ecumenical movement is precisely to pass, if God wills it and grants us to do it, from an invisible unity in Christ to a visible unity in the Church. Then, we would celebrate and communicate together. Until then, intercommunion is, alas, impossible.'[4]

---

[1] *Lund Report*, p. 40.
[2] *Intercommunion, Report*, 1952, p. 120, italics mine.
[3] On the development of ecumenism, cf. Bishop A. Nygren, *Christ and His Church*, English translation by A. Carlsten, London, 1957, pp. 116–17.
[4] *Report*, p. 151.

Professor L. Zander, Orthodox Oecumenical Patriarch (Exarchate for the Russians in the West), puts the dilemma:

> The problem of intercommunion is one of the most 'pessimistic' of ecumenical problems, apparently there can be no positive solution of it, for if Churches of different denominations enter into communion it means either that they renounce their own faith and accept the faith of the Church whose Communion Service it happens to be, or that they do not take the problems of faith seriously and substitute for the tragedy of Christian dividedness an emotional idyll of fine feelings and of psychological unity.[1]

Professor Zander, however, sees some hope in the fact that members of different Churches attend—even though in an extremely 'passive' way—one another's services; and he regards this presence with merely private prayer as 'a spiritual co-celebration (though only spiritual: that is the tragedy of our dividedness).' But this notion of 'a spiritual co-celebration', even though Professor Zander may think mainly of the presence of others at the Orthodox Liturgy, seems hard to reconcile with what he said earlier about the Eucharist: 'We cannot participate in Protestant sacraments precisely because they are *sacraments* of the separated Churches: to take part in them would mean entering into the very heart of Churches whose doctrine and worship we consider incorrect. This is why participation in another Church's Sacraments means in fact joining the Church and is a symbolic renunciation of the truth of one's own Church.'[2]

' The Thorn in the Flesh'

Many non-Catholics find the point of view expressed by Professor Zander and Père Congar hard to understand; they certainly do not think that by receiving Communion in a Church of which they are not members they thereby renounce the truth of their own Church. In the minds of some who advocate 'open' Communion, or occasional 'intercommunion', is the view that the invisible union between Christians who

[1] *Intercommunion, Report*, p. 350.
[2] *Ibid.* pp. 353-4.

accept Christ transcends all formulations of belief and all arrangements of Church administration; and that this union of hearts is rightly expressed, as it is fostered, by common reception of the Eucharist. Sometimes the meaning of the Eucharist is judged to be 'eschatological', that is, an outward sign not of present agreement and concord but principally if not exclusively of the union which lies, beyond history, in the world invisible. The Eucharist is thus conceived as a sign of the future, not of the present.[1] Sometimes it is said that 'the Table is the Table of the Lord' and no man can exclude from it.

The 'Catholic-Orthodox' tradition and conviction has always been that Holy Communion is a sign of full union with the Body of Christ, as that Body is manifest on earth in the visible Church. From earliest days those who held unorthodox beliefs, or refused obedience to the bishop, were cut off from Communion, for Communion was a sign, and an infinitely sacred sign, of agreement in faith and concord in government. Arians, Nestorians, Donatists and all heretics held this conviction with the same firmness as did the 'Orthodox'; and 'ex-communication' was mutual and was the outward sign of lack of concord. The general conviction was that disagreement in doctrine made 'intercommunion' simply unthinkable. This conviction many of our separated brethren share and I have misgivings lest appeals to 'charity' may sometimes be made a means of undue pressure upon them to surrender their convictions.

I feel obliged,—even though I recognize with pain that my words may offend some separated brethren for whom I have a genuine esteem and regard—to record here my feeling of shock and distress at some views held about 'intercommunion'. I do not mean to reflect in any way whatever upon the sincerity with which these views are held; but to me 'intercommunion' without doctrinal agreement is practically acting a lie. It is a declaration that there is agreement when in fact there is not.

[1] This is the view expressed by Reinhold Niebuhr in a conversation with Archbishop Temple in 1943; the Archbishop would not 'budge an inch' from his position against intercommunion. Cf. Iremonger's *William Temple*, pp. 493–4.

Many Lutherans hold that no one should communicate at the Eucharist who does not believe in the true bodily presence of Christ. The Orthodox and the Roman Catholics believe that it would be sacrilege to give the true body of Christ to those who believe that they receive no more than a wafer of bread, however symbolic it may be and however vivid may be the perception of Christ's spiritual presence.

But beliefs other than those about the Eucharist itself enter into the matter. For example: some believe that bishops are necessary for Orders and for preservation of true doctrine, and others believe that bishops are needless either for Orders or for true doctrine. If both communicate together at the same altar, or 'table', both equivalently declare that it does not matter what one believes about bishops, since together they have full union with Christ in spite of contradictory beliefs about bishops. After Communion, then, why should they continue to differ about bishops? One or the other ought to surrender his stand on episcopacy, since both have declared that episcopacy bears no relation to their union with Christ.

It is said—and I have heard it said with the most obvious sincerity and even piety—that 'it is the table of the Lord and no man can exclude any baptized person from it'. But on that principle, why should the unbaptized be excluded? Why exclude Buddhists or Hindus who have good will, a willingness to learn about Christ and have already a certain love for him? Yet their exclusion—even supposing that they wished to come —shows that the fundamental question is: 'What makes a table, or an altar, to be the table or the altar of the Lord?' Can any group of baptized Christians set up a table or an altar and declare it the table and the altar of the Lord? That would be a hard admission to make among the multitudinous split-up Christians of Africa. A table, or an altar, is a visible tangible thing, and it corresponds to the visible tangible body of the Church. Consequently, what one holds about the Church one ought to hold about the 'table' or the 'altar'. If there is division in the one, there must in honesty be division in the other. To appeal to a valid baptism is to deny the need of right faith, or else to declare, as the Disciples of Christ declare, that there should be no definition of doctrine. 'Intercommunion' might be a practical acceptance of the view that doctrinal definitions are needless, if not positively harmful; and so 'intercommunion' might well imply an acceptance of the belief of one group in the World Council and a rejection of the others.

Many of our separated brethren are opposed to 'intercommunion', because they judge it an impediment to real unity. It effectively declares that divisions at present existing are of small or no consequence and thus it undermines the very foundation of the effort to attain visible unity. If people can communicate together, there seems no reason to be disturbed about anything further, since their union with one another in Christ is visibly made manifest and all the rest assumes a very secondary or negligible proportion.

The position of the Church of South India is different from the position of people of different denominations gathered for a Conference. In the Younger Churches, such as that of South India, doctrine regarded as necessary has been declared, a liturgy has been accepted and there is willingness to accept episcopacy in practice and to learn more about it in theory. Yet even in South India, congregations need not, and many do not, communicate at the Eucharist of ministers not episcopally ordained. But in ecumenical gatherings many Churches are far from accepting such union among themselves as exists in the South India Church, and hence intercommunion takes on quite another aspect.

The most troublesome subject regarding the Church of South India has been about non-episcopally ordained ministers and about communion with the originating Churches, Anglican, Congregational, Methodist and Presbyterian. With episcopal Churches 'intercommunion' is not complete; and it is noteworthy that conversations between representatives of the Church of South India and of Lutherans and Baptists have not yet resulted in intercommunion, the difficulties proving doctrinal.[1]

There can scarcely be doubt that many a 'man of the world' even if interested in the ecumenical movement, would find this

---

[1] Cf. Rajaiah D. Paul, *The First Decade, an Account of the Church of South India*, Madras, 1958, ch. 4, 'Towards Wider Union', pp. 86–106. The details given in Mr Paul's book are insufficient on which to form any adequate theological judgement.

anxiety about 'intercommunion' a mere needless scruple, or else think it evidence that churchmen are occupying themselves with theological subtleties quite unrelated to the ordinary life of human beings. Harnack's idea that Christianity means merely 'the fatherhood of God and the brotherhood of man' is still latent in many minds. The following passage from G. K. Chesterton is pertinent:

Lastly and most important, it is exactly this which explains what is so inexplicable to all the modern critics of the history of Christianity. I mean the monstrous wars about small points of theology, the earthquakes of emotion about a gesture or a word. It was only a matter of an inch; but an inch is everything when you are balancing. The Church could not afford to swerve a hair's breadth on some things if she was to continue her great and daring experiment of the irregular equilibrium. Once let one idea become less powerful and some other idea would become too powerful. It was no flock of sheep the Christian shepherd was leading, but a herd of bulls and tigers, of terrible ideals and devouring doctrines, each one of them strong enough to turn to a false religion and lay waste the world. Remember that the Church went in specifically for dangerous ideas; she was a lion tamer. The idea of birth through a Holy Spirit, of the death of a divine being, of the forgiveness of sins, or the fulfilment of prophecies, are ideas which any one can see, need but a touch to turn them into something blasphemous or ferocious. The smallest link was let drop by the artificers of the Mediterranean, and the lion of ancestral pessimism burst his chain in the forgotten forests of the north. Of these theological equalizations I have to speak afterwards. Here it is enough to notice that if some small mistake were made in doctrine, huge blunders might be made in human happiness. A sentence phrased wrong about the nature of symbolism would have broken all the best statues in Europe. A slip in the definitions might stop all the dances; might wither all the Christmas trees or break all the Easter eggs. Doctrine had to be carefully defined within strict limits, even in order that man might enjoy general human liberties. The Church had to be careful, if only that the world might be careless.[1]

The judicious reader will, of course, understand that the possible suggestion that the word 'Church' in this passage

[1] *Orthodoxy*, London, 1908, pp. 166–7; the book has had fourteen reprintings.

should be applied to the World Council of Churches is one which the World Council itself would repudiate, as would the Roman Catholics, the Orthodox, and many others. Nevertheless the passage points, I think, to the heavy responsibility which lies upon those in the ecumenical movement, and to the unwisdom of hasty judgements either from within or from without the movement.

Dr Tomkins, in his account of the practice of 'Intercommunion' at the large gatherings, used almost the same metaphor as does Chesterton:

> There may be a danger that the Ecumenical Movement, prone to seek smooth running as all organizations tend to do, may try to find a formula which puts 'intercommunion' into its place, as one of the snags which are likely to occur and must be quickly and smoothly dealt with. But *fortunately* the problem is too alive for such easy resolution—or rather, the people who feel it are too alive *to be so easily tamed*. It has become 'a thorn in the flesh' for the Ecumenical Movement. Once again, it may be found the weakness in which strength is made perfect, the occasion to seek God's all-sufficient grace. When it is fully removed it will be because, by God's grace alone, the 'Ecumenical Movement' has ceased to be, and we have been given not 'intercommunion' but *communion* in an undivided Church.[1]

4. DIFFICULTIES IN FINDING A SUITABLE LANGUAGE

Tension between Frankness and Kindness

To learn a religion is, to some extent, to learn a language. New doctrines are contained in a religion and the doctrines need a language in which to express them. How true this is of the Eastern religions, all students know. Now the language used to express Christian truths has come to have a meaning which is accepted by most Christians if the meaning is kept very wide, but which, as soon as more exact definition and explanation is attempted, is understood quite differently. This is apparent in the use of words like the following:

Church, churches, ecclesiastical.
Unity, union, oneness, congregation, assembly.

---

[1] *Intercommunion Report*, p. 137 (italics mine, save the last).

Faith, faithful, assent of faith, assurance of faith, belief.
Grace, gracious, unmerited, gift, given.
Covenant, law, uncovenanted.
Justification, righteousness, sanctification, holiness.
Nature, human nature, supernatural, adoption, divine
    sonship.

This list could easily be enlarged. Each of the words in the
list would be defined differently by different Christian bodies,
and, although the differences between the bodies is far from
being a mere matter of words, nevertheless words have come
to have ramifying associations. The expressions 'righteous'
and 'righteousness' have a protestant ring in Catholic ears,
just as the words 'sanctifying grace' and 'merit' have a
catholic ring in Protestant ears. To speak of 'a gathered
Church' brings associations, to an English Catholic, of the
Free Churches, probably of Congregationalism; to speak of
'Church discipline' suggests Presbyterianism; of 'believer's
baptism' of the Baptists, and so on. Religious differences
affect terminology; 'transubstantiation' smacks of magic
to many a Protestant. Sometimes the same terms are used
without awareness that they mean different things to
different people: 'natural law' is a conspicuous example.
It means quite different things to a Thomist and to a legal
positivist. The word 'orthodox' and 'communion' are other
instances.

The World Council of Churches, wishing to compose
differences, and becoming acutely aware of the many pitfalls
connected with the use of this or that type of language, has
developed—within certain limits—a kind of language of its
own, which one may call 'ecumenical language'. To some
extent it is a language drawn from recent theological writings
which cut across denominational differences; for instance,
one often reads words such as 'eschatological', 'response',
'encounter', 'under judgement', 'dialectic', 'once-for-all
significance', 'kerygma', 'parousia', something 'given' and
so on. Words having an unpleasant association tend to be
avoided, such as heresy, heretic, heretical, schism, schismatic,
sect, sectarian. Conciliatory language is chosen, even when
differences are recorded. Ecumenists do not 'contradict' one

another, they 'express dissent'; they do not 'disagree', they 'place a different emphasis'.[1]

In religious discussion kindly language is most acceptable, especially in recording disagreements, and it is particularly justified in a movement such as the ecumenical movement whose aim is to promote unity among Christians. At the same time there arises a problem: how far does the use of such language cloak a disagreement, which in frankness ought to be brought to light; how far does it express a real agreement which in fact does exist beneath diverse emphases or expressions? The Council has had to attempt to solve this problem but there are different opinions about its success; generally the doubt has been whether the Council was too 'ecumenical', that is, whether it used such language as tended to blur, and not merely soften, the sharpness in difference of opinion and conviction, which ought to have been frankly stated and faced.

Here, again, one must record the differences between the earlier Conferences and the larger Assemblies such as Amsterdam and Evanston on the one hand, and the later publications of the Faith and Order Commission on the other.

The Evanston Report met criticism on ground of lack of clearness. In an article entitled 'Notes on Roman Catholic Writings concerning Ecumenism' in *The Ecumenical Review*[2] Dr Visser 't Hooft regrets the failure on the part of some Roman Catholics to realize the necessary limitations of language when speaking of such matters:

There is a curious impatience in some of these writings which contradicts the proverbial patience of the Roman Catholic Church. Even Father Tavard, whose book[3] shows at many points true insight into the life of the ecumenical movement and who warns so eloquently against 'negative attitudes', becomes 'negative' himself when he speaks (in reference to the Evanston

[1] Miss Helle Georgiadis in an admirable article 'Orthodoxy, Rome and Oecumenism', *Eastern Churches Quarterly*, xv, no. 8, Winter, 1956–7, says: 'The main obstacle to discussion between different Christian groups is that the same terms are used but these terms, so far as they apply to the Church, have altered their content as a result of historical pressure, in particular that of the Reformation. Moreover, the oecumenical movement has invested many terms which previously had a specific meaning (the word oecumenical itself for instance) with new significance'. P. 348.

[2] viii, no. 2, January, 1956.

[3] *The Catholic Approach to Protestantism*, New York, 1955.

Assembly) of 'a purely nominal overcoming of doctrinal diver-
gencies, by selecting an ambiguous terminology which, as such,
is no property of any one doctrinal tradition, but may be understood in various senses by all' (p. 48). Has Father Tavard then
not learned the simple A.B.C. of ecumenism, that there is no
ecumenical language which is completely unambiguous for all
concerned? And does he seriously believe that Evanston could
or should have chosen the language which is the property of
one particular doctrinal tradition for its mode of expression?[1]

Dr Visser 't Hooft is entirely justified in saying that Evanston
could scarcely have chosen the language of one particular
doctrinal tradition, for to have done so would have appeared
to be adopting a particular doctrinal standpoint and to be
rejecting all others. The purpose of the World Council is to
reconcile Churches and not to choose between them. At the
same time Dr Visser 't Hooft himself would probably agree
that many statements issued by Faith and Order are far
clearer, and not less conciliatory, than the Evanston Report
entitled 'Our Oneness in Christ and our Disunity as Churches'.
It is not only Father Tavard who has criticized this Report.
A group of Anglican theologians, appointed by the Church
Assembly's Council for Ecumenical Co-operation, while admitting 'the great value' of the Report and emphasizing
their general agreement with it, nevertheless make serious
reservations:

> We think that there are passages in the Report that suggest
> that the Church's duty of safeguarding the truths of faith are not
> sufficiently recognized.
>
> On page 8 we appear to be told that we involve ourselves in
> sin at every point where we take our stand, and honestly take
> our stand, on conviction. The meaning seems to be that our
> convictions themselves are infected with sin, because we are too
> disposed to value what is ours just because it is ours, and so
> mistake accidentals for essentials. The Report then goes on to
> say: 'Churches in their actual historical situations, may reach

---

[1] *Art. cit.*, p. 195. My impression is that the World Council can more easily
secure the services of biblical scholars than of trained canon lawyers. These latter,
of course, may tend to the obscurity of technical expressions. At the same time,
considering that the World Council has many complicated matters to deal with,
some of them bearing a relation to civil law, the services of men of civil and of
canon law ought not to be disregarded.

a point of readiness and a time of decision' where 'their witness-ing may require obedience unto death. They may then have to be prepared to offer up some of their accustomed, inherited forms of life in uniting with other Churches without complete certainty as to all that will emerge from the step of faith.' We miss here the safeguard that Churches have no business to give up their ac-customed inherited forms of life except where they have a clear conviction that this is what they are called upon to do, and they must not give up those inherited forms of life which they regard as matters of principle unless and until they undergo an intellectual conversion and change of mind on these points of principle.[1]

The citation of these words without their full context may perhaps give the impression that the Anglican group of theolo-gians were 'harsh and separatist', which they explicitly repu-diate. It should, also, be remembered that the Evanston Report on which they commented was merely a statement sent to the Churches for their consideration; and I imagine that most ecumenists would have smiled at the remark about Evanston attributed to Dr Fisher, Archbishop of Canterbury: 'We have done absolutely nothing,' he said, 'and have done it exceedingly well.'

But in fact, considering the size of the Evanston Assembly, the widely different outlooks and convictions of its members, the limited opportunities for previous consultation (opportun-ities necessarily limited by geographical distances and pressing occupations), the comparatively short time of the meetings themselves, the agreement shown at Evanston was surprising, and some criticisms were to be expected of the language used in its tentative statements. Evanston did give a stimulus to efforts towards unity; and there were many approvals, even from some quite outside the World Council of Churches. Père Boyer wrote:

'The Basis of the Council—that is, faith in the divinity of

---

[1] 'Notes on an Evanston Report', published in *The Church Quarterly Review*, clviii, no. 326, January-March, 1957, pp. 77, 78. The Anglican theologians say of the word 'repentance', used by the Report in connection with 'our divisions': 'Certainly there is an air of unreality about the use of the word, and it is liable to perplex and mislead the ordinary reader', p. 79. They also judge that the expres-sion *simul justus et peccator*, as applied by the Report to the Church, is apt to be misunderstood; and find obscurity in the use of the words 'manifest' and 'mani-fested', of the word 'concretely', of the expression 'to die with Christ', and of the phrase 'the ministry of the laity for Christian unity'.

Jesus Christ—was definitely professed, the end of man, which is to find God and save his soul, was strongly reaffirmed; and appeal to unity in the faith is clearly addressed to the congregations. Why should we not have hope?'[1]

5. Action as a Means to Understanding: Anglican-Presbyterian Relations

Mr T. S. Eliot has been quoted as saying that the Church of South India was built 'not on the principle of "we agree, therefore let us unite" but on "let us unite in the hope that we shall agree"'. There is a certain truth in the remark, but perhaps not complete truth. There are those who say:

'Our Churches are agreed in general about the doctrines of the sacraments, the ministry and the Church, in spite of the fact that our agreement issues in disagreement when we specify it more precisely. But our general agreement is far deeper and firmer than our specific disagreements. We can only come to understand how our agreements can dissolve our disagreements if we are prepared to sacrifice some of "our inherited forms of life" and unite with other religious bodies. Granted that matters of principle are not surrendered, it is only by uniting and living together that unity of specific belief can be attained.'

The Church of South India, for instance, has allowed both episcopal and presbyteral confirmation to continue side by side, in the hope that one may ultimately supplant the other, or that possibly some combination of the two may eventuate.[2]

---

[1] Quoted in 'Various Voices on Evanston', *Ecumenical Review*, vii, no. 3, April, 1955, pp. 261–74. Catholics regretted certain speeches made at Evanston, the prominence on book-stands given to Blanchard's book attacking the Catholic Church, and the pictures of Protestant churches destroyed in Colombia. I suspect that one such picture was of the church of Molinero, Dept. Atlántico. The *Bulletin* issued by the Evangelical Confederation of Colombia, no. 12, November 30, 1953, p. 9, claimed that this church had been blown up by a dynamite bomb; but Colombian Catholics maintain that an investigation by the authorities of Sabanalarga with the help of an engineer-architect and two master masons showed that the church had fallen because of weak construction and failure of the foundations. Eduardo Ospina reproduces the photograph and gives some account of the affair in *The Protestant Denominations in Colombia*, Bogotá, 1954, pp. 124–5, and appendix p. 4.

[2] Cf. Bishop Neill, 'Co-operation and Unity', *International Review of Missions*, xliv, no. 176, October, 1955, pp. 433–6. Bishop Neill seems to take the same view as Bishop Newbigin that certain forms of co-operation, although they may help towards understanding, may also become an impediment to organic unity.

Others, however, feel that such an outlook and method either surrenders principle or too easily leads to surrender of principle; or else it may result in mere external accord which will in effect hinder true unity.[1] This is an issue which became acute, perhaps unconsciously, in the proposals for closer relations between the Anglicans and the Presbyterians.

The Report on Relations between Anglican and Presbyterian Churches, published in May, 1957, can be said to be a fruit of the Ecumenical Movement.[2] Its authors, belonging to the Church of England, the Church of Scotland, the Episcopal Church in Scotland and the Presbyterian Church of England, acknowledged the mutual understanding and the assured friendship which association in the Ecumenical Movement had brought them and which inspired the Report.

The substance of the concrete proposals can be very briefly stated: the Church of Scotland was to accept 'Bishops in Presbytery', who were to be consecrated by bishops and who 'will hereafter act as the principal ministers of the Presbytery in every ordination and in the consecration of bishops'; they might have a final voice in matters of doctrine. The Church of England was to accept something akin to the office of a presbyterian 'elder', in the form of greater lay participation in the functioning of the Church, and the laity and the presbyterate were to be more closely linked with the bishops in the doctrinal and spiritual decisions of the Church; spiritual independence was to be secured by the Church of England in such matters as power to reform the liturgy and appointment of bishops on the recommendation of the Church, including lay representation.

The Report did not make clear the theoretical basis on

[1] Cf. the observations of the Anglican theologians cited above, pp. 111–12. Part of the difficulty is that some denominations have not settled definitely what exactly they regard as 'matters of principle'.

[2] A summary of this Report is given here in Appendix VI, pp. 305–11. This Report 'was the only church union scheme to be worked out directly in connection with the Commission (of Faith and Order) on Christ and the Church', as is said in the Minutes of the Working Committee of Faith and Order, July 15–20, 1958, Geneva, Switzerland, paper no. 26, p. 11, and cf. p. 28. Approval or disapproval of this Report must necessarily reflect approval or disapproval of an outlook which is held by many who are closely associated with the World Council of Churches, though perhaps it would be too much to suggest that Faith and Order did in fact 'promote or advocate' this particular scheme of unity.

which episcopacy was to be accepted; the 'Bishops in Presbytery' might be conceived as merely the delegates of the Presbytery, having in virtue of their office no essential pre-eminence over the ordinary presbyter; on this theory 'equality of ministry' would scarcely be in peril. The changes suggested in the English form of episcopacy tended to modify the concept of 'apostolic succession' in the direction of the presbyterian system. But the *Report* avoided exact definition of the nature of episcopacy.

The proposals for bishops in the Church of Scotland and for elders in the Church of England attracted popular attention, especially in Scotland. The most important newspaper in Edinburgh, *The Scotsman*, as soon as the *Report* was published, raised the objections which for three years have been repeated in many forms and by many voices in Scotland: 'simple lay-men will take the report as an admission that the Church of Scotland is defective in its orders and government and has been for almost centuries, and that it must now be reconstructed on the Episcopalian model'. The leader-writer seemed to think that intercommunion and exchange of ministers could take place at once, 'were there a generous fraternal spirit among all the Churches', and that the *Report* jettisoned 'the Presbyterian tradition of parity of ministers' and 'sacrificed the Presbyterian heritage'.[1]

It was the approach, the assumptions and the aims of the *Report* which were, and still remain, of greater importance than the concrete changes suggested:

(*a*) The *approach* is from the principle that the unity of the Church is fundamental, if not absolutely paramount.

(*b*) The main assumption, which has often been overlooked or misunderstood, is that full unity of belief will follow action and 'a living together'.

(*c*) The *aim* is not to secure immediate organic unity, but to make proposals of a tentative nature, which, after con-sideration and discussion, may lead on to organic unity.

(*a*) The *approach* is declared to be new. The *Report* does, indeed, take for granted the doctrinal agreement which pre-vious *Conversations* had accepted as actually existing between

---

[1] *Scotsman*, Edinburgh, April 30, 1957.

the Church of England and the Church of Scotland; what is new is the insistence upon the theological and practical need for unity.[1] The Biblical theology of the Church's unity is thus expressed:

'Unity is not a contingent feature of the Church's life, but is of the essence of it. One God, one People of God; One Christ, one Body of Christ; one Holy Spirit, one Fellowship of the Spirit—such is the incontrovertible logic of the New Testament teaching.'

The theology of ecclesiastical unity, the *Report* goes on, must set out from the unity of Christ: from his unity springs the unity of the Church and the unity of Christ must be reflected in the unity of his Body.

To this Scriptural and theological evidence about the nature of the Church is added the practical consideration that neither among the 'Younger Churches' nor in the lands of the older Churches can the Church's true being be made clear or its mission fulfilled as long as the 'Churches' remain in their separateness. 'Division in the Church distorts its witness, frustrates its mission, and contradicts its own nature. If the Church is to demonstrate the Gospel in its life as well as in its preaching, it must manifest to the world the power of God to break down all barriers and to establish the Church's unity in Christ.' The Church of South India is invoked as a practical

---

[1] The *Report* in Appendix I lists 'Things Believed in Common'; they include: Scripture as 'the supreme standard of faith and morals' and 'reverence for the Apostles' and Nicene Creeds as classic declarations of that faith and doctrine, which have served to unite the Church Universal on a common basis of Scriptural truth and fact and to protect it from fundamental error'; the Sacraments of Baptism and the Lord's Supper 'as effectual signs and seals of the saving grace of God'; the Ministry as a gift of Christ to the Church, belonging not to any section of the Church but to the Church Universal; admission to the Ministry through prayer and the laying on of hands by 'persons commissioned thereto'; the visibility of the Church, of which Christ is the one Head, and the obligation to seek and promote the visible unity of the Church wherever the pure Word of God is preached and the Sacraments are duly administered; the continuity of the Church from age to age and the unity of essential faith, which admits varying forms of devotion, service and thought; the obligation on the Church 'within its own spiritual sphere' to hold 'allegiance to its Lord alone' and the sovereign right of the Lord Jesus Christ to govern the whole of human life and conduct. Of the Thirty-nine Articles and the Westminster Confession of Faith it is said that the conferring Churches 'recognize as historic expressions of the Christian faith as they have severally received in later formulations (such as the Thirty-nine Articles and the Westminster Confession of Faith) which were evoked by later need' [*sic*].

demonstration that Episcopalians and Presbyterians 'can share the gifts which they have received along their historic line of tradition and take the like from others'; union of Episcopalians and Presbyterians is not a dream of theorists but a practical possibility.

(b) The main *assumption* of the *Report* is based upon the judgement, expressed by the *Report* of the Third World Council on Faith and Order at Lund in 1952 that 'a faith in the one Church of Christ which is not implemented by *acts* of obedience is dead. There are truths about the nature of God and His Church which will remain for ever closed to us unless we act together in obedience to the unity which is already won.' Accordingly, the authors of the *Report on Relations between Anglican and Presbyterian Churches* say that in the course of their discussions problems have arisen which they deliberately set aside or did not discuss to a conclusion, since the time for dealing with them will come only when unity is not merely discussed but planned. The essence of the outlook is contained in the following quotation:

> The whole Conference recognizes that besides such modifications as these in polity and structure (such as Bishops in Presbytery and elders) other and not less fundamental changes will or should come about in all the Churches concerned, changes *which will involve a revaluation of the place of the Word and Sacraments in the whole life, ministry and government of the Church.* But these can only come about as the Churches grow in spiritual fellowship together, and in understanding of one another's discipline. *It is of the nature of Christian truth that deeper understanding can only follow upon faithful obedience.* All the parties to these proposals recognize that there are many truths which we shall only appreciate after we have taken together the steps of faith which will set us free to enjoy gifts of God to His Church which we had previously undervalued or of which we had even been unaware.[1]

The changes proposed, the *Report* says, ought therefore to be understood and interpreted by each Church 'not in accordance with the *status quo ante* in its own tradition but in accordance with the plenitude of order and practice in the enriched Church of the future.'[2]

---

[1] *Report*, p. 28, italics mine.   [2] *Ibid.* p. 23.

5

(c) The *aim* of the *Report* is not immediate 'organic unity'. The four Churches are to remain 'Churches', but are to be in full communion with one another 'in the one Church of Christ', with fully authorized interchange of communicants and mutual recognition of ministries. This, the authors believe, would draw the sting from 'our unhappy divisions' and lead on to ultimate organic unity. The authors fully realize that 'these proposals in themselves leave unsolved a number of related problems of Church unity affecting various other Churches— Protestant, Orthodox and Roman Catholic'.

Criticisms of the Report

The *Church Times*, which has generally been regarded as representing the 'right' wing of the Church of England, gave a somewhat tepid approval to the *Report*, pointing out the gravity of the unresolved difficulties which the *Report* passed over: the nature of the priesthood, which in many ways is more fundamental than the episcopate; the co-existence in the same Church, at least for a time, of ministers episcopally ordained and those not so ordained; the interpretation of confirmation, and lastly, the acceptance of intercommunion as a means towards full organic unity rather than as an expression of that unity when achieved.[1]

Dr E. L. Mascall doubted whether the very method was correct, since it sought 'a synthesis by way of fastening together broken pieces'. Dr Mascall quoted *Catholicity* as declaring this method to be misleading:

> For when the unity of truth is broken it often happens that the result is not a number of fragments of truth, but a number of conceptions which are misleading, erroneous and heretical. We do not arrive at truth by fitting errors together.
>
> It is widely assumed that a synthesis can be reached by taking the agreed elements in 'our common Christianity' and by omitting matters on which there is deep disagreement. But to do this is to accept our common *distorted* versions of Christianity as a basis, without attempting to cure us all of our distortions. From the Highest Common Factor of several erroneous quotients, we get, not a true solution, but a result more erroneous still.[2]

[1] May 3, 1957, leader.   [2] *Catholicity*, p. 44.

Dr Mascall ends with the hope that the Church of the future will not be loaded 'with the incubus of our common unexamined inheritance from the past.'[1]

The Rev. Cyril John Newman, writing in the *Church Times*, was blunter; he said that after reading the *Report* he concluded that 'the pattern of South India has been adopted, viz: of leaving words and/or phrases capable of double meaning, unexplained, so that men of "differing traditions" can agree to the form of words while still holding their original and contradictory beliefs'. And, later, 'to issue statements which purport to show agreement, but which in fact hide disagreement, is dishonest.'[2]

This criticism, that the *Report* tried to cover up real differences under ambiguous formulas, has been repeated more than once. Taken generally, and taken *in the existing circumstances*, it seems to me unjustified.

The Orthodox or Roman Catholics could not approve such a *Report*, if it concerned themselves, since it left undefined matters whose definition is part of their faith and since it made a general statement about the method of achieving unity which is unacceptable alike to the Orthodox and to Catholics.[3] But the *Report* was not directed to the Orthodox or to Roman Catholics, with their clear definitions. It was directed to members of Churches whose faith is far less clearly defined and whose existing ideas about the Eucharist, the ministry and apostolic succession are not fixed and permanent, but—at least in many minds—are liable to revision and change. Very many members of these Churches admit the legitimacy of different opinions about things which Catholics regard as matters of faith. An instance of this is to be found in the *Notes on an Evanston Report* already mentioned; the group of Anglican theologians say:

We believe that the question of inter-communion ought to be re-examined theologically in the wider context of the life of the Church. The doctrines of the Eucharist, of baptism, of confirmation, or orders, would all be relevant but no aspect of any one of them should be regarded as automatically decisive, but

[1] *Church Times*, May 17, 1957, p. 11.
[2] *Church Times*, June 7 and 21, 1957, pp. 11–12, respectively.
[3] Cf. further, pp. 213–16.

each should be seen in its place within the larger whole. Only when this is done shall we be able to have a clear understanding of our own position and to interpret it effectively to other Churches. We do not wish to make any forecast about what the result of such an examination would be. We might be confirmed in our present attitude, or we might modify it towards greater relaxation or greater rigidity. *The conclusion we have reached is a confession of ignorance.*[1]

It may be sad that responsible theologians should confess ignorance on such matters. Nevertheless such a confession throws a different light on the *Report* about Anglican-Presbyterian relations. Many members of the Church of England and of the Episcopal Church in Scotland do not regard episcopacy as belonging to the essence of the Church but think that it certainly belongs to 'fulness' of the Church. Doubtless many others are confused and do not see clearly the exact import of episcopacy. The *Report*, it may be argued, took a realistic view of the uncertainty which exists in many minds and tried to lead them to firmer ground through consideration of the necessity of the unity of the Church and through the theology which is developing round that concept. It would certainly be dishonest to accept an ambiguous formula which permits contrary interpretations if the interpretations are regarded as matters of faith; but it does not seem in any way dishonest to accept a general formula if the possible interpretations are regarded as matters for investigation and if more light about them is being sincerely sought.[2]

It is here that the stress arises: should belief precede action or may belief follow action? The *Report* took the latter view and said clearly that only after action based upon a general agreement in a wide belief will people be able to grasp many

---

[1] *Church Quarterly Review*, clviii, no. 326, January–March, 1957, p. 82, Italics mine.

[2] It is difficult to see that the type of episcopacy advocated in the Report is contrary to Presbyterian principles; it is certainly not the type which was repudiated by the 'Solemn League and Covenant' of 1643–9, and it would not be an easy task to show that it is contrary to Scripture, though this has been asserted in *Glasgow Speaks, A reply to the Joint Report on Anglican-Presbyterian Relations*, Glasgow, 1959, p. 16. With this compare Professor Torrance's considered opinion that Presbyterians 'have not to my knowledge offered a single purely theological reason why the corporate episcopate, which they hold as firmly as Anglicans, *may not devolve upon individual men.*' *Conflict and Agreement in the Church*, vol. I, *Order and Disorder*, p. 72, italics in original.

specific truths which in separation they cannot grasp. Episcopacy, for example, will only be understood when it is
accepted in actual operation.

Anglo-Catholics, indeed, who believe that only a bishop can
transmit sacramental power, would find their consciences
burdened by some provisions of the *Report*.[1] Similarly, Presbyterians could not accept the implications of such a *Report*, if
they sincerely believed that 'parity of ministers' is a revealed
truth and that the Catholic, Orthodox and Anglo-Catholic
belief is contrary to the word of God.[2] But it was not and is not
clear how many members of the two Churches actually have
such firm doctrinal convictions. Consequently, it does not seem
to me to be fair to accuse the authors of the *Report* of being
unduly ambiguous or of seeking unity by placing together
conceptions which may be erroneous in order to attain a
fictitious unity. Might not acceptance of the *Report* have helped

[1] Those Roman Catholics who regard the Anglo-Catholics as fully representative of the Church of England may regard the *Report* as evidence that the Church
of England was turning away from Catholic principles toward a 'protestant'
attitude and influence. The Anglo-Catholics do, indeed, represent much that is
best in the Church of England, and their hold upon many Catholic principles
and their superior scholarship, especially in patristics, gives them very considerable
importance and influence. Yet the Anglo-Catholics were not and are not fully
representative of the Church of England: a fact insufficiently realized, for instance,
by Père Maurice Villain, to judge by some pages in his *L'Abbé Paul Couturier*,
Paris, 1957. An illuminating discussion of the position of the Anglo-Catholics in
the Church of England in the *Tablet*, April-October, 1955. Dr Norman
Sykes, *Old Priest and New Presbyter*, indicates the affinity which has always existed
between the Church of England and 'Protestants'. The position taken by some
who describe themselves as 'High Churchmen' may be seen in the volume edited
by the Principal of Westcott House, Cambridge, the Revd. Kenneth Carey,
entitled *The Historic Episcopate*, London, 1954. The authors of this book dismiss
discussion of episcopacy as of the *esse* or the *bene esse* of the Church, and hold that
it is the *plene esse*; hence they do not 'unchurch' those who have not had episcopacy, for there can be a Church without it, but urge that episcopacy is necessary
for the establishment of that universal unity said now to be lacking. The book was
criticized by A. L. Peck, *The Church of Christ. An Examination of Certain Presuppositions
in the Historic Episcopate*, London, 1955. Gotthard Nygren of Lund agreed with
Peck in thinking that *The Historic Episcopate* 'represents a vague compromise
solution', cf. *The Ecumenical Review*, x, October, 1957, p. 96.

[2] If there has been a reasoned Presbyterian rejection of the *Report*, based upon
Scriptural evidence and theological principles, I have not been able to find it;
most criticisms have taken the Presbyterian position for granted and argued whether or not it was sacrificed by the provisions of the *Report*. This is, I venture to
think, true of *Glasgow Speaks, A reply to the Joint Report on Anglican-Presbyterian Relations*, Glasgow, 1959. There is much in this pamphlet which would condemn
the Presbyterians who joined the Church of South India, and there is explicit
condemnation of the Plan of Church Union in North India and Pakistan, cf. pp.
22–4, as was frankly said by Professor J. Pitt-Watson, in the General Assembly of
1959.

to dissolve what are not really doctrinal convictions but are in fact prejudices associated with what is called 'our Presbyterian heritage' and 'our Anglican heritage',—prejudices due, perhaps, more to historical factors than to convictions about the Christian faith?

The General Assembly and the Lambeth Conference

In May, 1958, criticisms of the *Joint Report* were summarized by the Inter-Church Relations Committee of the Church of Scotland and presented to the General Assembly. This latter decided to remit the *Joint Report* to the Presbyteries for their theological judgement and to reconsider the matter in 1959. Meantime the Lambeth Conference Committee on Church Unity was made aware of Presbyterian objections and discussed them in its Report to the Lambeth Conference in the summer of 1958. Some Presbyterians may not realize that the Lambeth Conference is an unofficial body whose findings are not binding on any province of the Anglican communion, though no doubt considerable weight will be given to them by the constitutional authorities of the provinces. It will be convenient to state the Presbyterian reservations, which centred upon six points, and these Anglican answers.

1. In Presbyterian practice the Kirk Session is responsible for the admission to full membership, or confirmation. The *Joint Report* had overlooked this and simply suggested an association of the bishop and the parish minister acting together. In answer, the Anglican Committee, while saying that some members were apprehensive about safeguarding the incumbent's final responsibility, thought that Anglicanism might have something to learn from the Presbyterian practice and judged the question one which might be the subject of further conversations.

2. The Presbyterians expressed uneasiness about the authority assigned to the bishops and felt that the *Joint Report* left the matter too vague. There was anxiety lest the 'full and final authority of the General Assembly' should be undermined at important points. The Anglicans suggested that, so far as the General Assembly is concerned, the problem might be solved by allowing, on all matters of doctrine, separate votes in the

Assembly by bishops, by presbyters, and by elders. With this safeguard no one group could impose its will on the other two and any one of the three could veto proposals of the other two. In this suggestion the Anglicans probably had in mind the practice in the Church in Wales, the Church of Ireland and the Protestant Episcopal Church in the United States.

3. The Presbyterians found the *Joint Report* unduly vague about lay elders. The Anglicans answered that the lay eldership as it exists in the Church of Scotland ought to be considered seriously by the Anglican Communion, and suggested further study on the part of Anglicans.

4. The Presbyterians felt that the practical proposals of the *Joint Report* regarding Orders involved not mutual commissioning but merely an acceptance of episcopal ordination by Presbyterians. This seemed to them to fail to make plain that each Church recognizes the other as a true part of the One, Holy, Catholic and Apostolic Church and that neither explicitly or implicitly calls in question the spiritual effectiveness of the ministerial orders of the other. Some act of mutual recommissioning would have to be accepted, as, for example, by the laying-on of hands in a solemn act of rededication with prayer, such as is proposed in the 'Plan of Church Union in North India and Pakistan'.

The Anglican Committee judged that the Anglican Churches 'ought to be ready to recognize the Presbyterian Churches as true parts' of the Church and that the spiritual effectiveness of their ministerial orders ought not to be questioned in any way. The Committee believed that agreement might be reached as to some method of unifying the ministries, similar to that proposed for the Churches in North India and Ceylon.

5. The Presbyterians expressed regret that the relations between the Church of Scotland and the Episcopal Church in Scotland received scant attention in the *Joint Report* and felt that direct conversations between these two bodies ought to precede any general plans for intercommunion or organic unity. Organic unity is the ultimate aim and the organic unity ought to begin in uniting the two Churches, episcopal and non-episcopal, in Scotland. With this the Anglicans expressed entire agreement.

6. The Presbyterians effectively said, although they tried to use the most moderate language, that episcopalians ought to admit intercommunion as a preliminary to other suggested changes. This was not laid down as a prior condition to resumed conversations, but the very strong feeling among Presbyterian ministers and members was urgently represented.

Upon this point the Anglican answer was very definite. 'It must,' they said, 'be recognized as a fact that Anglicans conscientiously hold that the celebrant of the Eucharist should have been ordained by a bishop standing in the historic succession, and generally believe it to be their duty to bear witness to this principle by receiving Holy Communion only from those who have thus been ordained. The existence of this conviction as a view held among Anglicans clearly makes it in practice impossible to envisage the establishment of fully reciprocal intercommunion at any stage short of the adoption of episcopacy by the Churches of the Presbyterian Order, and the satisfactory unification of the Presbyterian and Anglican ministries.'

The different Presbyteries sent their theological judgements of the *Joint Report* to the Inter-Church Committee in December 1958. In the event, only one Presbytery was unreservedly in favour of the *Report*, 7 others reserved judgement and 39 definitely expressed their opposition to Bishops-in-Presbytery. In May, 1959, the General Assembly rejected a motion that the proposals of the *Report* were 'unacceptable in their present form,' and by 300 votes to 266 accepted a counter-motion that the proposals of the *Joint Report* 'were unacceptable, in that they imply a denial of the Catholicity of the Church of Scotland and of the validity and regularity of its ministry within the Church Catholic.'

In commending the motion which contained the words 'in their present form', Dr A. C. Craig had said:

If the Assembly adopted this recommended policy it would in effect be reaffirming the long-term policy authorised seven years ago in terms of which the recent conversations were held.

'Before the eyes of the Church, now far alerted, through two years of discussion, to the problems and sorrows of disunity, it will be holding up the vision of a reintegrated Christendom which has been the inspiration of the modern ecumenical movement. If it rejects this policy it will in effect be turning aside from the main stream of the ecumenical movement and retreating into a citadel of spiky Presbyterianism.'

Upon the rejection of the qualified motion and acceptance of the motion of the counter-proposal, Dr Craig resigned as Convener of the Inter-Church Relations Committee, a resignation which caused sorrow and distress to the members of the Assembly, as to many others.

The *Joint Report* was no more than 'an exploratory survey', a fact insufficiently stressed even by the Inter-Church Relations Committee of the Church of Scotland. Moreover the crucial importance of certain suggestions made by the Scots members to the Anglicans seem to have been overlooked, for instance, that the Church of England should attain 'such independence in spiritual things, as for example, to be able to reform its liturgy, or to have its bishops appointed on the recommendation of the Church, including lay representation', that large Bishoprics be divided into units capable of being adequately pastored by a single Bishop, and that Anglicans accept the office of eldership. Comments upon the *Report* not seldom showed slight appreciation of the 'new approach', of the theological considerations propounded in it, and of the missionary outlook.

The reception accorded the *Joint Report* and its rejection by the Assembly seems evidence that some of the leaders in ecumenical thought are in advance of the ordinary members and even of the ministers; and it is disconcerting that representatives should be appointed by a Church and their findings and suggestions afterwards generally rejected, the more so as no clear alternative has so far emerged.

The *Joint Report*, in spite of its vagueness about certain fundamental matters, such as the Eucharist and the priesthood, had several outstanding merits. It was marked throughout by the conviction that universalistic principles must apply in all discussions of Christian unity. It rose above immediate 'historical inheritances' and went back to the will of Christ and the principles of Church government judged to be inherent in the New Testament witness. It maintained that Christian unity must be outwardly visible and manifest. Its outlook was positive, not negative. It protested against nothing, save disunity, and says nothing that seemed designed to reject the doctrine of any body of Christians. It tried to by-pass the controversies of the sixteenth and seventeenth centuries and to lay down principles which antedate those controversies. It did not assume the individualistic idea that each man is alone in his quest for religious truth, but affirmed that religious truth can only be attained through obedience within the unity of Christ's Church. It accepted the doctrine that the Church's mission and authority derive, not from inspiration and guidance given to each individual, but derive from Christ through the Apostles and are continued through ordination in 'episcopé' or oversight. It did not positively accept, though neither did it explicitly reject, the concept that bishops may have authority in safeguarding truth and excluding error. It was anti-erastian, and looked to, if it did not actually demand, freedom from any spiritual control by the State. It recognized the missionary obligation of the Church, and, indeed, the missionary outlook is clear throughout. It insisted upon the need of humble prayer.

The *Report* caused controversy and heart-burning. But one may hope, in spite of its rejection, that it helped to open the eyes of many to wider perspectives, to dissipate misunderstandings and lessen acquiescence in positions, which, after all, are comparatively recent in the history of Christianity. In any event, it stands as a land-mark in the history of Church relations, and, in my opinion, its rejection is a striking instance of the influence of non-theological factors.

A Fundamental Assumption

Whatever be the ultimate result of this Anglican-Presbyterian démarche, its fundamental assumption ought not to be forgotten:

'A faith in the one Church of Christ which is not implemented by *acts* of obedience is dead. There are truths about the nature of God and His Church which will remain for ever closed to us unless we act together in obedience to the unity which is already won.'

This assumption underlies many proposals for 'reunion', notably the *Scheme* for reunion in Lanka (Ceylon) and the *Plan* for reunion in North India and Pakistan. It is, unquestionably, a somewhat precarious assumption and one which might be used to exert pressure against conscientious convictions. Some Anglo-Catholics have complained of the ambiguous language in the *Plan* for North India and Pakistan; they have felt that it is dishonest that the *Plan* retains, 'as worthy exponents of the Word of God, and as systems of doctrine to be taught in our Churches and seminaries', the Westminster Confession of Faith, the Confession and Canons of the Synod of Dort, the Heidelberg Catechism, Luther's Catechism and the Augsburg Confessions, documents not consistent among themselves. Anglo-Catholics have expressed themselves as shocked that the Lambeth Conference mentioned that these formularies were retained 'to secure the legal continuity of the united Church with the Churches from which its membership will be derived and for the safeguarding of property.' *Lambeth Conference*, pt. 2, p. 31.

But do not these Anglo-Catholics forget the latitude allowed to Anglicans in interpretation of their own formularies? The *Report* on *Doctrine in the Church of England*, 1938, approved a 'symbolic' interpretation of the Creeds which seems very strange to Roman Catholics and to the Orthodox; and the long history of 'the assent' given to the Thirty-Nine Articles seems to Roman Catholics to show a puzzling latitudinarianism. It must, in fact, be admitted that among our separated brethren there is a vagueness about matters of faith which is regrettable but which must affect judgement about these various 'reunions'. Even theologians of the different 'Churches' manifest a surprising vagueness about such concepts as validity of sacraments, the Eucharistic presence and sacrifice, and the nature of the ministry. Such vagueness, however, is compatible with a sincere love of Christ, strong faith in his divinity, a conviction of the need of grace, a reverence for the Eucharist and an active zeal to bring non-Christians to Christ. The Disciples of Christ, many Congregationalists and many

Methodists lay an emphasis upon personal adherence to Christ and upon personal 'conversion' which makes dogmatic matters seem to them comparatively of less importance. Indeed, the Disciples of Christ have traditionally rejected any formularization of the faith and for them it is an immense step to accept the formulae of these new ecclesiastical bodies.

The question about these plans is not: 'Is this plan for "reunion" a perfect plan?' The question is: 'Would it be better to leave the denominations as they have been?' If a Catholic examines the Constitutions and declarations of faith of these 'new Churches', and compares them with Catholic standards, he must conclude adversely. But he might judge differently if he compares the doctrinal formularies and the liturgies of these 'new Churches' with the formularies and the liturgies of the disunited bodies. Admittedly all such plans contain the danger of compromise in doctrine and of 'formulae' which conceal real differences; on the other hand, this danger must be judged in the light of the latitude already allowed in interpretation of denominational formularies. Judgement at best can only be approximate, but judgement ought to be made on the basis of the existing concrete situation and not merely on the basis of the fully articulated Catholic faith, which many of these denominations regard with dislike if not abhorrence. The 'reunions' are declared to be made with a will to learn, to develop and to work for the ultimate 'organic unity' of the whole of Christendom. Much in these 'schemes' and 'plans' tends to greater orthodoxy in faith and in liturgy; they look to universality as against 'denominationalism' and to this extent, at least, they tend to lessen prejudices and to open minds and hearts to the vision of true Catholicity.[1]

These observations, of course, are not meant to suggest that Anglo-Catholic criticisms are unfounded, for perhaps the Lambeth Committee might have used more measured language and Anglo-Catholic criticisms may supply a needed corrective.

[1] Cf. *Report of the Inter-Church Committee* of the General Assembly of the Church of Scotland, May 1958; *The Lambeth Conference 1958, The Encyclical Letter from the Bishops together with Resolutions and Reports*, London, 1958; *Plan of Church Union in North India and Pakistan*, ed. 3, Madras, 1957; E. L. Mascall, *Lambeth 1958 and Christian Unity* (published by the Council for the Defence of Church Principles), London, 1958.

But Anglo-Catholics have such firm hold on many Catholic principles, and yet can reconcile themselves to so much ambiguity in Anglicanism, that the consistency of their general position becomes a puzzle to many of their Roman Catholic brethren, in spite of deep sympathy and close friendship.

6. A Central Theological 'Obscurity': the Church as Visible and as Invisible

Is it possible to find one main principle at the root of the existing divisions among Christians? To attempt to do so may seem hopeless, for non-Catholic theologians hold a multitude of diverse opinions and use varying terminologies, as may be seen from even a hasty reading of the volume *The Nature of the Church*, published for the World Conference on Faith and Order in 1951.[1] Yet the meetings both at Amsterdam in 1948 and at Evanston in 1954 did attempt to indicate a central 'tension' and several writers familiar with the movement have done the same. The advantage of finding some central principle, even though it may be applicable only with reservations, is that it may give a main topic to which the varying opinions may be referred, and that, if it is really a root principle, to indicate it may help in overcoming the differences.[2]

The Amsterdam *Report* of 1948 saw 'our deepest differences' in the opposed 'catholic' and 'protestant' conceptions of 'Christian faith and life as a self-consistent whole'.[3] It may be that the Amsterdam Assembly had been influenced by the publication in 1947 of *Catholicity, A Study in the Conflict of Christian Traditions in the West* by a group of Anglican theologians of the 'Catholic' school of thought, who tabulated in striking fashion the 'catholic' and the 'protestant' convictions and outlook. The publication in 1950 by Dr R. Newton Flew and

---

[1] *Papers presented to the Theological Commission appointed by the Continuation Committee of the World Conference on Faith and Order*, edited by R. Newton Flew, London, 1952.

[2] A Catholic would doubtless say that the root principle is that of authority and I agree that this is so; but the question of authority goes back to further questions, which involve the very nature of the divine dispensation. Yet it is worth considering that a generally accepted central authority can permit, and even encourage, a diversity in local forms of government, custom and liturgy, which would be divisive without such generally accepted central authority. In the concrete, a central authority may protect liberty and not restrict it.

[3] Pp. 51-2.

Rupert E. Davies of *The Catholicity of Protestantism* may have tended to modify readiness to accept the 'catholic-protestant' antithesis, as the book objected strongly to the term 'catholic' being opposed to the term 'protestant'. The words, of course, are not used in this connection as meaning the 'Roman Catholic Church' and the 'Protestant Churches', since what may be called 'catholic' emphases exist among the Orthodox (who consider themselves as alone Catholic), among Anglicans, among some German and Scandinavian Churches, and, indeed, among some Presbyterians, just as some 'protestant' emphases exist among those who generally tend to 'catholic' views.[1]

The Evanston *Report* centralized the problem under the heading *Our Unity in Christ and our Disunity as Churches*, even though different opinions are held about the nature of 'our unity in Christ' and of 'our disunity as Churches'. One of the most common expressions is 'a given unity' and 'a manifestation of unity'; and Dr Visser 't Hooft judges that both these expressions are essential in ecumenical discussions 'but both are also ambiguous. Both need to be thought through in their full implications and in their relation to each other'.[2] The 'given unity' is the unity, speaking very generally, which God produces among the followers of Christ, and the 'manifestation of unity' is the unity which exists in the observable earthly order; the one is personal allegiance to Christ, the other to an organized church. To some extent the 'given unity' would correspond to what Catholics would call the union of all those who are in sanctifying grace, whether members of the visible Church or not, and 'the manifestation of unity' would correspond to outward profession of the same defined faith and life in the hierarchical Church with use of the same sacraments. Yet even this explanation would be inadequate, since both visible and invisible union are given

---

[1] Fr Edward Duff in *The Social Thought of the World Council of Churches*, London, 1957, accepted this 'catholic-protestant' antithesis as the source of the contrasting outlooks in social thought between 'an ethic of ends' and 'an ethic of inspiration'. Yet Père Georges Jarlot in reviewing the book accepted the general antithesis while omitting the words 'catholic' and 'protestant', a notable instance of the inadequacy of terminologies to cope with such heterogeneous elements. Cf. *Unitas*, viii, no. 4, Winter, 1956, pp. 346–50.

[2] 'Various Meanings of Unity and the Unity which the World Council of Churches Seeks to Promote', *Ecumenical Review*, viii, no. 1, October, 1955, p. 25.

by God and are by no means the result of merely human effort; and, moreover, Catholics agree that pagans may be in sancti-fying grace, whereas the 'given unity' and 'our unity in Christ' seem to refer only to Christians.[1] In fact, Dr Visser 't Hooft is profoundly correct in saying that the expressions 'given unity' and 'manifestation of unity' are ambiguous and need further thought to be made clear. The obscurity latent in them appears in the following citation from the *Report* on Anglican-Presbyterian Relations:

> Unity is not a contingent feature of the Church's life, but is of the essence of it. One God, one people of God; one Christ, one Body of Christ; one Holy Spirit, one Fellowship of the Spirit— such is the incontrovertible logic of the New Testament teaching. The Church, therefore, cannot be but one, its existence being grounded in that Divine realm where disunity is unthinkable; and of this fundamental unity God has given the separated 'Churches' a recovered awareness and experience, most of all in and through the Ecumenical Movement.
>
> Yet disunity visibly persists, and disunity in any measure contradicts the nature of the Church. In their visible separatedness the 'Churches' cannot but obscure and disfigure the face and form of the body of Christ. Hence the overcoming of disunity and the fuller manifesting of the Church's wholeness are not luxuries with which busy 'Churches' may dispense at their dis-cretion, but necessities of the Church's real existence and proper vitality (p. 12).

Everyone must welcome this assertion that the visible unity of the Church is a necessity and that 'Churches' must try to overcome their disunity. At the same time the passage is hard to understand. The Church has an existence 'grounded in' that Divine realm *where disunity is unthinkable.* But is this 'Church' one which we can recognize as existing in this world, which we can join, whose members we can know? Or is it a 'Church' which does not exist in this world of space and time, but only in 'a Divine realm' beyond our concrete perception? It would not seem to be merely the latter, a supramundane Church, because it has a 'fundamental unity' which can be experienced. Again, if the overcoming of disunity is 'a necessity for the

[1] Père C. J. Dumont has some thoughtful remarks on the expressions in his *Approaches to Christian Unity*, London and Baltimore, 1959, pp. 200–12.

Church's real existence', then if disunity is not overcome, the Church simply does not exist. Yet it is said that the 'fuller' manifesting of the Church's wholeness is a necessity of the Church's real existence and proper vitality. How 'full' must the manifestation be, in order that the Church may have a real existence and proper vitality?

These questions are not meant to be captious or controversial, but only to illustrate the obscurity which exists about the nature of the Church's visible unity. Several scholars, such as Père Dumont, Dr W. H. Van de Pol, Canon Hodgson and Bishop Newbigin, suggest that the radical obscurity in the ecumenical encounter is about the Church as invisible and as visible. Yet even these words are used in different meanings and confusion results which tends to cloud all discussion.

The Church Visible and Invisible

The misunderstanding of these terms was illustrated by an incident which happened at the Lausanne Conference in 1927, narrated in piquant style by Archbishop Temple:

> The Lutherans and the Orthodox combined in a demand that we must at all costs state concerning the Church that it is both visible and invisible. Now, there are not very many things that the Lutherans and the Orthodox hold in common concerning the Church, so we were delighted, of course, to fall in with this and nobody wished to dispute it. Then we had to add a footnote because, quite accidentally, it became apparent that according to the Lutherans the Church is visible indeed but only in its activities—preaching and administering the sacraments. In respect of its members it is quite invisible; nobody knows who are members of the Church; they are the elect. . . . But the Orthodox, of course, did not mean that at all. By the visible Church they meant the Orthodox Church and its members and by the Invisible Church they meant the deceased members of the same, and none of the rest of us were members in it at all. So, having first discovered this complete and enthusiastic verbal agreement between the Lutherans and the Orthodox we then, as I say, regretfully added a footnote to say that they meant not only different but diametrically opposite things by it.[1]

[1] F. A. Iremonger, *William Temple, Archbishop of Canterbury, His Life and Letters*, London, 1948, pp. 400–1.

In this citation Archbishop Temple certainly succeeded in making plain two meanings of the terms 'visible and invisible Church'. But in more recent times the Church is designated in 'eschatological' language, and sometimes it is hard to know whether the reference is to the Church visible on earth, with its discernible members, or the Church invisible in heaven, with members actually with it in heaven and some members on earth but not discernible to human judgement. 'Our unity in Christ' sometimes seems equivalent to our unity in the invisible Church, and 'our disunity as Churches' is sometimes spoken of as if a visible, recognizable Church on earth were perhaps too much to hope for.[1] Dr J. Robert Nelson gives a brief but excellent summary of the interconnection between views on eschatology and views about the nature of the Church. He divided views into three general classes:

(a) Thorough-going eschatology, according to which Christ and the New Testament writers thought that the end of the world was coming shortly, and hence the Church 'is a purely eschatological entity with no significance for the present'.

(b) 'Realized eschatology', according to which the Church is a reality which both transcends space and time and likewise is present in the visible gathering together of Christians in the 'Church' on earth. A brief but acute criticism of this view appeared in *Theology* in December, 1955, pp. 444-7, by A. W. Argyle, under the title 'Eschatology and Teleology'.

(c) 'The kingdom (not always identified with the Church), is both present and to come.' The Church on earth is the

---

[1] The literature on eschatology is immense. Cf., v.g., W. D. Davies and D. Daube, ed., *The Background of the New Testament and its Eschatology*, Cambridge, 1955; *Eschatology. Four Papers read to the Society for the Study of Theology*, by W. Manson, G. W. H. Lampe, T. F. Torrance and R. H. Whitehouse, Edinburgh, 1953; J. R. Nelson, *The Realm of Redemption*, London, 1953; the essay of Dr J. A. T. Robinson, 'Kingdom, Church and Ministry' in *The Historic Episcopate in the Fullness of the Church*, pp. 11-22; W. Manson, 'Church and Intercommunion', *Scottish Journal of Theology*, iv, no. 1, March, 1951; K. E. Skydsgaard, 'Kingdom of God and Church', *ibid.* no. 4, pp. 383-97; T. E. Torrance, 'The Nature and Mission of the Church', *ibid.* ii, no. 3, September, 1949, pp. 241-70; review of *Catholicity*, *ibid.* iv, no. 1, March, 1949, pp. 85-93; 'History and Reformation', *ibid.*, iv, no. 1, September, 1951, pp. 279-90; 'The Atonement and the Oneness of the Church', *ibid.* vii, no. 3, September, 1954, pp. 245-69; Barth, 'The Real Church', *ibid.* iii, no. 4, Sec. 1950, pp. 337-51. The list could be continued almost indefinitely.

beginning of the triumphant Church, but does not reveal its fulness or perfection.

Sometimes the 'eschatological' Church seems to be conceived as breaking through eternity and invisibility and being manifested in greater or lesser perfection in the temporal order. Professor J. H. Nichols says:

> There is general consensus that the unity of the Church is not something which we can bring about. If it is not already in existence, then we cannot hope to do anything about it. But it *is* already in existence and we have often sensed its present reality as the society of those called into the new household of God. This unity we cannot create, but we can manifest what is given to us. The task of the ecumenical movement is thus not to consolidate the churches as they are. It is to seek their renewal. Only as we grow together into Him who is our Head will we find the unity which is worth having.[1]

I must confess that I find Professor Nichols hard to understand. In what sense is 'the unity of the Church' already in existence? And in what sense are we still 'to find the unity which is worth having'? Is the unity of the Church in existence through common acceptance of Christ as God and Saviour and in the charitable convictions and feelings which this brings? Or is it in existence only as an 'eschatological' reality, as a Church united by the invisible acts of God?

Archbishop Temple declared bluntly: 'I believe in the Holy Catholic Church, and sincerely regret that it does not at present exist.'[2] Probably few ecumenists would agree with Archbishop Temple in his forthright declaration. The New Testament speaks of the Church as of a visible and recognizable thing, as so many analogies indicate: the Kingdom, the Vine, the Sheep-flock, the Building, the Net, the Temple, the People of God, the New Israel, the Ark of Salvation, the Body of Christ. The Lund Conference laid emphasis upon the need for a unity which non-Christians can easily recognize.[3] There seems to be very considerable agreement that the

---

[1] *Evanston: An Interpretation*, New York, 1955, p. 104.
[2] Iremonger's *Life*, p. 387. The reference given by Iremonger is to 'Addresses on Church Unity—*passim*'.
[3] Cf. above, ch. 2, and the Lund Conference, pp. 134-5.

Church's unity is meant to be visible and is in fact at present visible, but imperfectly, not in 'fulness'; but it must be confessed that there are many conflicting views about the nature of the perfection and the 'fulness' of the visible unity which is the desired goal. This is not said in criticism, but to point, if possible, to a central obscurity which may be clarified.

The Westminster Confession put clearly the difference between the Church invisible and the Church visible:

> Chapter XXV, Of the Church: 1. The catholick or universal Church, which is invisible, consists of the whole number of the elect that have been, are, or shall be gathered into one, under Christ the head thereof; and is the spouse, the body, the fullness of him that filleth all in all.

Several texts of St Paul which mention the 'body of Christ' are alleged in confirmation: Eph. i, 10; i, 23; v, 23, 27, 32; Col. i, 18.

> The visible Church, which is also catholick and universal under the Gospel (not confined to one nation as before under the law) consists of all those throughout the world that profess the true religion, together with their children; and is the kingdom of the Lord Jesus Christ, the house and family of God, out of which there is no ordinary possibility of salvation.[1]

This distinction made by the Westminster Confession is effectively renewed by not a few who write on ecumenical subjects, although their language often blurs the sharpness of the distinction. It is encouraging that the assertion is often made that 'the body of Christ' refers to the actual Church in space and time, composed of sinners as well as of saints. At the same time, hesitations and obscurities persist, and what Dr Tomkins wrote in 1946 remains substantially true:

'There are some who would dismiss the World Council from any serious meaning, because, taking refuge in a doctrine of the Invisible Church, they dismiss both the Churches and the meeting of the Churches as of no more than administrative convenience.'[2]

---

[1] *The Confession of Faith; the Larger and Shorter Catechism, with the Scripture-Proofs at large*, etc., Edinburgh, 1894, p. 85, and cf. pp. 125-7.
[2] 'The Present Position of the Unity Movement', *Theology*, xlix, no. 317, November, 1946, p. 329.

Dr Van de Pol, who is competent to make an appraisal of Reformed theology on the subject, gives his considered judgement in these words: 'The difficulty in realizing the Church of the Credo, the Body of Christ in the world, as a united, indivisible and incontestable reality of actual experience, is throwing its shadow over all the discussions and manifestations of the World Council of Churches'.[1]

The Rev. Dr J. Robert Nelson, speaking of bible-images in an illuminating article, 'Many Images of the One Church', in the *Ecumenical Review*, to some extent agrees with Dr Van de Pol:

> It is all too easy for certain words to become mere jargon of the ecumenical movement, so that each is susceptible of various and even contrary interpretations. Clearly this danger applies to the use of the term Body of Christ. It is undoubtedly significant, for example, that the delegates to the Lund Conference on Faith and Order, 1952, could agree on the sentence of the report which asserts: 'The Pauline image of the Church as the Body of Christ is no mere metaphor, but expresses a living reality.' (p. 12). But one would hardly have to have been a delegate to know that this statement, while expressing a wide agreement, also conceals some *profound and seemingly irreconcilable differences* in the concept of the Church held by various communions. Comparable divergences can be obscured by the over-casual use of such terms as the people of God, the royal priesthood, and the bride of Christ.[2]

Canon Hodgson, speaking about the continuity of the Church's unity, points out what he judges a radical divergence, which probably underlies the different concepts of the Church, of which Dr Nelson spoke:

---

[1] 'The Church as the Mystical Body of Christ in Reformed Protestantism', *Unitas*, vii, no. 3, Autumn, 1955, p. 133.

[2] *Ecumenical Review*, ix, no. 2, January, 1957, p. 107, italics mine. This brief citation does not do justice to the restrained but forceful urgency of the article. If the Churches do not take seriously the teaching of the New Testament about unity, says Dr Nelson, 'the flock remains scattered, the stones of the building become cold and lifeless, the heirs and brethren are estranged and even hostile, the members say, "I have no need of you", and we imply that these are several loaves which separately betoken the presence of Christ. So the scandal of division and the necessity of unity are proclaimed by the biblical images in such diverse ways that we should never merely take this teaching for granted and remain comfortable in schism.' P. 112.

He thought that there were two distinct points of view which it was impossible to reconcile. The one was that the Church was meant to be a body in space and time, the continuity being that of an actual historical body. The opposite view was one which maintained that the only continuity necessary was not in this space and time at all but was in the invisible sphere of our risen Lord Jesus Christ, the same yesterday, today and forever, Who embodies Himself as and when He will in this or that group of human beings whom He calls and who make the response of faith.[1]

Professor Torrance judged that 'the way in which Professor Hodgson has put the contrast is too sharp and does not appear to understand the "evangelical" insistence on the visible continuity of the Church', and, after four citations from Calvin, remarks: 'The difference does not lie therefore in a doctrine of historical continuity but in the form and nature of that continuity.'[2]

Professor Torrance here may be thinking primarily of Presbyterians, who traditionally have made more of order and of authority than have the English Independents, whom Dr Hodgson may have primarily in mind. These latter hold that the only continuity required in the ministry is the preaching of the apostolic and evangelical doctrine; among them the prophetic office is far more prominent than the pastoral. Dr Daniel Jenkins remarks, in his *Congregationalism: A Restatement*:

The popular notion among Catholics that Protestants in general and Congregationalists in particular believe only in an invisible Church, which becomes visible only in local congregations, is erroneous. Protestants have a different conception from many Catholics of how the Church becomes visible, a conception which faces the implications of the Ascension of our Lord and of the

[1] *Amsterdam Report*, p. 60. Dr Nelson cites from unpublished seminar notes of Canon Hodgson, Oxford, 1949: 'The fundamental cleavage in Christendom does not lie between those who hold differing views on the nature of the continuity of the visible Church, whether, for example, it is maintained by episcopal or presbyteral succession or by the continuous life of the whole body handing on the true faith from one generation to another. It lies between those who hold that there must be such continuity of the earthly body and those who hold that this is unnecessary.' *Realm of Redemption*, p. 157.

[2] 'The Nature and Mission of the Church', *Scottish Journal of Theology*, ii, no. 3, September, 1949, p. 251.

freedom of access to him which is now possible to all men through the Spirit, but they would insist as strongly as Catholics that visibility is an obvious characteristic of the Church in its earthly existence. Pp. 82–3.

Dr Jenkins, unless I misapprehend him, does not use the word 'visible' in the sense of 'recognizable'. In his *Tradition and the Spirit*, London, 1951, he says:

It is part of the New Israel's understanding of the terms upon which it exists in this world that it should frankly recognize that God may speak a word to His people not in contradiction to His decisive Word in Christ, but independently of, *and even in defiance of*, the official spokesmen of the Church's institutional manifestation. P. 136.

A little further on Dr Jenkins says:

The life of the true people of God may be held always to be found somewhere around that of the visible societies which strive to embody it, but they embody it imperfectly at best and sometimes hardly at all, while its true nature is often more vividly revealed *in the disturbances and schisms which rend that society* than in its steady, even movement. P. 137, italics mine.

Thus God may speak to his people even in defiance of the General Assembly or of any or even all of the Presbyteries, or in defiance of all the bishops. The norm by which 'disturbances and schisms' are to be distinguished from God's decisive Word in Christ is not clear, though presumably the decision must be left to the action of the Holy Ghost. The Church, then, may be visible, but is recognizable only with difficulties which appear disconcerting to one brought up in another tradition. There seems scarcely any doubt that many Baptists, Congregationalists and Disciples of Christ hold that the continuity of the Church is essentially that of the preaching of the true doctrine and the sole test of this is Scripture.[1]

[1] Cf., also, Dr Jenkins's *The Nature of Catholicity*, London, 1942, Canon O. C. Quick's observations in *The Journal of Theological Studies*, xliv, 1943, pp. 110–12, and Dr Jenkins's answer to these in *Tradition and the Spirit*, London, 1951. Cf., also, the volume edited by Dr Flew, *The Nature of the Church*, in which it appears that many of our separated brethren consider that 'continuity must be primarily a matter of witness to the true faith and the Spirit's guidance and enabling',

Bishop Lesslie Newbigin agrees in the main with Canon Hodgson: 'I have the impression,' he says, 'that the recent re-emphasis upon the eschatological character of the whole New Testament has been achieved at the cost of removing the whole group of ideas which we call eschatalogical from the realm of reality to that of symbol.'[1] Bishop Newbigin does not, of course, mean to reject the inherent eschatological element in the Church,—what Christian could do so, since clearly the Second Coming of Christ is in the Creed and there are few saints who have not felt a union with Christ which transcended the whole time order—but he has reservations about some expressions of it: 'We are risen with Him, yet we await the resurrection. We cry "Abba, Father", yet wait for our adoption. The Church is Christ's bride—yet she longs for the marriage feast. He is with us always—yet we cry "Come, Lord Jesus". Such must necessarily be the character of the life in this age—of the Church in the world.'

'Recent theological writings have made us familiar with this paradox. But I have a feeling that we often state it in a way which looks more like some kind of a conjuring trick with time and eternity than like something vital to our salvation.'[2] Bishop Newbigin finds, as did Dr Donald Baillie, a principle of solution in St Paul's 'I have been crucified with Christ, yet I live; and yet no longer I, but Christ liveth in me'. But Bishop Newbigin's stress on the missionary vocation of the Church leads him to desire that the Church be thought of as it

pp. 97, 111, 134–5, 141, 179, 207, 211, 242–3, 271, 287, 295, 297–8, 301. Some Lutherans hold a view scarcely dissimilar, cf. Eric H. Walstrom, in *The Nature of the Church*, p. 271. Professor Dr Edmund Schlink I find obscure in his account of Lutheran teaching in the same volume, pp. 54–70, and in 'Christ and the Church', *Scottish Journal of Theology*, x, no. 1, March, 1957, pp. 1–23. 'The unity of the Church', he says, 'is not primarily the unity of the members, but the unity of Christ who acts upon them all, in all places and at all times.' The problem, however, is how Christ acts differently upon Christians than upon non-Christians, and how he acts upon Christians, whether urging them to organic unity among themselves or leaving them free to be content with a cordial but unorganized fellowship of the Spirit.

[1] *The Reunion of the Churches*, p. 73.

[2] *The Household of God*, p. 122. The very moderate yet powerful criticisms of some presentations of eschatology by Dr Mascall in *Christ, the Christian and the Church*, London, 1946, do not seem to have lost their validity, pp. 101–8. His insight into the question of Christ's human knowledge might well have been pursued into the 'eschatological' question and into that of our incorporation into Christ.

practically affects the lives of Christians, and as it is knowable and visible in its appeal to people in non-Christian lands; and surely few can disagree with him here.[1]

Canon Hodgson and Bishop Newbigin illustrate the obscurity still persisting about 'unity in Christ' and 'disunity as Churches'; however great is the 'given unity' the manifestation of it is still deficient. Too great insistence upon 'eschatological' unity may tend to dismiss the 'manifestation' of unity to the end of this world. 'The Coming Great Church' may be regarded as essentially 'eschatological', that is, outside this world of sin and frustration, and so may induce acquiescence in existing divisions.[2] Pastor Pierre Maury, of the Reformed Church of France, expressed at Lund his fear lest interest in eschatology might result only in 'pious fancies and dreams for the future'.[3]

Yet an 'eschatological' outlook may be one possible solvent for loyalty to the letter of Reformation formularies and to 'heritages' not dissociated from national feeling. Such loyalties may be directed towards a wider loyalty by contemplation of the New Jerusalem, the city of God, where there is no possibility of divisions; the existing divisions ought to be viewed in the light of the triumphant Church, with its 'great multitude, whom no man could number, of all nations, and tribes, and peoples, and tongues, standing before the throne, and in sight of the Lamb'.[4] In this vision, loyalties which impede unity may be seen as in need of reappraisal; and sometimes insistence upon the 'eschatological' aspect of the Church appear to have this in mind.[5]

'We differ', says the Lund *Report*, 'in our understanding of the relation of our unity in Christ to the visible, holy, Catholic and Apostolic Church. We are agreed that there are not two

[1] On the question of the visibility of the Church Bishop Newbigin thinks that the Reformers were false to their own deepest insights, cf. *The Household of God*, pp. 55–8 on Luther, pp. 101–8 on Calvin.

[2] The expression 'The Coming Great Church' is not new, but was given greater prominence by Canon T. O. Wedel in his book under that title, published in New York in 1945.

[3] *Third World Conference on Faith and Order*, ed. Oliver S. Tomkins, London, 1953, p. 203.

[4] Apoc. 7 : 9.

[5] Cf. the address of Dr Visser 't Hooft at Lund, *op. cit.* p. 136 and of Professor E. W. L. Schlink, p. 161.

Churches, one visible and the other invisible, but one Church which must find visible expression on earth, but we differ in our belief as to whether certain doctrinal, sacramental and ministerial forms are of the essence of the Church itself. In consequence, we differ in our understanding of the character of the unity of the Church on earth for which we hope.'[1]

The difference in understanding the relation of the visible to the invisible appears again at Lund:

> The Pauline image of the Church as the Body of Christ is no mere metaphor, but expresses a living reality. All agree in finding the presence of Jesus Christ, the crucified and risen Lord, both living in and reigning over His Church. . . . We unite in affirming the solidarity between the Head and members and also the sovereignty of the Head over the members in the Body of Christ. But there are differing emphases among us as to the differing modes of participation of the members and the Head. The former view stresses the fullness of Christ as something already received by the Church, though not always consciously apprehended, the latter the manifestation of this same fullness at the Coming of the Lord in glory. In the present age, however, it is in the Church under the Cross that the fullness of Christ is realized.[2]

Towards a Solution

On the theoretical or doctrinal level the Conference at Lund indicated the true context in which the emphasis upon the Church as invisible can be reconciled with insistence upon the Church as visible. In its Report to the Churches, the Conference said:

> From the unity of Christ we seek to understand the Church in the light of Jesus Christ as God and man, and in the light of His death and resurrection. . . . Christ lives in the Church and the Church lives in Christ. Christ is never without His Church; the Church is never without Christ. Both belong inseparably together, the keystone and the temple, the Head and the Body. As members of His body we are made one with Him in the fellowship of His life, death and resurrection, of His sufferings and His glory. What happened to Christ uniquely in His once-

---

[1] P. 34; the differences appear about faith, p. 31, the Eucharist, p. 43, and sacrifice, p. 43, intercommunion, pp. 54–5, the ministry, p. 25, etc.
[2] *Ibid.* p. 79.

and-for-all death and resurrection on our behalf, happens also to the Church in its way as His Body.[1]

Making due allowance for the different images in which Scripture and tradition describe the Church, and remembering, too, that a metaphor must not be pressed unduly even though it denotes a reality, there does appear to be a principle of solution to the 'ecumenical deadlock'—at least on the theoretical level—in meditation and writings upon the union between Christ and the Church. Christ himself was 'visible' in many ways and not exclusively visible to human eyes and touchable by hands; through and in his human nature his invisible union with Father and Holy Spirit become attainable to us so that we may place our whole faith and trust in him. Keeping due proportion of likeness and unlikeness, what is true of the 'visibility' of Christ will be true of the visibility of the Church; and, a point never to be forgotten, mentioned by the Lund Conference, what is true of Christ's work of atonement and reconciliation will be true in its own order, and in complete dependence upon Christ, of the work of the Church in the world. All heresies and errors about the Incarnation and the Atonement will find their counterpart in mistakes about the Church; but to pursue the topic here would extend this book beyond all limits.[2]

For an outsider to estimate the general direction and trends in the movement is difficult and hazardous; however, merely tentatively, I venture to suggest the following:

1. In general, the appreciation of the 'non-theological factors' affecting disunion, and of their connection with 'doctrinal factors', has increased the tendency towards 'living together' and personal associations as solvents of congealed antagonisms or disunities. This explains, to some extent,

[1] *Lund Report* 1953, p. 18.
[2] The writings about the Church visible and invisible are almost innumerable; many useful references will be found in Mascall's *Christ, the Christian and the Church*, London, 1946, and in Henri de Lubac's, *Meditation sur l'Eglise*, Paris, 1953, excellently translated into English by Michael Mason under the title *The Splendour of the Church*, London, 1956. The fullest collection of texts from the patristic sources may be found in S. Tromp's *Corpus Christi, Quod Est Ecclesia*, Romae, 1946; 'De Nativitate Ecclesiae e Corde Iesu in Cruce', *Gregorianum* xvi, 1932, pp. 489–528; *De Sancto Spiritu Anima Corporis Mystici, 1. Testimonia selecta ex Patribus Graecis, 2. Ex Patribus Latinis*, Romae, 1932. The studies of Minear and Nelson on the images of the Church are valuable and illuminating.

what looks like less importance attaching to the Faith and Order Conferences. The period is, as Dr Visser 't Hooft put it, one in which there is need for 'cross-fertilization' between Churches.

2. Nevertheless the various Study Commissions of Faith and Order are proceeding with their investigations into 'Institutionalism', 'Worship', 'Christ and the Church', 'Tradition and Traditions' and allied subjects. At the meeting of the Working Committee in July 1958 in Geneva, a recommendation was made that Faith and Order should have an enlarged staff and should be given the status of a Division; and desire was expressed that 'Faith and Order should be more clearly seen to occupy a place in the structure of the W.C.C. which truthfully reflects its central and fundamental role in the whole ecumenical movement'.[1]

3. The study now in progress on 'Religious Liberty' is not under the aegis of the Faith and Order Commission, but of the Central Committee of the World Council. The proposals for the study make clear that it will investigate not only the thorny problems which surround the efforts of one Christian group to attract other Christians to itself, but also the diverse questions about the right of propagating Christianity and 'making converts' in lands not predominantly Christian.[2]

4. Regional meetings of the Faith and Order Commission have been encouraged, as the American meeting of Faith and Order at Oberlin in 1957 seems to have had considerable success. In smaller groups of more homogeneous character there is greater hope of understanding and progress than in larger groups, often different in language and historic 'culture'.

5. The 'Younger Churches' and their lands are daily as-

[1] Paper no. 26, *Minutes of the Working Committee 1958 Geneva, Commission on Faith and Order*, p. 52.
[2] *Proposed Study on Religious Liberty*, Central Comm. no. 16, August, 1958, a multigraphed paper. The scope of the study outlined is unrestricted; and those engaged in it will be faced with a task as difficult as it may prove useful. The philosophico-religious presuppositions underlying problems of 'religious liberty' in lands predominantly Buddhist, Hindu, Confucianist, Mahometan, and in lands behind what is called 'the iron curtain', will face investigators with grave difficulties; and these difficulties will be increased by the divergent views held among our separated brethren about the relations between faith and reason, and between grace and nature. In concrete situations it may be that good sense and good feeling can find solutions which abstract theory may not be able to pin-point.

suming greater importance and seem to offer larger hopes of attaining closer unity among Christians than appears to be the case in lands where a particular form of Church discipline or practice has become, rightly or wrongly, associated in the popular mind with national tradition and even prestige: the State connection of some of the 'older Churches', however liberally this be interpreted, has a restricting influence from which 'Younger Churches' are free. This seems a consideration in the minds of those who wish the World Council of Churches to be 'integrated' with the International Missionary Council.

6. In the case of the central agencies of bodies like the World Council of Churches and the International Missionary Council, strength may lie in restricting pronouncements to very general principles, without clear application to any particular situation or doctrine. But in the case of particular 'Churches' or 'traditions' it may be wise to have, at the outset of any 'conversations', a clear assertion of stands which cannot even appear to be questioned. The balanced and qualified statements made by theologians in conversations or in formal reports may not readily be understood by journalists avid for 'news value' or even sensation, and misunderstanding in the popular mind may result, as was the case in Scotland with regard to the Report on Anglican-Presbyterian Relations.

Here lies a consideration which must affect bodies like the Orthodox and the Roman Catholics, and justify a stand which at first sight may seem unduly intransigent but which may in reality be the wisest and most charitable.

Chapter Five

THE ATTITUDE OF ECUMENISTS TOWARDS 'ROME'

1. The Vista of Ultimate Reunion with 'Rome'

In so far as it is possible to generalize, those associated with the World Council of Churches tend towards two attitudes with regard to the Catholic Church:

1. There are those like Dr Karl Barth who declare plainly that the only attitude of Protestants towards Catholics and the Orthodox must be one of 'evangelism', that is, they are determined that both the Orthodox and Rome must drop our present devotion to our Lady and that Rome must drop the Pope. Sometimes this attitude amounts to real hostility, and a student of American Protestantism, Father Damboriena, writing in *Unitas*, 1956, expressed regret that not a few who take part in the ecumenical movement seem to 'give much of their lives to the ministry of antagonism', and ends by citing Father La Farge's warning that Catholics from Europe are not 'always alive to the subtler aspects of the Church's situation in this country (the U.S.A.).'[1] Mr Gilbert F. Cunningham, in the *Scottish Journal of Theology*, 1949, writing on 'Ecumenical Hopes and Fears' remarks that 'we have among our own churches the further difficulty that many Protestants, laymen in particular, hold very inaccurate views on the nature of Roman Catholicism, varying from an undiscerning tolerance to an equally indiscriminate hatred. Age-long prejudices distort men's minds; and the excesses of the Protestant Action League or the Orange Lodges may here and there be acutely embarrassing.'[2]

---

[1] 'Trends of the Ecumenical Movement in American Protestantism', *Unitas*, viii, no. 2 and 3, Summer and Autumn, 1956. As regards England, sometimes Continental Catholics seem to forget the Evangelical Anglicans and the Free Churches, not to mention the Presbyterians.
[2] *Scottish Journal of Theology*, ii, no. 4, pp. 409–10.

It is unnecessary here to speak further of this attitude, beyond saying that it has at least one good effect, for it damps any delusive hopes and exposes the unreality of suggestions of compromise. Whether this good effect outweighs the hurt to Christian charity is a matter for each man's conscientious judgement.

'*The* $64,000 *Question*'

2. Others associated with the World Council of Churches look to eventual 'reunion' with 'Rome', although doubtless many if not all hope that 'Rome' may be reformed or at least may explain away some doctrines in a way that will draw out their venom.

It is significant that the then Moderator of the Church of Scotland, Dr George MacLeod, speaking on television, October 27, 1957, put the question of eventual unity with Rome as 'the 64,000 dollar question'; the proposal of bishops in the Church of Scotland had roused memories of the 'Covenanters' and the accusation that the famous *Report* was really a betrayal of pure Presbyterianism to the superstitions of Anglo-Catholicism, and, much worse, of 'Rome'.

'Are we talking of unity with the Church of Rome?' Dr MacLeod asked.

'Well, in the ultimate we are, because the Body of Christ was one and for 500 years, nay 1,000 years, it was possible to have one Church.'

He referred to the Roman Catholic Archbishop of Liverpool and quoted him as saying: 'We have got to love each other until we are convinced of the same truth.'

'What is being sought after', went on Dr MacLeod, 'is not a coagulation of Protestant bodies in order to have a fight. The whole Church is about love. The whole Church is to teach charity.

'We must all stand for our principles. The Roman Church must stand for its principles. We must stand for our principles and yet we have got to go on loving each other.'[1]

The attitude expressed by Dr MacLeod is shared, to a greater

---

[1] Quoted in the *Scottish Daily Express*, October 28, 1957, p. 1.

or lesser extent, by many ecumenists. The Lambeth Conference of 1920 made the following statement, renewed by the Conferences of 1930 and 1948: 'We cannot do better than make our own the words of the *Report* of 1908, which reminds us of the fact 'that there can be no fulfilment of the Divine purpose in any scheme of reunion which does not ultimately include the great Latin Church of the West, with whom our history has been so closely associated in the past, and to which we are still bound by very many ties of faith and tradition.'[1]

Some, doubtless, would regard that statement as little more than a pious hope; others, however, would take it seriously, because they see that the Church must be one and that the idea of two ecclesiastical blocks is radically contrary to the New Testament teaching, and to immemorial Christian belief. At present they find many doctrines held by the Catholic and the Orthodox Churches so alien and odd that they find it hard to understand how intelligent men can really believe such things; yet they hope either that 'Rome' may change or that the doctrines and the 'system' may possibly look different when conditions in the world change. What is perhaps of greater interest is that a certain appreciation of the Roman Catholic Church is beginning to be found, not merely among Anglicans or Episcopalians, but among those of a Presbyterian tradition.

The Reverend Professor J. M. L. Haire, of Belfast, speaking after the Conference of Amsterdam in 1948 remarked that for some members of the Conference the Roman criticism of the Ecumenical movement in 1928 had much that was true in it as well as false, since the Stockholm Conference appeared to be seeking Christian unity without any theological basis.[2]

Bishop Newbigin judges that 'there ought to be nothing to prevent our looking now towards the restoration to the whole Church of a visible unity with a central organ of unity such as Rome was for so many vital centuries of the Church's

[1] *Conference of Bishops of the Anglican Communion, holden at Lambeth Palace, July 5 to August 7, 1920*, London, 1920, p. 12 and 144; Lambeth Conference of 1930, p. 131, and of 1948, p. 66.

[2] 'Amsterdam—What Are Its Implications?', *Scottish Journal of Theology*, ii, no. 3, September, 1949, p. 229. Professor Haire referred particularly to Professor E. Schlink, who wrote to the same effect in the *Ecumenical Review*, i, no. 2, p. 154.

history.'[1] Bishop Newbigin, to be sure, thinks that a far-reaching transformation would be required both of the Protestant Churches and of the Roman and Eastern before union could even be discussed; but it is interesting to see that a firm grasp of the need of unity leads to thought about some central organ of authority. Mr Gilbert F. Cunningham even goes so far as to contemplate the idea of an infallible authority in a future 'United Church'. His words are extremely cautious, yet it is clear that again the concept of unity in the Church carries thought forward to ideas which used to be regarded as abhorrent:

> At this stage, of course, it is hardly possible to foresee what kind of a constitution the United Church would possess, but doubtless anything resembling the Roman system would be abhorrent to nearly all the Churches concerned. *Yet, without any authority recognized as infallible,* and without some kind of internal discipline with sanctions to enforce it, one feels that, far from the World Council of Churches ultimately ceasing to be, as Professor Haire puts it, in order that the Church may appear again as one, it is more likely that it would have to remain in continuous, and not always harmonious session. We can hardly suppose that history will not sooner or later repeat itself, or that the United Church will no longer be
>
> > By schisms rent asunder,
> > By heresies distressed.
>
> The rebel who is condemned today may well still be the saint of to-morrow. We are but men, albeit men who claim to have the guidance of the Holy Spirit; and which of us will presume to judge between those whose interpretation of that guidance leads them in opposite directions? We know whither acceptance of Augustine's *Securus judicat orbis terrarum* has led, and may lead again; *but what is the alternative? This is not a question that can be settled once and for all;* our course seems always to lie between Scylla and Charybdis.[2]

Doubtless very many non-Catholics, if not all, would say that any alternative is preferable to 'Roman' Catholic in-

---

[1] *The Reunion of the Churches*, p. 189.
[2] 'Ecumenical Hopes and Fears', *Scottish Journal of Theology*, ii, no. 4, December, 1949, p. 407. Italics mine.

fallibility;[1] at the same time, as the Church is more and more recognized as essentially one, and visibly one, a certain 'institutionalism' and permanent authority is perceived to be inherent to a continuous unity. As the unity is understood to be necessarily 'organic' and as continuous throughout history, it becomes less easy to apply the forms of 'democratic' institutions to the Church, with elections, Committees and Sub-Committees, and inevitable reversals of policy and polity. It is significant that one defence of episcopacy made in Scotland is that the Kirk at present is being controlled by 'assembly committees' and that 'parity of ministers' leaves the individual minister without the help of a known, firm and permanent 'oversight' in the person of a bishop.

2. ECUMENICAL ACCOUNTS OF ROMAN CATHOLICISM

Very generally ecumenical discussions say very little about the Roman Catholic Church, except as a negative norm of what the Churches do not now want; this does not necessarily indicate complete opposition, but may indicate merely that discussion about 'Rome' is at present not worth while. Yet Catholic writings about the World Council receive considerable attention and it is a pleasure to record three accounts of the Church which are inspired by the sincere desire to explain to others what the Roman Catholic Church really is. In the volume *The Nature of the Church* appears an essay entitled 'The Church of Rome'; in the *History of the Ecumenical Movement*, 1954, appears an account entitled 'The Roman Catholic Church and the Ecumenical Movement'; and in the *Ecumenical Review* for July, 1955, is an article entitled 'Protestant-Roman Catholic Encounter an Ecumenical Obligation'. The first is by Dr R. Newton Flew, for long Head of

[1] Some non-Catholics have an imperfect conception of what infallibility means. It is not an infallibility 'over against' Scripture, but includes the Word of God in Scripture; nor is it an infallibility of the Pope as distinct from the whole Church. The doctrine takes seriously that the Church is the Body of Christ and therefore cannot lead men into error or fail to give due guidance; the bishops and the chief bishop speak for the Body, not as delegates for the Body, but as able to make articulate the common feeling and conviction which is inherent in the whole Body. Another misunderstanding arises over the canonical expression 'a perfect society', which some take as referring to moral or spiritual perfection, whereas it is really a legal term meaning that the Church is independent of the State.

6

Wesley House, Cambridge, the second is by Dr Oliver Tomkins, now Bishop of Bristol; and the third is by Professor Ernst Kinder, of the University of Münster, Germany, editor of *Evangelische Lutherische Kirchenzeitung*, a Lutheran Church periodical. These accounts of the Roman Catholic Church are written with scrupulous accuracy, with a spirit of kindliness and a desire to explain things as they are.

Dr Flew begins his essay like this:

> Those in other communions who have had the privilege of personal contact and unofficial discussions with scholars of the Church of Rome are eager that others should share in the charity, the sympathetic crossing of barriers, the sense of oneness in Christ, which usually characterize such encounters. The problems are not solved, but their harshness is mitigated. The following outline is for ministers and laymen in the communions represented by the World Council of Churches, in the hope that on certain outstanding problems they may be enabled to appraise more exactly the official doctrine of the Roman Church. It has been written, if I may borrow the famous distinction of St. Augustine, *non ut diceretur sed ne taceretur*—lest silence should be interpreted as forgetfulness or culpable neglect of the great place which the Church of Rome must occupy in the thoughts of all who are sorrowfully aware of the tragedy of disunion.
>
> A convinced Protestant must first present an apology for his temerity. The task is none of his seeking. He cannot produce any credentials. He has none, unless it be gratitude. He writes in gratitude for the inspiration and friendship of Friedrich von Hügel; in gratitude also for the kindness shewn to him many years ago by the teachers of the University of Fribourg, and especially by that great scholar, Pierre Mandonnet.[1]

But indeed Dr Flew has no need to apologise for temerity in undertaking a task which he did not seek. Competence, exactness and objectivity mark every line of his essay which is a triumph of impartial scholarship. The same is true of Dr Tomkins, though perhaps his sympathy goes out too manifestly towards those Roman Catholics who want to co-operate more closely with the ecumenists. Nevertheless Dr Tomkins's

---

[1] *The Nature of the Church, Papers presented to the Theological Commission appointed by the Continuation Committee of the World Conference on Faith and Order*, edited by R. Newton Flew, London, 1952, p. 17.

account is admirably complete and admirably balanced. He ends with the following significant words: 'What no historian can estimate is that which principally matters: how far, on both sides of this deep division between Christians, this is a story of the growth of that charity, without which all that has been recorded profiteth nothing.'[1]

Professor Kinder's article was a reaction against the growing rigidity, perhaps even hostility to Rome, manifested at the National Synod of the French Reformed Church of France at Strasbourg in June, 1955; among other things he says this:

> Any ecumenical thought and action, which definitely excluded the Roman Catholic Church because of the difficulties involved, would no longer be truly ecumenical; it would be pan-Protestant and anti-Roman, which is entirely different! If our thought and action are to remain truly ecumenical, we must bear the Roman Catholic Church constantly in mind, in spite of the fact that the attitude of that Church (though not always) and many (though not all) of its features and expressions are so difficult to understand and to accept, and sometimes make us feel completely hopeless. It is definitely not the mission of the World Council to become the official censor of the churches and of Christianity (by what standards could it do so?).[2]

An 'Inside' and an 'Outside' View

What follows is not meant to be a criticism of the genuine kindliness and careful scholarship of the three accounts just mentioned; it is only meant to illustrate what several ecumenists have emphasized, namely, the extreme difficulty of taking an 'inside' point of view when one is in fact on the outside. It may be said, too, that Catholics rarely write with knowledge of the intimacies of non-Catholic Churches, except perhaps in England of Anglicanism and in Germany of Lutheranism, and except for some American Catholics like Fr G. Weigel, who know the American religious field as well as it seems possible to know a field in which grow such a multitude and variety of crops. Fr Maximin Piette, the Franciscan, with his *John Wesley and the Evolution of Protestantism*, is almost

[1] *Op. cit.* p. 693.
[2] *Ecumenical Review*, vii, no. 4, July, 1955, p. 339.

an exception. Not infrequently Catholics tend to rely upon official statements because they wish to be accurate, and this inevitably gives 'an outside' as opposed to 'an inside' view.

To say, then, that the same is true of many accounts of the Roman Catholic Church given by non-Catholics is not meant to initiate controversy but only to try to increase understanding.

Marriage and Education

The day-to-day anxieties and interests of the ordinary Catholic bishop and priest tend to centre very much upon the question of marriage and education. They are both very thorny questions, on which the chasm between Catholics and non-Catholics has widened in post-Reformation times; and they are both questions which involve a whole fundamental outlook towards the very springs of life and the nature of human beings.[1] Yet in ecumenical writings about the Roman Catholic Church I do not remember to have seen any attempt to weigh or even to record the Catholic view on these matters. This may be due to a feeling that the questions are too prickly to be discussed without rousing high feelings; at the same time, it is a little surprising, because the ecumenical movement is connected so closely with the missions, and in the missions the Roman and the non-Roman views on marriage and education approach one another more closely than they do in Europe or America. It is not unknown for non-Catholics to say things about education and marriage which directly contradict the actual practice of missions which they support. Here, again, the duty of the Church to evangelize is the key to understanding, and it is in the light of this duty that questions of marriage and education must be faced.[2] That, however, is merely in passing; the main point is that the actual life of the Catholic Church is much concerned with marriage and education. No thoughtful

[1] I do not mean to suggest that the Catholic Church alone defends the holiness of marriage, since other Churches undoubtedly also do so; but the Catholic understands the holiness of marriage as excluding certain practices which very generally other Christians judge permissible.

[2] On the World Council and education Fr Duff has some pregnant remarks in *The Social Thought of the World Council of Churches*, pp. 102–4. At Evanston the question of education was discussed somewhat briefly; the American situation seemed much in the foregound and the 'Section' ended by referring the matter

Catholic is unaware that the stand of the Church upon divorce and upon purity in marriage is unpopular in the world; yet the Church remains firm. In ecumenical writings not very much is said about this aspect of the Catholic Church.[1]

The actual life of Catholics in many countries is much occupied with the practical question of education; and their struggle to maintain their schools absorbs so much of their attention—and rightly so—that other things sometimes tend to be judged in the light of it. How can one know the Roman Catholic Church without knowing the comparatively vast sums of money which the Catholic body, not conspicuously wealthy, pours out for the religious education of its children, and for the formation of its future priests? How appreciate the spirit of a religion without asking why the Catholic laity give so generously? Why do they pay for their schools, when there are schools which are free?[2]

3. THE DEFINITION OF THE ASSUMPTION

In his account of the attitude of Rome toward ecumenism Dr Tomkins refers to the definition of the Assumption of Our Lady, and says: 'The promulgation in November 1950 of the dogma of the Assumption of the Blessed Virgin served to

to the Central Committee, cf. *Report*, pp. 107–12. The matter is probably being studied at present. It may be added that the ecumenical outlook is bound to have an effect on the *Agreed Syllabuses* used in those English and Scottish schools which are entirely under government management. Dr D. Jenkins rejects the idea of 'a comprehensive education which is religiously neutral' and appears to favour schools 'which remain Christian while being freed from clerical control', *Congregationalism*, p. 127.

[1] Objections raised about 'nullities' are often very wide of the mark, as the most superficial acquaintance with the practice of episcopal Curias will quickly demonstrate. On the awkwardness of differing views about marriage held by the Churches cf. A. W. Phillips, *Survey of African Marriage and Family Life*, London, 1953, and the review of it in the *International Review of the Missions*, January, 1954, especially p. 11. An objective survey of Roman Catholic canon law on marriage would be a useful contribution to ecumenical literature.

[2] The Catholic stand on the matter of education is not confined to any country. Dr Bakaric, President of the Sobor (Council) of Croatia, in an interview given to a London *Times* correspondent in April, 1957, among other things said this: 'He found it natural and not disturbing that Catholic parents in this almost wholly Catholic republic should want their children brought up as Catholics, and he thought that more than 50 per cent of Croatian children were now receiving religious education through the Church. This high figure, which is believed to be increasing, contrasts with the corresponding position in Orthodox Serbia.' I cite this merely to illustrate the general Catholic point of view, and I know little about conditions in Croatia. *Times*, April 18, 1957.

underline the Roman claim to total obedience in matters of faith. Many commentators upon it in other communions deplored the way in which this decree erected one more barrier between Roman Catholic and other Christians.'[1]

I confess that this comment, because it seems so obvious to Dr Tomkins, depresses me greatly. Are we to think that a Catholic before the definition could have rejected the doctrine of the Assumption? The definition did not change the actual faith of Catholics, and the Church's faith was no different after than it was before. The definition may be compared to the definition by Nicaea in 325 that Christ is 'consubstantial with the Father', or to the assertion by Ephesus in 431 that our Lady is really Mother of God (*theotokos*). These Councils only made plain and manifest to all what the faith really was; they did not add anything to the faith but only gave clear guidance to any who were confused and cut off any who refused to admit the faith. The definition of the Assumption was a little different, because very few Roman Catholics, if any, doubted the doctrine; indeed they may be said to have expressed their faith in it whenever they said the Rosary, and petitions for the definition poured in from the whole Catholic world. Catholics thought that a definition would do more to honour the Mother of God and to make clear in Mariology another firm foundation on which to build.

The relevant theological issue was that of the development of doctrine and of 'tradition'; but in the background were the theological implications of the Motherhood of God, of her perfect virginity, of her holiness, of the resurrection of the body and, indeed, of the Church's whole attitude to sex, marriage and the human body. Increase in Catholic devotion to the Mother of God is, partly at least, an instinctive reaction against increased laxity in matters touching marriage and chastity. In some respects Catholic discussions about Mariology and non-Catholic discussions about eschatology deal with the same fundamental themes, although from a different aspect and in a different terminology. Basically, both discussions turn upon the worth of the body, the visible dispensation of the Incar-

---

[1] *Art. cit.* p. 690. The 'other commentators' mentioned as examples are Professor Alivisatos, an Orthodox, and a group of German Protestant theologians.

nation (the 'fulness of time' having come and being signalized by the breach in the merely natural continuity of human history made by the Virgin Birth) and upon the nature of Christian faith in the resurrection. This faith implies that Christians are not bound down and confined in the time-order in which alone our present bodies exist, but through faith already live a new life with the risen Christ; the Assumption is a token and a symbol of Christian superiority to death, just as the Mother of God is a symbol of the Church of God. The non-Catholic interest in eschatology approaches these themes more theoretically, the Catholic more concretely.[1]

It is fully understandable that non-Catholics do not agree with Catholic judgement about tradition and development of doctrine. It is understandable that they dislike more honours being paid to Mary,—although, if they hold that she is really the Mother of God, there seems little reason to boggle at lesser honours. But it is at least inadequate to say that the definition of the Assumption 'served to underline the claim of total obedience', and 'erected one more barrier'. That is purely an 'outside' view. It is as much an 'outside' view as if a Catholic were to suggest that Evanston applied the expression '*simul justus et peccator*' to the Church merely out of a desire to pay a compliment to Lutherans.

There were some Catholics who thought that a definition of the Assumption would be inexpedient, just as there were some Catholics who thought that the definition of papal infallibility in 1870 would be inexpedient; but in both cases Catholics understood that it was not any question of introducing 'new' doctrine but only of making clear what was in fact the existing doctrine. The Pope was no more infallible after 1870 than he was before. Our Lady was not any more taken up into heaven after 1950 than she was before. No Catholic imagined such a thing. Definitions do not make a thing part of revelation when it was not such before; they only

[1] For the literature cf. Dr Michael Schmaus, in the fifth volume of his *Katholische Dogmatik*, 'Mariologie', who gives a bibliography of 14 pages, pp. 385–99, which is by no means complete. In English two books worth consulting are G. D. Smith, *Mary's Part in our Redemption*, London, 1938, and George Dwyer and Thomas Holland, *Mary. Doctrine for Everyman*, London, 1956. For the Catholic feeling towards the Mother of God, cf. Frank Sheed's admirable selection from Catholic writers in *The Mary Book*, London, 1936.

make clear what was in fact, though possibly the fact was not realized by everyone, always contained in the revelation, in God's word to men. Suppose, however, that a non-Catholic tries to take an 'inside' view and says: 'I do not like the Roman Catholic Church; but I shall try honestly to answer this question: "Did the definition of the infallibility of the Pope weaken or strengthen that organization (which I repeat I do not like)?"'—what answer would he give? Would the Roman Church have been stronger had the question of infallibility been left undefined? I doubt if any one 'taking an inside view' would say that. Rather he would say that the definition gave clearness to what was already there, helped cohesion and concerted unreflective action and so strengthened the Church, just as the World Council's own effort has steadily been to clarify its own position and to define its relations to its constituent elements, and that body is the stronger thereby.

Neither the definition of Papal infallibility nor that of the Assumption created any 'new barriers'; they both, however, revealed clearly and unmistakably the 'barriers', if they are barriers, which were already there. They made it easier to know what the Roman Catholic Church really is. Greater and clearer knowledge may make people like it more or dislike it more; but at least their like or dislike is founded upon a more exact knowledge of the facts.[1]

4. 'Rome' as a System and as a Family

'Rome' is often regarded as a 'system', a body of doctrine, a kind of principle of authority (or tyranny),—in short as an abstraction. But in fact the 'Roman' Catholic Church is made up of living *people*. There are some 500 millions of them, of

---

[1] It is, of course, possible to object against any use of defining power that if everyone holds the doctrine, a definition is needless; if not everyone holds it the definition does not declare the faith of the whole Church. But the disjunction is incomplete. A definition may declare the ancient faith at a time when many are distorting the ancient faith, or it may merely affirm what the vast majority in fact hold, and affirm it in order to mark a stage in doctrinal development and to give a more clearly fixed point of departure for further development. But a definition, also, may be merely a glad occasion on which to rejoice in a beloved article of the faith. However, it is not easy to generalize and about the Assumption my point is exclusively that it was not a mere means of stressing a 'claim to total obedience in matters of faith'.

practically all nationalities, languages and races, and of ten different 'Rites', that is liturgical customs and canonical rule. They are a mixture of the most self-sacrificing and fervent people, of very 'middle-of-the-road' people, and of people who are Catholics in name only, and do not lead edifying lives. There are saints and there are sinners in the Church.

What keeps them all united as 'Catholics'? Catholics believe that it is no natural means, but the spiritual, the 'mystic' sacramental life which is signified and is caused by the Eucharist, in which Christ is really present. In this sense, the bond of union is invisible; but that bond has an outward visible expression in the chief Shepherd of the flock, the Bishop of Rome, who is equal to the other bishops in power of order but is the successor of him who, as St Ambrose says, Christ *was leaving behind for us as the vicar of His love*.[1] As the Eucharist is a sacrament of love, so, too, the Church is a sacrament of love, that is, an outward visible thing which at once tells us of the love of Christ and causes that love and unity to exist and persist. The primacy of the Bishop of Rome is, indeed, a primacy of 'jurisdiction', but the jurisdiction itself presupposes a free and loving acceptance, the self-committal of faith to Christ, and to Christ as he lives in his Body the Church.

Roman Catholics feel themselves a family, whether they live in the Pacific islands, or in Paraguay or in California or in Scotland; and they feel themselves one with the saints in heaven and with all those who, since the foundation of the world, have been taken to live with Christ. Now when one thinks of a family, one does not think of board-meetings or of committee-rooms; one thinks of people by name. When the Pope thinks of the Church, I suspect that he is apt to think of his saintly predecessors in his office, such as St Pius X, and to think of the individual bishops and faithful in definite localities. The Pope is, and is understood to be, the father of a family.

The Pope's power, though supreme, is exercised in accord with law and with immemorial custom and in union with the bishops. These in turn are obliged to 'take heed to the whole flock in which the Holy Spirit has placed you as bishops, to

[1] *Exposit. in Evang. sec. Lucam*, i, X, no. 175, Migne, *Patrologia Latina*, xv, 1942.

rule the Church of God, which he purchased with his own blood.' (Acts 20, 28.) The Pope is in constant consultation with the bishops, and although there is the considerable amount of form-filling inevitable in modern life, the relationship between the Pope and the bishops is not simply bureaucratic but retains a very considerable amount of personal contact. The bishops, in turn, rule by law and custom and not arbitrarily; and as a parish priest is at once supported and guided by his bishop, so, too, the bishops are supported and guided by the Pope. It is a complicated system, more flexible than is realized, with constant consultation; and decision of a definitive kind by the supreme authority is generally given only where there is difference of view and possible strife and disorder.

There is less centralization than is sometimes imagined; in aid to the missions, for instance, complaints have been heard that there is not enough centralization. A comparison would be interesting between the methods of the Catholic Church and those of the *International Missionary Council.*[1]

Conditions, of course, differ in different parts of the world; what is true of Germany need not be true of Ireland; what is appropriate in India may not be appropriate in France. Problems of 'unity' and 'uniformity', which so much exercise the minds of ecumenists, have been worked out by centuries of experience; and, though no Catholic would for a moment claim that the solution at any given moment is absolutely perfect, still the problems cause only minor and passing perturbations, as, for instance, the matter of the 'priest workers' in France. On the whole clergy and people live in mutual affection and respect all the world over, though, of course, there may be deficiencies more or less serious. The clergy come from the people and one great advantage of celibacy, which admittedly has its difficulties, is that the faithful feel that their priest is their own, devoted wholly to them.

The family spirit is very strong and becomes stronger when those outside the family make criticisms.

[1] Plans are maturing for the integration of the *International Missionary Council* with the *World Council of Churches*, cf. *The Ecumenical Review*, x, no. 1, October, 1957, pp. 72–81; and see further pp. 187–207.

A Very Delicate Matter

It is, of course, inevitable that non-Catholics should take a very different view of the Roman Catholic Church than do Catholics; as a particular instance, non-Catholics often feel that any definition of faith, or guidance given by the Pope, is a restriction on the intellect. Catholics feel that it is a liberation. When journeying through a foreign country, an accurate map is not a restriction on one's movements but a help; it saves one going down wrong roads or down roads which lead to a dead end. The Church is concerned with guiding men and women for whom Christ died, and so she feels that on the map which is to guide them the right road must be clearly marked. The comparison limps, as do all comparisons, for there is need of the pioneer and the explorer in theology as in every other science; yet even the boldest of explorers and pioneers generally needs to know what country is really unexplored, and in his exploration he needs at the very least a compass. The Church tells her theological explorers what country is only a barren desert or a series of swamps, and it provides a compass in unexplored country.

Catholics are truly convinced that Christ lives in the Church and that his Holy Spirit guides the Church, for the salvation and spiritual welfare of souls. This guidance, of course, takes different forms and it is the theologian's task to estimate exactly what degree of authority attaches to directions which are given; but they welcome the guidance and believe that our Lord is to be found in it. It is for this reason that they are grieved, and sometimes angry, when others write in a tone of disapproval about decisions from Catholic authorities or in a tone of approval of any Catholic who is imagined to be a little out of step with Catholic authorities. I deliberately refrain from giving any instances, not from lack of evidence but from fear of wounding charity. To a Catholic a tone hostile to his authorities is a cause only of increased loyalty. From an ecumenical point of view, which supposes that ultimately each 'Church' will bring its own contribution to a fully integrated Christendom, the contribution of the Roman Catholic Church would surely be its sense of authority and of obedience;

so to try from without to 'reform' the Church of Rome in this respect would be to try to destroy the very best thing which that Church could—on the hypothesis—contribute. Differences of fundamental convictions there certainly are and it is idle to try to disguise them. The refusal of the Catholic Church to join the 'ecumenical encounter' in any official way is sometimes taken—mistakenly, as I hope to show in the next chapter—as an implied reproach or evidence of hostility, and possibly in consequence of this there is a tendency to regard authoritative directions to Catholics about the matter as necessarily obscurantist or repressive. In the present circumstances, occasional manifestations of irritation or impatience, on one side or the other, are understandable enough; but surely those who love Christ and seek the unity which he wills can forgive everything, forget much and try harder to understand.

5. CATHOLIC ASSESSMENTS TOO NARROWLY THEOLOGICAL?

Regarding Catholic writings about the ecumenical movement Dr Visser 't Hooft makes an important observation:

It is interesting to note that the Roman Catholic writers, practically without exception, concentrate all their attention on issues of Faith and Order. For them the only ecumenical issue is the issue of the full unity of the Church in doctrine, in sacraments, in ministry. This is not astonishing from their point of view and is in many ways a healthy challenge to the churches of the World Council of Churches, which need to be reminded that the issues of Faith and Order are indeed the decisive issues. But it has the great disadvantage that the Roman Catholic ecumenists do not see the ecumenical movement as a whole and do not appreciate sufficiently that in the World Council matters of Faith and Order are discussed in the framework of a wider ecumenical process. To understand the significance of the World Council one must not only ask what specific progress is made to arrive at greater doctrinal agreement, one must at the same time watch to what extent the participating Churches are in fact engaged in a process of spiritual cross-fertilization, to what extent their life is renewed through more intimate contact with other churches, to what extent they learn to render a common witness to the world. It might be that we are in a period of ecumenical history in which the churches have to learn to live together and to grow together before they can take far-reaching steps in the realm of actual reunion.[1]

Dr Visser 't Hooft undoubtedly makes a useful remark here. In the existing situation among our separated brethren the doctrinal issues are very closely associated with, if not overlaid by, a whole host of things only incidentally connected with doctrine: historical and national traditions, customary ways, the power of an institution, social attitudes and status, manners in church and around the church, the choice of hymns, the preacher's selection of topics and even his intonation and mannerisms, the method of appointment of ministers and their promotion and pensions, the collection and administration of church funds, the influence of boards of trustees and of lay committees—a whole host of matters which are intangible but really constitute a dividing force which may have to be lived down and cannot be reasoned down.[2] Religion is largely a life and to modify a religion is to modify life, and life usually changes slowly. Moreover the World Council of Churches is engaged upon very considerable charitable works, and is closely associated with the International Missionary Council.

And yet Dr Visser 't Hooft might perhaps appreciate more fully the difficulties facing a Roman Catholic writer on ecumenism. Certain matters it would be impertinent to attempt to assess: has the ecumenical movement helped to greater seriousness of religious purposes, to greater purity of intention, to more humble service of Christ our Saviour, to more earnest prayer? Only God can judge such things. But even in matters which fall under the legitimate estimation of students of the religious scene, an appraisal is exceedingly difficult, for judgement must be comparative and the comparison between the

[1] 'Notes on Roman Catholic Writings concerning Ecumenism', *Ecumenical Review*, viii, no. 2, January, 1956, p. 192.
[2] Cf. Walter G. Muelder, 'Institutional Factors Affecting Unity and Disunity', *Ecumenical Review* viii, no. 2, pp. 113–26. And cf. books like H. F. L. Crocks, *The Nonconformist Conscience*, London, 1944; J. Marlowe, *The Puritan Tradition in English Life*, London 1956; D. Jenkins, *Congregationalism: A Restatement*, London, 1954.

past and the present requires a wide knowledge which is not easy to obtain. This is one reason, I think, why Catholics look at the sweep of ideas and concentrate upon formulated doctrine; for the movement of life and the 'cross-fertilization' will show itself sooner or later in ideas and doctrine. It is clear that the ecumenical movement has brought new outlooks and a wider charity and that the World Council of Churches, in seeking to overcome divisions among Christians, is unquestionably trying to fulfil the purpose of Christ; but to make determinant estimates of its progress or regress over, say, five year periods, is most extremely difficult.

Dr Visser 't Hooft's observation is only another illustration of difficulty in assigning priority to action or priority to conviction; and it is generous of him to say that he thinks that Roman Catholic comments constitute a healthy challenge. It may be remembered that at the time of the Malines conversations it was Archbishop Davidson, the Anglican, who insisted upon putting the dogmatic issues in the first place;[1] and general opinion has, I venture to think, supported him in this.

Dr Jenkins has a remark about a typical Catholic theologian which I read with a certain rueful amusement: 'He gives the impression, especially if he is a cleric trained in one of the great religious orders, of being a cold and bloodless thinking machine moving remorselessly from one position to another with faultless logic, without ever making the effort to stand outside his own system and ask himself whether his first principles are valid. He is convinced, in Hodges' words, that thought is the master of life and not life of thought.'[2]

Even, however, at the risk of seeming to place thought above life, I venture to ask whether there is not a tendency among ecumenists, or at least among those interested, to make theology to fit the situation, and not to try to make the situation fit the theology? If this is so, then is not such a tendency dangerous in the long run for the cause of ultimate unity? Action such as that in South India, and as the proposed action

[1] Cf. G. K. A. Bell, *Christian Unity; the Anglican Position*, London, 1948, pp. 72–77.
[2] *Tradition and the Spirit*, London, 1951, p. 117. The reference to H. A. Hodges, 'The Crisis in Philosophy' in *Reformation Old and New*. London, 1947, p. 185.

in Ceylon and India, may find a temporary justification in present doctrinal uncertainties and divergences and in the founded hope that time and experience may resolve them; but in the long run life must be conformed to truth, and charity and truth cannot be divided, any more than Christ himself can be divided.

It cannot be too often or too strongly asserted that conformity to truth does not mean constraint but liberation and that unity in faith does not mean a dead uniformity. Too often it is imagined that the unity of the Church involves what Dr Visser 't Hooft has called 'a centralized, authoritarian, monopolistic and politically minded ecclesiastical system'.[1] This, no doubt, describes what many imagine the 'Roman system' to be and what they fear the World Council of Churches might become. Their imagination and their fears are vain.

Truth and freedom are inseparable. Christ said: 'You shall know the truth and the truth will make you free.'[2] Unity with Christ means unity at once with his truth and with his freedom. The norm of Christian liberty must derive from Christ's liberty, just as the norm of Christian holiness derives from Christ's holiness. Men fear, indeed, that they may lose liberty were there only one Church. They forget that they have already largely lost liberty through the barriers of denominationalism and divisions, for each division means a barrier which others are not free to cross. How much time, thought and effort is consumed merely in the effort to overcome divisions. And it is partly through Christian divisions that many non-Christians are cut off from Christian freedom, precisely because divisions hinder perception of the truth of Christ, and hinder more effective efforts to make that truth known in the world.

[1] 'The Super-Church and the Ecumenical Movement,' *Ecumenical Review*, x, 4, July, 1958, p. 383.
[2] John 8: 32.

Chapter Six

THE CATHOLIC ATTITUDE TOWARDS ECUMENISM

1. The General Background

Pope Pius XI was invited to the Lausanne Conference of 1927 and courteously declined. Since then the leaders of the ecumenical movement have issued no formal invitation to the Roman Catholic Church, yet have given signs that they do not wish to shut the door in Rome's face but realize that Rome does not consider participation in the meetings to be wise. If Rome gave signs of a desire for formal participation, there might be some in the World Council who would be opposed, but one can conjecture from the Toronto statement of 1950 that an invitation would be extended. Many, if not all, in the movement are very deeply convinced that there ought to be a real unity of *all* Christians; many, if not all, would, like Dr MacLeod, oppose anything in the nature of 'a coagulation of Protestants to have a fight'; and some, if not many, feel that perhaps there is something to learn from Rome and that a counterpoise may be acceptable against a tendency to attempt union without a firm doctrinal basis.

At Edinburgh in 1937 and at Lund in 1952 Catholic 'observers' were present, and could not speak too highly of the courtesy extended to them. At the conference of the Faith and Order Commission at Oberlin, Ohio, Sept. 3–10, 1957, among the observers were two Roman Catholic theologians who were present in an unofficial capacity. They were the Rev. Gustave Weigel, S.J. of Woodstock, Maryland, and the Rev. John Sheerin, editor of the *Catholic World*. Catholic co-operation in theological work is welcomed, and the Section on Mariology in the Lund Theological Commission's book *Ways of Worship* was a clear indication of a desire to understand, as well as a kind of compliment to the Orthodox, and indirectly to Roman Catholics, which roused the wrath of some thorough-going Protestants and caused accusations of 'Romanizing'. The leaders have been most correct in their official attitude towards the Roman Catholic Church and it is right that this should be cordially acknowledged.[1]

The authorities of the Catholic Church have declined to take any official part in the various Conferences; but in directions given to members of their own communion there has been a different emphasis as the ecumenical movement itself has changed and developed. Pius XI in his Encyclical on *Fostering True Religious Union* (*Mortalium Animos*) spoke firmly against ecumenism of a liberal type, which had lost grip on the necessary dogmatic foundations of Christian unity.[2] In 1949 the Holy Office said: 'The Catholic Church, although she does not participate in "oecumenical" conferences or meetings, nevertheless has never ceased, as may be seen from many papal documents, nor ever will cease from following with deepest interest and furthering with fervent prayers every effort to attain the end which Christ our Lord had so much at heart, namely, that all who believe in Him "May be made perfect in one."'[3] The reasons for this abstention are not strictly and directly dogmatic, as if there were something in the faith which forbade discussion with dissident bodies about restoration of communion. Reunion with the Greeks was discussed at the Council of Lyons in 1245, and at the Council of Florence which was in session from 1438 until 1445; and there have been talks with other dissident bodies, such as the Jacobites of India. Although, however, there is no article of

---

[1] Cf. Tomkins, 'The Roman Catholic Church and the Ecumenical Movement', *History of the Ecumenical Movement*, pp. 685–9; J. M. L. Haire, 'Amsterdam—What Are the Implications?', *Scottish Journal of Theology*, ii, no. 3, p. 229.

[2] It is interesting to compare the account of this Encyclical given by Dr Tomkins in the essay cited in the last note, pp. 682 ff., with that given by Père Congar, in *Divided Christendom*, pp. 131–3. It may be added that Archbishop Davidson, as regards the Malines Conversations, showed practically the same attitude as Pius XI showed towards the general ecumenism of the period.

[3] The Latin reads: Ecclesia Catholica, etsi congressui ceterisque conventibus 'oecumenicis' non intervenit, numquam tamen destitit, ut ex pluribus documentis Pontificiis colligitur, neque unquam desistet intensissimis studiis prosequi assiduisque precibus fovere omnes conatus ad illud obtinendum, quod tantopere Christo Domino cordi est, videlicet ut omnes qui credunt in Ipsum, sint consummati in unum'. Ioan. xvii, 28.

faith which forbids conferences or meetings with non-Roman
Christians, there are, nevertheless, dogmatic principles involved which the Church must preserve clearly and unmistakably. Since the publication of the *Instruction* of the Holy Office
in March, 1950[1], the World Council has made one of its most
important declarations, that at Toronto in 1950, and has
published the *Report* of a Theological Commission on Faith
and Order in the form of a small volume entitled *The Church*.[2]
Both these documents affirm that membership in the World
Council in no way involves the acceptance of any doctrine
about the nature of the Church and that member Churches
need not consider one another as 'Churches' in the full and
proper sense.[3] Consideration, then, of the attitude of the
Catholic Church to the World Council must now take account
of these declarations. Before, however, attempting such consideration, a few words are necessary about the difficulty of
giving an explanation of the attitude of the Catholic Church.

2. DIFFICULTIES IN EXPLAINING

The first difficulty is that both the Roman Catholic Church
and the World Council of Churches are large and international bodies, and adequate judgement about their attitudes
can scarcely be formed exclusively on a basis of the official
pronouncements made by either. The Catholic Church, for
instance, has declined any official participation in the World
Council and its proceedings; but has taken formal cognizance
of the movement, has issued instructions to Catholics about the
right principles to follow, and has given marked signs of approval to the Roman Unitas Association, which tries to combine fraternal affection with evangelical candour. Individual
Catholics, while accepting most loyally the instructions from
Rome, lay different emphasis upon different aspects of the

[1] Fr Maurice Bévenot noticed that the *Instruction*, although dated 20 December
1949, was not published until March, 1950, cf. 'The Recent Instruction on the
Ecumenical Movement', *Eastern Churches Quarterly*, viii, no. 6, Summer, 1950,
p. 357.
[2] London, 1951. The Chairman of the Commission was Dr Newton Flew and
the Secretary was The Rev. Canon Kenneth Riches.
[3] The Toronto Statement will be found, at least in its main affirmations and
explanations, together with comments of my own, in Appendix IV of this book.

matter, and show a feeling varying from the distinctly warm to the distinctly cold.[1]

As regards the World Council of Churches, and the ecumenical movement in general, the matter is more complex for several reasons. The movement has not yet reached its full development. The World Council of Churches has not yet finally settled all the involved questions which arise concerning the relations of member Churches to the various divisions and commissions of the World Council. The integration now in process of the International Missionary Council into the structure of the World Council is bound to have reciprocal influence upon both.[2] Then, as has so often been said by ecumenists, there is a whole complex of matters which are imponderable; the experience of worship together, which touches minds and hearts, personal contacts and friendships, the sense of a common task, the awareness that the World Council of Churches is an agency not only for doctrinal confrontation but also for works of charity both spiritual and corporal—in short, that 'cross-fertilization' of which Dr Visser 't Hooft spoke, which can only reveal its effects gradually and after some years have passed. To estimate the weight of all these elements, many of them intangible, is extremely difficult, making exact judgement impossible and any general judgement hazardous. This seems to me one of the most fundamental considerations in appraising the attitude of Rome towards the movement.

A General Commendation of 'Rome'?

There is a second general difficulty which faces a Catholic when he tries to explain the attitude of his Church towards ecumenism: his explanation may appear like an attempt, under guise of explaining one point, to commend the whole Roman Catholic position. This book is not meant to be an

---

[1] This book deliberately abstains from giving an account of Catholic writings on the subject, not from lack of respect for others' judgement, but from lack of time and space to do justice to the varying emphases, which sometimes reflect the different religious and doctrinal climates of different countries. But I would like to express my gratitude for the light and help received from the authors of the books and articles mentioned in the Bibliography.

[2] Cf. below, pp. 187–207.

apologia for Rome's attitude; it is meant to explain the principles by which Rome's attitude is guided. At the same time, there are three reasons which make such an explanation difficult, (*a*) the close interconnection of Catholic doctrine; (*b*) the nature of the act of faith as conceived by a Catholic, which accepts doctrine because taught by the Church; and (*c*) the *emotional* connection between doctrines, which affects, though in differing ways, both Catholics and non-Catholic alike.[1]

(*a*) The close interconnection of all doctrines is not something peculiar to Catholicism, for ecumenists are well aware that all Christian doctrines are interconnected. The *Report* of the Theological Commission on *The Church* observes that 'some points of difference, small in themselves, may actually be matters of major importance, because divergent positions represent diverse *total systems*. Conceptions of the Church differ not only at specific points, but give rise to rival *systems* of Christian faith and practice.'[2]

Minor points do indeed involve a whole system. Differences about the ministry may involve differences about the inspiration of Scripture and about the nature of Christian faith itself. Differences about intercommunion involve the question of apostolic succession, the nature of the Eucharist and even the nature of the hypostatic union. While this is true of Christianity in general, it is perhaps more particularly true of Catholicism. In a famous passage in his *Development of Christian Doctrine*, Newman, after giving illustrations to show how many Catholic doctrines 'are members of one family, and suggestive, or correlative, or confirmatory, or illustrative of each other', ends by remarking: 'You must accept the whole or reject the whole; attenuation does but enfeeble, and amputation mutilate. It is trifling to receive all but something which is as integral as any other portion; and, on the other hand, it is a solemn thing to

[1] Here, as so often, words are a trouble; I use the word 'non-Catholic' as meaning those who do not accept the Pope's primacy of jurisdiction, although the Orthodox, many Anglo-Catholics and others would dislike being classed as 'non-Catholics'. In many respects it is quite wrong to use the expression 'non-Catholic' of them, especially since they accept, to a large extent, the principles on which the Roman Catholic attitude towards ecumenism is based. They will please understand, then, that the term 'non-Catholic' is used in a relative sense, meaning 'those who do not accept the primacy of the Holy Father and who diverge, in wider or narrower degree, from the Roman Catholic position'.

[2] *Op. cit.* pp. 22–3. Italics in original.

accept any part, for, before you know where you are, you may be carried on by a stern logical necessity to accept the whole.'[1]

Of this 'stern logical necessity' many non-Catholics complain. It seems to them to put logic before the large dumb certainties of life. In fact, the intimate coherence of all Catholic doctrines is taken by Newman, and by most Catholics, as evidence pointing to the oneness of truth; it is an inherent 'logic' arising from the unity of truth itself and from the wholeness of God's revelation, and is not the mere verbal logic of a logician. However this may be,—whether Catholics are right or wrong on the point—it remains true that it is very hard to explain one point of Catholic belief or practice without explaining all.

(b) Catholic belief involves not only doctrines which are themselves interconnected, but involves a faith which is accepted as a whole or is really not accepted at all. It is, indeed, a general Christian doctrine that faith involves an unconditional and total surrender to God, and that faith means acceptance of God's revelation as a whole. The self-surrender of faith gives a certainty which nothing can shake; and on this there is no difference between Christians. Members of the World Council, for instance, accept Christ as God and Saviour, and accept this in faith; they are, consequently, sure beforehand that none of their discussions could ever lead them to believe that Christ is *not* their God and Saviour. All Christians agree that there are 'temptations to unbelief'. As an instance, in the book *The Church* we read: 'Whenever a Christian is placed in a radically un-Christian environment and is permanently cut off from Christian fellowship, worship and witness, his temptations to slip back into unbelief are immeasurably increased. It is not surprising that many slip back into apostasy.'[2] The conception of 'a temptation to unbelief' involves necessarily the conviction that a Christian possesses a certainty which he knows nothing ought to shake, in spite of the obscurity of faith and in spite of all objections which non-Christians might urge against Christianity.

But it is here that Catholics make an application of the

[1] Ch. 2, sect. 3, no. 2.
[2] *The Church*, Faith and Order Report, London, 1951, p. 32.

common principle of faith's complete and unconditional self-surrender which many non-Catholics think is unwarranted, false and even superstitious: the Catholic commits himself to Christ *in the Church*, and makes that self-committal as absolutely and finally as a non-Catholic makes his self-committal to Christ as God and Saviour. In acceptance of the principle there is no difference: all Christians should have an antecedent certainty which nothing can shake. But the Catholic extends that to the Church, while the non-Catholic, *insofar* as he differs from the Catholic, separates his self-committal to Christ from his self-committal to the Church. Both agree that Christians must resist 'temptations to unbelief', but the difference lies in assignment of the boundaries where unbelief begins. The Catholic sees the boundaries as drawn by Christ living in the Church and its visible head, whereas the non-Catholic—again *insofar* as he differs from the Catholic—sees the boundaries as drawn by Scripture alone, or by Scripture as understood by tradition, or as understood under the personal guidance of the Holy Spirit, or, at least, does not admit that the boundaries between belief and unbelief are drawn by the visible Church and its visible head. Many feel that the boundaries are to be drawn by sound scholarship, a variable norm, indeed.

Here is a source of radical misunderstanding, even in explaining the Roman Catholic attitude to the World Council. Catholics are partly grieved and partly bewildered when they hear anyone say that they could accept one doctrine but not another, could accept, for instance, the Catholic teaching on marriage but not the teaching on the sacrament of penance, or could accept the Catholic teaching on the inspiration of Scripture but not on the sacrifice of the Mass. The Catholic accepts the whole because the Church teaches it, and he is apt to imagine that our separated brethren can 'believe what they choose', quite forgetting that many non-Catholics feel themselves as firmly bound by Scripture as the Catholic feels bound by the Church. Some, if not all, non-Catholics look upon this conviction of Catholics as making the Church superior to the Gospel and even superior to Christ, forgetting that it is integral to the Catholic's faith that Christ is one with the Church. Both agree that faith means a 'giving-away of self' and a liberation of self; but the deep abyss of divergence lies in the conception of the union of Christ with the actually existing, or 'the empirical', Church.

But, it cannot be repeated too often, the principle which both accept is the same. For those outside the Roman Catholic Church, to doubt the Gospel would be to doubt and betray Christ; for a Catholic to doubt the teaching of the Church would be to doubt or betray Christ. For any Christian, face to face with non-Christians, even to *appear* to doubt the Gospel would be to betray Christ; for a Catholic, even to appear to doubt the Church would be to betray Christ. There are ramifying applications of this difference between Catholics and non-Catholics; the latter can, quite consistently with their principles, take a different view of worship together with those not of his own denomination. He can take a view quite different from a Catholic's on the question of participation in un-denominational, or super-denominational, bodies such as the Young Men's Christian Association. 'Indifferentism' in religion has different connotations and applications. Not seldom the non-Catholic thinks that the Catholic is hopelessly ob-scurantist and narrow-minded, not to say uncharitable; not seldom the Catholic thinks that the non-Catholic relies on a formula as a substitute for real unity and extends his liberty as a Christian man beyond all reasonable bounds. The diver-gence is growing less, as Catholics understand better the sincere and deep longing of many non-Catholics for visible unity and the charity which inspires it, and as non-Catholics appreciate better that Catholic 'intransigence' springs from a deeply rooted conception of the Church as the Body of Christ. But as things stand at present, a Catholic would find his con-science burdened were he a member of an organization which published literature on Christian unity which he could not conscientiously circulate among his fellow-Catholics. The valley between the high peaks may be rising and the path from one peak to the other may be becoming clearer and easier; but the valley is still very deep.[1]

[1] On a Catholic layman's conception of the 'liberty' of thought among non-Catholics, cf. the letter of Mr T. S. Gregory, *Tablet*, October 15, 1955, p. 378, and the answer from the Rev. J. W. Walker, of Kilmersdom, Bath, October, 22, 1955, p. 410,

(c) Not merely theological 'systems' but 'emotional-theological systems' make a chasm across which it is difficult to make one's voice carry. Religion is not merely a theological system but is a devotional life. It may appear trite to repeat a truth so obvious; but the applications are pertinent to the difficulties of explaining the Catholic attitude towards ecumenism. The Orthodox, for instance, like the Roman Catholics, and like not a few Anglo-Catholics, have a sincere and deep devotion to the Mother of God and this devotion tends to colour their whole religious outlook. I recall a phrase of Dr Parker's in the volume *Ways of Worship:* 'Never to think of God without thinking of Mary and never to think of Mary without God is a safe rule.'[1] The Orthodox certainly follow that rule and in Conferences sometimes introduce the subject of the Mother of God in contexts which others think most inept and inappropriate; but in this the Orthodox show a sense of an emotional connection between things which seems almost unintelligible to those who do not share the Orthodox feeling and instinctive devotions. Many a Protestant regards this devotion to our Lady as superstitious. He thinks that the Orthodox, and the Catholics, and even the Anglo-Catholics, put Mary into Christ's place; whereas the Orthodox thinks that the Protestant often reduces Christ to Mary's place instead of keeping him at the right hand of the Father. But the diversity is not merely in the logical order, it is also in the emotional order.

Matters such as the ministry, the sacraments, and the norm of faith are not merely theological. A thorough-going Protestant recoils with a sense of shock from things like the priesthood, the Mass, devotion to the Blessed Sacrament, prayers for the dead, and, perhaps particularly, to 'infallible pronouncements' from the Pope. Yet the Catholic loves all these things and they are woven into the texture of his religious life. Similarly, not a few Catholics are unaware of the tenderness and depth of much Protestant devotion, perhaps particularly devotion to the Eucharist, for a Catholic is apt to imagine that rejection of his concept of the real presence empties out all real de-

[1] 'Mariology (Anglican)', by the Rev. T. M. Parker, reprinted from the volume *The Mother of God*, ed. E. L. Mascall, London, 1949, in *Ways of Worship, Report of a Theological Commission of Faith and Order*, ed. Pehr Edwall, Eric Hayman, William D. Maxwell, London, 1951, p. 286.

votion. Both sides, of course, try to respect feelings, even though they do not understand them. But there remains an emotional cleavage which it sometimes seems impossible to bridge.

Consequently there is a chasm to cross in explaining the attitude of the Catholic Church towards the World Council of Churches. Rome's refusal to take part in discussions with other Christians about the restoration of broken Christendom seems to many to be a proud and arrogant demand for nothing less than 'submission'. To the Catholic it seems the greatest humility, because the faith committed to the saints is not his, and the sincerest charity, because he knows that the heart of charity is the centre of unity and that centre is Christ united indissolubly with his body, the visible Church. The Catholic tends to see the multiplication of denominations as caused by the principle of private judgement and he feels he must not even seem to approve that principle; the non-Catholic is likely to think that readiness to consult with others is at least some concession against the absoluteness of private judgement.

Feeling is most acute about the Papacy, non-Catholics tending to regard the Popes as avaricious tyrants, or at least as slaves of a system, and to regard Catholic devotion to the Pope as an abdication of responsibility which a Christian ought manfully to accept; whereas Catholics associate the Pope with the humble and loving St Peter, with the martyred Popes of the early Church and see him as a 'common Father' for whom they have a deep affection, to obey whom is submission to Christ. Here, too, agreement in principle should be noted and fostered: both agree upon the principle of authority, in spite of disagreement as to its seat, and both agree that faith demands obedience and humility. In the agreement is the hope of reconciliation. We must all obey him who was obedient unto death, even the death of the cross, by whose obedience many are to be made just.

3. ALOOFNESS AN ADVANTAGE TO THE WORLD COUNCIL?

It is not true charity to fail to point out a serious, even a fatal, danger, or to encourage misleading hopes or misguided enthusiasm. The persistent influence of Rome has been against any tinkering with the problems and against any tendency, condemned and repudiated so often by ecumenists, 'to conceal difficulties under the cloak of a formula'.[1] The Roman authorities, not without advice from all over the world, judged that by maintaining official aloofness the Catholic Church could best serve the greater and the wider good. Some Orthodox judged that a limited participation—for they do not enter into discussions or vote—would help more, and considering their conditions and circumstances, which are different from Rome's, the Orthodox seem to have had 'a wholly beneficial influence on the World Council of Churches'.[2]

Dr Oliver Tomkins has observed that 'Roman Catholics may claim that their contribution to the Ecumenical Movement has been, by their abstention, to compel non-Romans to reconsider the meaning of authority, ministry, sacraments, and dogma'.[3] This is perhaps said with too great kindness,

[1] The words are Dr Newton Flew's, and their context may be quoted: 'The fear has often been expressed, usually by those who have had little experience of Faith and Order discussions, that such gatherings tend "to conceal difficulties under the cloak of a formula". I do not think that any reasonable person will level that reproach against the following pages.' Foreword, *The Church*. Dr Newton Flew is perfectly correct about the later published proceedings of Faith and Order and about the Report produced under his chairmanship, entitled *The Church;* at the same time, such fear was not chimerical in the earlier stages of the movement. Stockholm did appear to be seeking unity without any solid theological basis, and even now, has all danger vanished of despair of doctrinal agreement and of seeking a refuge in common good works?

[2] Cf. Avery R. Dulles, 'The Orthodox Churches and the Ecumenical Movement', *Downside Review*, no. 239, January, 1957, pp. 38–54. Nicolas Zernov has a most illuminating account of 'The Eastern Churches and the Ecumenical Movement in the Twentieth Century' in *History of the Ecumenical Movement*, pp. 645–74. As an instance of 'non-theological factors' which affect the situation the following may be quoted: 'This history of the Eastern Churches has always been closely linked with the destiny of their nations and states, and the majority of their members find it hard to draw a line between the religious and national communities to which they belong. It is equally difficult for them to visualize any Western ecclesiastical body independent of the interests of one or another of the Great Powers. Bitter and long experience has taught Eastern Christians, especially in the Near East, to look upon Roman Catholics as agents of France, upon Anglicans as spokesmen of Great Britain, upon Protestants as emissaries of Germany, and, more recently, of the United States. It is only natural, therefore, that when representatives of the ecumenical movement approached the Eastern Churches, the latter identified them with the supposed imperialistic schemes of the Anglo-Saxon democracies, and welcomed or refused co-operation with them according to their own political sympathies.' Pp. 669–70. The restrictive resolutions adopted by the Conference of Autocephalous Orthodox Churches held at Moscow in July 1948 were certainly only doubtfully based upon purely doctrinal considerations, though it should be added that many of the Orthodox have opposed participation in the ecumenical movement upon doctrinal grounds.

[3] 'The Roman Catholic Church and the Ecumenical Movement', *History of the Ecumenical Movement*, p. 693.

since in any event these doctrines would have had to be re-considered, for there were already deep divergences among non-Catholics about them and whatever Rome did the differences would have had to be faced.

Professor Kinder says:

> We cannot do without the Roman Catholic Church. We must remember that *all* the real problems of ecumenism spring from the split in the Church at the time of the Reformation in the sixteenth century. All later divisions were merely the outcome of this first split. That is why we must always go back to the Reformation as the source of our divisions, if they are ever to be overcome. If we seek their source elsewhere, the solution will not prove sound and permanent. Then the Roman Catholic Church occupies a special, indispensable place in a truly ecumenical movement; and its very existence compels us to go to the Centre and not to take the easiest course. If we let the Roman Catholic Church go, we shall thereby lose a certain salutary obligation to go to the root of the problem; we shall also lose a valuable barrier against the free play of certain forms of humanism, pietism and dynamism which are latent in Protestantism. Whenever Protestantism has been definitely opposed to Roman Catholicism, it has become over-liberal and has lost its essential message. We seem to need discussion with the Roman Catholic Church as a sort of *katechon*, (check-point, 2 Thess. 2: 7).

A little further on, Professor Kinder develops his contention:

> Finally we must not hesitate to admit that there are many essential things which we Protestants must learn from the Roman Catholic Church and from their comments on what we do— things that are essential for us to know and that we would scarcely have an opportunity to learn without them. We need the Roman Catholic Church also as a corrective, simply in order to see things realistically. When confronted by Roman Catholicism, we perceive more clearly the dangers and mistakes to which we Protestants are prone. If we are horrified by many dangerous secular and even pagan elements in the Roman Catholic Church, we should be equally horrified by similar elements in our own Church—instead of going to the other extreme (secularism and humanism). The danger of condensing the Christian message into metaphysical and legal forms is no less great than that of its

dispersion in personalistic and activistic forms. Our first task is not to judge the Roman Catholic Church, but to judge ourselves in the light of our own consciences.[1]

Professor Kinder, in his general attitude, does not stand alone. 'It seems absurd', says Father Damboriena in *Unitas*, 1956, 'to think of any true ecumenism without the active participation of that [the R.C.] Church. There are, undoubtedly, American ecumenists who have that minimum of respect for the Church of Rome; this I have discovered during the time and study devoted to the preparation of this paper.[2] Bishop Angus Dun, for example, and other writers such as Leiper, Van Dusen, and Bennett are among those who are respectful in their references to the Catholic position. It is a duty for me, in particular, to give an acknowledgement to Professor K. S. Latourette, whose understanding and appreciation of what the Catholic Church is and holds takes him much nearer to us than most of his colleagues'.[3]

To a considerable extent the Roman position acts as a kind of 'catalyst', which is defined as 'a substance which without change itself aids a chemical change in other bodies'. The Roman doctrine, whether it be liked or disliked, is at least clear-cut in many matters, especially matters on which there is divergence among ecumenists. At the same time this clearness ought not to be exaggerated, as if the Catholic Church regarded all questions as already settled and closed. This is

---

[1] *Art. cit.*, *Ecumenical Review*, vii, no. 4, July, 1955, pp. 342 and 344.

[2] 'Trends of the Ecumenical Movement in American Protestantism', *Unitas*, viii, nos. 2 and 3, Summer and Autumn, 1956.

[3] *Art. cit.* p. 155 and cf., also, Eva Maria Jung, 'Roman Catholic Impressions of the Evanston Assembly', *Ecumenical Review*, vii, no. 2, January, 1955, p. 123. There are certainly many in these islands to whom tribute might well be paid for their courtesy, charity and understanding of a position which they do not accept; but to attempt to do so here would take undue space and, besides, it would raise the question of those whose courtesy, charity and understanding seem, to Catholics, at least, not always to attain the fullest measure. Jules Lebreton is quoted by Henri de Lubac as saying: 'Surely when it is a question of two Christians sincerely discussing their faith, there can be nothing more between them than a passing misunderstanding born of the darkness of the human condition and due to be dispersed on the morrow by the light of God?', *The Splendour of the Church*, English translation by Michael Mason of the second edition of *Méditations sur l'Eglise*, London, 1956. Lebreton means that our religious misunderstandings, and, much more, antagonisms, will all disappear when we pass *ex umbris et imaginibus in veritatem* and that we must measure our conduct here below by the standard which Christ will apply when he comes to judge us all.

particularly true, for instance, in the matter of biblical studies. Pope Pius XII

makes clear that biblical scholars must not be treated with suspicion when they face difficulties valiantly in their efforts to find interpretations consonant with the teaching of the Church and in harmony with the certain conclusions of the secular sciences. Indiscreetly zealous critics of those hard working labourers in the Vineyard should remember 'that among the many matters set forth in the legal, historical, sapiential and prophetical books of the Bible there are only a few whose sense has been declared by the authority of the Church, and equally few concerning which the opinion of the Holy Fathers is unanimous. There consequently remain important matters, in the explanation of which the sagacity and ingenuity of Catholic interpreters can and ought to be freely exercised, so that each in the measure of his powers may contribute to the common good, to the ever-greater advancement of sacred learning, and to the defence and honour of the Church.'[1]

There is, too, a wider latitude in theological discussion among Catholic theologians than is sometimes imagined.[2] This granted, it remains true that the 'Roman' position on many matters is sharply defined, so that it can act as a kind of standard of comparison, even when people wish to avoid it; on the theological map the area is clearly marked: 'here be popery', or, as Catholics believe, 'here is the authentic faith of the saints'.

'Roman', and the Orthodox, doctrine as a firm point of comparison appears manifestly in the chapter entitled 'The

[1] Encyclical *Divino afflante Spiritu*, AAS, xxxv (1943), p. 313, cited by William Leonard and Dom Bernard Orchard in *A Catholic Commentary on Holy Scripture*, art. 'The Place of the Bible in the Church', p. 10. The following words might also be noted: 'All modern Catholic exegetes are directly or indirectly indebted to the tremendous stream of non-Catholic works on biblical subjects, which flows universally over the western world, for their suggestive ideas, scholarly exegesis and broad and bold hypotheses. These when tested by the Rule of Faith have yielded, and continued to yield, valuable lights and fresh illustration of the truth of God's Word,' *ibid*. p. 8. Cf. also, E. F. Sutcliffe, 'The Replies of the Biblical Commission', and particularly the quotations from the *Letter to Cardinal Suhard* of 1948, *ibid*. p. 74.

[2] Part of the failure to appreciate the width of discussion among Catholic theologians is due to the fact that many have written and still write in Latin; this has its disadvantages, but it contributes much to clearness. It is far harder to be vague in Latin than in modern languages; and it is noteworthy that it would be easy to turn into Latin the Toronto declaration of the World Council, and the Report entitled *The Church*, but far harder to find a Latin adequate for Evanston.

Nature of the Church: Agreements and Disagreements', of the *Report* of the World Council Commission of Faith and Order, *The Church*. On this Commission were theologians from over twenty 'Churches'[1] and their desire was to make plain the nature of the doctrinal differences between 'Churches'. They selected general subjects and listed the varying views in order. In almost every case they first placed the 'Roman Catholic' doctrine, next the Orthodox, and then the doctrine of others.[2]

Part of the reason for placing the Roman Catholic and the Orthodox positions in the first place may have been that on the subject of the Church the non-Catholic denominations simply reject certain elements and consequently there was little to say about their doctrines; at the same time, this

---

[1] The theologians who were members of the Commission belonged, according to the Appendix, to the following ecclesiastical affiliations: Methodist Church, Lutheran, American Episcopalian, Church of England, Evangelical Church in Germany (Lutheran), Orthodox Church, Society of Friends, Reformed Church of the Netherlands, Reformed Church of France, Swiss Protestant Federation, Disciples of Christ in North America, Church of the Augsburg Confession in Alsace and Lorraine, Church of Scotland, Church of South India, Congregational Christian Churches in the U.S.A., Northern Baptist Union, Baptist Union of Great Britain and Ireland, Methodist Church of Ceylon, Congregational Union of England and Wales, Evangelical and Reformed Church, U.S.A., Old Catholic Church, Churches of Christ in Great Britain, Reformed Church of Hungary, Augustana Evangelical Lutheran Church, U.S.A.

[2] (a) *The Limits of the Church and the Mode of its Definition:* 1. the Roman Catholic doctrine; 2. the Orthodox; 3. the Old Catholic; 4. the Anglican communion; 5. the Lutheran; 6. the 'Reformed' (i.e. of the Calvinist or Presbyterian tradition); 7. the 'other Protestant communions'.

(b) *The Continuity of the Church:* 1. the Roman Catholic; 2. the Eastern Orthodox, the Old Catholic and 'many portions of the Anglican communion'; 3. the Lutheran and Reformed; 4. the Methodist; 5. the other Protestant communions.

(c) *The Unity of the Church:* 1. the Roman Catholic Church, the Orthodox Church, the Old Catholic Church and 'many Anglicans'; 2. the 'main Reformation tradition'; 3. 'other Protestant communions'.

(d) *The Goal of the Reunion Movement:* 1. Roman Catholics; 2. the Orthodox; 3. the Old Catholics; 4. Anglicans; 5. Lutherans and Reformed; 6. 'other Protestants'.

(e) *The Number and Nature of the Sacraments and their Relation to Membership of the Church:* 1. the Roman Catholic Church; 2. the Old Catholic Church; 3. the Orthodox Church; 4. 'Protestants of the Lutheran and Reformed tradition'; 5. the Anglican communion. There follows an account of baptismal teaching according to the varying traditions,—Lutheran, Reformed, Methodist, Congregationalist, Baptist and Disciples of Christ.

(f) *Scripture and Tradition:* 1. Orthodox; 2. Roman Catholics; 3. Church of England; 4. Old Catholic; 5. 'the Protestant Churches'.

(g) *Infallibility:* 1. Orthodox; 2. Roman Catholic; 3. 'the non-Roman communions'.

(h) *Priesthood and Sacrifice:* 1. Roman Catholic; 2. Orthodox; 3. Old Catholic; 4. 'the Protestant Churches for the most part'. *Op. cit.* pp. 14–20.

was not true of matters like the unity of the Church, and the goal of the reunion movement. On all the topics selected the Catholic position was clear and could serve as a point of departure and of comparison. It may be noted in passing that in every instance the doctrine of the Catholic Church was presented accurately, although not one of the theologians was a Roman Catholic and some probably had strong feelings against the Roman Catholic positions.

Père Congar said of the Catholic Church: 'Her way of helping the cause of oecumenism is simply to be herself. In refusing to enter the movement she has done more for it than the partial groups which compose it, and the more recent developments of the movement owe much to the uncompromising attitude taken by the Catholic Church.'[1] The English translation of Père Congar's book appeared in 1939 and there have been some changes in the ecumenical movement since then, which demand consideration.

4. THEOLOGICAL ASSUMPTIONS OF THE WORLD COUNCIL

One main development in the ecumenical movement has been the repeated effort of the Central Committee of the World Council of Churches to make clear that churches enter the Council without any compromise of their principles. The Central Committee at Toronto in 1950 and the Commission on the Church in 1951 insisted that the Council 'does not prejudge the ecclesiological problem'. In the *Report* entitled *The Church*, are listed six 'theological assumptions', together with explanations of them, the main lines of which are as follows:[2]

'(1) The Council assumes that God wills a unity between Churches greater than that which at present exists. There may be Churches participating in the Council which do not consider that God wills any closer unity than is already possible

---

[1] *Divided Christendom*, London, 1939, p. 133. Père Congar refers to K. Barth's *The Church and the Churches*, p. 48.

[2] The explanations given by this Theological Commission under the chairmanship of Dr Newton Flew are in one or two points clearer than the Toronto statement, though not contrary to it. The main declarations made at Toronto may be found in this book, *Appendix IV*.

through the kind of co-operation which the Council now affords. Nevertheless, they are members of a body which is pledged "to proclaim the essential oneness of the Church of Christ and the obligation of the Churches to manifest that unity".[1]

'(2) The Council assumes that every known view of the nature of the Church's unity has a legitimate place within it, and that it is within the Council that any or all of these views may be brought into living confrontation with each other.' But Christ must be recognized as the divine Head of the Body, and the explanation ends: 'The fact of Christ's Headship over His people *compels* all those who acknowledge Him to enter into real and close relationships with each other, even though they differ in important points.' (N.B. Italics mine.)

'(3) The Council assumes the faithfulness of Christ's promise to be with those who meet in His name and the gift of the Spirit to those who seek it. *This is a crucial assumption. There is no reason why those Churches which believe that God has finally committed to them the fulness of the Catholic Church should not be in the Council as the point of contact at which the Holy Spirit will convince others of the truth which He has already revealed to them.* The same applies to those who believe that the unity of the Church is wholly a "unity in the Spirit" before which all differences of sacrament and ministry shrink into insignificance. The one demand which the member Churches make on one another is the belief that all, others as well as themselves, are sincere in calling Jesus Lord, involving the responsibility to be obedient to Him and to remain sensitive to the leading of the Holy Spirit. This is why the only ultimate assumption of the World Council is that it is "a fellowship of Churches which accept our Lord Jesus Christ as God and Saviour". (Italics mine.)

'(4) Member Churches recognize that the question of the limits of membership in the Catholic Church needs further

[1] At the end of the explanation of this first 'theological assumption' an important observation is made: 'It is essential to distinguish sharply between what the Council says about the Council and what it says about the Church. For example the statement (Official Report, p. 127) that "the Council disavows any thought of becoming a single unified church structure" refers to the Council, and leaves entirely open whether the Church should ever be "dominated by a centralized administrative authority".' The Council has steadily disclaimed any idea that it is to become a Church and maintained that it is only a means by which churches can come into useful contact with each other.

exploration. Both Roman Catholic and Orthodox theologians recognize, in different ways, that salvation is possible for persons not associated in the visible organization. This recognition finds expression, for example, in the fact that with very few exceptions the Christian Churches accept the Baptism administered in other Churches as valid.[1] What consequences are to be drawn from this teaching? The underlying assumption is that each Church *has a positive task to seek fellowship with all those who, while not members of the same visible body, belong together* as Churches which accept our Lord Jesus Christ as God and Saviour. (Italics mine.)

'(5) The Council assumes that membership does not imply that each Church must regard the other member Churches as Churches in the full sense of the word. Differences of faith and order exist, but the Churches recognize one another as serving the One Lord, and they wish to explore their differences in mutual respect, trusting that they may be led by the Holy Spirit to the recognition of the full truth and to the manifestation of their unity in Christ.

'(6) The Council assumes that member Churches enter into spiritual relations through which they seek to learn from each other and to give help to each other in order that the Body of Christ may be built up and that the life of the Churches may be renewed. It is the common teaching of the Churches that the Church as the temple of God is at the same time a building which has been built and a building which is being built. The Church has, therefore, aspects which belong to every structure and essence and cannot be changed.[2] But it has other aspects which are subject to change. Thus the life of the Church, as it expresses itself in its witness to its own members and to the world, needs constant renewal. The Churches can and should help each other by a mutual exchange of thought and experience. This is the significance of the World Council and of many other of its activities. There is no intention to

[1] The use of the word 'valid' here may be compared with its use by non-Catholic theologians as regards Orders. Here does it mean more than 'not to be repeated'? Some Anglican theologians regard Baptism as necessarily in need of Confirmation for such Christian initiation as admits to the other sacraments.

[2] 'Belong to "every" structure and essence' seems an awkward phrase; should it read 'belong to its very structure and essence?' There may be a number of 'structures', but surely there can be only one 'essence'?

7

impose any particular pattern of thought or life upon the Churches, but whatever insight has been received by one or more Churches is to be made available to all the Churches for the sake of the "building up of the Body of Christ".[1]

Obscurities and Unexpressed Assumptions

Now it is the duty of a Christian to interpret the statements of another in the best meaning possible: 'It must be pre-supposed that every good Christian must be more ready to excuse the proposition of another than to condemn it; and if he cannot save it, let him enquire how he understands it: if the other understands it wrongly, let him correct him with love; if this suffice not, let him seek all possible means in order that the other, rightly understanding it, may save it from error.'[2] The following comments, then, made only by an individual, are intended in a spirit of charity and not of contention, and if they seem intransigent, the reason is not unfriendliness but the demands of sincerity.

Is there not an assumption, unexpressed but manifest, that the way in which the World Council seeks the unity of Christendom is the only right way? It is, indeed, right that the World Council should explain its purposes and its own nature; but do not the words of the Theological Commission go beyond this? Do they not suggest that the Commission has examined certain Christian doctrines and deduced therefrom the only proper means of healing the schisms among Christians? Do not the words used in the *Report*—no doubt unintentionally —call in question the right of the Church to make its own decision about how best it can further the cause of the unity of Christendom? The second theological assumption says that *all* who recognize Christ's Headship *are compelled* to enter into 'real and close relations with each other'. The fourth deduces from the acknowledgement of the validity of baptism the conclusion that each Church 'has a positive task to seek fellowship with all who belong together as Churches which accept our Lord Jesus Christ as God and Saviour'

[1] *Op. cit.*, pp. 53–5.
[2] St Ignatius of Loyola, *Spiritual Exercises*, Preliminary note, ed. London, 1913 p. 11.

The sixth, after referring to the 'renewal' of the Churches, argues from 'the common teaching' that Churches *should* help each other, and the assumption is that this involves 'entering into spiritual relations with each other'.

Some of these phrases are vague: 'real and close relations', 'seeking fellowship' and 'entering into spiritual relations with each other'. Perhaps they do not absolutely signify joining the World Council of Churches. Perhaps, too, the theologians of the Theological Commission intended to state the principles on which they themselves act rather than to lay down principles on which every Church ought to act. Yet the statements are made in universal form and can readily be taken to mean, even if they do not really mean: 'This is the best way to promote the unity of Christendom.' The statements of the Commission imply—doubtless without conscious intention—that the method it judges best is the method which all ought to judge best; and a reproach is implicit. Now the Roman Catholic Church, as regards herself and her members, has hitherto rejected this method. It is a method inspired by the best of intentions, but it easily permits the tacit assumption of false principles and certainly has special dangers in it. Admission of 'fellowship' because of faith in Christ as God and Saviour can weaken convictions about the supreme importance of the one true faith and the obligation of accepting it in its entirety. It can, for instance, incline to ready acceptance of an 'agreed syllabus' in schools, or even of the exclusion from schools of religious teaching, as is the case in many parts of America.

The implications of the Headship of Christ and of the admission of the validity of baptism may be understood differently. The Roman Catholic Church, together with several other Christian bodies, does not understand the obligation in the same way as the Theological Commission appears to do. The history of the Church shows that not seldom the best way of dealing with dissidents was judged to be refusal of 'real and close relations' and of normal Christian fellowship; and there are some theologians associated with the World Council who are prepared for such a method of refusal.

The group of Anglican theologians who commented upon

the *Evanston Report* gave a clear indication that the negative method is not to be universally reprobated: 'It should be recognized', they say, 'that unity may have to be achieved by exclusion as well as by inclusion.'[1] Admission of 'real and close relations' may consolidate divisions and refusal of such relations sometimes may help to bring home the evils of schism and division.

This does not mean that refusal of 'close relations' is invariably the best way to heal schisms. Nor does it imply that the members of the World Council of Churches are not following a method which, in their circumstances and conditions, may be best for them. Much less does it mean that frank and calm discussion, under due conditions, may not be of the greatest help to perception of the truth. But it does mean that some of the statements in the *Report* of the Theological Commission on the Church, and in the Toronto statement, are worded too broadly, and,—almost certainly contrary to their authors' intention—suggest that those who stand aloof have a mistaken or imperfect understanding of the Headship of Christ and of the meaning of Baptism, and hence by implication these statements reproach those who judge that in their own case another method is suitable. How hard it is to keep clear of *odium theologicum*!

This said in general, the statements made by the Central Committee at Toronto and by the Theological Commission on the Church call for a reassessment or restatement of reasons sometimes alleged to justify the aloofness of the Roman Catholic. For instance, an assertion that membership in the Council would be a tacit admission that all 'churches' have equal rights, or that no 'church' has supreme authority, could be met by the explicit and official assertion that a Church can join the World Council with the declared intention of persuading the other members that it and it alone has the 'fulness of the Catholic Church'. The Orthodox have participated in the Council with this explicit aim.

Nor would the doctrine of any Church be compromised: none of the statements made by the World Council in any way

[1] 'Notes on an Evanston Report', *Church Quarterly Review*, clviii, no. 326, January–March, 1947, p. 78.

bind the member Churches, which are perfectly free to qualify acceptance of such statements, or to reject them entirely, as the Orthodox often reject them. As regards doctrine, the Council is purely and simply a meeting-place for discussion and mutual enlightenment; and in this sense it is perfectly true that the World Council 'does not prejudge the ecclesiological problem'.[1]

5. Assessment of the Concrete Situation. Proposed Integration of the World Council with the International Missionary Council

Dr Visser 't Hooft has remarked that Catholics who write about the World Council pay excessive attention to the doctrinal side and overlook broader aspects and the general 'cross-fertilization' which is taking place among the Churches. Although that may be true of theologians who have written, I doubt if it is true of the Church itself in regulating its attitude towards ecumenism. Many factors need assessment as a whole; and among them appear to be the following:

1. *The mission of the Catholic Church to all men, which demands consideration of the mentality which exists among many men.* 'Religious indifferentism' is not a chimera. Competent observers from various parts of the world, including Great Britain and America, have remarked upon the 'atomic individualism' and the subjectivism in religion which is too often taken for granted. 'Liberalism', though in many theological writings declared to be dead, nevertheless still persists in the popular mind, which is often inclined to regard Christianity as no more than 'the Fatherhood of God and the brotherhood of man', and to think that religion is above all a matter of practical charity.

---

[1] Yet this wording is open to misunderstanding: in what sense can one speak of 'the ecclesiological problem'? The Orthodox and the Roman Catholics would say that the only problem is that involved in helping confused minds to see the one true Church of Christ. But the expression 'the ecclesiological problem' might be understood as meaning or as implying that we really do not know what Christ willed for his Church and that we have to investigate in order to find out. I think that the intention of the theologians of the Theological Commission was to permit the Orthodox-Catholic understanding of the term, since they certainly intended to avoid any prejudgement whatever; and so it would be preferable to say 'does not prejudge ecclesiological doctrines' rather than 'the ecclesiological problem'. This may sound unduly meticulous; but, as Chesterton said, much may hang upon exact expression, and language used with the best of intentions may contain unexpressed assumptions or suggestions.

The 'demythologizing of the Bible might be understood as meaning that the Bible contains only fairy stories and 'myths' in the popular sense; 'scientific humanism' regards many teachings of Christianity as positively injurious to mankind. There has, indeed, been a theological revival, with greater attention to dogmatics; how far it has affected the man in the pew is doubtful. Sometimes ecclesiastics of non-Catholic denominations speak publicly about Christianity in a way which shocks many sincere believers. In his account of the Church of Scotland in 1952, Mr C. Stewart Black said: 'The "Apostles' Creed' would no longer be generally acceptable in Scotland; it contains too many points that are debatable, and are in no way essential to Christianity.' *The Scottish Church*, Glasgow, 1952, p. 268. I sincerely hope that Mr Black, who was Provost of Paisley, is mistaken about Scotland; but his remark is not without significance as to the mind of many.

It is against this background of religious subjectivism that the Catholic Church has to consider her mission to all men and to judge such questions as association in the ecumenical movement. The officials of the World Council have tried to make clear that they do not stand for union by a watering-down of doctrine and acceptance of a lowest common denominator; yet, owing to circumstances not under their control, ordinary people are often confused. The Reverend Rosewell Barnes, Associate General Secretary of the American National Council of the Churches of Christ, is reported in the popular periodical *Time*, September 16, 1957, as having said that 20 per cent of American families change religious affiliation each year, which he thought would lessen denominational differences and smooth the path towards Christian unity. Some delegates to the American Conference on Faith and Order in 1957 thought that competition between churches within one big church might be a good thing, on the analogy of the competition between Chevrolet and Pontiac within the same corporation, General Motors. It is scarcely necessary to say that some few delegates to a regional meeting do not represent the mind of the World Council; nevertheless striking phrases such as that quoted can set up mental associations between 'ecumenism' and latitudinarianism.

A 'man of the world' may easily think or say something like this: 'Why can't the Churches iron out their differences by give and take? It is the method we use in business and in relations between employers and employees. Why make such a fuss about insignificant trifles of doctrine? Let the Free Churches concede episcopacy, the Anglicans concede occasional lay celebration, the Baptists concede infant baptism and so on. Let the Pope be President of a democratic set-up. In this way they could all get together and stop squabbling.'

That may be an exaggeration; but the fact remains that the aims and methods of the World Council are very generally misunderstood. The Toronto Statement is not known, or not appreciated, sometimes even by students of the movement, and membership in the Council is mistakenly taken as a tacit admission that we do not know what Christ wills for his Church and must consult together in order to find out. The World Council has most explicitly repudiated the suggestion that any Church surrenders its claim to uniqueness by joining the Council; but unhappily this repudiation is not well known and very considerable confusion exists in many minds. This is a fundamental fact which must influence the Roman Catholic Church in her conduct towards the Council.

2. *The changing and developing character of the World Council of Churches.* The Council has certainly developed and the period of its development is by no means ended. It is now proposed to 'reconstitute' the World Council of Churches by integration into it of the International Missionary Council; and it is as yet uncertain what would be the effects, or the imagined effects, of such an integration.[1]

---

[1] The phrase 'a reconstituted W.C.C.' is used by Dr Ernest Payne and Dr David Moses on p. 25 of their *Why Integration? An Explanation of the proposals before the World Council of Churches and the International Missionary Council*, published by the Edinburgh House Press, London, 1957. This is a most useful booklet; it prints the Constitution of the W.C.C. and of the I.M.C., and the list of members of each, besides containing much valuable information about the proposed 'integration'. For accounts of the International Missionary Council, cf. K. S. Latourette, History of the Expansion of Christianity, vol. iv. ch. 4 'Processes', pp. 64–107; *ibid.* 'Ecumenical Bearings of the Missionary Movement and the International Missionary Council' in R. Rouse and S. C. Neill's *History of the Ecumenical Movement*, pp. 353–405; W. R. Hogg, *Ecumenical Foundations, A History of the International Missionary Council and its Nineteenth Century Background*, New York, 1952. To list books on the history of the various non-Catholic missionary societies is here impossible.

The International Missionary Society has a structure almost more complex than that of the World Council of Churches. It is 'a Council of Councils'. Its members are not Churches, but national and regional councils. These fall into several different categories. Some of the oldest and most influential councils are associations of missionary agencies in the U.S.A. and Europe; others—chiefly in Asia and Africa—are councils with a mixed membership of churches, missionary agencies and such bodies as the Y.M.C.A. and the Student Christian Movement. Still other councils, as in India and Indonesia, restrict their full membership to Churches: in these councils the missionary agencies are only indirectly represented. Some of the missionary agencies referred to above are under Church authorities and others are independent bodies governed and supported by groups of individual Christians. The Methodist and Presbyterian missions, for instance, belong to the first category, being under the authority respectively of the Methodist Conference and of the Presbyterian General Assembly; whereas the Church Missionary Society and the London Missionary Society are independent bodies, though this latter is effectively Congregational.

The general purpose of the I.M.S. is 'to further the effective proclamation of the Gospel of Jesus Christ, as Lord and Saviour.' Among its functions are the following:

to strengthen its member organizations and encourage evangelism,

to stimulate thinking and investigation on missionary questions,

to make the results available for all missionary societies,

to co-ordinate the activities of various evangelical bodies,

to seek to unite Christian public opinion in support of freedom of conscience, including liberty of worship, the right to educate and persuade, and the right to change religious allegiance,

to help to unite the Christian forces of the world in seeking justice in international and inter-racial relations,

to call missionary conferences,

to be responsible for publications such as the *International Review of Missions*, to act in association with the World Council of Churches in the promotion of the common purposes of both.

In considering the effect of the proposed 'integration' it must be remembered that the two bodies are already in close association. Members of the I.M.C. had a considerable share in founding the W.C.C.; on the notepaper of the W.C.C. appears *In Association with the International Missionary Council*; the two bodies together formed the Commission of the Churches on International Affairs, which, since 1948, has represented both the W.C.C. and the I.M.C. with governments and the United Nations; they have had a joint Secretary for Asian affairs since 1949 and are in process of enlarging the functions of the Asian Secretariat; they have co-operated closely in Inter-Church Aid and its ramifications; since 1954 they have had a common Division of Studies; most of the missionary societies and boards 'closely identified with' the I.M.C. are connected with European or American Churches which are members of the W.C.C., as, for instance, the Church Missionary Society and the Society for the Propagation of the Gospel. 'Churches of Asia, Africa and Latin America have played an increasing part in all the concerns of the ecumenical movement. Many of these churches are now related to both the world bodies.' Certain churches, however, like the Gereformeerde Church of Holland are connected with the I.M.C. but refuse membership in the W.C.C. The functions and the membership of the two bodies are to a large extent inter-locked and inter-dependent. Integration is urged upon grounds of administrative efficiency and upon the theological ground that the unity of the Church and the mission of the Church to evangelize are inextricably connected.

Misgivings

Some of the 'fundamentalist' Protestant Churches have been associated with the I.M.C. but have kept aloof from the W.C.C. because they think that this latter organization tends to weaken convictions about the autonomy of the local congregation and is too acquiescent in its attitude towards Romanism, Modernism and Communism. Some of these bodies might withdraw from the I.M.C. were integration accomplished, as is clear from Sir Kenneth Grubb's discussion of the matter in an article entitled 'I.M.C.-W.C.C. Relations—A Personal View'.[1] Sir Kenneth says that the W.C.C. is held in some suspicion 'by groups of conservative evangelical outlook' who might withdraw their support from the integrated body. Yet Sir Kenneth thinks that the integration 'is bound to come'.

It is not, perhaps, fully realized by the Orthodox and by Roman Catholics that many of the Protestant 'missionary' bodies stand apart from both the I.M.C. and the W.C.C. Professor Latourette, the distinguished author of *The Expansion of Christianity*, pointed out that there has been a rapid growth in Asia, Africa and Latin America of groups and denominations which do not co-operate in the ecumenical movement. In this category are more than half of the Protestant missionaries in Japan and in Taiwan; and many in the Caribbean, South America and the Philippines.[2]

The 'groups' not in association with the I.M.C., apart from 'fringe' bodies such as Jehovah's Witnesses and Independent Tabernacle Churches, have been listed as follows:

(a) *The Interdenominational Foreign Missions Association of North America* includes some 35 'mission boards' of denominations, some of which have an income of three million dollars a year, and it is responsible for approximately 4,800 missionaries from North America.

(b) *The Evangelical Foreign Missions Association of the National Association of Evangelicals*. This Association arose from opposition to what was regarded as the 'liberalism' of the Federal Council of the Churches of Christ in America (an organization no longer existing, though many of its members formed the

---

[1] *International Review of Missions*, xlvi, no. 183, July 1957, pp. 299–305.

[2] '*Re-thinking Missions* after Twenty-five Years', *International Review of Missions*, xlvi, no. 182, April, 1957, pp. 165–70, especially, p. 168. Professor Latourette thinks that the prominence of these non-co-operating bodies should 'compel those churches who join in the oecumenical movement to re-appraise their methods and message in drastic fashion'. I think some limitation is needed here, cf. below, pp. 235–6, regarding the attitude of Roman Catholics toward the Pentecostals in Chile. On 'groupings', that is associations of missionary bodies, which do not co-operate with the W.C.C. or the I.M.C., cf. H. Lindsell, Dean of Fuller Theological Seminary, Pasadena, California, 'An Appraisal of Agencies not co-operating with the International Missionary Council Grouping', *International Review of Missions*, xlvii, April, 1958, pp. 203–9, and Dr Norman Goodall, 'Evangelical and W.C.C.-I.M.C.', *ibid.* pp. 210–15.

National Council of the Churches of Christ in America). It contains non-denominational mission boards, as well as boards under the jurisdiction of churches; Pentecostal and Holiness groups belong to it, and, though none of its members admit association with the American arm of the I.M.C., they do permit the presence on occasion of 'observers' or 'consultants'. It supports about 4,400 missionaries and proportionately to its numbers its contribution to missionary activity both in men and in money is greater than that of the denominations from which its members withdrew. This seems particularly true of the conservative Baptist Foreign Mission Society, a group which withdrew from the American Baptist Convention because of alleged modernism.

(c) *The International Council of Christian Churches* includes only 'denominations', and its most influential members belong to the General Association of Regular Baptist Churches. It takes what is described as 'a militantly fundamentalist' stand on questions of co-operation with other bodies of Christians, insisting upon complete separation from what they describe as 'apostasy'. This organization is militantly opposed both to the National Association of Evangelicals and to the National Council of Churches, on the ground that the latter is apostate, and the former has compromised its position by not insisting that its members break all connection with the so-called apostate denominations. In Scandinavia it has spread accounts of the W.C.C. which are regarded as misrepresentations, to speak mildly.[1]

(d) *The Southern Baptist Convention* supports more than a thousand missionaries; it stands aloof both from the W.C.C. and from the American National Council which belongs to the I.M.C.

(e) *The New Tribes Mission* has about 400 missionaries and is said to be 'radical in its principles and practice of missions'; but information about it is scanty.

It is well worth noting that few, if any, of these bodies would accept the principles of the W.C.C. about 'proselytism', and that it is partly because of the alleged willingness of the

[1] Cf. the account given by Dr Goodall in his article ' "Evangelicals" and W.C.C.-I.M.C.', *iam cit.*

W.C.C. and the I.M.C. to 'compromise' with 'Romanism' that they stand aloof.

Orthodox and Roman Catholic Misgivings

On the other hand, the Orthodox and the Roman Catholics view the proposed 'reconstitution' of the W.C.C. with the following misgivings:

Hitherto the World Council of Churches has been a Council seeking the unity of the Church: the 'reconstitution' would turn it into a body supporting what are in fact Protestant missions.

'Integration' would mean a more formal and more conspicuous association of the W.C.C. with organizations of a pronounced 'Protestant' character, of whom some are engaged in 'proselytism' in Spain, Italy, Latin America and the Middle East'.

The importance of the Faith and Order Commission would be lessened, and in that Commission the Orthodox and the Roman Catholics see the greatest hope for healing divisions. The 'reconstitution' might swing interest and effort in the direction of co-operation without firm doctrinal basis.

The effort to retain in the integrated body the 'evangelistic' organizations, which suspect the W.C.C., might tend towards acceptance of a diluted 'undenominational' form of Christianity. The basis of the W.C.C. is acceptance of 'our Lord Jesus Christ as God and Saviour',[1] whereas the I.M.C. uses the formula 'proclamation of the Gospel of Jesus Christ, as Lord and Saviour'.

In short, the fear is that the integration may tend towards what Dr George MacLeod called—only to repudiate it—'a coagulation of Protestant bodies to have a fight'.

The Eastern Orthodox Churches deserve special sympathy in their fears of a consolidation of Protestant and Western bodies which try to attract non-Christians, and sometimes Orthodox Christians, to their beliefs. The Eastern Orthodox Churches hold a very special position in the 'Middle and Near East', which all Christians ought to recognize with gratitude. It was in the 'Near East' that Christ was born, lived, died and

[1] Dr Visser 't Hooft gives the history of the adoption of this basis in *History of the Ecumenical Movement*, pp. 702–5.

rose again. In the 'Near East' the Apostles received their mission and their vision and passed it on to their successors, and to men like Polycarp, Irenaeus, Clement of Alexandria, Denis of Alexandria and countless saints and martyrs. In the 'Near East' Athanasius stood against the world in defence of faith in Christ as God and Saviour. In the 'Near East' that faith was defended, clarified and deepened by holy and wise men like Basil, Gregory of Nazianzus, Gregory of Nyssa, Cyril of Alexandria, Epiphanius, Chrysostom and so many Syrian and Byzantine saints, doctors and apostles. From them the faith was carried to Russia; and Christians in the 'Near East' for centuries endured oppression and yet kept the tradition of the one true faith.

In the last century a number of Protestant bodies entered the Levant, until in 1954 there were 74 different Protestant denominations and some 1,400 missionaries, with schools, colleges, hospitals, orphanages, agricultural institutes and churches. These have shown, indeed, that Western peoples do not go to the Middle East merely for commercial reasons, and educational and humanitarian work has been impressive. The missionaries may, also, have helped to stimulate the religious sense of Muslims and even of the Orthodox.[1] Yet who could fail to understand the Orthodox recoil from any suggested intensification or consolidation of this Non-Orthodox religious effort? The Protestant emphasis upon individualism—'the right of every man to make his own religious decisions', as Dr Badeau puts it—is deeply alien to the Orthodox conception of 'Tradition', which sees the individual carried on, though not submerged, by the stream of religious life in the Church past, present and future, and sees all the faithful as united to the Mother of God and to the saints. Many Protestant bodies in lands traditionally Orthodox have

[1] Dr John S. Badeau of the Near East Foundation, New York, formerly Dean of the American College, Cairo, gives an account of these missions, 'The Role of the Missionary in the Near East', *International Review of Missions*, xliii, no. 172, October, 1954, pp. 397–403. Dr Norman Goodall, after a visit to the Near and Middle East in 1956, alludes to 'the infinite variety of "evangelicals" whose differences cannot, with the greatest charity, be ascribed solely to the rich diversities inherent in a unifying Evangel'. 'Some Reflections on the Near and Middle East', *International Review of Missions*, xlvi, no. 181, January, 1957, p. 7. Dr Goodall's account of the many Christian divisions is afflicting to read since it is so objective and the situation so tragic.

used methods not in accord with the best missionary theory, to put it mildly, and the 'conversions' gained have been, in Orthodox eyes, to something 'Western' as well as to non-Catholic and non-Orthodox doctrine. The Orthodox 'Rite' is not merely a matter of ceremonies and language, it is a whole institutional and cultural complex which is characteristic of each of the non-Latin churches among the Orthodox.[1] Orthodox fears regarding what seems like further support for what they regard as 'proselytism' are natural and ought to be received with the utmost sympathy.

Are the Fears Justified?

It is difficult for one who is admittedly an 'outsider' to do more than conjecture about the effects of an integration of the W.C.C. and the I.M.C., if it eventuates. Speaking, then, in some ignorance, it would appear that the fears of the evangelical Protestants, of the Orthodox and the Roman Catholics are *too late*. The plan for integration appears rather a stream-lining of existing association than an initiation of new relationships. Many both in the I.M.C. and the W.C.C. are convinced that the unity of the Church and the missionary obligation of the Church are indivisible; and both bodies seem committed in many lands, especially in Asia, to continue to help the formation and development of 'Younger Churches'. I doubt if the momentum of this movement can be stopped, even though it causes the I.M.C. some loss.

The effect on 'Proselytism'

As regards 'proselytism', the World Council of Churches has for some time been interested in the subject and the problems it presents; and the Central Committee of the W.C.C. has expressed the opinion that 'those churches which are concerned about the problems arising from the activities of missions carried on by other churches in their own areas will be in a

---

[1] Cf. the illuminating article by Dom Polycarp Sherwood, 'The Sense of Rite', *Unitas*, ix, no. 3, Autumn, 1957, pp. 168–85. Many Encyclicals of the Popes have insisted that the Orthodox must never think that they need surrender their own legitimate rites and institutions, and notably Pope Pius XII, in his Encyclical on the 15th centenary of the death of St Cyril of Alexandria, *Acta Apostolicae Sedis*, xxxvi, 1944, pp. 137–54, especially pp. 137–8.

better position to deal with such problems in an integrated Council than they are at present.' The statement, issued by the W.C.C. in 1956 entitled 'Christian Witness, Proselytism and Religious Liberty in the Setting of the World Council', expressed the desire and the hope of finding 'truly Christian solutions in local situations, solutions which are based on the loyalty all must show to the Great Commission of Matthew xxviii, 19–20, yet avoid that kind of proselytism which is a corruption of true Christian witnessing.'

There are, of course, different views about 'a corruption of true Christian witnessing' and the subject is thorny in the extreme. Would integration of the two non-Catholic bodies cause more thorns to grow and make the thorns longer and sharper? It is not clear that it would. The International Missionary Council owes its origin to the Edinburgh Missionary Conference of 1910, from which agencies carrying on 'evangelization' in countries already Christian were excluded. Since its foundation one of the aims of the I.M.C. has been to lessen the scandal caused by competing missionary activities in non-Christian lands. It has done this largely through negotiating 'comity' agreements, which divided territories among agencies; but such 'comity' agreements are quite outmoded in the modern world and their practical and theoretical breakdown has been a potent factor in the impulse for Church unity, especially though not exclusively in Asia.

In recent times the inter-relation of missionary bodies makes general statements likely to be misleading. Bodies which have missions in Orthodox and Roman Catholic countries tend to keep their distance from the I.M.C., and still more from the W.C.C. Many of them have their strongest supporting bases in the U.S.A., where there exist at least two big national organizations which provide more congenial company for them than would the Division of Foreign Missions (of the National Council of the Church of Christ) which is the American member unit of the I.M.C. These two organizations are the Evangelical Foreign Missions Association (related to the National Association of Evangelicals) and the Interdenominational Foreign Missions Association. The latter tends to be aggressively hostile towards the I.M.C. and the W.C.C. The

former includes groups which are well disposed towards the
I.M.C. but uneasy about its present association with the
W.C.C. and apprehensive about the integration proposal.

In Spain and Italy the most active 'evangelistic' bodies
are the Southern Baptist Convention (U.S.A.), the Brethren
(Plymouth, more or less) and the Assemblies of God. The first
two of these have no formal links with the I.M.C. but both
W.C.C. and I.M.C. have contacts with the small Methodist
and Presbyterian Churches in Italy as well as with the Waldensians, the Lutherans and the Mennonites.

In Latin America the pattern is still more complex. There
are various national or regional councils comprising in their
membership churches and missionary agencies. A few of these
—Brazil, Mexico, Cuba, Puerto Rico and the River Plate
Confederation which covers Argentina, Paraguay and Uruguay
—are in membership with the I.M.C. Others, such as the
Evangelical Confederation of Colombia, are not in direct
membership with the I.M.C., but most of these Latin American Councils have indirect links with the I.M.C. through
the Committee on Co-operation in Latin America which is
connected with the I.M.C. through the Division of Foreign
Missions of the National Council of the Churches of Christ
in U.S.A. Some Latin American Churches are members of
the World Council of Churches.

In the Near and Middle East the pattern is somewhat
similar to the Latin American; the more zealously 'evangelistic' the body the less its connection with the I.M.C.

Within the membership of the I.M.C. there is, however, a
somewhat loosely organized federation called the Near East
Christian Council with a membership drawn from a vast
area including: Egypt, Iran, Israel, Jordan, Lebanon and
Syria, Sudan, Ethiopia, Greece, Iraq, Arabia and Turkey. No
Orthodox Churches are in membership with this Council but
Orthodox churchmen very frequently attend its meetings
as fraternal visitors or speakers. The possibility of linking the
work of this Near East Christian Council more closely with
some of the Orthodox Churches is under discussion. Recently
all Christians in Egypt have united in protest against restrictions and discriminations against them.

The question of formal relations between 'missionary' bodies is really of less importance than the personal relations existing between the leaders of these bodies. Even though missionary groups may not be officially connected, even indirectly, there may be cordial personal relations between individuals; sometimes these cordial relations exist in one country and not in another. Moreover, it must not be imagined that an indirect link of some small missionary body with the I.M.C. is indicative of support given by the I.M.C. to this body; personal relations may not exist or may not be cordial. The matter, in short, is too complex for hasty judgement.[1]

The spirit of the I.M.C. can, to some extent, be judged by the personalities of those who are associated with it or take an interest in it. Fr Damboriena has been cited about the attitude of Bishop Angus Dun, Dr H. P. Van Dusen, Professor John Bennett, Dr Henry Leiper and Professor K. S. Latourette.[2] All of them have been connected with the I.M.C. Dr Van Dusen is Chairman of the Joint Committee of the W.C.C. and the I.M.C. Professor Latourette has for years been on the editorial board of the *International Review of Missions* and up to 1952 took a leading part in most of the assemblies of the I.M.C. Professor John Bennett undertook special investigations in Asia for the I.M.C. and is in close touch with its officials. Dr Henry Leiper has been a missionary in China and is at present on the staff of the American Board of Commissioners for Foreign Missions, associated with the I.M.C. President John Mackay of Princeton has just been succeeded in the Chair of the I.M.C. by Bishop J. E. L. Newbigin of the Church of South India. Bishop Newbigin is also Vice-Chairman of the Faith and Order Commission of the W.C.C. It should be

---

[1] Dr Norman Goodall, secretary of the Joint Committee of the W.C.C. and the I.M.C., most kindly sent me detailed information about a number of 'evangelistic' bodies which work among peoples already Christian. It would require another book to detail the exact number of these bodies, their numbers, spirit, the geographical location of their 'missions', their success and the methods which they use. 'Protestants' vary from the conservatism of Anglicans and Episcopalians, who have churches in some Catholic countries, but exclusively for people who are already their members, to the obtrusive and persistent zeal of the Witnesses of Jehovah and others, who have small acquaintance with the culture and history of the countries to which they go and have a fierce antagonism to everything save Protestantism as they understand it.

[2] Cf. above, p. 176.

remembered that the I.M.C. is a purely consultative body and has no authority whatever over its constituent members; its influence is purely by information and persuasion.

Doubtless there are persons associated with the I.M.C. who have prepossessions or prejudices against the Orthodox and Roman Catholics. The same is true of the W.C.C. In the summer of 1957, at the meeting of the Central Committee of the W.C.C., which numbers about one hundred, some members of the Committee spoke without accustomed ecumenical moderation about the Roman Catholic Church and religious liberty. Bishop Sante Uberto Barberi proposed a resolution that the Council strongly condemn the persecution of Protestants in predominantly Catholic countries. To the honour of the Council this offensive proposal was not accepted, and several officials expressed themselves in a contrary sense. Finally Dr Geoffrey Fisher, Archbishop of Canterbury, was instrumental in having approved a more moderate motion, although it was scarcely 'ecumenical', that the Executive Committee be instructed to arrange for a study of 'the problem of religious liberty arising in Roman Catholic and other countries'.

Roman Catholics of many lands expressed their displeasure in no uncertain terms, and in *Istina* Père Dumont voiced the opinion that a *faux pas* had been committed. In October, 1957 Dr Visser 't Hooft wrote to Père Dumont saying that the vast majority of the Central Committee disagreed with the views held by only a few and that the desire of the Committee as a whole was to reject any 'aggressive' proposal but to accept proposals for a peaceful and objective enquiry into the whole question of religious liberty.[1]

In the background of this discussion in the W.C.C. almost certainly was the situation in Colombia, which the 'Evangelical

---

[1] An account of the matter is given in *Unitas*, ix, no. 3, Autumn, 1957, pp. 196–200, with citations from members of the Central Committee who disagreed with Bishop Barberi, from the U.S. National Catholic Welfare Conference, from a prominent newspaper correspondent who had experience of Colombia, from the *Tablet* of August 17, the Duke of Norfolk's letter to the Colombian Chargé d'Affaires in London and a letter in answer from the Colombian Ambassador. In the same number of *Unitas* is printed a statement from the Colombian Bishops, and from Cardinal Luque, pp. 225–6. Dr Visser 't Hooft's letter to Père Dumont is printed in *Vers l'unité chrétienne, bulletin catholique d'information mensuel, centre d'études 'Istina'*, 25 Boulevard d'Auteuil, Boulogne sur-Seine, no. 97, p. 97.

Confederation of Colombia' represents as real persecution, but which Catholic Colombians represent as civil war followed by bandit war, conjoined with a campaign of calumny by certain Protestant bodies.[1] Even among the officials of the W.C.C. there are some who are antagonistic to the Roman Catholic Church. Would the proposed reconstitution increase the number of such members? Would it give a more effective sounding-board to critics hostile to Roman Catholicism and to Orthodoxy? It is difficult to answer these questions.

At present the W.C.C., in appointment of Presidents and members of the Central and Executive Committees, takes account not only of personal qualifications but also of 'confessional' and geographical representation. The new plan would increase representation of those with missionary knowledge and experience. In the Assembly of the I.M.C. representation follows somewhat the same pattern, although the Administrative Committee must be drawn from at least four continents and ten member organizations, account also being taken of a principle of rotation among the regions of the Council. Competent members of the Committees of both the W.C.C. and the I.M.C. become implicated in a numerous variety of organizations and tend to be overburdened;[2] and administrative simplification is a powerful argument for the new plan. This, and the steady convergence of missionary concerns, are the reasons advanced in favour of integration. If the 'reconstitution' were in fact to result in greater influence for those antagonistic to Catholicism, this would be an accidental by-product.

[1] For a Catholic account of the matter cf. Eduardo Ospina, *The Protestant Denominations in Colombia, A Historical Sketch with a Particular Study of the So-called 'Religious Persecution'*, Bogotá, 1954, and Eugene L. Culhane, 'Colombia and U.S. "Missionaries"', *America*, March 8, 1958. After a visit to Colombia the Rev. E. L. Culhane speaks of 'the systematic slandering of Colombia in the world Press by certain U.S. Protestant agencies as a persecutor of religious minorities', and ends his article by saying that Crisanto Cardinal Luque, Archbishop of Bogotá and Primate of Colombia, would welcome 'a mixed commission of Protestants and Catholics of known probity to visit Colombia, investigate the position and declare its findings.'

[2] Cf. Dr Norman Goodall, Secretary of the Joint Committee of the W.C.C. and the I.M.C., 'The Limits of Co-operation', *International Review of Missions*, xliv, no. 176, October, 1955, p. 449. Dr Goodall gives an alarming list of 'Conferences', 'Departments', 'Groups', 'Commissions' and 'Committees'.

Less Attention to Doctrine?

Would integration lessen the influence of the Commission on Faith and Order, in which the Orthodox and Roman Catholics tend to place the greatest importance of the W.C.C.? The Faith and Order Commission certainly made a great advance, notably in relating all theological problems to the doctrine of the unity of the Church; nevertheless its deliberations show that the outlook of the theologians is in advance of that of the ordinary Church member and that there is no present prospect of doctrinal agreement. Ideas have, of course, seeped down from the theologians to the pews and the changed outlook toward Eucharistic worship is evidence of it. At the same time the conviction has grown that 'unity will only come by action'.

Ever since the coalescence in 1948 into the W.C.C. of 'Life and Work' and 'Faith and Order', the latter organization has been recognized as only one element in the World Council. The original impulse towards unity sprang in great part from the missionary organizations, as the Edinburgh Conference of 1910 and its consequences show. The missionary organizations—the term includes some Churches—grasped the fact that denominational issues which divided European and American Churches were largely meaningless on the missions[1]; and in consequence they tended to underestimate the importance of doctrine in favour of an undenominational proclamation of 'the Glorious Gospel of the blessed God'. They were, too, children of their age, the age of the Wesleyan and Evangelical revival, taking for granted that 'Rome' was pernicious and that only Protestants could preach the true Gospel. Time and experience appear to have led them to closer union with ecclesiastical bodies, which themselves grew more centralized, such as the 'Conferences' of Free Churches, and to an appreciation of the intellectual void which might be left by an undiscriminating abandonment of denominational teaching. They came to see that this void must

[1] An enquiry among Congregationalist missionaries in 1952–3 evoked answers that much Congregationalist theory and practice was scarcely applicable in places like the Gilbert and Cook Islands, Madagascar and parts of India; for instance, the Church meeting, lay celebration of the Eucharist and women ministers, cf. Dr Goodall's *Congregationalism—Plus*, London, 1953.

be filled by doctrinal principles of universal application; and there was a general rejection of the 'liberalism' in the famous report of American laymen who investigated missions, and published their findings in a book, *Re-Thinking Missions*[1]. A sharp reaction to *Re-Thinking Missions* appeared at the meeting of the I.M.C. at Madras in 1938, when Dr H. Kraemer produced his forceful *The Christian Message in a Non-Christian World*, which applied the Barthian theology to missionary theory.[2] These two contrasting missiological theories caused considerable stir among all those interested in missions.

Consequently the missionary organizations welcomed the efforts of the Faith and Order Commission, though perhaps they tend to be impatient with the apparently dilatory procedures of the theologians. It is doubtful whether interest in doctrine will decline through a union of the W.C.C. and the I.M.C. At the meeting of the *Ad Interim* Committee of the I.M.C. at Whitby, Ontario, in 1950, the need for 'research' was recognized as involving 'a radical examination of first principles together with a realistic grasp of the facts now confronting missions and churches' and the way was prepared for the joining of the W.C.C. and the I.M.C. in one Division of Study. In further illustration of the attention paid by the I.M.C. to the Faith and Order Commission the 'Findings of the Willingen Meeting of the I.M.C.' in 1952 are relevant. A report on 'The Pattern of Missionary Activity' includes a section headed 'Ecumenical Co-operation': the following paragraphs are extracted from the recommendations of this section:

That Christian councils should consider afresh their responsibility in relation to the cause of Christian unity within their own areas. It is not the purpose of the ecumenical movement to set up an ecclesiastical superstructure, and action in matters

[1] A brief account is given in Professor Latourette's *Expansion of Christianity*, vol. vii, pp. 51–3.

[2] Published in New York and London, 1938. Dr Kraemer has since modified his missiological views somewhat in *Religion and the Christian Faith*, London, 1956. The Right Rev. Sabapathy Kulandran, Bishop of the Church of South India, expressed courteous yet forceful reservations about Kraemer's apparent denial that there is a bridge between Christianity and other religions, cf. 'Kraemer Then and Now', *International Review of Missions*, xlvi, no. 182, April, 1957, pp. 170–81.

of faith and order must remain the responsibility of the churches. Nevertheless within the co-operative activity of the Christian councils the disunity of the churches continues to hinder the fulfilment of the Church's mission.

That the member councils of the International Missionary Council should consider fresh ways of relating their experience and concern for unity to the deliberations and actions of the churches within their membership, and to the Commission on Faith and Order of the World Council of Churches.[1]

The Rev. Charles W. Ranson, General Secretary of the International Missionary Council, in 1953 referred to theological questions affecting the missions and said: 'They are questions on which, in the process of re-thinking, in a modern context, the meaning of the Church's missionary obligation to the world, we greatly need and ardently desire the active collaboration of theological faculties of many lands.'[2]

There is some evidence that the more the missionaries come face to face with the problems involved in establishing a universal Church, the more they tend towards a range of ideas approaching the Orthodox and the Roman Catholic. This is true, I think, of South India; and in Uganda, the Rev. J. V. Taylor, undertaking for the International Missionary Society the first of their studies of the Younger Churches, recommends for the Anglican Church in Uganda the following: a lessening of the Evangelical and Protestant emphasis associated with the earlier days of the mission, in favour of 'Catholic insights', more liturgical life, some form of the confessional, exorcism and a recovery of 'the sense of a supernatural dimension'.[3]

Nevertheless, the fears expressed by some Roman Catholics lest the W.C.C. is tending towards less real interest in unity of doctrine seem to be shared by Dr Visser 't Hooft, who remarked

[1] *Missions Under the Cross:* edited by Norman Goodall—Edinburgh, 1953; p. 224.
[2] 'The Christian World Mission in the Perspective of History', *International Review of Missions*, xliii, no. 172, October, 1955, p. 389.
[3] *International Review of Missions*, xlvi, no. 182, April, 1957, p. 142. The Reverend J. V. Taylor, of the Church of England, formerly Principal of Bishop Tucker College, Uganda, was seconded to the International Missionary Council by the Church Missionary Society for this 'study'. His article is a brief forecast based upon only part of his investigation, but is of unusual interest.

at Oberlin in 1957 that the World Council is engaged in many activities which have no direct relevance to the furtherance of the unity of the Church. Concern for unity, he said, has now become only one of a large number of concerns of the W.C.C. But it is not absolutely evident that integration with the I.M.C. will tend against furtherance of unity, though the change certainly deserves careful study. I have heard and read opinions about the effects of the proposed integration which were obviously based upon imperfect knowledge of the nature of the International Missionary Council and of its past and present relations with the World Council of Churches. Such opinions are not necessarily incorrect, for there may be a kind of intuition which can seize the truth even upon knowledge which seems inadequate; but at the same time it would seem wise to seek information and to base opinions, as far as is possible in such complex matters, upon objectively ascertained facts.

The Voice of the I.M.C.

The International Review of Missions, published quarterly by the I.M.C., has an editorial outlook similar to that shown by Professor K. S. Latourette in his well-known volumes *The Expansion of Christianity*. Its articles, reviews and, above all, bibliographies, which list articles as well as books, make it invaluable to every missiologist. It is certainly as devoted to the cause of Christian unity as is the organ of the W.C.C., *The Ecumenical Review*, and, with an exception to be mentioned, it shows the same attitude towards the Orthodox and the Roman Catholics as does the *Ecumenical Review*. In both, of course, the editors allow contributors to express their own views with freedom and take no responsibility for the views expressed. *The International Missionary Review* almost every year carries a well-informed and sympathetic account of Roman Catholic missionary activities, sometimes written by Roman Catholics,[1] and its references to the Orthodox and to Roman Catholics are generally most acceptable. For instance, the Fordham Conference of Mission Specialists, of 1953, was

[1] For instance, Fr John J. Considine, 'Missions of the Catholic Church, 1948', vol. xxxviii, no. 150, pp. 164–81. Fr Considine is a Maryknoll Missionary.

reported fully, and the Rev. David M. Paton said 'missionaries of other churches will find this conference report of absorbing interest. . . . Rome is in a fertile, creative and almost unpredictable state in many parts of the world to-day, reacting to fresh situations with remarkable elasticity; and (almost) anything is possible in the way not, indeed, of alteration, but of adaptation of order to new circumstances.'[1]

The reviewer of H. Burn-murdoch's *The Development of the Papacy* had an opportunity to express antagonism to Rome, if he felt any. The *Downside* reviewers of the book said that Mr Burn-murdoch's attempt at fairness reminded them of Dr Johnson's reply when asked if he treated the parties fairly in his 'reported' speeches in Parliament: 'Yes, but I took care that the Whig dogs did not have the best of it.'[2] Yet the reviewer in the *International Review of Missions* took occasion to ask whether the ecumenical movement does not involve acceptance of 'the papal principle of a visible centre of unity'. 'From the time of Peter and Paul', said Professor E. R. Hardy of Berkeley Divinity School, New Haven, 'the faith of the Roman Church has been the inspiring centre of much of the Christian mission—a tradition which certainly need not disappear from the Church's memory.'[3]

The *Review* does not fail to criticize, even forcefully, some aspects of Protestant missionary activity and theory.[4] Some Roman Catholic readers, however, may judge that with regard to events in Colombia, the *Review* departed somewhat from its normal objectivity and charity. The editorial *Surveys* of 1952, 1953 and 1954 (which include sympathetic accounts of Roman Catholic missions) record in a regretful tone 'active persecution in Colombia at the instigation of local Roman Catholic

---

[1] 'Missiologists in Conference', *ibid.* xlv, no. 178, pp. 228–9.
[2] Dom Ralph Russell and Dom Cyprian Stockford 'The Development of the Papacy', *Downside Review*, lxii, no. 228, April, 1954, p. 245.
[3] *International Review of Missions*, xliv, no. 176, October, 1955, p. 467.
[4] For instance, Dr Charles W. Ranson, Secretary of the I.M.C., 'In this period it was the forces of the Counter-Reformation which kept alive, within the Church, the vision of a universal missionary obligation. While Francis Xavier was burning himself out in his intense missionary labours in Asia, some Protestant theologians were arguing that the command to preach the Gospel to all nations was given only to the original apostles and expired with them. This view was to persist within Protestantism for more than two centuries.' 'The Christian World Mission in the Perspective of History', *ibid.* xliii, no. 172, October, 1954, p. 383.

leaders'; and the Survey of 1952 speaks of the 'soberly assembled and authenticated documents' circulated by the Evangelical Confederation of Colombia—which Roman Catholics in Colombia and elsewhere regard as nothing less than 'a campaign of calumny'.[1] In the meeting of the Central Committee of the W.C.C. at Lucknow in December, 1952, the Director of the Commission on International Affairs, in reporting to the Committee the difficulties facing his Commission, mentioned requests from certain churches for action about Colombia, but said that 'in a comprehensive approach' there would be need *'of independent verification of reports'* from Colombia (italics mine), and this, together with correlation of publicity efforts and approaches to governments, etc., would be beyond the resources of his Commission. On April 9, 1953, the Central Committee of the W.C.C. asked the Colombian government to inquire about the alleged persecution of Protestant Evangelicals in that country, basing itself upon reports received from the Evangelical Confederation of Colombia. The results of this request, if any, are not known to me. One has the impression that the *Ecumenical Review*, the organ of the W.C.C., was more circumspect in acceptance of the *Bulletins* from the Evangelical Confederation of Colombia than was the *International Review of Missions*, the organ of the I.M.C., but that the feeling was practically the same in both bodies.[2]

---

[1] *International Review of Missions*, xlii, no. 165, January, 1953, p. 51; xliii, no. 169, January, 1954, p. 56; xliv, no. 173, January 1955. Dr Alberto Rembao, Research Consultant of the Committee on Co-operation in Latin America, New York, in an article entitled 'Protestant Latin America: Sight and Insight', makes the statement that in Colombia, Spain, Mexico and Bolivia 'the clergy, as a rule, from archbishops to the parish priests, both officially and in their pastoral letters and orally from their pulpits, have incited the masses to violence against the heretics.' *Ibid.* xlvi, no. 181, January, 1957, p. 34. No proof is given of this astonishing statement. Roman Catholics would question the objectivity of certain other appraisals made in the *Review*: the article 'Evangelical Education in Colombia' by the Rev. Alvin L. Schumaat, Colegio Americano, Bogotá, who takes his statistics from the Evangelical Confederation of Colombia, and the review by Sir Kenneth Grubb, C.M.G., of J. D. Hugley's *Religious Freedom in Spain*, London, 1955, cf. *International Review of Missions*, xliii, no. 172, October, 1954, pp. 429–35 and lxv, no. 178, April, 1956, p. 234. The Rev. Alvin Schumaat is a missionary of the Presbyterian Church in the U.S.A.; Sir Kenneth Grubb, President of the Church Missionary Society, is Chairman of the Commission of the Churches on International Affairs, a joint body of the W.C.C. and the I.M.C.

[2] Obviously more could, and indeed should, be said about the accusations of persecution in Colombia, but this book is not the place for it. About an impartial

Regarding the 'reconstitution' of the World Council of Churches, the legal maxim may be recalled that justice must be done and must appear to be done. There is much ignorance and misunderstanding about both bodies. In the Near East, as Dr Goodall wrote in 1957, the W.C.C. is regarded as representing the Orthodox and the I.M.C. as representing the Evangelicals[1]; in the United States, the connection of certain Mission Boards on the one hand with the I.M.C. and on the other with 'evangelical' bodies whose 'evangelism' in Latin America Catholics regard as often 'a corruption of true Christian witnessing', tends to diminish confidence in the I.M.C.[2] It is unquestionable that certain evangelical bodies regard Roman Catholicism as a pernicious error and Roman

investigation by a visiting Commission appointed for the purpose, I confess that reflection has made me doubtful. It would be difficult to find members trusted by both parties, conversant with Spanish, of a judicial temperament, and with the time and health required. If such could be found, it would be excellent, though their task would not be enviable. Meantime, useful work could be done in collecting and summarizing the publications circulated by the Roman Catholics and by the Evangelical bodies, with attention to their tone and spirit. The publications of Jehovah's Witnesses, for instance, declare the Trinity a myth and a fraud; and an examination of the monthly *Aurora* might throw light upon Roman Catholic resentment, though it is strongly denied that resentment degenerated into persecution. A model which might be used in such examination of publications in Colombia, is the Academic thesis of the Methodist minister, the Rev. Ralph Lloyd Roy, published in 1953, with the title *Apostles of Disruption*, and the subtitle 'a study of organized bigotry and disruption on the fringes of Protestantism'. The Rev. S. M. Berry, Secretary of the International Congregationalist Council, in reviewing the book remarks: 'If in this wild, anarchic scene, one tries to select the more settled antagonisms, it must be admitted that it is *the honoured and trusted leaders of American Protestantism who take the hardest and bitterest knocks*. The old Federal Council of the Churches and the National Council of the Churches which has now taken its place are characterized in language which used to be regarded as the proud possession of Billingsgate. To them are ascribed all the ills which have fallen upon the Church and the nation. They are accused of being Communists in very thin disguise.' Roman Catholics, Jews, Communists and Negroes, of course, come in for their share of vituperation. *International Review of Missions*, xliii, no. 171, July, 1954, p. 357. Italics mine.

[1] Dr Goodall, 'Some Reflections on the Near and Middle East', *International Review of Missions*, xlvi, no. 181, January, 1957, p. 9.

[2] The Presbyterians in Colombia are connected with the U.S. Presbyterian Board of Foreign Missions, and in Colombia with the Evangelical Federation. This latter includes: Assemblies of God; Calvary Holiness Church; Christian and Missionary Alliance; Conference of Mennonite Brethren; Cumberland Presbyterian Mission; Evangelical Union of South America; Foursquare Gospel Mission; Gospel Missionary Union; Independent Evangelical Church of Vallarrica; Independent Gospel Tabernacles of Casanare; Inter-American Mission; Mennonite Mission in Colombia; South American Indian Mission; United Evangelical Tabernacles of Colombia; Wesleyan Methodist Church; World-Wide Evangelical Crusade. Such was the list in 1950; some may have left the Confederation and others joined since that date.

Catholic countries as proper spheres of missionary activity. Whether the integration of the W.C.C. and the I.M.C. would give such bodies a wider influence, or whether it would tend to moderate their anti-Orthodox and anti-Roman zeal, I am unable to judge. It must be frankly acknowledged that both the World Council of Churches and the International Missionary Council are very largely made up of those who in fact are 'Protestant', or, at least, who derive from a 'Protestant' tradition. My own impression is that the Missionary Council is more likely to insist upon universalistic principles, as it is in more concrete touch with non-Christians, than is the World Council, and that therefore fears about 'integration' are not only too late, but unfounded, *considering the concrete situation*. Nevertheless, the objection stands: hitherto the World Council has had for its objective the unification of Christians, and the 'integration' will commit it to a support, however 'ecumenical' and moderate, of agencies which in fact are 'Protestant' and some of which consider it a duty to 'convert' Roman Catholics and Orthodox to 'Protestant principles'. Much will depend upon the language used at the time of the consummation of the 'integration'. If striking declarations were made of absolute ecumenicity and of charity towards all, many misgivings might be allayed, and anxieties relieved, about a possible 'Protestant bloc' in opposition to the Orthodox and the Roman Catholics.

However that may be, the developing character of the World Council shows that the Roman attitude of reserve has been wise.

An 'essential indivisibility'

Apart from questions of organization and of official statements, account must be taken of the intangible yet real connection between various manifestations of ecumenism. Dr Normal Goodall, speaking primarily of the relations between the W.C.C. and the I.M.C. makes an observation which seems to me true in general: 'Behind this historical inter-relatedness of organizations there lies that ecumenical movement which is a movement of thought and spirit which is essentially indivisible.'[1] This may be illustrated in the following examples:

(a) Proposals made for federations, amalgamations or reunions of Churches show a distinct similarity of language to that used in diverse 'ecumenical encounters'; and not seldom the persons who sponsor essays at reconciliation of Churches have been and are active in the ecumenical movement in general. The World Council of Churches takes no responsibility whatever for any proposals or actual 'reunions', and the officials of the World Council have more than once issued warnings against unsound plans and a *Report* was submitted in 1957 at Oberlin renewing the warnings. Nevertheless, when charges are made that such plans or proposals involve compromise of principle, there is a repercussion, in the popular mind, perhaps unjustly, upon the general outlook of the World Council of Churches.

(b) The idea has increasingly been spread that no organized body called a 'Church' fulfils Christ's will for his Church, but that each 'Church' is defective in one way or another and all 'orders' are consequently defective. No 'Church' has what is essential to make the being of the Church, but all have elements which when united together will manifest the 'fulness' of The Church. The word 'fulness' is applied to the ecclesiastical situation in a way that suggests a metaphor derived from the broken pieces of a material object, which have to be joined together in order to restore the whole, almost like scattered bits of a jig-saw puzzle each of which contains parts of a picture but must be put together in order to manifest the 'fulness' of the picture. This use of the term 'fulness' is really unscriptural, for St Paul uses the term as a metaphor drawn from the growth of a human being, which presupposes the individual already living in his essential unity.[2]

---

[1] 'W.C.C. and I.M.C. Relationships: Some Underlying Issues', *Ecumenical Review*, ix, no. 4, p. 397.

[2] The meaning of the term 'fulness' as applied to the Church cannot be ascertained apart from the Pauline meaning of 'the body' and of the nature of the union between Christ and the Church which the metaphor of 'the body' expresses; cf. L. Cerfaux, *La théologie de l'Eglise suivant saint Paul*, Paris, 1948, pp. 235 and 244–8; the Revd. C. F. D. Moule, '"Fulness" and "Fill" in the New Testament', *Scottish Journal of Theology*, iv, no. 1, March, 1951, pp. 79–86; A. Feuillet, 'L'Église Plérôme du Christ d'après Ephés. I, 23', *Nouvelle Revue Théologique*, lxxviii (1950), pp. 449–67 and 593–620. These works contain ample references to other authorities.

It would be most unjust to say that the World Council officially endorses this idea that the Church of Christ is dispersed among many different bodies and hence no longer exists in the essential nature which Christ gave it and continues to give it. At the same time, the use of such expressions as 'Churches in the *full* sense of the word' and the constant expression 'manifestation of unity' suggest that the idea of 'Churches in a partial sense' is not alien to that 'movement of thought and spirit' which, as Dr Goodall says, is 'indivisible'. The use of polite language ought not be pressed and interpreted in strict legal fashion to force from it enunciation of a theory, when those who use the language explicitly disclaim the intention of propounding or presupposing any theory whatever; nevertheless, the use of such language and the practical necessity to treat all 'Churches' as being independent and equal, inevitably carries with it the suggestion that no one body constitutes by itself alone the Church which Christ willed.

(*c*) Within the Council there is a radical difference of outlook between those who favour 'liberty of the spirit' and those who favour authority embodied in visible form, as in bishops, and who favour greater adherence to tradition.[1] How these different outlooks will be reconciled is as yet uncertain. If the movement for 'unity' advances, the result may be the formation of 'federations' of Churches upon a vague doctrinal basis which may perpetuate real divisions, or, conceivably, it might be the formation of unions or a union with a doctrinal basis sufficiently firm to make a real unity and sufficiently vital to permit growth towards the universalistic position. The World Council has said that it exists in order to bring about the death of the denominations, and that is an admirable aim. But it is not yet clear into what grave the denominations

[1] Cf., for instance, the views expressed by Professor Walter M. Horton—not to be confused with Professor Douglas M. Horton, of Harvard Divinity School, recently elected chairman of the Faith and Order Commission—and by Dr Winifred E. Garrison in *The Nature of the Church, Papers presented to the Theological Commission appointed by the Continuation Committee of the World Conference on Faith and Order*, ed. R. Newton Flew, London, 1952, pp. 278–9, 287–8; cf., also, D. Jenkins, *Tradition and the Spirit*, London, 1951, S. C. Hendry, *The Holy Spirit in Christian Theology*, London, 1957 and *Glasgow Speaks, A reply to the Joint Report on Anglican-Presbyterian Relations*, 1959, pp. 9 and 11.

will be buried or what will be the form of their resurrected body.

Such uncertainties and obscurities must influence the Roman Catholic Church in regulating her attitude towards the World Council of Churches. The uncertainties and obscurities are not created by the leaders of the ecumenical movement but are elements of a sad situation with which every Christian body has to deal; and the fact that the Roman Catholic Church judges wiser a policy of official aloofness indicates only that she is acutely aware of the inherent difficulties of the situation and of the obligations which it places upon her, without in any way reflecting upon the sincerity and aims of those whose theological convictions and general situation are different.

Lastly, there is the practical consideration that Rome's lack of desire for official participation saves the leaders of the World Council from considerable embarrassment. 'Some Churches', said Dr Tomkins, 'hold that the Church of Rome has so far departed from the truth of the Gospel that no other attitude can be taken up towards it than that of resolute and uncompromising opposition. Such contacts as the ecumenical movement has had with the Roman Catholic Church have exposed it to criticism from some of the more strongly Evangelical bodies, and have been among the reasons advanced by them for not joining the World Council of Churches. Other Churches and groups . . . feel that until Rome is other than she is her co-operation would represent rather a danger than an advantage. . . . There are, however, many in the constituency of the World Council of Churches who would agree with the line taken by such ecclesiastical statesmen as Archbishop Davidson and Archbishop Söderblom—that the very life-blood of the modern ecumenical movement is the search for fellowship with all those who name the name of Christ with sincerity; that therefore the door to co-operation with Rome must at all times and in every possible way be kept open.'[1] Dr Tomkins was writing of the state of things up to the year 1948, but the tone of the Theological Commission on *The Church* and of the Toronto Statement of 1950 gives no hint of a

[1] *History of the Ecumenical Movement*, pp. 686–7.

decrease in the number or the influence of those who agree with the line taken by Archbishop Davidson and Archbishop Söderblom. Yet, all told, the aloofness of the Roman Catholic Church probably saves embarrassing discussion in the World Council.

A Catholic, conscious of the unity of his own Church, sees among his separated brethren unity in desire and in effort, but bewildering disunity in fact. Those outside the World Council are split into countless sects; those within are also divided: Orthodox and 'Protestant', episcopalian and non-episcopalian, presbyterian and congregational, 'evangelical' and 'liberal'. Within the denominations individuals and groups are deeply divided. A Catholic, viewing these divisions with sincere grief, cannot even appear to approve principles from which he believes disunity springs, or neglect of principles on which alone he believes unity can subsist.

There are, however, reasons for hope: the widespread conviction that divided Christendom is contrary to God's will and is a scandal; constant appeals for prayer and for repentance; a renewal in religious studies, biblical, doctrinal, liturgical, ascetic and historical; a greater share taken by the laity in the apostolate; interest in forms of Christian worship and readiness to make changes; growing respect and understanding among Christians, fostered by diverse frank and charitable 'encounters', personal and written; appreciation of the non-doctrinal factors causing divisions, and of the urgency of Christian consolidation in the face of the growing preponderance of non-Christians in the world. These signs are solidly hopeful.

Recently Professor Oscar Cullmann has called attention to another aspect of the problem of disunity: the need of renunciation and of self-sacrifice in the cause of unity. No community can be united without self-sacrifice. Christianity was founded by the sacrifice of Christ, and without share in that self-giving no one can rightly claim the name of Christian.

Chapter Seven

CATHOLIC PRINCIPLES RELATIVE TO ECUMENISM

The first and universal principle which must guide individual Christians and the Christian Church is the principle of charity: the love of God and the love of our neighbour. Christ declared: 'On these two commandments, all the law and the prophets depend.' St Peter admonishes: 'But above all things have a constant mutual charity among yourselves, for charity covers a multitude of sins.' St Paul says: 'If I should speak with the tongues of men and angels, but have not charity, I have become as sounding brass or a tinkling cymbal.'

Charity is a gift of God, for to love God is his gift to us; and this gift is closely connected with the gift of wisdom. St Thomas Aquinas well says: '*Blessed are the peacemakers, for they shall be called the children of God*. Peacemaking, which brings peace to oneself and others, is the fruit of wisdom. It is the result of setting values in their proper order, for peace, says Augustine, is the tranquillity of order. To set things in order is wisdom's office; its role is eirenical.'

Amid the multitude of conflicting opinions about the causes and the cure of the divisions among Christians the need of wisdom is thrown into clearer relief; charity must be wise, for charity must extend real and not apparent good things to others.

The attitude of the Catholic Church towards the ecumenical movement is based, in my best judgement, upon the charity of true wisdom; and has been guided by principles which are sometimes unknown and sometimes misunderstood. To state them in brief form, even without justification of them, may help towards clearness and towards 'the tranquillity of order' which is the eirenic role of wisdom guided by charity. What seems to some to be harsh intransigence is only humble faith-fulness to belief about the nature of Christ's union with his Church.

1. THE FOUNDATION BY CHRIST OF ONLY ONE CHURCH

THE ROMAN CATHOLIC CHURCH CLAIMS TO BE AND IS THE ONLY HOLY CATHOLIC AND APOSTOLIC CHURCH FOUNDED BY JESUS CHRIST

The claim to be the one sole Church of Christ is not made exclusively by the Roman Catholic Church; the Orthodox Church makes it, and only in comparatively recent times have Churches ceased to make it. It is hard to see how the claim can fail to be made by any Christian body which believes that it derives from Christ its commission to teach 'all things what-soever I have commanded you' and to bring all men into Christ's flock.

Christ founded only one Church. 'Upon this rock I will build my Church and the gates of hell shall not prevail against it.'[1] That Church is to have one faith, just as it has one Lord and one baptism and one God[2]; and it is to be 'the pillar and ground of truth'[3]. Faith comes by hearing and the hearing comes through the Church; as the faith is to be enduring through the centuries, the hearing of the Church must be enduring through the centuries, and so the Church must be reliable. Christ promised that it would be reliable: 'behold I am with you all days, even to the consummation of the world.' 'But the Advocate, the Holy Spirit, whom the Father will send in my name, he will teach you all things, and bring to your mind whatever I have said to you.'

Unhappily, the multiplications of 'denominations' has obscured this plain fact that Christ founded only one Church. A number of 'Churches' claim to be the one Church, and confusion of mind arises, so that some have recourse to an 'eschatological' fulfilment of Christ's promises, since they do not see which among so many claimants is the genuine heir of the promises. Yet is a multitude of claimants any reason to deny that one claim can be true and to affirm that all claims

---

[1] Matt. 16: 18.   [2] Eph. 4: 5.   [3] 1 Tim. 3: 15.

8

must be false? Miss Helle Georgiadis, of the Orthodox Church, speaking of the exclusive claims made both by Rome and the Orthodox Church, makes a remark which is astringent but bracing:

> Many people argue that because the Orthodox and the Church of Rome both claim to be *the* Church, it follows that neither claim can be wholly true if true at all, an argument which is commonly used against the papacy on the grounds that at a certain time in history two rival 'popes' both claimed to be the supreme pontiff.
>
> This way of thinking, if one can call it thinking, is an evasion of the problem at issue. For if two men claim to be the father of the same child it does not mean that the child has more than one father, nor that it is altogether unnecessary to have a father at all. The difficulty in determining which claim is true cannot affect in any way the actual relationship of the real father to the child.[1]

It is one measure of widespread doctrinal 'haziness'[2] that this claim to be alone the one Church of Christ is regarded by so many as arrogant. At Evanston some who were present at the meetings could scarcely bring themselves to believe that the Orthodox really meant what they said, and were depressed when they realized that the Orthodox were in earnest.

The claim of the Orthodox and the Roman Catholics has, of course, many difficulties to meet. But still greater difficulties face those who admit Christ's divinity, admit his promises to the Church, and then attempt to say that all Churches are wrong. There is no escape in applying Christ's promises only to the 'eschatological' church and not to the 'empirical' church. Scripture, in spite of one or two obscure texts, gives this theory no support; the promises were made to the new

---

[1] 'Orthodoxy, Rome and Oecumenism', *Eastern Churches Quarterly*, xv, no. 8, Winter 1956–7, p. 347. This article is a defence of 'traditional ecclesiology' and contains many most penetrating observations.

[2] The word was used by the Rev. A. G. Reynolds, of the United Church of Canada, speaking at a Board Meeting, February 24, 1955; Dr Reynolds also said that many Protestants were 'tiring of the unchartered freedom of churches with practically no discipline', cited in Irené Beaubien's excellent account of the Catholic Inquiry Forum of Montreal, entitled *Towards Christian Unity in Canada, A Catholic Approach*, Montreal, 1956, p. 26.

people of God', to the flock of Christ. Others imply that all churches are partly right and partly wrong but still make a combination which fulfils Christ's promises. The logic of this is not evident. The older 'branch theory' has been dropped, probably because it is associated with 'Ritualism' and 'Puseyism' and because the Orthodox, the Roman Catholics and the Evangelicals repudiated the metaphor, aware that it did not fit the facts. Yet the metaphor had the advantage of being drawn from a living thing, which manifests unity amid variety, and which grows.

The expressions more recently used to escape the difficulty is 'givenness of unity' and 'manifestation of unity', 'unity in Christ', and 'disunity as Churches'. The expressions to some extent meet the present situation, in which there is great good will and devotion to Christ, yet almost insuperable difficulties in attaining outward visible unity. Dr Visser 't Hooft has said: 'Our task is to speak adequately about the intermediate situation which while having a real unity we have not that greater unity which Christ desires us to have. In other words, we need a theology of the abnormal situation in which we are today.'

The Orthodox and the Roman Catholics welcome such declarations that the present religious situation is 'abnormal'. They understand, at least to some extent, the distressing problems with which ecumenists have to deal and appreciate the need of patience. Yet 'a theology of the abnormal situation', if it seems convincing or persuasive, may tend to 'a static conception of inter-church relations' and to maintenance of the *status quo*. The Orthodox and the Roman Catholics do not believe that there can be such a thing as a satisfactory theology of this abnormal situation. Their position with regard to one another is clear: the Church is the pillar and ground of truth, and therefore if one or the other Church teaches even one false doctrine, it has thereby ceased to be the Church of Christ, however many truths it may have preserved. The difficulty of determining what doctrine is false is no reason for denying the principle that Christ's Church must not teach a single false doctrine and must not fail to teach all that Christ willed his Church to teach.

The Orthodox, then, and the Roman Catholics do not consider themselves either impatient or arrogant in insisting that only one Church can be the one holy apostolic Church of Christ. Nor do they consider that they are governed by an inhuman logic unrelated to the actual situation of divided Christendom; they feel convinced that the situation ought to be made to conform to the theology of the Church and not the theology of the Church made to conform to the situation. In this, they judge that they are following the will of Christ for his Church and that to 'hedge' in any way on their claims would be a betrayal of Christ, and a betrayal of the duty which they have to separated brethren whom they love in Christ.

2. The Visible and Recognizable Unity of Christ's Church

THE CATHOLIC CHURCH BELIEVES THAT CHRIST WILLED HIS CHURCH TO HAVE SUCH A VISIBLE UNITY THAT MEN CAN SEE IN IT A SIGN OF HIS INVISIBLE PRESENCE IN THE CHURCH

The ecumenical movement has brought clearer perception that the unity which Christ willed for his Church is a recognizable unity, such as can lead non-Christians to the truth of Christianity. In the New Testament the Church is designated under a multitude of images: the body of Christ, the bride of Christ, the kingdom of Christ, the people of God, the new Israel, the holy nation, the royal priesthood, the temple of God, the vine, the sheep-fold, the family and household of God, the net, the tree, the seed, the sole ark of salvation, and many others also. All of these imply a visible cohesion. In a remarkably clear and penetrating article, Dr J. Robert Nelson, after commenting upon the study of these images which is going on, proceeds:

Such study can well serve the cause of unity in so far as we always keep in mind the concrete, historical reality of the Church for which these images stand, and do not indulge in such unreal speculations about it as these would seem to permit. When the Bible speaks of members of the body, of living stones, branches, sheep, salt, light and leaven, it refers basically and simply to human beings who are inwardly transformed by the power of

Christ and united with him. When these figurative words are supplemented by such human images as saints, pilgrims, slaves and disciples, it is still the flesh-and-blood members of the Church who are designated. This is to say that the biblical figures of speech do not refer to a Church which is figurative and fanciful, wholly invisible and therefore docetic, but to the visible and sensible Church of which our countless congregations and members are living parts.[1]

Dr Nelson does not mean to imply, I think, that all members of all congregations are living parts of Christ's one Church, but only to insist that Scriptural images of the Church are meant to apply to the Church as visible, and not merely as invisible.

In this application of the Scriptural images to the Church as a visible 'empirical' body there is a mystery involved. As the mystery, and the 'scandal', of Christ lies in the unity which he has *as man* with the Father, so, too, the essential mystery of the Church, and the 'scandal' of the Church, lies in the unity which the Church, as a visible institution and a corporate human entity, has with God in Christ. The mystery is not so much the union of the triumphant Church with Christ as the union of the militant earthly Church with God in Christ.

The union of Christ with the Church is not exclusively a union of human beings 'who are inwardly transformed by the power of Christ', but is a union which remains essentially unchanged in spite of the sinners and hidden hypocrites in the Church. Most Christian Churches have rejected the Donatist heresy, which makes the visible Church a congregation of people who are in the grace of God, but not all accept the implications of a rejection of Donatism. Sinners and hypocrites can remain members of the mystical body, and,—an implication which few outside the Roman Catholic Church accept,—sinners and hypocrites can *become* members of the mystical body. The Donatist position can scarcely be rejected by the

[1] 'Many Images of the One Church', *Ecumenical Review*, ix, no 2, January, 1957, p. 108. Dr Nelson is a Methodist. He gives a warning against urging unduly any one image, to the neglect of the implications of other images, and I conjecture that he would think that the Roman Catholic Church lays undue emphasis upon the images which suggest organization, but this is, of course, the merest conjecture.

sole evidence of Scripture; how prove from Scripture alon
that 'the unworthiness of the Ministers hinders not the effect o
the sacraments'?[1] Unconsciously many assume that member
ship in the mystical body of Christ means the inward tran
formation which Catholics call 'sanctifying grace'; but th
fact must be faced that the union of Christ with the Churc
means union with a body which contains sinners as well a
saints.[2]

On the question of 'membership' in the Church too muc
attention seems to me to have been paid to the question of th
salvation of individuals. It is now generally admitted tha
individuals can be saved without visible union with the Churc
but it is not sufficiently realized, or preached, that peop

[1] On the supposition that the effect of the sacraments is exclusively psychol
gical, the unworthiness of the minister need not hinder the effect; but less and le
is the purely 'psychological' theory of the effect of the sacraments being ma
tained. For a discussion of the implications of St Augustine's stand against t
Donatists, cf. *Principles of Sacramental Theology*, chs., 4, 5 and 6.

[2] Anglican theologians of the eighteenth century were well aware of the teachi
that the Holy Spirit is the soul of the Church. Waterland cites with approval t
following from Sherlock's *Vindication of the Defence of Stillingfleet*: 'And it must ma
a *fundamental Change* in the Doctrine of divine Grace and Assistance, to deny t
Divinity of the Holy Spirit. For, can a *Creature* be the *universal* Spring and Founta
of divine Grace and Life? Can a finite *Creature* be a kind of *universal* Soul to t
whole Christian Church, and to every sincere member of it? Can a *Creature* ma
such close Application to our Minds, know our Thoughts, set Bounds to o
Passions, inspire us with new Affections and Desires, and be more intimate to
than we are to ourselves?' (*Sic*). It is noteworthy that Sherlock and Waterla
take as an accepted fact that the Holy Spirit is a soul 'to the whole Christi
Church and to every sincere member of it'. They distinguish the action of t
Holy Spirit on the Church as a whole and upon the members of the Churc
the action of the Holy Spirit is restricted, in the latter case, to 'sincere' membe
Cf. Daniel Waterland, *The Importance of the Doctrine of the Trinity asserted in Re
to some late Pamphlets*, London, 1734, pp. 62–3.

[3] There is an admirable discussion of Roman Catholic teaching on the po
in Dr Newton Flew's account of the Roman Catholic Church in *The Nature
the Church*, London, 1952, pp. 33–40. And cf. H. de Lubac, *The Splendour of
Church*, London, 1956, pp. 77–8, especially note 1, p. 78. A more detailed accou
is given by R. Lombardi, *The Salvation of the Unbeliever*, English translation
Dorothy M. White, London, 1956. Christian salvation, of course, is neither pur
individual nor purely other-worldly; we are saved in this world from fears a
superstitions and hatreds, and saved through our relationships with others. '
Christ said 'This night they will require *thy* soul of thee', and each one will
judged, to go to everlasting life or to the second death. Unhappily the doctrine
the judgement often degenerates into the question: 'how many others will
condemned?' The real question is: '*I*, do *I* deserve to be condemned?' It is a
how many other people go to damnation, but that *I* may go to damnation. '
have, of course, boundless trust in the goodness of God and the merits of Chr
trust that excludes worry and anxiety; but even St Paul chastized his body a
brought it into subjection lest having preached to others he should be disquali
in the contest for eternal life. I Cor. 9: 27.

can be damned who have lived all their lives in the visible Church, though we may devoutly hope that none are. This means that God's grace has a broader incidence than the sanctification of individuals as individuals; in view of the sanctification of the body it is given to those who as individuals may be unworthy and wicked. In this sense it is correct to speak of the enlightenment of the common mind. There is deep significance in the expression *sensus Ecclesiae*, the mind and feeling of the Church, of which the *sensus fidelium*, the instinctive judgement of the faithful, is one criterion, and of which the bishops and the chief bishop are the authentic spokesmen. That unified mind and feeling is one important element in the union which the Church, as a Church and not merely as a conglomeration of individuals, has with Christ. Fr Charles Davis has well said: 'The true vision of the Church's teaching authority sees it in the mystery of the Mystical Body.'[1] A sinner still remains a member of the mystical body and may still retain faith and hope, even though he has lost charity.

This doctrine is very practical, especially in the lands of the Younger Churches. Preaching based upon the 'salvation experience' or upon the 'I-Thou' relation to God or upon the 'personal response' to God, though these have an element of truth, nevertheless may lay stress upon the union of the will and feelings with God and tend to overlook the union of the intellect with God. Yet in sin, the intellect may still retain a certain true union with God which can be used by God to help the return of the whole man to God. This is the basis of the sacrament of penance, rejection of which inevitably lessens the importance of the visible Church. Men sin and know that they sin. If they can return to God independently of his visible Church, the conclusion must be that they can in general be saved without the visible Church. The sacrament of baptism, if carefully examined, implies the sacrament of penance; for without the sacrament of penance, baptism must either make Christians sinless for the future—which is false to experience —or else declare that in a Christian sins are unimportant. The truth is that neither sins before baptism nor after baptism can be remitted, in normal circumstances, without recourse

[1] *Clergy Review*, xxxviii, 1953, p. 411.

to Christ, and to Christ in his visible Church. The result of rejection of this sacrament is that in sophisticated lands the psychologist undertakes the exorcism of 'guilt-complexes', and in the lands of the Younger Churches many 'tumble-down half-Christians', as the Rev. J. V. Taylor calls them, fall into practical despair and feel that 'Christ is too much for us'. True, 'Anglicans say, "God will forgive me"; Roman Catholics say, "The priest will release me". One of the most universally acknowledged attributes of the Christian God is that "He does not get angry".'[1] Yet well-trained and devoted confessors can do much for such people and can help them against the practical despair of giving up the struggle. Probably there are too few such confessors, for missionary priests are all too few and are overburdened; but the basis of the real help lies not in the qualities of the individual confessor and director, though he needs a sound instruction and training, but, ultimately, in the firm belief that God acts through him and in the knowledge that all confessors have the same law by which to judge. Here is one very practical application of the doctrine that the visible church consists of sinners as well as of saints. Among Lutherans and among the French Reformed the practice of confession is increasing.

Catholic belief is that the unity of the Church, though it may shine forth with differing degrees of clearness at different periods of the Church's history and even in different regions, remains nevertheless always sufficient to be a means by which non-Christians and dissident Christians can perceive that the cohesion, taken in its entirety, cannot be accounted for unless Christ, the Son of God, has been and is with the Church. Christ's prayer was 'that they also may be one in us: *that the world may believe that thou hast sent me.*' 'The unity of the Church in God', says Professor C. K. Barrett in his *The Gospel according to St John*,[2] 'is the supreme testimony to the truth of the claim that Jesus is God's authorized emissary. The existence of such a community is a supernatural fact that can be explained only as a result of a supernatural cause.'

[1] 'The Uganda Church To-Day. Some Impressions Gained During the First of the "Younger Church Studies"', *International Review of Missions*, xlvi, no. 182, p. 139.
[2] London, 1955, p. 427.

The union of Christ and the Father is not only a union of love but is a union also of intellect and understanding: 'my doctrine is not mine but his who sent me'[1], 'the things I have heard of him, these same I speak in the world',[2] 'I do nothing of myself, but as the Father hath taught me, these things I speak'[3] and 'Do you not believe that I am in the Father, and the Father in me? The words I speak to you, I speak not of myself, but the Father who abideth in me, he doth his own works.'[4] So too the union of Christians who abide in Christ and in the Father must be a union of intellect and of understanding and not merely a union of charity—if, indeed, it is possible to maintain a union of charity where there is discord of mind. The Catholic insistence upon the primacy of union in faith and in doctrine is based upon the Scriptural teaching that Christ is the Word of God, the Light of the world, the revealer of the Father, the bestower of the Spirit of truth: and that is one main reason why the Church from its earliest days regarded true doctrine as essential to union with Christ: 'We are of God. Whoever knows God listens to us, and he who is not of God does not listen to us. By this we know the spirit of truth and the spirit of error.'[5]

One of the most striking Scriptural images of the Church is an image not resting upon the comparison to a lifeless construction which can be broken up into parts and then reassembled, but the image of a living man, who may be disfigured, sick, bruised and wounded, but who always retains his recognizable identity. The Catholic Church has readily admitted her need of 'reform'. Some of her most loyal children have declared the need of reform in forceful language[6] and the usual term 'Counter-Reformation' expresses a reality. Yet the 'reform' was never conceived as the unification of different elements to make manifest what had become invisible or unrecognizable, but the restoration to good condition of a being whose identity was never in question. The present efforts to bring 'unity to the Churches' is an implicit admission that the principles from which have derived such diversity of

[1] John 7: 16.   [2] John 8: 26.   [3] John 8: 28.
[4] John 14: 10.   [5] I John 4: 6, Revised Standard Version.
[6] De Lubac gives some striking citations in *The Splendour of the Church*, pp. 213–14.

convictions about the nature of Christ's Church must have been mistaken.

Here lies a cruel dilemma for ecumenists. They are obliged to affirm that 'we are united in Christ' and yet that 'we are divided as Churches'. Many are acutely aware that these two assertions are almost contradictory to one another, and aware that insistence upon 'our unity in Christ' may tend to perpetuate' our 'disunity as Churches', and that insistence upon 'disunity as Churches' may tend to lessen 'unity in Christ'. Many see that unity in Christ cannot exist except in unity with his one holy catholic Church, and consequently speak in a way which seems to Catholics to be confused: they appear to assert that oneness in Christ has never been lost and imply that this oneness is visible, and yet they insist that visible unity is Christ's will and is something still to be attained. I do not say this to score a debating point, but rather to stress the need, often stressed by ecumenists, and notably by Dr Visser 't Hooft, for most serious study and thinking on this fundamental issue.

Catholic belief is clear: the essential unity of Christ's Church has not been and cannot be lost; and that unity is recognizable as a sign of Christ's presence. Individuals, of course, and even groups may in fact not recognize it. But the same is true of the claims of Christianity itself and few Christians would admit that these claims are in themselves so obscure as to be unrecognizable.

3. The Unity of the Roman Catholic Church

THE ROMAN CATHOLIC CHURCH HAS A VISIBLE AND A MANIFEST UNITY. THE VISIBILITY INCLUDES OUTWARD PROFESSION OF THE SAME FAITH BY ALL MEMBERS, THE SAME SEVEN SACRAMENTS, OBEDIENCE BY ALL TO THE VISIBLE HEAD OF THE CHURCH, AND THE CONTINUITY OF THE BISHOPS NOT ONLY IN MATERIAL SUCCESSION BUT ALSO IN FULL SACRAMENTAL AND DOCTRINAL SUCCESSION.

Few would deny that the Roman Catholic Church has a visible unity; but non-Catholics would say that such unity is not the unity which Christ willed for this Church. Many hold that the Roman Catholic Church has corrupted the true doctrine of Christ; many deny that there are more than two sacraments; many deny legitimate succession in the case of the bishops who, they think, have corrupted the work of God, or deny the need of sacramental succession; and almost without exception non-Catholics repudiate the authority of the Pope. To enter into controversy on all these subjects is far from the purpose of this book; but two observations may be made:

First, the unified existence of the Roman Catholic Church is a phenomenon which merits the serious consideration of all sincere Christians, especially of those who seek the unity of Christendom. The Roman Catholic system is often rejected out of hand as being an obvious imposture, or as being a 'rigid institutional structure' foreign to the true spirit of the Gospel. On the other hand, not all Catholic apologetic has full exactness and discrimination. For instance, Catholics often point out that though there are a multitude who reject the Catholic Church, still they urge contrary and often contradictory reasons. Opponents vary from the Orthodox and the Anglo-Catholic, who accept all save the primacy of jurisdiction of the Pope, down to the 'black' Protestant who rejects a thing merely because it seems to him to be 'popish'. Some say the Catholic Church is too strict, others that it is too lax; some that Rome exerts too rigid a control over her subjects, others that she does not, especially in certain countries, exert control enough. Some say the Catholic Church is sunk in old-fashioned traditional ways, others that she introduces new doctrines; some that she neglects Scripture, others that she holds too closely to the 'propositions' of Scripture. Some say her corruption began in the third century, others in the sixth, others in the tenth, others in the twelfth, and others only at the Council of Trent. Some in reality accept seven outward ceremonies as means of grace, others entirely reject all outward observances as confining the Spirit. In short, the objections cancel one another out.

Now such a method of apologetic may give pause to an opponent who has not really made a thorough analysis of his objections to Rome, and it may lessen the imposing effect of an apparent *consensus* against Rome. Yet it does not prove that none of the objections are founded, for among contradictory and conflicting reasons one may be true. Nor does it prove that there may not be a revulsion correct in substance yet difficult to make precise in particular; for as the Catholic faith holds together as a whole, so the rejection may be of the whole, without, so to say, specification of the parts: although no particular point of rejection may in itself be conclusive, still it is the convergence of various lines of argument and the emotional consistency (and not all emotion is wrong) which moves the mind, just as it is the convergence of various lines of thought and their consistency which moves a believer to believe, as Father M. C. D'Arcy so well points out in *The Nature of Belief*. This, of course, makes the apologetic problem in some respects more difficult; but the argument from contrary and contradictory reasons should not, I think, be urged as more than a reason why the Roman position should be examined impartially and as a whole.

Similarly, arguments from the suitability of having an authority in the Church should not be pressed unduly. Sometimes Catholics urge that a visible body must have a visible head; but this might be to lay too much stress upon one image, forgetting the rest of the images which Scripture uses to describe the Church. The authority of the Church derives from no human reason of convenience or of suitability; it derives from the will of Christ, or else it has no Christian foundation. Pope Leo XIII pointed this out very clearly in his Encyclical on the Unity of the Church. Speaking of the external principle which should secure correct interpretation of Scripture, he said: 'Assuredly the infinite power of God is not bound by anything; all things obey it as so many passive instruments. In regard to this external principle, therefore, we must enquire which one of all the means in His power Christ did actually adopt.'

And, again, speaking of the authority which the Church is to have, 'the nature of this supreme authority, which all Christians are bound to obey, can be assertained only by finding out what was the evident and positive will of Christ.'[1]

[1] *The Great Encyclical Letters of Pope Leo XIII*, New York, 1906, pp. 360-1 and 372.

Pope Leo XIII, of course, did not mean to say that each individual is reduced to investigating Scripture for himself in order to discover what was Christ's will. On the contrary, it is possible to come to see Christ's will fulfilled in the Church by a variety of perceptions, and by the perception of the characteristics of the Church as manifesting a more than human power at work. But Pope Leo XIII did mean that the Church cannot be considered apart from Christ: in him and with him and through him are all things, and without him is made nothing in the Church. The unity of the Church is indeed visible, knowable, susceptible of a certain 'proof' from observation and reason. But this is not the unity of the Church in which we *believe*. When St Thomas said to our Lord: 'My Lord and my God', Christ answered; 'Because thou hast seen me, Thomas, thou hast believed. Blessed are they that have not seen, and have believed.'[1] What Thomas saw was the visible body of Christ, with the glorious wounds; what he believed— and he did believe—was the divinity which he did not see. Similarly, we see the visible unity of the Church in the earthly order, and that gives us reasonable ground on which we can make our act of faith in Christ as one with the Church, that is, in the invisible presence of Christ in the Church. The unity of the Church is a *sign*, which, like the 'signs' that Christ manifested during his earthly life, lead us on to believe in the things to which the signs point.

Granted, however, that some attacks upon the Roman Catholic Church and some defences of it have lacked sobriety, it still remains true that that Church is a phenomenon unique in religious history and unique in the religious world of today. How does it happen that so many millions are united in the same faith and in loving obedience to the same authority? The more corrupt the doctrine, the more surprising that so many who are not unintelligent accept it; the more arbitrary or unfounded is the authority, the more astonishing that it should be so widely obeyed and so warmly defended. The Roman Catholic Church is, contrary to hasty assertions, less 'clerical' than the major Protestant denominations, that is, the proportion of the laity to the clergy is greater than among

[1] John 20: 29.

Protestants, and this is particularly true in the British Isles and the United States, where the proportion of practising lay people to the number of the clergy is higher than among non-Catholic Christians. And, especially in English-speaking countries, it is noteworthy that the Roman Church has been loved most and served perhaps most effectively by those who, like Newman, were brought up in an entirely different tradition.

The second observation on the existing unity of the Roman Catholic Church is this: a Catholic's feelings for the Church are very like the feelings of the members of a family for one another, perhaps especially the feeling of a son towards his mother, about which men rarely speak. Catholics, of course, are very numerous and have astonishingly different outlooks, even on spiritual matters. Yet 'Confession and Holy Communion' convey to all much of the same sense of the mystery of life, of the contradiction of losing life to find it, of being taken into Christ's self-giving and Christ's obedience to the Father in the Spirit of love. Many non-Catholics, thank God, have great reverence for the Sacrament which has deep and tender meaning for them; but for the Catholic the Eucharist is more closely connected with the Church. 'Let a man prove himself and so let him eat of that bread and drink of that chalice. For he that eateth and drinketh unworthily, eateth and drinketh judgement unto himself not discerning the body of the Lord.' A Catholic 'proves himself' in the Church. If he had committed a serious sin, he would, before Holy Communion, go to Christ in the Church that he might receive forgiveness from one to whom he confesses as to Christ: 'Receive the Holy Ghost, whose sins you shall forgive they are forgiven.'

The Catholic feeling towards the Church is one of glad union with the mind of the Church. When he recites the hymn *Gloria in excelsis Deo*, he says: 'For thou only art holy, thou only art the Lord'; but he understands that Christ is holy in the Church, is the Lord in the Church. In uniting his mind with the mind of the Church, a Catholic no more feels that he is resigning 'his power of personal decision' or his liberty as a child of God than Peter did when he said:

'To whom else shall we go? Thou hast the words of eternal life.' A Catholic believes that Christ in the Church has the words of eternal life. 'Thou art the Christ, the Son of the living God.'

Such a union with Christ in the Church lifts human judgement to union with the judgement of Christ, which no man can accuse of lack of independence as regards this world. 'But we have the mind of Christ', said Paul, than whom no one was more bold in rejecting the foolishness of human wisdom. St Athanasius stood alone against the world, than whom no one was more affectionate, no one keener in detecting the subtle fallacies of a worldly wisdom or more zealous in making plain and manifest the truth of Christ. The Church is a home and we are children with the freedom of the children of God, knowing that the Spirit breathes where he wills, but knowing, too, that he will never breathe against the Word through whom he, the Spirit, is sent. 'But when the Paraclete cometh, whom I will send you from the Father, the Spirit of truth, who proceedeth from the Father, he shall give testimony of me. And you shall give testimony.' A Catholic believes that the Holy Spirit is with the Church, and that consequently in the Church he can learn of Christ, who is meek and humble of heart, but yet who alone knoweth the Father and reveals the Father to us in the Church. 'You shall know the truth and the truth shall make you free'; it is the truth in the Church and freedom in the Church.[1]

[1] In recent years no one has expressed better the feelings of a Catholic towards the Church than Père de Lubac, *The Splendour of the Church*, in ch. vii, 'Mater Ecclesia', pp. 174–207, which glows with humility, wisdom and charity. The book is a mine of useful references, but would be greatly improved in usefulness by the addition of an index. Chanoine Gustave Thils in *Les notes de l'Église dans l'apologétique catholique depuis la Réforme*, Gembloux, 1937, gives a bibliography of some 35 pages and contains most interesting matter about Catholic explanations of the notes or marks of the Church. *L'Église est Une*, Paris, 1939, ed. Pierre Chaillet, contains a series of essays by MM. Sertillanges, Adam, Goyau, Bardy, Bihlmeyer, Ranft, Geiselmann, Loesch, De Montcheuil, Congar, Tyszkiewicz, Bierneisel, Pribilla, Jungmann, and has useful matter, but is now a little 'dated'. Cf., also, Dupont, J. *Sun Christoi, l'union avec le Christ suivant S. Paul*, Bruges, 1952; Braun, F. M., *Aspects nouveaux du problème de l'Église*, Paris, 1942, Tyszkiewicz, S., *La sainteté de l'Église christoconforme*, Rome, 1945; Jaki, S., *Les tendences nouvelles de l'ecclésiologie*, Roma, 1957, especially pp. 139–50, on the impact of ecumenism on Catholic ecclesiology. Jaki's summary of C. Lialine's comments on eirenic methods is most useful. Much fruitful work is published in periodicals devoted to Scripture, such as *Biblica, Revue Biblique*, etc., but I cannot attempt to list it all.

4. Missions, Religious Liberty and Proselytism

THE ROMAN CATHOLIC CHURCH DOES NOT SEEK UNITY FOR HERSELF, BUT SHE IS OBLIGED BY HER COMMISSION FROM CHRIST TO TRY, WITH CHRISTIAN ZEAL AND PRUDENCE, TO DRAW OTHERS INTO THE UNITY WHICH CHRIST HAS GIVEN AND PRESERVED.

'The lost treasure of Christian unity'. Unity is indeed a treasure and most precious, more precious even than unity in families or than unity among nations, since all other unities among men derive from the unity which Christ came on earth to bring, unity with the Father, the Son and the Holy Spirit.

But Roman Catholics hold that Christian unity has not been lost and cannot be lost. The Theological Commission of the World Council were well aware in 1951 that the Orthodox and the Roman Catholics believe that God 'has committed to them the fulness of the Catholic Church', and therefore believe that Christian unity has not been lost. Catholics, even where they are overshadowed in numbers by non-Christians or by Christians who are not Roman Catholics, are conscious that there are some 500,000,000 (or more) people in the world who believe that the Roman Catholic Church is one and unique.

The Roman Catholic Church, therefore, is obliged, by being herself, to assert, and in no way to obscure, the claim that heresy and schism[1], though they may inflict grevious wounds upon the Church, nevertheless cannot dismember her so that she is no longer the body of Christ. Here, again, the 'intransigence' of the Orthodox and the Roman Catholics, as likewise of some 'evangelical' bodies, has disconcerted ecumenists; but it has, also, helped to deeper examination of the nature of the Church of Christ, and, here, again, neither the Orthodox nor Roman Catholics feel that the intransigence is either arrogant or unfriendly.

Many ecumenists and 'missionary' bodies have stressed the essential missionary vocation of the Church. Bishop Newbigin

---

[1] Though the words be disliked, all Christians must agree that the reality is possible. Unitarians, for instance, could not conscientiously join the World Council of Churches, nor be admitted into it. Docetism, Donatism and Pelagianism are usually rejected as 'heresies' by non-Catholics. It is noteworthy that the *Instruction* of the Holy Office does not use the words 'heresy' 'schism' or their derivatives.

has insisted—and others, too,—that the missionary vocation is not merely of the *bene esse* of the Church, but of its *esse*, part of its essence. Nor is it merely of the *plene esse* either; it is acceptance of Christ's words: 'As the Father has sent me, I also send you.' As the Father sent his beloved Son on a mission of redemption which meant suffering and death, so, too, the Church is sent on a mission which means suffering and has meant the death of countless martyrs.[1]

In modern times, when 'the era of missions in the old sense is over',[2] the Orthodox, the Roman Catholics and the Churches connected with the W.C.C. and the I.M.C. face the same problems: a changing civilization, a nationalism which often sees religion identified, both in their own people and in foreigners, with race, culture or nation; attempts to enforce teaching of non-Christian religion in Christian schools and

---

[1] On Roman Catholic missionary activity, Latourette's bibliographies are useful, and Mgr. S. Paventi, an official of the Roman Congregation *de Propaganda Fide*, in his *La Chiesa Missionaria*, Roma, 1949, gives a summary of Catholic teaching and law relative to the missions, and has excellent bibliographies. He takes account of the meetings at Tambaram, Madras, in 1938 and at Jerusalem in 1928. Cf., also, J. Schmidlin of Münster, *Catholic Mission Theory*, published in translation from the German by the Mission Press, Techny, Ill. U.S.A.; Pierre Charles, *Études Missiologiques*, Louvain, 1955, a posthumous collection of representative essays made by Père J. Masson, sympathetically reviewed by Dr W. T. Ingram, of the Cumberland Presbyterian Theological Seminary, Tennessee, in the *International Review of Missions*. Many religious orders publish valuable matter about missions,—Dominicans, Franciscans, Jesuits, Society of the Divine Word, the White Fathers, etc. etc. I may be permitted to mention *Studia Missionalia*, published by the Gregorian University, Rome, from 1943 onwards. Cf., also, E. Loffeld, *Le problème cardinal de la missiologie et des missions catholiques*, Rheness, Holland, 1956; N. Dunas, 'Perspectives d'une théologie missionnaire. Missions extérieurs et missions intérieurs', *Parole et Mission*, Paris, 1958, pp. 342–66. This new missiological periodical, *Parole et Mission. Revue de théologie missionnaire*, carried in the October number an excellent bibliography, and in the April number a list of missionary periodicals.

[2] A remark made and accepted by all in the 'East Asian Christian Conference', March, 1957, at Prabat—which means 'a meeting-place'—near Lake Toba in Sumatra. There, under the auspices of the W.C.C. and the I.M.C., representatives gathered from Pakistan and India, Ceylon and Malaya, Vietnam and Hong Kong, Korea, Japan, Taiwan (Formosa), the Philippines, Indonesia, Australia and New Zealand, for the purpose of co-ordinating their Christian efforts. Cf. *International Review of Missions*, xlvi, no. 183, July, 1957, p. 308, and pp. 306–13. Cf., also, *The Ghana Assembly of the International Missionary Council 28 December, 1957 to 8 January 1958*, ed. Ronald K. Orchard, London, 1958. One of the most important statements of the Central Committee of the World Council was at Rolle, Switzerland, in 1951, 'The Calling of the Church to Mission and to Unity', printed, with exception of the last section on relations between the W.C.C. and the I.M.C., *Ecumenical Review*, lv, October, 1951, pp. 66–71. An excellent bibliography of non-Catholic writings on missiological theory is to be found in W. Andersen, *Towards a Theology of Missions*, an *I.M.C. research pamphlet*, London, 1955.

Universities[1]; restrictions on entry and activity of missionaries in more than one part of the world, and, in general, the attitude of those 'who suspect the supra-national loyalties that foreign missionaries may evoke and are resentful of the claim to higher appreciation into spiritual truth than their own countrymen have attained.'[2]

In the East, of course, missionaries from the West have received much kindness from non-Christians and assurances of appreciation of their self-sacrificing lives and their contribution to the welfare of the people; often an ideological antagonism is much modified in practice by personal kindliness and good will. It may be remembered, too, that Mohammedanism, Buddhism and Hinduism have historically been 'expansive' religions and in modern times are trying gradually to exert their influence in the West, as may be seen from the places of worship which have been opened in recent years in England.

Religious Liberty

In the present period of rapid social change, ideas of 'proselytism' and of 'religious liberty' need deeper examination. The older 'liberalism' which regarded the individual as intellectually autonomous, with 'a right to think as he pleases', is proving inadequate to sustain Christian rights in non-Christian lands. This is indicated by Dr Charles W. Forman, of Yale Divinity School, in a stimulating article entitled 'Freedom of

---

[1] In Pakistan in 1954, such a request from the Advisory Board of Education for Muslim pupils received a negative reply from Catholics and the request was not urged. But both Catholics and non-Catholics seem to agree that teaching of Muslim cultural history is not only permissible but desirable. The views of Fr V. Courtois, who publishes in Calcutta 'Notes on Islam', a quarterly Bulletin about Islam with special reference to India and Pakistan, and of Dr J. W. Sweetman, the learned author of *Islam and Christian Theology*, so far three volumes, London, 1945, '47 and '55, seem to agree fully as to the right approach to Islam in Pakistan, cf. for Courtois 'How to Present the Christian Message to the Muslims', *Christ to the World, International Review of Apostolic Experiences*, English edition, vol. 1, no. 6, pp. 62–73; Sweetman, 'Problems and Prospects in West Pakistan', *International Review of Missions* xliii, no. 171, July, 1954, pp. 301–10. In some countries Roman Catholics in danger of losing their schools entirely have permitted non-Christian pupils to be taught a non-Christian religion; in others plans have been made to receive in future only Roman Catholic children, though this means financial loss.

[2] Cf. K. A. Ballhatchet, 'Asian Nationalism and Christian Missions', *International Review of Missions*, xlvi, no. 182, April, 1957, pp. 201–4, who refers especially to Sardar K. M. Panikkar's *Asia and Western Dominance*, New York, 1953, *Asien und die Herrschaft des Westens*, Zürich, 1954.

Conversion: the Issue in India', which reviews the attitude of different Indian thinkers on the question of conversion. He quotes Radhakrishnan's defence of tolerance: 'toleration is the homage which the finite mind pays to the inexhaustibility of the infinite'[1] and points out that the dominant tendency in Hindu philosophy today is of 'full tolerance of religion but not of conversion away from the basis on which that tolerance is established', which is, roughly, that all religions are more or less equally good. This basis for toleration points the 'liberal' dilemma in meeting Communism and other tyrannies: can toleration be given to a teaching which denies the basis on which toleration is justified?[2]

In fact, toleration cannot be divorced from truth and charity. How can a reasonable theory of toleration be built upon a denial that human reason can by due exercise come to a knowledge of the true God and can recognize the 'signs' of God's revelation? To deny this capacity of the human mind leaves no common ground between Christians and non-Christians, for there is no common truth which they recognize, and without recognition of some common truth how can there be reasonable toleration? When Christians join together in a protest against discrimination against them, as they recently have done in Egypt, they can only appeal in the name of natural justice and human dignity to the laws of God, recognized alike by Christians and non-Christians. For this reason I think that a Barthian outlook, laudable as it is in its rejection of liberalism, and stimulating as it is on so many points, fails and will fail to meet the situation as it is developing in non-Christian lands conscious of their new-found freedom.

'Proselytism', 'toleration' and the 'right to change religious allegiance' never exist in the abstract, but always in concrete circumstances; and hence a doctrinaire application of ideas of 'religious freedom' will fail to meet the facts. The 'right to change religion', for instance, though it is an undoubted right, must be exercised with due regard to existing

---

[1] *Eastern Religions and Western Thought*, London, p. 317.

[2] Dr Forman's article strikes me as one of the best presentations of the problem which I have seen. It is well documented and calm, *International Review of Missions*, xlv, no. 178, April, 1956, pp. 180–93; cf., also, A. Hartmann, *Toleranz und christlicher Glaube*, Frankfurt a/M., 1955, French ed., *Vraie et Fausse Tolérance*, Paris, 1958.

obligations and to the seriousness of the step involved. Every one has a right to marry; but the right must be exercised with due prudence and with realization of the gravity of the obligations contracted. It is, with due limitations, the same with the right to change religion. What is true in England and in the United States, where a considerable amount of economic individualism reigns, may not be true in communities which can exist only by their cohesiveness. Sound missionary practice insists upon the catechumenate and upon proper instruction of prospective 'converts'.[1] Conditions differ so much in various parts of the world that it may be misleading to speak of 'rights' in the abstract and without consideration of the concrete circumstances in which they are to be exercised.

In the meeting of Faith and Order at Oberlin, Ohio, in 1956, Dr Visser 't Hooft deplored the attitude of those who were content with the existence of the present variety of 'Churches, on the ground that individuals can choose what suits them best. This, said the General Secretary of the World Council, presupposes the mistaken idea that the Church exists merely in order to satisfy a specific need of men and that the Church therefore can be fashioned by men's plans and desires.'[2]

Dr Visser 't Hooft was right to deplore such a view, since it implicitly denies the divine institution and constitution of the Church. He might also have added that in deepest truth man does not choose the Church: 'You have not chosen me,' said Christ to his apostles, 'but I have chosen you.' Christ says the same to all those who have the gift of faith: 'No one can come to me unless the Father who sent me draw him'. God chooses us, God draws us, but through our own free will. It is not we who first choose him but he who first chooses us: 'what have you that you have not received?' The gift of faith is really a gift, not, indeed, given independently of our own intelligence and free will, but the more a gift because it enables us and draws us to use rightly our intelligence and free will.[3] Augustine's comment on John 6: 44 is famous:

[1] Cf. *The Training of Converts: Proceedings of the Fordham University Conference of Mission Specialists.* Ed. J. Franklin Ewing, New York, 1953.

[2] Cited in *Unitas,* ix, no. 3, Autumn, 1957, p. 211.

[3] John 15: 16; 6: 44; and I Cor. 4: 7–8, a favourite text of St Augustine which he urged repeatedly against the Semi-Pelagians.

No man comes to me, save whom the Father shall draw. Do not imagine that you are drawn against your will: the heart is drawn even by love. We ought not to fear the objections of men who weigh words nicely but are far from real understanding of divine things. They object against the energetic words of this text and say to us:

'How can I be said to believe with my own good will, if I am drawn?'

I answer: 'You are drawn, not merely by will, but—which is more—even by pleasure.'

What is the meaning of 'to be drawn by pleasure'?

Delight in the Lord and he will give thee the requests of thy heart. There is a pleasure of the heart to which the bread of heaven is sweet. Yes, and if the poet could say, *trahit sua quemque voluptas.*

'Each has his dear delight which draws him on',

not necessity, but pleasure, not obligation, but delight: how much more strongly ought we to say that a man is drawn to Christ, when he delights in truth, delights in blessedness, delights in justice, delights in everlasting life,—all which Christ is?

If the senses of the body have their pleasure, is the heart and the mind to be left with no pleasure of its own? If the mind has no pleasure, why is it said

'The sons of men shall trust under the shelter of thy wings:
They shall be inebriated with the plenty of thy house:
And thou shalt give them to drink of the torrent of thy delight:
For with thee is the fountain of life:
And in thy light we shall see light.'

Give me one that loves, and he feels what I say. Give me one that longs, one that hungers, give me one that is on pilgrimage in this wilderness, and thirsts and pants after the fountain of his eternal home: give me such a one, and he knows what I would say. But if I speak to one who is cold, he does not understand what I say. *No one,* says Christ, *can come to me unless the Father draws him.*

It is God who draws us to the Church, and the Church is God's building, not man's. Only some form of Pelagianism could lead men to imagine that they can have a Church such as their own natural desires would fabricate. The foolishness of God is wiser than men.

The West, unhappily, is riddled with Pelagianism, and that is why change of 'religious affiliation' is taken so lightly. The 'turn-over' in America is surprising. Of the situation both in

England and America, Dr Daniel Jenkins, in his *Congregationalism*, points out that 'many Protestant sects of a very primitive type and comparatively recent origin', such as the Pentecostals, the Assemblies of God, the Nazarenes, Jehovah's Witnesses, and similar bodies, are not able

> to keep their new-found members in their fold for very long, unless they themselves undergo considerable changes. Either the Church itself develops in maturity and spiritual understanding and becomes a respectable and recognized member of the family of Churches, as several of the smaller Baptist denominations have, or else those who were converted by the raw and narrow sect move on, as their experience develops, to another and more spacious part of the Church.
>
> This is the most typical form of religious migration in the English-speaking countries and the chief way in which new Christian families are brought into circulation among the churches, but there are other kinds. The person brought up in a very liberal church reacts against what he conceives to be the indefiniteness or religious superficiality of his environment into fundamentalism or, more commonly, into a form of Catholicism. The person brought up in a pious household which has been deeply involved in the life of a particular church often seems to find it necessary to make his spiritual home in another communion, perhaps in order to convince himself that his soul is his own. As a very rough generalization, it might be said that churches in the liberal Protestant tradition like the Congregationalist and many of the Methodist and Presbyterian churches flourish at the expense of the new sects or the more conservative bodies, and that the more liturgically developed and aristocratic churches, like Anglicanism and the metropolitan forms of Roman Catholicism, flourish at the expense of these same Liberal Protestant churches.[1]

Dr Jenkins' remark has a bearing upon the concern which many ecumenists are expressing relative to the increase of

---

[1] Dr Jenkins is himself a Congregationalist. He adds that churches ought to have a new humility towards each other: 'The prosperity of a particular church is intimately bound up with the success or failure of another church which might feed it or draw people away from it; and a church's prospects cannot be adequately assessed except in the setting of the movement of church life as a whole.' *Op. cit.*, pp. 138–40. Dr Jenkins has objections to Roman Catholicism, but they are at a deeper and a calmer level than those which used to be urged in the older type of controversial writings.

'Pentecostal' bodies on the 'fringe', so to say, of the larger Protestant bodies, and without connection with the Younger Churches, such as the Church of South India. In *Christ to the World*, first issue of 1958, Fr Prudencio Damboriena made a study of the Pentecostalists in Chile: 'A Very Active Protestant Sect in Chile: The Pentecostals'. In the introduction to the article the editor, Fr F. Legrand, an ex-missionary from China, makes these remarks:

> The fact that the Pentecostals, with a very poor insight into the Gospel, succeed in obtaining from their numerous converts *a deep feeling of their Redemption by Christ, a real detachment from material goods, great zeal, great generosity*, shows us *what we ourselves could obtain* from them by teaching them to know and appreciate the real message of Christ. They could be trained *to become very devoted lay apostles* who would give precious, indispensable collaboration to a clergy that is overwhelmed by the immensity of the task.
>
> On the other hand, the article also shows *the negative characteristics* of the sect, such as its excessive emotional element, the trances and hysterical phenomena to which it leads, and the poverty of its doctrinal teachings, shortcomings which, sooner or later, will detach its converts from it and *facilitate their return to the Church*.[1]

The agreement between Dr Jenkins and Fr Legrand, each writing from an entirely different experience, is striking. In the course of his interesting and accurate article Fr Damboriena cites Walter G. Muelder as saying: 'it seems also that, as the social and economic conditions improve, the extremely emotional and the unconventional elements in their beliefs and practice, gradually disappear.'[2] Fr Damboriena agrees that the sect can scarcely remain as it is, but will either be transformed, or will, in the second or third generation, see its members abandon all religion, or even join the Communists. Fr Damboriena recommends as the best way of dealing with them: 'Not only have we to pray, but we should also *show personal kindliness* (how it grieves them to feel themselves despised by Christians!), to contact them and distribute

[1] *Christ to the World*, vol. 3, no. 1, 1958, pp. 111–12. Italics in original.
[2] *Op. cit.*, p. 121.

pamphlets and leaflets.' Further, preventive measures must be taken with luke-warm Catholics: instruction, contact with the priest, active participation in liturgical life and in the *lay apostolate* and a *reading of simple pamphlets*.[1] Perhaps the only 'bridge' which can be built to meet these 'evangelical' bodies is personal kindliness and a direction of efforts to make known to them that the form of Christianity which they experience is not the only or the authentic form.

Aggressive Methods?

Before leaving this subject of the Roman Catholic claim to be the one and only Church of Christ and the duty it involves of drawing others into its unity, a word may be said about the charge of 'aggressive methods' said to be used by Roman Catholics. Any one who is seriously concerned about the charge may see the methods recommended to Roman Catholics in the pages of *Christ to the World, An International Review of Apostolic Experiences*, published in Rome, which is written to foster apostolic zeal among Roman Catholics, and anything 'aggressive' in Roman Catholic attitudes, if there were such, would be sure to appear in this periodical.[2] By reading it, a non-Catholic would be in a position to eavesdrop, as it were, upon Roman Catholic plans or plots.

An enquiry conducted in the United States, some results of which were summarized by Fr J. A. O'Brien, and reprinted in *Christ to the World*, 1957, no. 3, revealed that Roman Catholics

---

[1] *Art. cit.*, p. 121. Italics in the original.

[2] Available in Britain by application to Rt Rev. F. Walsh, Bishop of Aberdeen, Clydeside and North Bank, 226 Union St., Aberdeen, Scotland. Occasionally Protestants are exhorted to convert Roman Catholics. Mr C. Stewart Black, Provost of Paisley, wrote in 1952: 'Hamilton and Wishart, as they pass among us, seeing though unseen, must wonder sadly why no one now takes pity, as they did, on the unfortunates who still are thralls to the superstitions of Rome. Not the most enthusiastic of our evangelists seems ever to give them a thought. The official attitude of the Church [of Scotland] appears to be one not merely of tolerance towards the Romanists but of ignorance of their very existence. There are home missions and foreign missions, missions to pagans both here and abroad, missions among Jews, Mohammedans and Buddhists, but not a single missionary is dedicated to the conversion of the Romans. Yet among them would perhaps be found the most fruitful field of all. When our Commandos have realized that fact, and set themselves to the task of exploiting it, it may well be that they will reap a harvest that will astonish even the most sanguine among them.' *The Scottish Church*, Glasgow, 1952, p. 263. I think that the leaders of the Church of Scotland have more knowledge and wisdom than Provost Black imagined.

are less zealous in trying to win converts than are Protestants. His conclusions are as follows:

1. The overwhelming majority (72 per cent) of Catholic lay men and women have never so much as lifted a finger to win a convert for Christ.

2. Protestants are more than twice as active in seeking to win converts, 59 per cent against 28 per cent.

3. Catholics need to learn effective techniques of winning converts, as only 28 per cent who tried were successful, as compared with 59 per cent of Protestants who tried.

4. The chief difference between the two groups in convert-making effectiveness, however, is that the percentage of Protestants who try to win converts is more than twice as large as the percentage of Catholics.[1] The table, printed in *Christ to the World*, is reproduced on p. 238.

In spite, however, of this lack of zeal among the Catholic laity, the number of Catholics in the United States increased from 31,476,261 in 1954 to 34,563,851 in 1958, an increase of more than 3,000,000 in four years. As regards apostolic zeal on the part of the laity, to what extent conditions in England

---

[1] The survey was made by a commercial firm, Ben Gaffin and Associates, of Chicago, 'specialists in the art of sounding public opinion by means of approved scientific techniques, independent of every religious sect'. Yet its accuracy may be only approximate. It gives figures showing that between 1932 and 1952, 1,896,000 'Protestants' became Catholics, 1,434,000 'Catholics' became Protestants, while 16,926,000 persons abandoned all practice of religion; 12,926,000 of these had been 'Protestant', 2,529,000 had been 'Catholic', and 528,000 had been 'Jews'. Probably many of these had held only nominal membership in churches or the Synagogue. The total population of the United States in 1954 was 163,210,000, of whom 31,476,261 were Catholics. These figures were reproduced by the editor of *Christ to the World*, 1957, no. 3, pp. 404–7, in his preface to an article entitled 'A Prejudice that Paralyzes our Apostolate: Results of an Enquiry in the United States', pp. 405–10. The 'prejudice', which exists among Catholics, is that the apostolate towards non-Catholics is the exclusive affair of priests and that priests do not train our people to be apostles and may not be sufficiently familiar with newer methods. Yet, all the same, the number of converts in the U.S. has steadily increased; and there are factors not mentioned in the article, such as antagonisms against the Roman Catholic Church, its known stand on divorce and birth-control and the recognition of greater finality in becoming a Catholic than in becoming a member of another Protestant denomination. Cf. ch. 8, 'Conversion and Proselytization' of Claris Edwin Silcox and Galen Fisher, *Catholics, Jews and Protestants, A Study of Relationships in the United States and Canada*, published in 1934 for the Institute of Social and Religious Research, New York and London. This book was written before the new methods of sounding public opinion were developed; but the authors bring evidence that seems convincing that Protestant missions to Catholic immigrants into Canada and the United States have not proved a success, cf. pp. 291–8.

Percentages of Church Members who Promote Their Faith

Religions	Millions of People This Represents	Tried to Get Someone to Join %	Succeeded %	Did not Suceed %	Don't know if succeeded %	Never Tried to Get Anyone to Join %
Catholics	20.6	28	17	9	2	72
Protestants	53.3	59	43	10	6	41
Jews	1.8	27	24	3	0	73
Baptists	13.9	67	50	10	7	33
Methodists	12.7	56	39	8	9	44
Lutherans	6.1	49	28	19	2	51
Presbyterians	5.7	59	52	5	2	41
Episcopalians	2.3	53	45	6	2	47
Congregationalists	1.0	32	19	10	3	68
Other Protestant Denominations	11.6	61	44	11	6	39

and Scotland resemble those in the United States, is unknown as similar figures are not available. My own impression is that Roman Catholics are perhaps too shy, that we are apt to imagine prejudice exists where it does not and that there is need to arouse more apostolic zeal to try to reach the immense numbers who are lost to every Church.

Religious Correspondence Courses

One method of spreading knowledge of their faith used by Roman Catholics in the United States, Canada, Indonesia, India, Holland, Mauritius and England is that of Religious Correspondence Courses.[1] Mr Daniel-Rops, of the French Academy, has advocated such courses in France; but they do not exist, Fr Legrand thinks, in France, Germany, Italy, Spain, Austria, Belgium, Portugal, Switzerland, nor in any country in Eastern Europe. I believe there is such a course in Ireland. The English course was described in *Christ to the World* by Fathers G. P. Dwyer (now Bishop of Leeds), M. O'Connor and F. J. Ripley. A sample of the advertisements put in newspapers is the following:

> *The Catholic Enquiry Centre* has been set up because many of our non-Catholic friends want to know us better. We cannot give you the Faith. But we can give you facts about the Faith and remove misunderstandings. You may intend never to become a Catholic. But we can still help you. It is always worth while to learn something new. Send today for the explanatory brochure giving details of a full course of leaflets which will be sent to you free if you are further interested.[2]

---

[1] Cf. *Christ to the World*, 1955, no. 1, pp. 37–48, for the United States and China: 1955, no. 4, pp. 40–2, for Indonesia; 1957, no. 1, pp. 85–93, for India, Holland and Mauritius. The issues of 1955, no. 2, pp. 37–44, 1956, no. 3, pp. 51–60, and of 1957, no. 1, pp. 6–15, make suggestions for increased efficiency in methods. Fr J. Vos, after a study of the Voice of Prophecy World-Wide Bible Correspondence School (Seventh-Day Adventist), which has numbers variously estimated as between 300,000 and one million, concludes: 'These Protestants have succeeded in utilizing for their propaganda the results of psychological, pedagogical, catechetical and typographical research. From the technical point of view, their Course is obviously the fruit of long experience and deep study. *We believe it is better than ours*. (Italics mine.) Cf. *Christ to the World*, 1956, no. 3, pp. 51–60.

[2] *Christ to the World*, vol. 2, no. 3, 1957, p. 370; the article is from pp. 370–8, and describes financial difficulties and the method of overcoming them, the type of enquiries made by those who take the Course and the results obtained as far as these can be ascertained. The list of newspapers is given in which advertisements have appeared; some most interesting comments by enquirers are recorded. For

This method of apostolate is free from the objections which are urged against 'proselytism'. Those who read the advertisements must take the trouble to write for the Course and are free to drop the Course at any time. Many do so, as the following figures show:

1. Requested explanatory brochures   67,056
2. Enrolled for Course of instruction   36,643
3. Referred to priest for instruction   3,345
4. Received into Church as a result of
   the Centre's work   1,513

The Centre has enlisted the help of 'sponsors' and 'promoters', and of existing Organizations. Thus it aids in bringing home to ordinary Church members the truth which the World Council of Churches and the International Missionary Council have recognized so clearly, namely, that Christianity is essentially missionary. In fact, in the matter of Correspondence Courses, Roman Catholics only followed the example of Protestants who initiated them. Such Courses demand clarity of doctrine and call attention to the grave duty incumbent upon ecumenical and other theologians to secure doctrinal unity.

5. THE VISIBILITY OF THE CHURCH IN SCRIPTURE. THE OBLIGATION TO AVOID OBSCURITY

THE ROMAN CATHOLIC CHURCH HAS A DUTY, TO HER OWN MEMBERS, TO DISSIDENT FELLOW-CHRISTIANS AND TO THE WORLD TO ASSERT HER CLAIM OF UNIQUENESS, UNITY AND VISIBILITY, AND NOT TO ALLOW IT TO BE OBSCURED

Scripture depicts the Church under several images which signify that God wills his means of salvation to be not only knowable but to be conspicuously manifest.[1] Isaias had said:

---

instance one writes: 'I came to no other decision than to try to follow Christ as a Protestant.' 'As an old age pensioner, I am too old to change my religion now.' Others were saved from atheism, many mistaken notions corrected, and results doubtless obtained which are impossible to estimate.

[1] There are images which illustrate other aspects of the Church, as the treasure hidden in the field, the seed which grows together with the weeds, the leaven which works silently, the net which the fishes do not notice; but the images must be taken in their sense and bearing, to see exactly what they are intended to illustrate. They do not contradict one another.

And in the last days the mountain of the house of the Lord shall be prepared on the top of the mountains, and it shall be exalted above the hills and all the nations shall flow into it.[1]

Our Lord, perhaps referring to this passage of Isaias, said: 'A city seated on a mountain cannot be hid'.[2]

Ezechiel uses the figure of a tree:

Thus sayeth the Lord God: I myself will take of the marrow of the high cedar and will set it up . . .

on the high mountain of Israel will I plant it, and it shall shoot forth into branches, and shall bear fruit, and all birds shall dwell under it and every fowl shall make its nest under the shadow of the branches thereof.

Our Lord, likewise, uses the metaphor of a tree, but of a mustard tree, the seed of which

when it is grown up, it is greater than all the herbs, and becometh a tree, so that the birds of the air come and dwell in the branches thereof.[3]

What the Old Testament says of a sign lifted up among the nations, the New Testament applies to Christ, and has generally been applied also to the Church. Isaias says: 'He will lift up a sign to the nations.' That sign our Lord sees in the Book of Numbers:

Make a brazen serpent and set it up for a sign. . . .

Moses therefore made a brazen serpent and set it up for a sign: which when they that were bitten looked upon, they were healed.

Christ said:

As Moses lifted up the serpent in the desert, so must the Son of Man be lifted up. . . .

And I, if I be lifted up from the earth will draw all things to myself.[4] 'And this child is set', said Simeon, enlightened by the Holy Spirit, 'for a sign that shall be contradicted.[5]

---

[1] Isaias 2: 2; cf., also, Mich. 4: 1–2, and the commentaries of Augustine, Origen and Chrysostom on these passages.

[2] Matt. 5: 14.   [3] Ezech. 17: 22–4; Matt. 13: 32; Dan. 4: 20–2.

[4] Is. 5: 26; Num. 21: 9; John 3: 14; 12: 32.

[5] Luke 2: 34. St Luke also tells us that the shepherds were given a sign: 'And this shall be a sign to you: you shall find the infant wrapped in swaddling clothes and laid in a manger.' 2: 12. The mystery of the Word Incarnate's involvement in human conditions during his natural human infancy and life corresponds to his involvement in human conditions in his mystic life in the Church.

The Church is meant to be a sign, even though it be contra-dicted.

The image of the Shepherd is strongly yet tenderly expressed by Ezechiel:

> Behold I myself will seek my sheep and will visit them. As the shepherd visiteth his flock in the day when he shall be in the midst of his sheep that were scattered, so will I visit my sheep,
> and I will deliver them out of all the places where they have been scattered in the cloudy and the dark day.
> And I will bring them out from the peoples, and will gather them out of the countries, and will bring them to their own land.

Christ's claim to be the Good Shepherd is intimately con-nected, in chapter ten of St John's Gospel, with his giving his life for his sheep and with his unity with the Father; yet a most important point is that 'them also must I bring, and *they shall hear my voice*, and there shall be one flock and one shepherd'.[1] The shepherd is one whose voice the sheep recognize: and the Shepherd gathers his scattered flock together.

Isaias uses the image of light to picture the new Jerusalem, and its light is to be shed upon 'the holy people, the redeemed of the Lord':

> Thou shalt be called: a city sought after, and not forsaken.
> Arise and be enlightened, O Jerusalem; for thy light is come and the glory of the Lord is risen upon thee.
> For behold darkness shall cover the earth and a mist the people: but the Lord shall arise upon thee, and his glory shall be seen upon thee.
> And the gentiles shall walk in thy light, and kings in the brightness of thy rising.[2]
> For Sion's sake I will not hold my peace, and for the sake of Jerusalem I will not rest, till her just one come forth as brightness and her saviour be enlightened as a lamp.[3]

Christ was foretold by Simeon as 'a light to the revelation of the Gentiles' and Christ himself said: 'I am the light of the

---

[1] Ezech. 34: 11–14; John 10: 16, Westminster version.
[2] Is. 60: 1–3.
[3] Is. 62: 1.

world: he that followeth me, walketh not in darkness, but shall have the light of life.'[1]

In turn Christ said to his Apostles:

You are the light of the world. . . .

Men do not light a candle and put it under a bushel, but upon a candle-stick, that it may shine to all that are in the house.

So let your light shine before men that they may see your good works and glorify your Father who is in heaven.[2]

When Christ told his apostles that they were to be the light of the world, he referred primarily to good works: but in the case of the Apostles, their main good work was to be 'witnesses to me in Jerusalem, and in all Judea, and Samaria, *and even to the uttermost parts of the earth.*'[3] If they are to be witnesses, they are to carry the light and the light must not be extinguished.

The metaphors, then, of the mountain of God, of the city set on a hill, of a great tree affording shelter, of a sign lifted up among the nations, of a shepherd whose voice the sheep recognize, of a light not to be hidden but to enlighten the darkness, all apply to the Church, signifying that the Church must be clearly and unmistakably recognizable and not shrouded in mist and darkness. Of the confusion which God permits and of the causes which have made it difficult for many to recognize the one true Church, it is not ours to judge, nor for the moment to discuss. But the duty of the Church remains: not to do anything which would tend to obscure her visibility or to make herself less of a 'sign' or to render her uniqueness harder to recognize.

If Rome Did Change

Sometimes hopes or desires are expressed that 'Rome will change'. It is worth considering whether it would be in the best interests of the declared aims of ecumenists if Rome actually did change. The change most desired, it may be conjectured, would be a change in the supremacy and infallibility

---

[1] John 8: 12. The image of light runs through the whole of St John: 1: 4, 5, 8, 9; 3: 19; 9: 5; 12: 35, 36, 45; 1 John 1: 7; 2: 9; Apoc. 21: 23, 24; 22: 5.
[2] Matt. 5: 14–16, and cf. parallel passages in Mark 4: 21 and Luke 8: 16 and 11: 33. The application of the metaphor in these passages varies somewhat.
[3] Acts 1: 8.

of the Pope. If that were changed, would not the Roman Catholic Church disintegrate into a number of autocephalous churches, with no racial or national cohesion such as helps to keep the Greeks and the Slavs united, and the result would be still greater disunion among Christians and diminished hopes for a real union of Christendom. It is belief that papal supremacy and infallibility is a revealed doctrine which makes the cohesion of the Roman Catholic Church, and were that belief given up, exactly the same state of things would be seen as among the numerous independent 'Protestant' bodies. Could some kind of a permanent conciliar plan be adopted as an alternative? In fact, the Church has had long and varied experience of Councils; to put things merely on a human level, there seems no antecedent reason why a council, whose composition offers considerable difficulty, should be more effective in constitutional administrations and in religious decisions than one individual who is believed to administer and to decide by divine guidance and authority. On a supernatural level, it is not obvious that there is greater reason to trust the guidance given by the Holy Ghost to a constitutional group, permanently in session, than to trust that guidance given to one man whose duty and practice it is to consult the whole Church in any grave matter. Thus on grounds merely of expediency, so to speak, the arguments against papal supremacy and infallibility are not convincing. But belief in the position of the Vicar of Christ rests on no grounds of expediency, but solely on grounds of revelation and faith.

The Central Committee of the World Council of Churches disclaims any authority whatever over the member Churches; and yet, in the exact degree in which Committees of the World Council try to voice the common mind of the Churches, as, for instance, on Korea, Egypt and Hungary, they are approximating to the Roman concept of the Holy Father voicing the common mind of the Church. Such statements from permanent officials of the World Council, of course, have no authority to bind the member Churches; it is the inherent reasonableness and the expression of the authentic mind of Christians which alone gives weight and authority to any such declarations from the World Council, as Archbishop Temple said. The Churches can reject such statements, and this makes an abyss of difference from the Roman concept. Yet the principle is not radically different, namely, that the common feeling and judgement of Christians can be expressed by a group or by an individual as spiritually one with the Church. The definition of the infallibility of the Holy Father made in the Vatican Council reads:

> We teach and define that the Roman Pontiff, when he speaks *ex cathedra*, that is, when in discharge of the office of Pastor and Doctor of all Christians, by virtue of his supreme Apostolic authority he defines a doctrine regarding faith or morals to be held by the Universal Church, by the divine assistance promised to him in blessed Peter, is possessed of that infallibility with which the divine Redeemer willed that His Church should be endowed for defining doctrine regarding faith and morals: and that therefore such definitions of the Roman Pontiff are irreformable of themselves, and not from the consent of the Church.[1]

Both Fr Tyszkiewicz and Père de Lubac point out how the expression *ex sese, non autem ex consensu ecclesiae,*—definitions 'irreformable of themselves and not from the consent of the Church'—have been misunderstood as if they meant that the Pope as separate from the Church is infallible, whereas the definition explicitly says that the infallibility of the Pope is not different from the infallibility of the Church, although it may be said to be concentrated in him as the authentic voice of the whole Church.[2] The expression *ex sese et non ex consensu ecclesiae, of themselves and not from the consent of the Church,* is a technical expression drawn from the Gallican *Articles* of 1682, the third of which asserted a religious nationalism which is basically contrary to the spirit of ecumenism: 'The exercise of the Apostolic power is to be regulated by the canons of the Church, and in France by the laws and customs of the Gallican Church.'

[1] Vatican Council, translated in Cuthbert Butler's *The Vatican Council*, London, 1930, ii, p. 295.
[2] Tyszkiewicz, S., 'La théologie moehlérienne et les théologiens pravoslavs' *L'Église est une*, ed. Chaillet, P., Paris, 1939, p. 292; de Lubac, *Splendour of the Church*, p. 202, and note 2.

9

Following this third article, and to be understood in conjunction with it, is the assertion in the Gallican *Articles* that the Pope's judgement 'is not irreformable unless the consent of the Church is given to it'. This was the view which the Vatican Council rejected, and in ultimate substance, the issue was the same as the issue which divides many ecumenists today, namely federation as against organic union. The World Council has encountered many difficulties in its search for the unity of all Christians, and nationalism is certainly one of them. Here, as so often, there is an underlying common principle between ecumenists and Roman Catholics, which in this case is acceptance of the idea that the common mind of Christians can be expressed, and that the unity of the Church is impeded by nationalistic rivalries and the consequent danger of interference by the State. Is the Church of Christ to be a multitude of independent national churches, in federation with one another?

In suggesting the possibility, then, that 'Rome should change', care ought to be taken that the basis of ecumenical principles are not implicitly denied, and that the state of Christendom be concretely envisaged if the Roman Catholic Church actually did dissolve, through abandonment of its fundamental principles, into divided and rival independent bodies.[1] Catholics, of course, believe that this could never

---

[1] On the Gallican *Articles*, cf. Cuthbert Butler's *Vatican Council*, i, pp. 27–34; ii, 126, 157. The exposition of Bishop Gasser's interpretation of the Pope's infallibility, especially as 'separate', is of great interest, cf. pp. 134–48. All at the Council 'vehemently repudiated the assertion that they were isolating the Pope or separating him from the *magisterium* of the Church. They would all have said that when defining a doctrine *ex cathedra*, he certainly defines *ex magisterio ecclesiae*: but they were bent on killing the Gallican *ex consensu ecclesiae*, and were perhaps hypersensitively shy of anything that could give any kind of countenance to it.' P. 146. How easy it is to misunderstand the phrase *ex sese, non autem ex consensu ecclesiae* is illustrated by Sergius Bulgakoff, who says: 'It is absurd to imagine that an oracle exists which dictates the truth of revelation to the Church. Such a notion is contradicted by the nature of the Church and that of revelation itself. If such an oracle were to exist it would stand above the Church and outside it. This is our main theological difficulty in accepting the Vatican dogma of the Pope as infallible *ex sese, non ex consensu ecclesiae*, in so far as his prerogative bears on the present and the future, and is not confined to the past.' He adds a note saying that a pre-eminence of position as representative of the Church would make the Pope mouthpiece of the Universal Church, which agrees with the 'general trend of tradition in the Church in relation to the primacy of the Roman see. It is quite compatible with the conception of the *sobornost* of the Church, which becomes hierarchically organized from top to bottom.' But he thinks that the Vatican

happen, because of the union between Christ and his Church; but suggestions about changes in Roman doctrine ought to be analysed carefully to see if they do not finally lock doors which later experience may prove had been better left open. The World Council of Churches has accepted one infallible definition, namely, that Christ is God and Saviour; when the Council expresses agreements, these are accepted because they represent the common mind, or nearly the common mind, of Christians, for instance about the validity of baptism in all denominations, a thing which cannot easily be established from Scriptures. There is much that is implicit in these agreements and in the manner of reaching them.[1] The 'ecumenical idea' has closer affinities to the 'Roman idea' than is sometimes appreciated.

6. The Spontaneous and Free Obedience of Faith. Corporate 'Reunion'. 'Vestigia' Theology

IT IS MISLEADING TO SAY THAT ROME'S ONLY ATTITUDE TOWARDS SEPARATED BRETHREN IS 'TO DEMAND SUBMISSION'. SHE INVITES THEM OF THEMSELVES BY GOD'S GRACE TO RECOGNIZE CHRIST IN HIS UNIVERSAL CHURCH, AND SPONTANEOUSLY TO BRING TO HIM ALL THEIR GIFTS AND ALL THE GOOD WHICH THEY POSSESS. THE ONLY 'SUBMISSION' IS SUBMISSION TO CHARITY AND TO THE OBEDIENCE OF FAITH

Although the phrase 'demand submission' need not have a sinister connotation, it may easily carry one. It suggests a

---

definition effectively introduced a dogmatic oracle. 'Catholic theology, however at its best, does not wish to abandon the principle of *sobornost*, and attempts to combine it with the Vatican dogma even though the arguments used appear unconvincing.' *Revelation*, ed. John Baillie and Hugh Martin, London, 1937, p. 166. It is unhappily too little known that the famous phrase is technical and rejects the Gallican conception, which rests upon a nationalism quite alien to *sobornost*. Cf. G. Dejaife, '*Sobornost* and Papacy', *Eastern Churches Quarterly*, x, 1953, pp. 28–38; 75–85; 111–24; 168–78.

[1] It should be added that in the published proceedings of the World Council I do not remember finding any rejection of the Roman Catholic position, save here and there by possible implication or unexpressed assumptions; and, of course, the remarks made by individuals at diverse meetings cannot be taken as representing the Council itself or even a majority of its members. Individual ecumenists, however, feel free to associate their ecumenism with opposition to Roman Catholicism, an association, again, which is no sense commits the general body.

conflict, or even a war, in which the vanquished put their necks under the yoke in sign of defeat, and so it suggests an enforced obedience. But the obedience which the Church asks is the obedience of love, the glad giving of oneself, not to a man or a group of men, but to Christ. If there is 'submission', it is submission only to Christ as he lives in his Church. The Roman Catholic Church is obliged to affirm the truth about her own nature, just as Christ, in obedience to his Father, was obliged to affirm the truth about his own nature. But in both cases the 'demand' is the demand of truth and of love. Insofar as 'Rome's' claim is conceived or represented as springing from a desire of worldly domination, it is a claim which ought to be strongly rejected; but it ought not to be so conceived or so represented. To argue that the claim is unfounded is, of course, quite another matter which may be reasonably and calmly discussed in an atmosphere free from emotion. Rome's attitude towards separated brethren forms part of her belief in the union of Christ with the Church, and should be calmly discussed in that light, and not rejected in emotional language as a demand 'for submission' or for 'a confession of inferiority' or for 'acceptance of unilateral conditions'.[1]

Reconciliation 'Corporate' and 'Individual'

Sometimes an antithesis is made between 'corporate re-union' and 'individual reconciliation'; but, more especially of recent years, it may be doubted if the distinction, or anti-

---

[1] Among the non-theological factors making for division, choice of language ought to be added. Thus to say that Orders are invalid or defective is sometimes said to be 'unchurching' people, or 'asking them to repudiate their heritage'; and what ought to be a calm theological examination becomes charged with emotion and associated with imputation of not having served God properly, or of not having produced good spiritual fruits, or of being disloyal to some implied allegiance. Partly to avoid evoking such emotions, language is used, or theories excogitated, which in effect 'unchurch' every Church and invalidate all Orders. In sober fact, any Church which exists by the very fact of its existence 'unchurches' every other Church, or else unchurches itself and suggests that Christ's Church will only exist at the Parousia. The little volume produced by the Theological Commission of the Commission on Faith and Order, which met in 1951, entitled *The Church*, published in 1952, has a chapter 'The Background of our Divisions', which faces the difficulties squarely, says much that is pertinent to the situation, avoids the vague expressions 'givenness of unity' and 'manifestation of unity' and ends by saying courteously but sufficiently clearly that some must admit that there is something 'amiss' in their Churches.

thesis, is quite so sharp as it appears to be. On the one hand, no 'corporate reunion' can absolve an individual from his personal responsibilities or from his own act of faith; on the other, men are influenced not only as individuals but also as members of groups, especially in non-Christian lands, and the ecumenical movement has been making strenuous efforts to overcome the 'atomic individualism' of the older 'liberal' outlook. A word on each of these subjects.

An illuminating article, entitled 'Mar Ivanios and the Reunion of the Syro-Malankarites with Rome', written by Fr Alphonsus Raes, points out that this 'reunion' took place through the reconciliation of two Bishops with Rome and then, only with difficulty, the reconciliation of the larger body of the faithful:

> This cannot strictly be called corporate reunion; but on the other hand it is more than an individual reconciliation in view of the position of the person who comes into the Church. It is a method which presupposes a movement beginning at the top and working downward. It is certain, however, that when individuals become less gregarious and more conscious of their worth and personality, such a method becomes more difficult of application, if not impossible. In very many cases, there will be more preference for the other method which consists in preparing the faithful for reunion by neutralizing the prejudices which one element nurses against the other. This can be accomplished by an appeal to the objective facts of history and by frankly acknowledging those values of genuine Christianity which separated groups have conserved and which Pope Pius XI compared to pieces broken off gold-bearing rock.[1]

The movement to Rome started by Mar Ivanios encountered great difficulties; but it was helped by the unitive power of the ancient Rite, by the personality of Mar Ivanios himself, by aid given by the Syro-Malabar Church in the form of property and priests, and by the support of the Holy See. It was not, then, strictly a 'corporate' reunion, and yet neither was it merely a series of independent individual reconciliations.

Efforts for the reunion of Anglicans, Congregationalists,

[1] *Unitas*, viii, no. 2, Summer, 1956, pp. 93–101, citation, p. 98.

Methodists and Presbyterians into the Church of South India took over fifty years to attain their goal. In Lanka (Ceylon) it seems that it will take less to unite Anglicans, Baptists, Congregationalists, Methodists, and Presbyterians; and in North India and Pakistan, Anglicans, Baptists, the Brethren, the Disciples of Christ, Methodists (episcopal and non-episcopal), and a union of Congregationalists and Presbyterians. The example of South India has had an influence, as has, likewise, the changed political situation in these Eastern countries. The political break with Europe has had repercussions upon the 'Younger Churches', and has led to a desire to be independent of the parent 'missionary' bodies. Moreover, the tradition of the uniting bodies has had less exacting doctrinal standards than those of the Roman Catholic Church. At the same time, it would be unrealistic not to take account of a changed outlook with regard to ecclesiastical matters; there has been far more emphasis upon 'corporateness', and a very considerable amount of discussion in common among leaders of Churches, so that judgement of affairs as they were twenty years ago may not be reliable. Nor should judgement be made merely on a European or an American experience; no one can tell what may happen in the East or in Africa within the next fifty or one hundred years.

The Holy See has closed no doors, as its dealings with the Eastern Orthodox make plain. Various matters, such as the celibacy of the clergy, the language and form of the Liturgy, and similar things, are not matters of defined faith, as everyone ought to know. But they are not the central questions in any discussion of 'reunion', which in the last analysis involves the question of the ultimate bond of visible unity. Roman Catholics believe that this bond is unity with the Vicar of Christ on earth; while this belief is rejected other matters are secondary and to place things like canon law and custom in the forefront assumes an air of tinkering with the problem. During the Malines Conversations it was Archbishop Davidson who insisted upon this, saying: 'But prior to all these (other questions), and far outweighing them in importance, stands the fundamental question—Is there, or is there not, a Vicar of Christ upon earth, who possesses *jure divino* a distinctive authoritative position in relation to the whole of Christendom?'[1]

'Unity' and 'Uniformity'

Nevertheless it would be a mistake to suppose that the Roman Catholic conception of the unity of the Church is defined adequately merely by reference to the ultimate authority of the Church. The bishops have true and very real authority; and both the authority of the Pope and that of the bishops presupposes and relies upon the action of the Holy Spirit in the Church. Among the norms by which the faith is determined is the *sensus fidelium*, the instinctive judgement or feeling of the faithful; neither bishops nor Pope are separate from the faithful but are united with them in a unity which truly corresponds to the organic unity of a body. Admission of a supreme authority, however, permits a diversity of custom which would be divisive without that authority; and it helps to solve many of the questions which the World Council has found troublesome, which centre round the general question of 'unity' and 'uniformity'. A book like Donald Attwater's *The Christian Churches of the East*, volume one, *Churches in Communion with Rome*, published in Milwaukee, 1948, shows that the Roman Communion not only allows but encourages a diversity which may surprise those familiar only with the Western or Latin Rite. These Churches in the East belong to five different 'Rites': Alexandrine, Antiochean, Armenian, Byzantine and Chaldean, and have liturgies in more than ten different languages. A quite different canon law applies to them; many do not sing the *Filioque* in the Creed, the words of consecration are chanted in the anaphora, leavened bread is used, Communion is given under both kinds, baptism is by immersion and confirmation by the priest immediately afterwards, more than 50% of the priests are married, and in some, as in the Melkites, the Holy See has 'neither voice nor part in

---

[1] G. K. A. Bell, *Randall Davidson, Archbishop of Canterbury*, London, 1952, p. 1298. This account of Archbishop Davidson throws most interesting light on the Malines Conversations, but might be read in conjunction with Ernest Oldmeadow's *Francis Cardinal Bourne*, vol. 2, London, 1944, W. H. Frere's *Recollections of Malines*, London, 1935 and F. J. Lockhart's *Viscount Halifax*, part II, 1885–1934, London, 1936.

the appointment of bishops'. The loyalty to the centre of unity on the part of these Eastern Christians, who number probably between 9,000,000 and 10,000,000, is striking, the more so as they are not highly esteemed by the dissident Eastern Churches, and as administrative relations with Rome are naturally not without possibilities of misunderstanding, as, for instance, on questions connected with emigrant members of these Churches, and on matters of precedence. In spite of vicissitudes, due to the lack of perfect wisdom in human nature, the Holy See has made plain a sincere esteem for the Eastern rites and customs, and the influence of the Holy See, has been, on the whole, to protect them from attempts at 'Latinization' on the one hand, and from disorder and relaxation on the other.

It can be asserted with confidence that the Holy See, in its dealings with the Eastern Orthodox, has not been 'a central-ized ecclesiastical institution of world-wide character which seeks to impose unity and uniformity by means of outward pressure and political influence', as some seem to fear the World Council might become. Certainly, uniformity of faith and of recognition of the centre of unity is essential; but uniformity of custom, liturgy and canon law is not essential, at least where diversity has not been introduced in opposition to principles of the faith, but has grown up within the one faith. The question of the language of the liturgy, for example, is in itself quite indifferent, as history and present practice show; but it can assume doctrinal overtones when a doctrine has been pro-pounded asserting that the effect of sacraments is purely psychological and that *therefore* the liturgy must be in the vernacular. The celibacy of the clergy is certainly only an ecclesiastical law and not an evangelical law; but it has different aspects where, as among the Eastern Orthodox, virginity is highly esteemed as an ideal, and where, as in the West, virginity has sometimes been held to be a less perfect state, in itself, than the married state.

The multitude of religious orders and congregations in the Catholic Church, and their variety of outlooks, their different rules and customs, together with almost innumerable Asso-ciations, Confraternities, Sodalities, Legions, etc., and a growth

of 'secular institutes' in recent times, are evidence of a unity
without uniformity which only acceptance of a firmly acknowledged centre of unity could keep in harmony. In the
Interim Report of the Conversations between the Church of
England and the Methodist Church, Dr Norman Sykes and
Dr E. Gordon Rupp quoted Macaulay's famous remark to the
effect that had John Wesley been a Roman Catholic he would
have been 'the first General of a new Society devoted to the
interests and honour of the Church'; they add that recent
research has greatly modified Macaulay's picture though they
do not repudiate it entirely. In fact, the 'marks' of Methodism
given in the *Interim Report* strike a Catholic reader as almost
typical of characteristics of the different religious orders among
us, though no doubt there may be underlying differences
which closer acquaintance might reveal. The religious orders
and congregations have, within the one faith and obedience, a
difference of spiritual emphasis and of customs which might
surprise those to whom they are unknown.

One conviction which I think is common both to the ecumenical movement and to the Roman Catholic Church is this:
the approach made to the problems connected with bringing
all Christians into unity should not be on too narrow a front,
and should not be confined to an immediate and foreseeable
future. Rome shows this by her attitude towards the Eastern
Orthodox Churches, setting up Institutes like the Oriental
Institute and the Russian College at Rome, encouraging some
priests of Western origin to accept an Oriental 'Rite', and
above all, encouraging serious study of all problems, remote and
immediate, connected with missions and with the unity of all
Christians. The ecumenical movement, likewise, has the
Institute at Bossey for purposes of study, and encourages all
aspects of investigation bearing upon Christian unity. Some
of the manifestations of ecumenism, such as the idea that the
truth will only come home to people if they religiously 'live
together', have been questioned; their defence, I think, must
rest upon the existing situation among our separated brethren,
among many of whom doctrinal convictions are fluid and
undetermined. One of the best services to be rendered to the
cause of Christian unity is the patient and exact labours of

scholars, which bears fruit only slowly; and in this field much is progressing.

'Vestigia' of the true Church

A *vestigium* in this connection is understood as a 'trace', an 'impress', an 'element', a 'characteristic' or 'gift', which exists in a separated Church, but exists there in isolation from other such 'impresses' or 'characteristics' or 'gifts' all of which together ought to mark the one Church of Christ. Some who hold this conception suggest that the Body of Christ has been dismembered and its members so scattered among various 'Churches' that the Body of Christ can no longer be recognized as a living and actually existing organism. Such a conception really buries Christ in the historical order, for on that hypothesis no Church has the essential principle of oneness within it, and hence unity must be secured, if it can be secured at all on this earth, by a new intervention of God; the finality of Christ's revelation is implicitly denied and the sufficiency of his redeeming death. The view is radically Arian, for it subjects Christ to the created order. Because it is hard to discover where the principle of unity exists, supporters of this outlook tend to say that it does not exist at all, at least in the visible order.

But the *vestigia* question is put in another and quite different way by some Roman Catholics, who seek to find in it a real ecumenical principle. Separated bodies, they say, may retain certain gifts, like the gift of baptism, certain truths and insights; these are really Catholic, but in separation are mingled with falsity, or at least lack balance and security. The problem, then, is to discover what are these 'gifts' and true insights and to show separated brethren that on return to Catholicism they can retain their own special *vestigia* or imprints of the true Church and that they lose nothing but only regain unity, balance and security.

Now it is clear that heretics and schismatics, when they leave the Church, may retain many of the good things which they had when they were within the unity of the Church: valid, and when received in good faith, even fruitful sacraments, true faith in the Trinity and many other such things, the number of them varying with the degree of abandonment of Catholicism.[1] Père Boyer has well said that 'in themselves these elements are good and can serve toward the sanctification of those who with sincerity make use of them. Speaking on one occasion of the separated communities of the East, the late Pope Pius XI declared: "Pieces broken off from gold-bearing rock, themselves bear gold."[2] Those who have been baptized and draw their inspiration from the Gospel undoubtedly possess something very precious.'

Père Boyer continues,

An individual who comes to acknowledge these vestiges as such and who enters the Church of Christ is not renouncing anything which had previously aided his sanctification. Quite the contrary, he will now rediscover it in a fuller measure, protected and reinforced by the native milieu itself from which those elements had been detached. Finally, those elements which are found outside their natural setting can be compared to exiles who are tormented by nostalgia. By their very nature they are inclined towards their native land. And since they are not against Christ, they are for Him.

There is a truth which all of us may reflect upon: all elements of good existing in separation are not against Christ but for him. One of these elements is certainly the desire for visible unity. We need not, then, be niggardly in glad recognition of every good which exists among our separated brethren.

---

[1] A study of Arianism shows the retention of much of Christianity, including missionary zeal, but shows, too, the insecurity of such retention; Ulfilas, the Arian, translated the Scriptures into Gothic, and Arians 'converted' many of the Visigoths, Vandals, Lombards and others to the Arian version of Christianity. Yet Arianism, after flourishing in varying degrees for more than 500 years, eventually died. Cf. Le Bachelet, art. 'Arianisme', especially cols. 1847–9, in *Dictionnaire de Théologie Catholique*, vol. I, Paris, 1903, cols. 1831–63; and Gwatkin, H. M., *Studies in Arianism*, London, 1900. Newman, J. H., *The Arians of the Fourth Century, their Doctrine, Temper, and Conduct, as Exhibited in the Councils of the Church between A.D. 325 and A.D. 381*, London, 1833, is by no means out of date. Cochrane, C. N., *Christianity and Classical Culture*, Oxford, 1940, ch. x, shows the deficiencies of the Arian fundamental conceptions. Newman wrote as an Anglican and at the end of this book compared the Church of Rome, which he considered really began 'with the fatal Council of Trent', with the Arian domination of the Church, and suggested if not predicted the same end for Rome as for Arianism. He little imagined when he so wrote that he himself was to be one of the most effective defenders of the Church of Rome.

[2] Massi staccati da una roccia aurifera sono auriferi anche essi. 'Discorsi agli Universitari', *Studium*, Romae, 1932, p. 28.

The Rev. Charles Davis, Professor of Dogmatic Theology at St Edmund's College, Ware, ends an article entitled '*Faith and Dissident Christians*' as follows:

What must characterize ecumenical activity is the recognition of Christian faith and life in those to whom it is directed. An objective assessment of the task it faces must include an acknowledgement of the Christian elements present in the dissident communities. That determines its immediate aim, which must be to foster and encourage all that is true and valuable in the separated Churches and to assist in eliminating errors. This is a wider task than that of making converts. Those to whom God gives the grace of conversion are to be helped and welcomed by us. Their return is often a providential aid to the Church in her ecumenical activity. But an over-eagerness to make converts must never lead us to despise or to trample upon anything that is truly Christian in the separated Churches. The Christian elements they retain belong really to the Church, and it is our duty to cherish them. Apart from this, healing is always achieved by the strengthening of life; our separated brethren will be brought to the fullness of life by the growth of the life they possess and not by its decay. And when the fruits of their Christian life and traditions are brought eventually within the unity of the Church, her life will be enriched. We know well enough that the Church, in her unbroken unity and indefectibility, has lost nothing essential by the damage inflicted by heresy and schism, but this does not exclude the fact that the return of all Christian gifts, not found in a state of separation, will be a real benefit to her life. Part of our task is to see that these gifts do not meanwhile perish.

The missionary work of the Church requires a sympathy, knowledge and appreciation of all that is sound in the customs and traditions of the peoples to whom it brings the Gospel. What sympathy, knowledge and appreciation are needed when confronted with the fruits of Christian faith in our separated brethren! The fact that these are marred with the fruits of error does not mean that we can be content with an attitude of opposition. What is called for is a work of delicate discernment, which will enable us to encourage what is true and combat what is false. The task demands an enlightened Christian charity. How far are we in this country fulfilling it?[1]

[1] *Clergy Review*, xliv, no. 4, April, 1959, pp. 219–20. The whole article will repay the most careful study.

While agreeing wholeheartedly with all that Father Davis says, nevertheless I have some doubts about possible applications of this 'ecumenical method', particularly by our separated brethren as among themselves, and should stress the need of 'enlightened' charity. First it is not easy to discern precisely what are the good religious elements in diverse Churches; and secondly, as I think ecumenical experience tends to show, concentration upon the specific good elements in particular Christian bodies may easily miss the expansive force—*bonum diffusivum sui*—of these good things and cling to them as they actually exist, that is, in separation from others.

As to the first point, the difficulty lies in estimating the precise *religious* values held in separation. An Anglican or a Presbyterian, for instance would not find it too easy to determine the exact values contained among the Plymouth Brethren or Jehovah's Witnesses. God gives gifts of nature as well as of grace; and he may give gifts of a charismatic kind, for instance the gift of preaching, which are not primarily for the sanctification of its individual possessor. In members of divided churches there is a complicated intermingling of factors: religious, racial, national, philosophical, historical, social, and to segregate the specifically religious factors is difficult. How make such a judgement about the Free Churches or the Anglicans or the Presbyterians? There is development going on, and national and historical influences mingle with the religious, so that the good which undoubtedly exists among them is not easily distinguished as specifically religious. It proves very hard indeed to determine exactly what each denomination 'stands for', what is its 'distinctive witness' and there is not always agreement on the matter even among members of the same denomination. The Rev. Farid Auden tried to classify the good qualities which he thought each denomination might bring to the 'united Church' of our ideals[1]; but the qualities were exclusively moral and their connection with doctrine was overlooked. There is a complicated interplay between natural good qualities, national and group circumstances and religious inspirations. It is recognition of this fact that leads

[1] Cf. above, p. 93.

serious missiologists to a study of non-Christian religion, culture and history.

Secondly, as experience shows, insistence upon 'distinctive witness', 'historical heritage', in short, upon the distinctive 'something' which each denomination must preserve and contribute to the 'Great Church', may easily tend to solidify the actually existing outlooks and religious frameworks and settings. The point of view tends to concentration upon particularity and to loss of vision of the greater whole. There are indications that a broader and deeper method is being recognized as more promising. What is needed is not so much an exact appraisal of the specific religious goodness in each divided body, but a principle which will, so to speak, bypass the reasons for division and find a principle of unity. Dr A. C. Craig, commending the famous Report in his Speech to the General Assembly of the Church of Scotland, declared:

> But in the providence of God a grain of mustard-seed was sown at Lund—the suggestion and the hope that a genuinely new beginning might be made in the Faith and Order Movement if the parties to it would consent, for the moment at least, to stop comparing and contrasting and defending *ex parte* the historic traditions which had landed them on opposite banks of a broad river, and if they would travel upstream together to its headwaters; to speak without metaphor, if they would seek to subordinate the variant ecclesiological doctrines developed in the course of divergent traditions to the doctrine of Christ as the one King and Head acknowledged by all the separated Churches, and therefore try to see how the former looked in the light of the latter.[1]

In that statement, it seems to me, is contained a clear indication that 'distinctive witness' ought to yield to common witness and that 'our historic tradition' ought to yield to the universal tradition. It is, indeed, right to welcome every possible truth and goodness which exists in dissident bodies; and right to try to show how truths which are held ought to lead

---

[1] *The Lost Treasure of Christian Unity*, Edinburgh, 1957, p. 11. Yet Dr Craig did not wish Scottish or English 'character and accent, ecclesiastical and national' to be destroyed; 'these rich and racy historic differentiations should not be blurred or rubbed out, but should be conserved as far as is consistent with unity in Christ Jesus.' P. 9.

on to other truths and to a wider synthesis. At the same time, to erect 'the *vestigia* theology' into an ecumenical method may easily tend to blunt the sense of the evil of divisions. The multitude of different doctrines and of 'traditions' surely makes plain that not all can be right and that some are definitely mistaken. 'True insights' may be vitiated by admixture of falsehood, and elements of truth may be made a means of overlooking or even of supporting elements of falsehood. If a religious body teaches even one false doctrine, or fails to teach even one truth of Christ, it has thereby ceased to be the Church of Christ, the pillar and ground of truth. This may sound a hard saying and perhaps an impatient one. Nevertheless, the ecumenical movement has not yet entirely escaped the danger of overlooking the primacy of true doctrine as a prerequisite for unity, and the danger of trying to escape from intractable dogmatic questions by interest in works of charity and in assurances of mutual good will. It can scarcely be too often repeated that a plurality of Churches is contrary to the plain teaching of the New Testament and contrary to the will of Christ.

To return, however, to the principle stated at the beginning of this section: it is natural enough that separated brethren should feel that Rome claims the right to lay down unilateral conditions and that this—say what Catholics like, argue as they may—is basically an arrogant and even uncharitable stand. In spite, however, of awareness that her attitude appears at present self-sufficient and separatist, especially to those who look upon Rome merely from the outside and have little acquaintance with the flexibility of the Roman organization, nevertheless Catholics feel that the Church's attitude is part of her loyalty to Christ, springing from her belief about the unity of the mystical body of Christ. Yet Catholics believe, also, that faithfulness to this belief will in the long run do most for the union of all Christians. Meantime, disagreement need not diminish charity; indeed disagreement, the more radical it seems, can be the occasion of a charity equally radical.

The Interconnection of Intangibles

The Roman Catholic Church, like the Orthodox and some others, esteems and encourages observance of 'the evangelical

counsels' over and above observance of the evangelical pre-
cepts. She normally has, save in some Eastern Rites, a celibate
clergy, and she has a multitude of different orders and congregations of monks and nuns. The Catholic Church also has
firm convictions about the nature of the holiness of marriage,
convictions which contrast sharply with many views current in
the world today. Now the Catholic outlook upon both these
matters forms part of a whole; in the mystical body of Christ
there are different gifts and functions, the life of contemplation
as well as the life of action. Most Catholics have the conviction that the holiness of marriage can best be secured in a
body which esteems vows of celibacy, and that there is an
intangible but real connection between attitudes towards the
one and attitudes towards the other. Monasteries, convents
and clerical life, as the history of the Church shows, can become relaxed in tone and discipline. Yet an ill state of religious
life often is a reflection of a bad condition in society generally,
and sometimes of secular interference in religious matters;
and in any case there is no need to kill a patient because he
falls sick. Catholics feel that to a large extent her convents solve
the problem, existing in many Churches, of the 'ministry of
women' and gives scope and standing to women's service in
God's Church. It would not be easy to detail the debts which
the Church, and indeed humanity, owes to their humble, self-
sacrificing and intelligent work, especially, though by no means
exclusively, in education, nursing and medical missions. The
influence of African nuns upon the African outlook towards
marriage and towards the relation of the sexes might well
prove a fruitful subject for investigation. Without the spiritual
writings of saints like St Teresa of Avila, St Margaret Mary
Alacoque, St Terèse of Lisieux, the world would be the poorer.
In recent times women, including nuns, are taking a larger
share in the intellectual and directly spiritual apostolate.

The spiritual writings of Thomas à Kempis, St John of the
Cross, St Francis of Sales, St Ignatius Loyola, of the Flemish
and English mystics, and of many others, form part of the
heritage not merely of the Roman Catholic Church but of
Western Christendom: and inspiration to missionary zeal of
men like St Francis Xavier, Charles de Foucauld, Cardinal

Lavigerie, Cardinal Vaughan and many others has not been limited to the Roman Catholic Church, but has extended to many Christians who have felt the expansive force inherent in the Gospel of Christ.

Now the Catholic Church is well aware of the danger of the infiltration of lax ideas about marriage and of general religious 'indifferentism'. The Catholic population is not immune from the subtle temptations of the world; and although by God's grace there are most encouraging signs of real holiness and intelligent zeal to be seen in all the various manifestations of Catholic life, still the maintenance and encouragement of this holiness and zeal depends upon a complicated interaction of intangible factors. Conditions differ in different parts of the world. The Church commits judgement on all such intangible, —and tangible—factors to the Bishops, who, of course, are in consultation with the clergy and laity. Among such intangible factors are relations, especially anything approaching official relations, between Catholics and other religious bodies. Not every individual Catholic, layman or priest, has consummate knowledge and wisdom; and so it is reasonable that 'ecumenical encounters', of whatever kind, should be guided by the Bishops, or, if the 'encounter' may have national or international repercussions, by the wider authority, which is kept informed of conditions in different countries by its representatives who are in consultation with the Bishops.

There is evidence that many non-Catholics are appreciating more the responsibility of the Bishops in doctrinal matters, and are tending more to conclude that Bishops should represent a heritage not merely of 400 years or so but of the whole of Christianity since the time of the Apostles. The Constitution of the Church of South India says this:

> The office of a bishop is essentially a teaching office, and he should do all that is in his power for the edification of the ministers and congregations over whom he has oversight by instructing them concerning the truths of the Christian faith.
>
> On each bishop in his own diocese, and on the bishops as a body, is laid the responsibility of publicly stating, as need may from time to time arise, the doctrine of the Church Universal as understood by the Church of South India, and its application

to the problems of the age and country. But the bishops acting as a body shall only issue such statements after consultation with representatives of the presbyters and laity to be appointed for this purpose under rules laid down by the Synod of the Church; and no such statement shall have any force as a rule of the Church unless and until it be adopted by the Synod as such.

The Committee appointed by the Archbishop of Canterbury, under the chairmanship of the Bishop of Derby, made its fourth recommendation 'that there should be a modification of the rules for synodical procedure, clarifying and properly safeguarding the position of bishops'. The American Delegation which visited the Church of South India in 1956, comments upon this recommendation of the Derby *Report*:

> It is true that, in principle, the bishops of the C.S.I. can be overruled on matters of faith and order by the clerical and lay members of the Synod. After quoting the Synodical procedure by which a decision of the bishops could be overruled, the American Delegation continue: 'Even though it is quite unlikely that any proposal which did not have the bishops' approval could survive such synodical procedure, we agree that there might well be a modification of this constitutional provision.[1]

7. CATHOLIC INTEREST AND MANIFESTATIONS OF SINCERE GOOD WILL

THE UNITAS ASSOCIATION. DIRECTIONS FROM ROMAN AUTHORITIES

Abstention from formal participation in the Conferences and in the World Council of Churches by no means signifies lack of interest or of sympathy, as many non-Romans are aware. At Lund in 1952 the Secretary of the Commission on Faith and Order, Dr Oliver S. Tomkins, said: 'Although the Roman Catholic Church does not co-operate formally in our work, the manifest concern of Roman Catholics, both clergy and laity, has never been absent from my thoughts in everything that I have said.'[2] Such declarations could be multiplied. There are many evidences of Catholic concern—books and

---

[1] *Constitution of the Church of South India*, p. 22; *Report on South India*, Joint Commission on Ecumenical Relations, New York, 1957 (not dated, but 1957 was most probably the date of publication).

[2] *Lund* Report, p. 173.

articles written by Roman Catholics and information privately exchanged by scholars for mutual help,—but for the sake of brevity I shall refer mainly to the *Unitas Association* founded at Rome in 1945, whose aims and principles will be found explained in Appendix III. It is 'an international organization whose purpose is to promote the spiritual union of men and especially of Christians'. It 'keeps in close touch with the Ecumenical Movement, and endeavours to aid it in its quest for unity'. 'Across the imperfections of men, it tries to make evident that spirit of fraternal affection and faithfulness to the teachings of Christ which is at the very heart of the Church's life and the manifestation of the Holy Spirit at work in her.'

The Association received the blessing of Pope Pius XII when it began in 1945 and its tenth anniversary in 1955 was the occasion of significant marks of approval at Rome. The celebration lasted three days and those attending received a cordial message and a blessing from the Pope at the beginning, the members of the *Unitas Association* going to Castel Gandolfo to receive a special blessing at the end. The Rev. Father Louis Ciappi, O.P., Master of the Sacred Palace and the Theologian of the Holy Father, gave an address on 'Pius XII's Appeals for Unity'. The following Cardinals were present in person at the meetings:

His Eminence, Eugene Cardinal Tisserant, Dean of the Sacred College and Secretary of the Sacred Congregation for the Eastern Church.

His Eminence, Joseph Cardinal Pizzardo, Prefect of the Sacred Congregation for Seminaries and Universities.

His Eminence, Valerio Cardinal Valeri, Prefect of the Sacred Congregation for Religious Orders and Congregations.[1]

His Eminence, Celso Cardinal Costantini, of the Congregations of the Council and of the Propagation of the Faith.

His Eminence, Benedict Cardinal Aloisi Masella, Proprefect of the Sacred Congregation of the Sacraments.

His Eminence, Gaetano Cardinal Cicognani, Prefect of the Sacred Congregation of Rites.

Cardinal Costantini gave an address on 'The Summons to Unity and the Missions' and Père Charles Boyer one on

[1] These play a very large part in missionary work.

'The Ecumenical Movement and Unitas'. The sessions were attended by visitors from all over the world, America, Belgium, England, France, Germany, Holland, Italy, Poland and the Ukraine, and from numerous dioceses and religious orders and congregations. The celebration was the occasion of striking marks of approval of the aims and spirit of the Unitas Association, and from the highest quarters in the Vatican. The periodical *Unitas*, published in Rome, under the editorship of Père Boyer, shares the interest in all ecumenical matters manifest in other Catholic periodicals, such as *Irénikon*, in Belgium, *Vers l'Unité Chrétienne* and *Istina*, in France, *Una Sancta*, in Germany, and *The Eastern Churches Quarterly*, in England.[1] *Unitas* is published in a French, an Italian and an English version.[2] To some extent its comments share the authority of the editor, who has held and still holds positions of responsibility in Rome. The attitude it commends to Roman Catholics is as follows:

'ACROSS THE IMPERFECTIONS OF MEN TO TRY TO MAKE EVIDENT THAT SPIRIT OF FRATERNAL AFFECTION AND FAITHFULNESS TO THE TEACHINGS OF CHRIST WHICH IS AT THE VERY HEART OF THE CHURCH'S LIFE AND THE MANIFESTATION OF THE HOLY SPIRIT AT WORK IN HER.'

The Great Charter of Catholic Ecumenism

This is the *Instruction* from the Holy Office (which corresponds, roughly, to the Faith and Order Commission of the World Council) of December 1949. It was Père Charles Boyer who called it the 'great charter'.[3] He was right and I regret that the account given in the *History of the Ecumenical Movement*

[1] Dr Tomkins says of some of these periodicals: 'The articles show a scrupulous desire to understand the intention of ecumenical writings, and indeed they sometimes exhibit an ingenuity of deep interpretation which credits the ecumenical committees or authors with subtleties never intended by them. The ecumenical writings are assessed and evaluated in terms of the orthodox Roman Catholic position, with courtesy and charity where agreement is impossible.' *History of the Ecumenical Movement*, p. 692. It is plain that good intentions are not enough.

[2] The English version of *Unitas* is published by the Graymoor Press, Peekskill, New York; the annual subscription in English money is 15/-; the agents are Duckett, 140 Strand, London, W.C. 2.

[3] *Unus Pastor*, Italian ed., Rome, 1950, p. 57.

tends to leave a reader with the impressions that the document is 'repressive'. This impression, I believe, would be quite mistaken, for there is scarcely anything in the *Instruction* which could not be reproduced, though in a different terminology, from the writings of leading ecumenists.

1. The *Instruction* gives formal recognition to the ecumenical movement and declares it to be a matter of concern to the whole Roman Catholic Church. It not only permits but actually encourages a certain Catholic participation in the movement.

2. The growing desire for unity is attributed to the action of the Holy Spirit and to the prayers of the faithful.

3. At the end it is said:

This excellent work of 'reunion' of all Christians in the one true faith and in the Church should daily assume a more significant place within the Church's universal pastoral care and every Catholic should pray ever more earnestly to God for this object.

It will prove a great help if the Faithful are suitably instructed, for example, by pastoral letters about these questions and the steps being taken, together with the Church's instructions on this matter and the reasons underlying them. All, *especially priests and religious, should be encouraged to take an ardent interest* and to do everything in their power, by prayer and sacrifice, to work for the success of this cause. (Italics mine)

Finally, all should be reminded that the best commendation of their religion by Catholics is an edifying life in accord with their faith.

4. Bishops are exhorted 'to make a special object of their care and attention this work of "reunion" which is a particular charge and duty of the Church'. They must at once encourage this work of 'reunion' and guard against possible dangers. They should keep themselves well informed and appoint suitable priests 'to make a special study of the movement and everything connected with it.'

In the *Clergy Review*, which is widely read by the clergy of England, Fr Charles Davis, Professor of Dogmatic Theology at St Edmund's College, the Seminary of the Westminster Diocese, in a review of Fr Henry St John's *Essays in Christian Unity*, London, 1955, said very frankly:

'The chief impression left by the book is the need of a wide-spread ardent desire among Catholics for the reunion of Christendom. This condition is imperative, but does not yet adequately exist.'[1]

Fr Gustave Weigel, in his book *A Catholic Approach to the Ecumenical Movement*, London, 1958, urges more Catholic study of non-Catholic positions. Pius XII in *Humani Generis* condemned both 'bogus ecumenism' and 'theological xeno-phobia'. 'If the Pope's counsel was good for Catholic thinkers everywhere in the world, it was perhaps most timely for American theologians, who by and large have not been too aware of their obligations, even though most pressing in our cultural climate, of which pluralism is the specific note.' Perhaps the same has been true in these islands.

Fr Weigel notes a decline from the standards of theologians like St Robert Bellarmine, Francisco Suárez and Johann Adam Moehler. 'With a spirit of unconcealed hostility the later men reduced the serene work of their predecessors to a ludicrous caricature of the original positions, and for many years this caricature was palmed off to innocent and ignorant tyros as the whole truth. Is it too fantastic to think that, for many a Catholic student of theology, *pecca fortiter sed fortius fide* is the formula which genuinely, adequately and loyally expresses the thought of Luther? Today, fortunately, we find a widespread dis-comfort with this kind of presentation.' P. 70.

In the present state of theology, especially biblical and patristic, scholars must consult the work of other scholars, whoever they may be. The best hope lies in serene scholarly work, undertaken with aims neither controversial nor 'eirenic'; theological impatience is a poor counsellor. Study undertaken with the purpose either of refuting or of conciliating 'adver-saries' may have its place; but in the long run this place will not be primary, though it is important, and sometimes urgent.

5. Gatherings 'at which Catholics and non-Catholics *meet as equals* (italics mine) and discuss matters of faith and morals, each one putting forward the teaching proper to his Creed, are not absolutely forbidden but may be held only with the ap-proval of the competent ecclesiastical authorities.'

---

[1] *Clergy Review*, xl, 1955, 'Notes on Recent Work', p. 597.

6. The restrictions placed round the gatherings mentioned in (5) do not apply to mixed gatherings where Catholics and non-Catholics meet, not to discuss matters of faith and morals but to take counsel together concerning the defence of the fundamental principles of Christianity and the natural law, 'nor does it apply to occasions when they meet to deal with the rebuilding of the social order and similar questions'. This would apply, for instance, to meetings of all Christians to consider policy when governments make regulations affecting religion, such as, for instance, regulations about the entrance of foreign ministers of religion into a country. This is a very practical question and promises to become more so.

7. At all such conferences and meetings [including (5) and (6)], it is not forbidden to open or close the gathering with the common recitation of the Lord's Prayer or some other prayer approved by the Catholic Church.

The *Instruction* adds a number of regulations, the principal of which are these.

1. In interdiocesan, national or international conferences the permission of the Holy See is needed, and details must be given of what is planned.

2. The Bishops are to regulate what is to be done in their own dioceses in the way of co-operation.

3. For theological discussion only competent priests are to be assigned.

These regulations in fact are very much the same as those followed by the Church of England, in which the Church Assembly appoints a 'Council for Ecumenical Co-operation' which then appoints whom it chooses to act as its representatives on the various organs and commissions of the World Council or to discuss relations with the Presbyterians or the Free Churches. Dr Tomkins says that the Executive Committee of the World Council regretted these regulations of the Roman *Instruction* as lessening 'the informal and spontaneous character of such meetings [*which* meetings is not clear] on which much of their value depends. There will be less room for the pioneer.' But the World Council must and does make a careful scrutiny of the credentials of representatives from different Churches to ensure that they are duly appointed; and would the Presbyterians or the Free Churches give great welcome to self-appointed 'pioneers' in initiating discussions with members of other Churches?

It seems fair that people who are to speak for a body and to explain its aims and character should be approved by the officials of that body and should not act merely on their own initiative and unseconded. In fact a compliment is paid to the ecumenical movement, since dealings with it must have official recognition. A very superficial knowledge of the practice of the Foreign Office, or of the Services, would surely throw light upon these regulations. Self-constituted diplomats are regarded, generally, as a nuisance and who has ever heard of a self-constituted liaison-officer? The comparison, of course, is not absolute, but is close enough to give pause before regarding the regulations of the *Instruction* as merely 'negative'. Personal relations, of course, are a different matter, but these are not in question; they may be a consideration in making appointments in all walks of life, but they cannot suffice to make an accredited spokesman. If relations are desired with any organization one must take that organization as it is and not as it is imagined to be or said to be.

Conditions differ greatly in different countries and dioceses; what is suitable in Holland or Germany may not be suitable in Spain or Canada or the United States. The Bishops know the character of their people and what is wise or unwise under the existing conditions.

At the time of the Malines conversions had such regulations been in force on both sides, there would have been far less confusion. As it was, the conversations were neither wholly private nor wholly public; no one appeared to know in what way those taking part represented their respective communions, and the result was a general recognition of the amiability of all concerned and of the purity of their motives, but perhaps not very much else. The Free Churches wondered if the Church of England were turning away from them and 'Romanizing' and the subsequent reaction was away from the Anglo-Catholics. The English Roman Catholics, not aware of all the facts, were somewhat bewildered and wondered if their

Continental brethren thought them lacking in charity or in competence to explain the faith to their fellow-countrymen. Judgements about Malines have differed widely and doubtless still differ; but had clear regulations existed beforehand considerable confusion and misunderstanding might have been avoided.

The *Instruction* gives a number of warnings, not really dissimilar to those to be found in the proceedings of Faith and Order Conferences and meetings of Commissions, though perhaps they are expressed in different language.

1. There must be frankness and completeness in stating the whole doctrine of the Church.

This is certainly desired by the World Council; and some non-Catholic theologians have noted that differences small in themselves may sometimes reveal a difference of total system.

2. There must be no attempt to patch up accord by slurring over points of disagreement, whittling down the faith or being apparently indifferent to objective truth.

The ecumenical movement itself has shown that there can be a spirit of too great conciliation which in the end defeats its own purpose; and many leading ecumenists can be cited to this effect. In 1957, at Oberlin, Ohio, for instance, one of the reports warned against too facile a manner of promoting unitive plans. It gave cautions against undue haste and pointed to the 'necessary and often painful' adjustments which may have to be made. Steps towards unity, said the report, should be preceded by careful consideration of both the theological and sociological factors which impinge upon the issue. Further training in ecumenical consciousness must be pursued before any general plan of union can hope to be effective in North America.[1]

3. In dealing with the Reformation it must not be suggested that the 'Reformers' had all the virtues and the Roman Catholics all the faults. The principle that schism and heresy are wrong must not be obscured.

This is far from suggesting that history should be written in a partisan spirit; on the contrary, impartiality, as far as it can be attained, is desired. The writing of history is not a science

[1] Cited in *Unitas*, ix, no. 3, Autumn, 1957, p. 299.

but an art, as is, I think, being more and more realized; but
the art is to convey as far as possible the facts and the meaning
of the facts. Probably many Protestants would think that
Catholics and Protestants will always differ on their interpretations of the 'Reformation'. I venture to disagree, for time
brings changes. Meantime, this seems undeniable: many
history books, especially some written for schools, try to inspire
a hero-worship of the 'Reformers' which sets up mental barriers
to such suggestions as Dr Craig's of 'a genuine new beginning',
in which there is surcease from 'comparing and contrasting
ex parte the historical traditions which have landed us on opposite sides of a broad river.' Such history books raise barriers
not merely between 'Catholics' and 'Protestants', but between
various groups of Protestants. Dr Craig referred, I think,
mainly to the historical traditions which impede good relations
between the Church of Scotland and the Church of England;
but the same 'historical traditions' come into play in many
'Church-relationships', notably in the case of the Baptists
and of various of the Free Churches.

An example may aid in illustrating the importance of the
presentation of history. Suppose an ecumenist, deeply concerned that the Younger Churches should be really united in
the true Christian faith, were asked by the authorities of a
Far Eastern University: 'We are deciding on recommendation
of a "set book" on the history of Christianity: we have two
such before us, Harnack's *History of Dogma* and Latourette's
History of the Expansion of Christianity. Which do you recommend?'
What answer would the sincere ecumenist give? I imagine
that for undergraduate work he would recommend the latter
and not the former, because it gives a more complete
picture.

The words 'heresy' and 'schism' are disliked; and an imputation that the 'Reformers' initiated either heresy or schism
is apt to be resented. Ecumenists, however, have admitted that
they did, but express the fact in altogether different language.
Take, for instance, the very names by which 'denominations'
are known: there are over 300 of them in Europe and America
and a countless number in Africa. Some ecumenists have said
that these names must disappear, and the disappearance is

the logical conclusion of the ecumenical movement. These names fall into three main classes:

(*a*) Names derived from the founders of the 'denomination', as 'Lutherans', 'Calvinists', 'Wesleyans', etc.

(*b*) Names derived from doctrinal convictions, such as Baptist, Evangelical, Reformed, Church of the Augsburg Confession, Episcopalian, Congregationalist, Presbyterian, Pentecostalist, Seventh Day Adventist, and so on. It is sad that names originally taken with a desire to avoid denominationalism have come to have a denominational association; such is the case with the Disciples of Christ and with the Brethren of Christ.

(*c*) Names associated with nations, or regions, the Church of England, the Church of Scotland, the Church of South India, the United Church of Canada, etc. These may perhaps be unavoidable in present circumstances; but would it not be better if the term 'Church *in* South India', 'Church *in* Australia', could be used instead the preposition 'of' which carries the suggestion that the Church somehow belongs to the country named?

Now ecumenists by wishing to abolish 'denominationalism' (without, of course, abolishing reasonable diversity in language, custom and accidental matters) and in deprecating the narrowness and prejudices associated with denominationalism, are in effect saying the same thing in different words which the *Instruction* said. Schism and heresy are grievous in their effects; and some of these grievous effects are most manifest in bodies which are aggressively hostile to both the World Council of Churches and to the International Missionary Council. In passing, I wonder if it might not be possible to make clear which Churches are members of the World Council by some manifest means, such as an addition to notice boards outside their church buildings? Perhaps 'ecumenical' or 'member of World Council of Churches' added to all notices would avoid the confusion which undoubtedly exists between members of the World Council and members of other bodies whose tendencies are almost equally aggressive against the World Council, as against the Orthodox Churches and the Roman Catholic Church. This might help to dispel some of the ignorance which most certainly exists.

5. The *Instruction* from the Holy Office then says that larger gatherings are said to produce little good and much danger.

Some of the difficulties encountered at Amsterdam and at Evanston about 'intercommunion' tend to confirm this, and it may be doubted if meetings so large are as productive of lasting good results as the more sober and smaller meetings such as the meeting of Faith and Order at Lund or at Oberlin. No doubt the larger meetings may arouse considerably more interest, but certainly there were those who experienced a great sense of disappointment at least at certain moments at Evanston. An effort to apply methods too democratic in ecclesiastical affairs has dangers. It is noteworthy that the Church of South India has avoided 'majority votes' on matters of concern to the Church, and tries to secure general consent by allowing time for consideration and advice by the Bishops and leaders.

Some ecumenists seem to regard the *Instruction* of the Holy Office as unduly restrictive. Yet had the Holy Office gone to the theologians who drew up the Toronto declaration and said to them: 'You know our position and our circumstances. From your own experience inside the movement, what would you advise us?' the answer, from conscientious men, might well have been something like this: 'We do not agree with your beliefs and we do not think that your conception of authority is founded. In short, we wish you would stop being the Roman Catholic Church. But if you insist on holding to your beliefs and on being the Roman Catholic Church, then consistently with all you believe, you ought to do thus and so' —and the net result would not have been very much different from the *Instruction*. On similar principles, Bishop Newbigin, who is by no means an Anglo-Catholic, advised Anglo-Catholics to be intransigent, for the purpose of avoiding temporary and hollow agreements which break down quickly.

In short, the Roman Catholic Church tries at once to be faithful to her divine commission and to show real fraternal affection to our separated brethren; and she judges that these two efforts do not conflict with one another but rather each strengthens the other.

The announcement by Pope John XXIII of the convocation of a General Council has given added impetus to interest, zeal and prayers for the overcoming of divisions between Christians. The very fact of convening a Council stresses the association of the Head of the Church with the members, of the Pope with the Bishops. Moreover, Pope John XXIII has made plain that unity among Christians is one of the aims of the Council. The Vatican Press Office in January 1959 released the following communiqué in which news of the prospective council was made known:

> On the occasion of the visit made this morning to the patriarchal Basilica of St Paul Outside-the-Walls, and after having attended a prayer service in the papal chapel, His Holiness John XXIII delivered an allocution to the cardinals who participated in the ceremony.
>
> His Holiness spoke on several points concerning the most important apostolic activities which have been suggested to him by the first three months of his Pontificate and which concern his responsibilities as Bishop of Rome and Supreme Shepherd of the Church Universal.
>
> As Bishop of Rome, the Holy Father stressed the considerable growth of the city over these last decades and the serious problems posed by the spiritual assistance of the population.
>
> As Supreme Pastor of the Church, he alluded to the dangers which especially threaten the spiritual life of the faithful in our day, that is to say, those errors which insinuate themselves here and there, and the excessive attraction of material things, spread abroad more than ever by technical progress.
>
> In order to confront these pressing difficulties of the Christian people, the Sovereign Pontiff, drawing inspiration from the age-old practice of the Church, has announced three events of the greatest importance, namely: a diocesan synod for Rome; the celebration of an Ecumenical Council for the universal Church; and the bringing up to date of the Code of Canon Law, preceded by the proximate promulgation of the Code of Canon Law for the Eastern Church.
>
> Apropos of the Ecumenical Council, it will not only have for its end the spiritual good of the Christian people, but in the mind of the Holy Father it will serve also as an invitation to the separated communities towards the quest of that Unity to which so many today aspire in all parts of the world.

Clarifications

This announcement by the Pope was, apparently, mis-understood by some journalists; and the editor of the *Osservatore Romano*, in the issue of February 1, 1959, made some corrections: the Council was in no sense a political matter regarding relations between the State and the Church; nor was it an attempt to consolidate Christian unity 'under the assault and the fear of Communism'. This latter may be only one form of the neo-paganism characteristic of our present age, but it certainly was not specifically envisaged in the announcement of the convocation of the Council. It is not fear but charity which inspires the convocation of 'a Council for Unity'; and the motives are purely religious. After a modest reference to the massive cohesion of the Catholic Church which increases its force towards return and forgiveness, the editor turns to correct certain journalistic sensationalism which wrongly attributed to the Pope the statement that 'the Catholic Church had committed faults' in matters relative to the unity of the Churches. The expression was not used by John XXIII, declares the editor; the faults were not those of the Church but of Catholics.

Confiteor

'We Catholics, too,' says the editor, 'say our *Confiteor*. . . . The faults, of which Catholics are not, alas, free, lie in our not having prayed enough to God to smooth the ways that converge on his Church; in not having felt this charity to the full; in not having always practised it towards our separated brethren, preferring the rigour of learned, logical, incontrovertible arguments, to forbearing and patient love, which has its own compelling power of persuasion; in having preferred the philosophical rigidity of the lecture-room to the friendly serenity of the *Controversie* of St Francis of Sales. We can say our heartfelt 'Confiteor' for our selfishness in being satisfied with having certainty in the dogmas taught us by the Catholic Church, without feeling any urge or anxiety to help those to share in it who envy us for it and do not know how to come by it,—the selfishness of those who, sitting at the door of a sheltering home, watch a storm coming down on a wayfarer who, whether he is caught unawares, or bears up against it, is in any case struck by it. We are to blame for not having listened with sympathy and apostolic zeal to the constant appeals of the Popes, as if these were a mere repetition of academic platitudes, and not a call to action as insistent as other papal appeals for truth and for peace. . .

The Council, then, is a Council for unity, a Council for reconciliation, for the commonweal of Christians; and a Council of evangelical charity: Concilio dell'unità dunque, Concilio del perdono, Concilio della civiltà; Concilio di carità evangelica. . . .

The announcement of the Council has been greeted by our separated brethren with a ready welcome and with lively hope. If anyone felt an inclination to hasty and bitter repudiation, that very impulse of aversion should make him doubt about the 'truth' he holds, in accordance with the aphorism of St Francis of Sales, which is borne out by experience: 'a truth which is not charitable is a truth which is not true'. May God grant that in such meditations, minds and hearts may turn to a more conciliatory and Christian attitude.[1]

There have been, very naturally, speculations about the subjects which the Council might take into deliberation, and speculations about the relation of the Council itself to those not in communion with the Catholic and Roman Church. I write this in May, 1959, and by the time this book is printed, some of these speculations will have been confirmed, others modified and others, perhaps, corrected. Consequently, I only repeat here that the convocation of the Council has very manifestly been made in a generous and large-hearted spirit. Difficulties are undoubtedly great and perhaps humanly insuperable; nevertheless a supernatural charity may be able to overcome obstacles before which merely human wisdom is helpless. The Holy Spirit of God will be present at the Council and will guide its deliberations and conclusions; it is in that Holy Spirit that our hopes must principally rest.

[1] *Osservatore Romano*, Domenica 1st Feb., 1959, pp. 1, 2.

EPILOGUE

In this study of the ecumenical movement I am sadly aware that, in spite of sincere efforts, some things may have been omitted and other things not rightly said. If any reader feel aggrieved at omissions or misrepresentations, I can only offer my sincere apologies and an assurance of willingness to do my best to put matters right. My own convictions may be summed up:

1. The divisions among Christians are so intractable, and so tragic, that we must have incessant and intense recourse to the mercy of our loving God that he may accomplish what seems humanly impossible. God can do what we poor men cannot do. Our hope must be in him.

2. Charity can be, and should be, reconciled with firmness to principle. The union of these two is difficult, but a spirit of magnanimity, received from our Saviour's Holy Spirit, can achieve it.

Dr MacLeod did well to cite Dr Heenan: We must love each another until we come to see the same truth. We must stand to our principles, and yet we must go on loving each another. 'Now there remains these three: faith, hope and charity. But the greatest of these is charity.'

3. Theologians and thinkers should search for unrealized principles of agreement beneath and behind the disagreements. There is acute need of vigorous yet calm theological study, since an impatient desire for quick if not spectacular results will defeat itself. Yet patience must not degenerate into slothful acceptance of divisions.

The very desire for unity, vague though it may be, unfruitful of concrete results though it may seem, should at all costs be clung to and fostered.

4. Our eyes should never close upon the vision of the Church as one with Christ the Light of the world and the Saviour of the world. By baptism all Christians are marked and sealed with Christ as kings and priests and prophets. Therefore they share in the sending of Christ by his Father, who desires all men to be saved and to come to the knowledge of the truth. All questions of 'disunion', all questions of theology, must be

viewed in the light of the appeal of Christ to non-Christians to enter, of themselves, freely and gladly, into their royal and eternal inheritance with Christ.

A corrective for possible wrong perspectives is to turn our eyes and hearts towards the millions and millions of men for whom Christ died, whom Christ now loves, with whom Christ suffers, yet who do not know him and love him. Is it in any way due to us that they do not know or love him?

But, at the end, with St Paul we must humbly say:

> We preach Christ crucified:
>> Unto the Jews indeed a stumbling block
>> And unto the Gentiles foolishness:
> But to them that are called, both Jews and Greeks,
> Christ the power of God and the wisdom of God.
>> For the foolishness of God is wiser than men;
>> And the weakness of God is stronger than men. . . .
> For the foolish things of the world hath God chosen,
>> That he may confound the wise:
> And the weak things of the world hath God chosen
>> That he may confound the strong:
> And the base things of the world,
> And the things that are contemptible
>> Hath God chosen:
>> And the things that are not:
> That he might bring to naught the things that are:
>> That no flesh may glory in his sight.[1]

[1] Cor. 1: 23–30.

APPENDIX I

The Meaning and Use of the Word 'Church'

In the Report, published in 1950, of the conversations between representatives of the Archbishop of Canterbury and of the Evangelical Free Churches in England, the following is said about the word 'Church':

> We are agreed that the modern use of the words 'Church' and 'Churches' to mean the different denominations or communions into which Christendom is now divided corresponds to nothing in the Bible. The New Testament Church did not consist of a number of separated bodies comparable to our 'Churches', but was one single Communion. When the word 'Church' is used of some one Church as distinct from others (e.g. the Church at Ephesus or at Corinth) there is no suggestion of one body being denominationally different from another. There was one Church of which all Christians were members. In each place the local Church was the congregation of all the Christians in that place. All were in communion with one another and with all other Christians elsewhere. We have to face the fact that neither in Christendom as a whole, nor in most of our towns and villages, is there any body which corresponds to the New Testament idea of the Church as the fellowship in which all the Christians of the place are united in their Christian life and worship.[1]
>
> In the course of time words change their meanings. It is impossible to avoid the modern usage, and to confine our use of the words 'Church' and 'Churches' to describe what they mean in the New Testament. We have to do two things: (i) recognize frankly that our modern usage is unbiblical and that therefore we must be careful how we seek to find in New Testament passages the answer to our present-day problems, and (ii) be careful, in considering any modern statement, to determine from the context the sense in which the word 'Church' is being used. (P. 20).

[1] This is, of course, an assertion which would be qualified by both the Orthodox and the Roman Catholics. St John speaks of those who 'went out from us' in his first letter 2, 19, and the Church in the first five centuries, certainly never considered the existence of schisms or of heresy as something that denied the substantial unity of the Church. The unity may, indeed, shine out more conspicuously at one period than at another, but it can never be lost, and was not lost even at the time of the Arian controversy or of the schism of the West. But this remark is incidental to the use of the word 'Church'.

Dr Oliver Tomkins, Secretary of the Conference on Faith and Order at Lund in 1952, put the distressing position caused by the existence of present divisions as follows:

I suspect that there will be many members of this conference who have not yet quite grasped the implications of being in a fellowship in which not all the Churches are prepared to say of other bodies in it that they consider them to be *Churches* in the full and true sense of the word. It is equally embarrassing to have one's own Church treated as though it were not really a Church, and to have to treat bodies which one does not believe to be Churches practically as if they were. But to wish to have it otherwise would be to reduce the Council to an association of bodies (whichever they might be) which are already in virtual agreement. Such an association might serve quite useful purposes, but it would not be the Council into which we have in fact been led. No, this Council has come to be as it is not primarily because we liked each other, or agree together, but because God has called us into it in spite of ourselves.[1]

In the Report of the Lund Conference, 1952, submitted to the Churches for consideration, it is said:

Membership in the World Council of Churches implies a measure of recognition in that the Churches recognize one another as serving one Lord. But differences of faith and order still exist and membership in the Council does not imply that one Church must regard all other members as Churches in the full sense.[2]

Dr Newbigin, until recently Bishop in Madurai, says:

One may summarize the situation as this document (Dr Newbigin refers to the document issued at Toronto in 1950, which does not in this matter differ from the Lund statement of 1952 just quoted) states it by saying that the World Council of Churches gives institutional embodiment to the conviction that the Church ought to be one, while remaining neutral as to the proper form of that unity. It thus provides a place in which very diverse views as to the unity which the Church ought to have can confront one another in fruitful conversation. There are those who

[1] *The Third World Conference on Faith and Order, Lund, 1952*, ed. Oliver S. Tomkins, Chairman of Working Committee Faith and Order Commission, London, 1953, p. 164.
[2] *Ibid.* p. 33.

hold that the divinely willed form of the Church's unity already exists in their own communion (whether in assent to doctrines as formulated in a particular confession, or in acceptance of a particular historic order) and who therefore cannot regard bodies outside their own communion as, in the full sense, Churches.[1]

A Catholic hesitates, however, to say that separated bodies only fail to be Churches 'in the full sense' as if bodies could be 'Churches' in a partial or 'less full' or 'less true' sense; but the expression 'our separated brethren' used by Roman Catholics in public and private prayers and very generally in discussion, is a better expression, showing a real feeling of affection and coming nearer to the truth than any more abstruse formula propounded by theologians seeking for exquisite doctrinal accuracy about 'membership in the Church'. As Père Congar has shown, the Popes have spoken of the dissident Eastern bodies as 'Churches'.[2]

Thus the very words used in talking about the existing situation of Christendom at once raise most thorny theological questions. Many claim that the World Council of Churches exists in order to abolish the use of the term 'Churches' and to restore the use of the word 'Church' to its sole true meaning, that is, to designate complete unity in faith and order of all who bear the Christian name. However this may be, I have tried to avoid controversies about words and titles, in hopes that readers will understand that choice of words has no doctrinal implication.

It is commonly known that many non-Romans object to 'Roman Catholics' speaking of themselves as 'Catholics', whereas 'Roman Catholics' desire to be called simply 'Catholics'. Similarly, the 'Anglo-Catholics' have difficulties about being so called, and (at least some of them) would regard themselves as the Catholic Church in England. Thus words raise deep problems. I use the word 'Church' and 'Churches' of dissident bodies, because the title 'Church' has in fact been taken by so many of our separated brethren,

---

[1] *The Household of God*, London 1953, reprinted 1954 and 1955, p. 20.
[2] Cf. *Divided Christendom*, London, 1939, Appendix iv, pp. 294-5.

because its modern usage has only remote doctrinal connotations and because it is so very hard to find any alternative.

The word 'Catholic', for instance, raises other acute difficulties. Speaking broadly, people generally understand the
main lines of division between 'Catholic' and 'Protestant', at
least in the West; the touchstone of difference is often regarded
as adherence to the Bishop of Rome as Head of the Church,
but this is by no means the universal understanding. The
Eastern Orthodox Churches are certainly recognized as
'Catholic' and not 'Protestant', in spite of their rejection of
the supreme authority of the Papacy; and when one begins to
talk of 'Catholic' and 'Protestant' traditions, the matter
presents more awkwardness than is at first sight apparent.
In 1947 a group of Anglican theologians wrote a booklet
entitled *Catholicity, a Study in the Conflict of Christian Traditions
in the West, being a report presented to His Grace the Archbishop of
Canterbury*, London, 1947, in which they contrasted the 'Catholic' and the 'Protestant' tradition. But Dr R. Newton Flew
and Dr Rupert Davies wrote an answer, entitled *The Catholicity
of Protestantism*, London, 1950, in which they contended that
those who are called 'Protestants' have in fact maintained the
'Catholic' faith and practice more faithfully than have those
called 'Catholics'.

This is not the place to enter into the merits of this disagreement; but it may be worth pointing out that there is a
certain 'tradition' among English-speaking Roman Catholics
(I use the term 'Roman Catholic' without prejudice, for
clearness) which is nearer to the Free Church tradition than to
the Anglican; it is a tradition springing from memories of
persecution and of exclusion from rights and opportunities,
which membership in the Church of England—the State
Church—would have given. The Oxford movement and the
attitude of the Free Churches on education did much to
change this tradition, but have not entirely eradicated it.
John Henry Newman, who has been so influential among
English-speaking Roman Catholics, sprang from an 'evangelical' background and much that he wrote as a Catholic seems
to have an 'evangelical' savour.

APPENDIX II

On March 4, 1950, *The Tablet* published the following Instruction from the Holy Office to Local Ordinaries on the Ecumenical Movement:[1]

The Catholic Church although she does not participate in 'ecumenical' conferences or meetings, nevertheless, as may be seen from many papal documents, has never ceased, nor ever will, from following with deepest interest and furthering with fervent prayers every effort to secure what Christ our Lord had so much at heart, namely, that all who believe in Him 'may be made perfect in one.' Indeed, with the true love of a mother she embraces all those who return to her as to Christ's one, true Church. The fullest approval and encouragement is always given to all those plans and enterprises which have been undertaken, with the consent of ecclesiastical authority, either for the instruction of those seeking the faith or for the further instruction of those already received.

The present time has witnessed in different parts of the world a growing desire amongst many persons outside the Church for the reunion of all who believe in Christ. This may be attributed, under the inspiration of the Holy Ghost, to external factors and the changing attitude of men's minds but above all to the united prayers of the faithful. To all children of the true Church this is a cause for holy joy in the Lord; it urges them to extend a helping hand to all those sincerely seeking after the truth by praying fervently that God will enlighten them and give them strength.

Yet is it clear from experience that so far certain attempts of various individuals or groups to bring about this reconciliation of dissident Christians with the Catholic Church have not always been founded upon sound principles, even though inspired by the best of intentions. Even where the principles are sound, special dangers are always present. For this reason this Supreme Sacred Congregation, whose care it is to watch over and preserve intact the deposit of faith, considers it opportune to issue a reminder of the following points and to enjoin their observance:—

I. Bishops, whom 'the Holy Ghost has placed to rule the Church of God,' ought to make a special object of their care and attention this work of 'reunion' which is a particular charge and duty of the Church. They must not only use great diligence in

[1] I have made one change in the translation of the Latin, namely in the first sentence.

keeping all this under effective supervision, but give it prudent encouragement and direction with the twofold purpose of assisting those who are in search of truth and the true Church and of shielding the faithful from the dangers which so easily accompany the progress of this movement. In the first place they must fully acquaint themselves with the past and present activities of the movement in their own dioceses. For this purpose they shall appoint suitable priests to make a special study of the movement and everything connected with it. These studies shall be along the lines laid down by the Holy See and in accordance with papal teaching (e.g. in the Encyclical letters *Satis cognitum*, *Mortalium animos* and *Mystici Corporis Christi*), and the priest shall duly report back to the Bishop from time to time.

Any form of publication on this subject by a Catholic calls for special vigilance; the Bishops will insist upon strict observance of the Canon Law 'On previous censorship and prohibition of books' (canons 1384 *et seq.*) The same applies also to publications of non-Catholics on this subject if they are intended for publication, reading or sale by Catholics.

Moreover the Bishops will see that facilities are provided for non-Catholics seeking knowledge of the Faith, and that there are centres where specially appointed persons may be visited and consulted by non-Catholics. They will also make provision for those who have already been received into the Church to be further instructed in the Faith and the practice of their religion. This may be done by suitable conferences, study groups, retreats and other spiritual exercises.

II. As to the method to be followed in this work, the Bishops themselves will prescribe what is or is not to be done, and they will see to it that all obey. They should be on their guard against those who under false pretexts stress the points on which we agree rather than those on which we disagree. Such an approach may give rise to a dangerous indifferentism, especially amongst those who are not so well versed in theology or the practice of their religion. They must be on their guard, too, against the so-called spirit of 'eirenicism' which, looking in vain for a progressive assimilation of the various creeds, subjects the tenets of Catholicism, whether dogmas or truths connected with dogma, to a process of comparative study, whittling them down and bringing them into line with non-Catholic teaching. In this way the purity of Catholic doctrine is jeopardized and its original and true meaning obscured.

Certain dangerous modes of expression also must be avoided, inasmuch as they give rise to false opinions and misleading hopes which can never be fulfilled: saying, for example, that what the Popes have written in their Encyclical letters about the return of our separated brethren to the Church, about the Mystical Body or about the constitution of the Church, is not to be taken too seriously, for after all not everything is *de fide;* worse still, saying that in the realm of dogma not even the Catholic Church yet possesses the fulness of Christ, but can be perfected from other sources. The Bishops will pay special attention to the manner in which the story of the Reformation is presented and will take a firm stand against any exaggeration of shortcomings on the Catholic side coupled with a glossing over of the Reformers' errors. They will guard against the undue focusing of attention on side issues so that the real point, a falling away from the Catholic faith, is obscured and barely perceived. Finally they will take care lest harm, rather than good, may be done to the cause by the excessive and over-zealous activity of misguided enthusiasts. Catholic teaching is therefore to be set forth and explained whole and entire and none of its truths must be passed over in silence or cloaked in ambiguity; for example, the truths concerning the nature and means of salvation, the constitution of the Church, the Roman Pontiff's primacy of jurisdiction and the certainty that true reunion can only come about by the return of dissidents to the one, true Church of Christ. Non-Catholics may certainly be told that, should they return to the Church, such good as the grace of God has already wrought in their souls will not be lost, but will be completed and brought to perfection. But they must not be given the impression that by their return they are contributing to the Church something essential which formerly she lacked. All this must be stated clearly and openly since they are seeking the truth and real union will never be found outside that truth.

III. Mixed gatherings and conferences of Catholics and non-Catholics such as have been initiated in the past few years for the purpose of fostering 'reunion' call for exceptional vigilance and control on the part of Ordinaries. Even though they provide a welcome opportunity for speading knowledge of the Faith among non-Catholics, who for the most part are more or less ignorant of Catholic teaching, there is a real danger that the Catholic participants may become tainted with indifferentism. Where there is hope of good resulting the Ordinary will see that such meetings are properly conducted and will appoint priests best qualified for this work to put forward a suitable exposition and defence of Catholic doctrine. The faithful, however, may not attend these meetings without first obtaining special permission from the ecclesiastical authorities and this will only be granted to those who are known to be well instructed and firmly grounded in the Faith. Where on the other hand there is no such hope of good resulting or where special dangers arise from the particular circumstances, the faithful must prudently be prevented from attending and the meetings themselves be either suspended as soon as possible or gradually brought to a close. Experience shows that as a rule little good results from larger gatherings of this character, and that they are in fact a source of danger only to be permitted after most careful investigation.

For discussions between Catholic and non-Catholic theologians only priests are to be sent and these must have proved their fitness for such tasks by their knowledge of theology and by their close adherence to the Church's principles and regulations in this matter.

IV. All such gatherings and conferences, whether public or private, large or small, are subject to the Church's prescriptions to which attention was drawn in the warning *Cum compertum*, issued by this Sacred Congregation on June 5, 1948. These gatherings, at which Catholics and non-Catholics undertake to meet as equals and discuss matters of faith and morals, each one putting forward the teaching proper to his creed, are not absolutely forbidden but they may only be held with the approval of the competent ecclesiastical authority. This warning does not apply to catechetical instructions, even when these are given to a number of persons together; nor does it apply to conferences at which Catholic doctrine is explained to prospective converts. This holds good even if on such occasions opportunity is afforded to the non-Catholics to expound the beliefs of their own denominations so that they may see clearly and accurately how these agree or disagree with Catholic teaching. Nor does the warning of 1948 apply to those mixed gatherings where Catholics and non-Catholics meet, not to discuss matters of faith and morals, but to take counsel together concerning joint action in the defence of the fundamental principles of Christianity and the natural law; nor does it apply to occasions when they meet to deal with the rebuilding of the social order and similar questions.

In the case of conferences and meetings which come within the terms of the warning explained above but which are purely local in character, local Ordinaries are hereby given the faculty for three years from the publication of this Instruction to grant the requisite permission of the Holy See on condition that: (1) There is absolutely no *communicatio in sacris;* (2) The discussions themselves are duly supervised and controlled; (3) At the end of each year a report is sent to this Supreme Congregation giving a list of the places where such meetings have been held and an account of what experiences have been gained.

With regard to theological discussions the same faculty is granted for a similar period to the Ordinary of the place in which the discussions are to be held, or to the Bishop whom the other Ordinaries have, by common consent, appointed to assume the direction of such activities. The conditions are as above with this addition: That each year this Sacred Congregation is to be informed of the questions discussed, the names of those present and the speakers on both sides.

For interdiocesan, national or international conferences, special permission must be obtained each time before the event from the Holy See itself. The petition must specify the questions to be discussed and give the names of the proposed speakers. Moreover, before this permission has been obtained, no one may begin public preparations for such a conference or make any approach to non-Catholics engaged in similar work.

V. Although every sort of *communicatio in sacris* is to be avoided at all such conferences and meetings, it is not forbidden to open or close these gatherings with the common recitation of the Lord's Prayer or some other prayer approved by the Catholic Church.

VI. It is the right and duty of each Ordinary to direct and take the lead in promoting this work in his diocese but the co-operation of several bishops may be useful and even necessary in setting up offices and organizations to observe, examine and direct this work as a whole. It will be for these Ordinaries to consult together and decide the most suitable means of obtaining uniformity and concerted action.

VII. Religious superiors must be watchful, and secure from their subjects strict and loyal obedience to the injunctions of the Holy See and all local Ordinaries.

This excellent work of 'reunion' of all Christians in the one true Faith and in the Church should daily assume a more significant place within the Church's universal pastoral care, and every Catholic should pray ever more earnestly to God for this object. It will prove a great help if the faithful are suitably instructed, for example, by pastoral letters, about these questions and the steps being taken, together with the Church's instructions on this matter and the reasons underlying them. All, especially priests and religious, should be encouraged to take an ardent interest and do everything in their power, by prayer and sacrifice, to work for the success of this cause. Finally, all should be reminded that nothing will contribute more towards preparing the way for our separated brethren to embrace the Faith and enter the Church than the living by Catholics of edifying lives in accord with their Faith.

Given at the Palace of the Holy Office, in Rome, the 20th day of December, 1949.

FRANCIS CARD. MARCHETTI-SELVAGGIANI,
Secretary

Alfred Ottaviani,
Assessor

APPENDIX III

The Unitas Association

The Unitas Association is an international organization whose purpose it is to promote the spiritual union of men and especially of Christians. It was founded in Rome in 1945 by a group of professors and writers, priests and laymen; and in June of that year received the blessing of Pope Pius XII. Fr Charles Boyer, S.J., Dean of the Theological Faculty of the Gregorian University in Rome, was elected president of the Association and also serves as editor of its organ *Unitas* which appears in three editions: English, French, and Italian.

Established at the centre of Catholicity, the Unitas Association in carrying on its activities endeavours to follow with studied perfection the guidance of the Holy See. In striving to fulfill its purpose, it attempts to regulate its mission in accordance with the following principles:

To Catholics it recalls the benefits of the unity which they enjoy and the duty which is incumbent upon them to pray for those who are deprived of it. The Association invites the active co-operation of Catholics and exhorts them to keep ever before them the advice of Pope Pius XI: 'This unity ought to be promoted less by discussion or other means than by the example of a saintly life'.

To its separated brethren of the Eastern Churches, it speaks of those long glorious centuries of union when the Doctors of the East illumined the universal Church and triumphed with their Latin brethren over the most subtle and distressing heresies. Unitas lays stress upon all that the separated East has preserved in common with Catholics: the priesthood, the Sacraments, the cult of the Blessed Virgin Mary. It makes clear the duty of union and strives to eliminate the barriers which prejudice and resentment have in the course of the centuries erected between Christians of the East and West.

To Anglicans and Protestants, Unitas reveals the genuine character of the Roman Catholic Church. Across the imperfections of men, it tries to make evident that spirit of fraternal affection and faithfulness to the teachings of Christ which is at the very heart of the Church's life and the manifestation of the Holy Spirit at work in her. Finally, Unitas keeps in close touch with the Ecumenical Movement, and endeavours to aid it in its quest for unity.

*   *   *

The Unitas Association has affiliated groups in Italy, France, Belgium, Canada, and Turkey. All that is necessary to form a group of this kind to further the aim of Christian unity is that a small number of persons of good will plan their organization, obtain the approval of their bishop, and then make their step known to the Central Committee of the Association in Rome.

APPENDIX IV

THE PASTORAL LETTER OF THE DUTCH HIERARCHY ABOUT THE AMSTERDAM ASSEMBLY OF 1948

The Archbishop and the Bishops of the Netherlands to the clergy and faithful entrusted to their charge.

Blessedness in the Lord.

Dear Brethren,

From August 22nd until September 5th next the 'World Council of Churches' will come together in a congress to discuss the theme: 'God's Design and Man's Disorder'. This Congress, which is going to be devoted to a subject of such present-day interest, and which moreover is going to be held in our own country, namely in Amsterdam, will certainly also draw the attention of many Catholics in this country. For this reason, apart from all others, we have considered it to be our duty to address you in a common pastoral letter telling you about this congress.

For quite a considerable time non-Catholic Christians have been alarmed at the religious divisions existing between Christians. They understand that this disunity is contrary to the commandment of our Lord Jesus Christ and must needs have fatal consequences with regard to the salvation of mankind. The so-called Oecumenical Movement found its origin in this alarm and is striving towards a new religious unity among all those who are willing to accept Jesus Christ as their Lord and Saviour. Shortly before the outbreak of the last world war this movement acquired more definite shape through the foundation of the so-called World Council of Churches, and the congress which will now be held at Amsterdam will be the first fully attended meeting of this World Council of Churches.

Beloved brethren, also the Catholic Church—no less than any one else—deplores the religious disunion between the Christians. She, too, realises how fatal are the consequences of this disunion. Also she is quite ready to acknowledge that this endeavour towards a new religious unity is inspired by the best intentions of many people. But notwithstanding all this, she feels compelled to stand aloof and thus there can be no question of the Holy Catholic Church taking part in the congress at Amsterdam.

This aloofness is not based on any fear of losing prestige or any other merely tactical consideration. This attitude solely proceeds from the conviction of the Church that she must be unshakably true to the task with which Jesus Christ has entrusted her. For she is the one holy catholic and apostolic Church which was founded by Jesus Christ in order that His work of salvation might be carried on through her unto the end of all times; she is the mystical Body of Christ; she is Christ's Bride. In her this unity exists imperishably; for Christ has promised her that the gates of hell should not prevail against her (Matt. 16: 18).

That is why the divisions between the Christians can only be put an end to in one way: by a return to her; by a return within the unity which has always been preserved within Her. If, however, the Catholic Church were to participate in the endeavour towards a new religious unity and this on an equal footing with the others, then by doing so she would in fact admit that the unity, willed by Christ, does not continue within her and that, therefore, there really is no Church of Christ. Indeed, it is just by her very aloofness that she must not cease to manifest that within Her the unity as willed by Christ has always been preserved and that within Her this unity remains accessible to all.

This duty to keep aloof is also shown in another way. Genuine unity is not possible without unity of faith. This is also realised more and more clearly by a growing number of people within the Oecumenical Movement. But how is such a unity of faith safeguarded? Our Lord Jesus Christ has charged Peter and the other Apostles and their successors to preach the Gospel in His Name and on His Authority. 'Whosoever hears you, hears Me; whosoever despises you, despises Me' (Luke 10: 16). For this purpose He promised them the help of the Holy Ghost. In the power of this Holy Ghost, the Popes and Bishops as successors of Peter and the Apostles have preserved the revealed Truth unimpaired and preached it with infallible authority; and they will continue doing so until the Lord comes again. Who accepts their Word accepts Christ's word and by doing this enters into the unity of faith. Now, how would it be possible for the Pope and the Bishops to consider, together with others, whether perhaps they have misunderstood the Word of God's Revelation and have preached human inventions as Divine? What would this mean but want of faith in Christ's promise or doubt of the power of the Holy Ghost? No, they can only go on preaching Christ's teaching with infallible authority and, in this manner, preserving the unity of faith.

Therefore, there can be no question of the Holy Catholic Church taking part in the Amsterdam congress. But we will certainly follow the proceedings of this congress with the greatest possible interest.

For this congress has been born out of a great and sincere desire for the unity willed by Christ on the part of many who are prepared to accept Him as their God and their Saviour. And how could we, who have been charged by the Holy Ghost, under the guidance of St Peter's successor, to preserve and extend the Church in Her unity, carelessly ignore a sincere longing for unity? Nor can it be a matter of indifference to us whether this congress will mean a step forward or a step backward: a step forward if the congress will lead to a strengthening of the yearning for the Mother Church and the unity which is given in Her; a step backward, if the result should be that many are satisfied with a unity which is still far removed from the unity which Christ has brought. A return to the Mother Church, this it is, dear brethren, by which true unity can be achieved. But we know that there are deeply rooted prejudices which stand in the way of such a return. We know that, owing to the abuses which existed at the time of the schisms and also owing to growing estrangements, the gulf and alienation have become so great that the voice and the language of the Holy Church are no longer understood by her separated children. We know that for many a return is not possible without a severe inner struggle and great personal sacrifices. We know that a wholehearted return will never be possible, unless God by His Grace enlightens human intelligence and moves the human will. And finally we know that God wants His grace to be asked for.

That is why we urgently call upon all of you, priests and people, to join us in fervent prayer. During these days, pray for all those who take part in this congress and for the many other non-Catholic Christians, who longingly look out for unity, who truly follow Christ and live in His love and who—although they are separated from Christ's flock—yet look to the Church—be it often unconsciously—as the only haven of salvation. Especially pray for those who act as leaders of the non-Catholic Christians, and who carry such a heavy responsibility because the simple faithful are dependent upon their attitude and often cannot attain the right insight by themselves. Pray Our Father in Heaven, 'Whose will it is that all men should be saved and be led to recognise the truth' (I Tim. 2: 4). Pray to Him through Jesus Christ, 'Who lives to be our Mediator' (Hebr. 7: 25). Pray to Him in the one Holy Ghost who is the lifegiving soul of the one mystical Body of Christ. Pray that all may share in the true unity, which is not made by men, but which has been brought into this world by Jesus Christ Our Lord.

Do not forget, however, dear brethren, that your example is

necessary as much as your prayer. In early times the un-Christian lives of many Catholics have furthered the apostasy from the Church. At the Council of Trent the Church Herself has brought this apostasy to an end through a wholesome reform, 'in head and members'. In the same way the return to the Mother Church will best be promoted if we show forth the holiness of our faith in the holiness of our life and work.

And if in the past, when defending the Catholic unity, not all Catholics have always been led by love and therefore have not always been mindful of the word of the Apostle: 'veritatem facientes in caritate; preserving the truth in love' (Eph. 4: 15) and therefore are not free from guiltiness in respect of the alienation which has arisen between ourselves and non-Catholic Christians, then this certainly has not been according to the spirit of our Mother, the Holy Church.

She Herself always is and remains the Holy Church. She remains Holy in Her Liturgy, Her Sacraments and Her Sacrifice and in the life of grace, which She mediates thereby. She remains Holy in Her teaching, which comes from God and leads back to God. She remains Holy in Her laws, which are directed only towards the Honour of God and the salvation of mankind. She remains Holy because at all times She brings forth great saints. By this holiness She continuously proves Her Divine origin. But all Her members are and remain human beings; in them human nature—sometimes all too human—may manifest itself; and these human, all too human, weaknesses may sometimes be a source of scandal and the cause also of the fact that many are not able to see the real holiness of the Church.

That is why in these times a heavy responsibility rests upon us, Catholics. Now that many, who acknowledge Christ, have shown to have felt a strong and real longing for unity, it is of a great importance, that our lives should be permeated entirely by the spirit of Christ and that, in all our activities, in every sphere of life, we should not seek anything but Jesus Christ and the spreading of His Kingdom. More than ever before we should now obey Christ's command: 'Your light must so shine before men that they can see your good works and glorify your Father, Who is in Heaven.' (Matt. 5: 16). More than ever before we must now make the holiness of the Church visible in our own lives. May God give that all understand this duty; and may the Holy Ghost Who is the Spirit of Christ, come to the aid of our weakness in the fulfilment of this duty (Rom. 8: 26).

Finally, beloved brethren, We prescribe that in all churches belonging to the Church Province of the Netherlands and in all chapels where a rector has been appointed, on Sunday August 29th next, a solemn, or at least a sung Holy Mass shall be celebrated to obtain from God that all may share in the unity of the Holy Church. For this purpose the form which is indicated in the Roman Missal as Votive Mass for the ending of schism (*Missa ad tollendum schisma*) is to be used. We trust that all of you will unite yourselves as closely as possible with this Holy Sacrifice.

And this our pastoral letter shall be read from the pulpit in the usual manner and at the appointed time during all Holy Masses on Sunday, 22nd next in all churches belonging to the Church Province of the Netherlands and in all chapels where a rector has been appointed.

Given at Utrecht, July 31st 1948.

JOANNES CARDINAL DE JONG, Archbishop of Utrecht
P. A. W. HOPMANS, Bishop of Breda
DR. J. H. G. LEMMENS, Bishop of Roermond
J. P. HUIBERS, Bishop of Haarlem
W. P. A. M. MUTSAERTS, Bishop of 's-Hertogenbosch

APPENDIX V

In Toronto in July, 1950, the Central Committee commended for study a statement entitled 'The Ecclesiological Significance of the World Council of Churches.' This document was an attempt to answer questions which arose subsequently to the 1948 Assembly at Amsterdam and was made 'especially in the face of a number of false or inadequate conceptions of the Council which are being presented'. The document makes thirteen brief assertions, printed in heavy type, with explanations of each. I give all the assertions or 'articles', but only some of the more important explanations with an occasional comment of my own.

Part I

What the World Council is Not

1. The World Council of Churches is not and must never become a Super-Church.

Membership in the Council does not in any sense mean that the Churches belong to a body which can take decisions for them. Each Church retains the constitutional right to ratify or to reject utterances or actions of the Council. The 'authority' of the council consists only 'in the weight which it carries with the Churches by its own wisdom.'[1]

2. The purpose of the World Council of Churches is not to negotiate unions between Churches, which can only be done by the Churches themselves acting on their own initiation, but to bring the Churches into living contact with each other and to promote the study and discussion of the issues of church unity.

3. The World Council cannot and should not be based on any one conception of the Church. It does not prejudge the ecclesiological problem.

[1] William Temple.

The World Council exists in order that different Churches may face their differences, and therefore no Church is obliged to change its ecclesiology as a consequence of membership in the World Council.

4. Membership in the World Council of Churches does not imply that a Church treats its own conception of the Church as merely relative.[1]

5. Membership in the World Council does not imply the acceptance of a specific doctrine concerning the nature of Church unity.

In particular, membership in the World Council does not imply acceptance of the doctrine that the unity of the Church consists in the unity of the invisible Church. Thus the statement in the Encyclical *Mystici Corporis* concerning what it considers the error of a spiritualized conception of unity does not apply to the World Council. The World Council does not 'imagine a Church which one cannot see or touch, which would be only spiritual, in which numerous Christian bodies though divided in matters of faith, would nevertheless be united through an invisible link.' It does, however, include Churches which believe that the Church is invisible as well as those which hold that visible unity is essential.

Part II

Positive assumptions which underlie the World Council of Churches and the ecclesiological implications of membership in it.

1. The member Churches of the Council believe that conversation, co-operation and common witness of the Churches must be based on the common recognition that Christ is the Divine Head of the Body.

In the explanation is said: 'The fact of Christ's Headship over His people *compels all those who acknowledge Him to enter into real and close relationships with each other* (italics mine) even though they differ in many points.'

Some commentary upon this 'positive assumption' has been given in the text of this work, pp. 182–5.

---

[1] The explanation of this article has been given on pages 180–1.

2. The member Churches of the World Council believe on the basis of the New Testament that the Church of Christ is one.

The ecumenical movement owes its existence to the fact that this article of the faith has again come home to men and women in many Churches with an irresistible force. As they face the discrepancy between the truth that there is and can be only one Church of Christ and the fact that there exist so many Churches which claim to be Churches of Christ but are not in living unity with each other, they feel a holy dissatisfaction with the present situation. The Churches realize that it is a matter of simple Christian duty for each Church to do its utmost for the manifestation of the Church in its oneness, and to work and pray that Christ's purpose for His Church be fulfilled.

Naturally there are differing conceptions of the way in which each Church can 'do its utmost', and this explanation does not suggest the contrary. Nor need it suggest that Christ's purpose for his Church has been frustrated, but only that it is not in every respect completed and perfected. But we walk on slippery ground here. The Roman Catholic Church, like the Orthodox, holds that Christ's purpose has been 'fulfilled', save in accidentals, and that there *is* already 'a manifestation of the Church in its oneness'. The explanation does not say that the Church is not manifested in its oneness, but only that each Church should do its utmost 'for' that manifestation. The word 'for' is ambiguous. 'To do its utmost for the manifestation of the Church in its oneness' may mean that the oneness is not now manifest and the Churches must strive to make it so, or it may mean that the Churches must co-operate with God's grace to maintain and make still more manifest the oneness which in fact exists. The Roman Catholic Church rejects the first meaning and accepts the second. The difficulty might easily be avoided by making the article read: 'it is a simple Christian duty for all individuals and groups to do their utmost for the unity of Christendom', etc.

3. The member Churches recognize that the membership of the Church of Christ is more inclusive than the membership of their own church body. They

seek, therefore to enter into living contact with those outside their own ranks who confess the Lordship of Christ.

All the Christian Churches, including the Church of Rome, hold that there is no complete identity between the membership of the Church Universal and the membership of their own Church. They recognize that there are church members 'extra muros', that these belong 'aliquo modo' to the Church, or even that there is an 'ecclesia extra ecclesiam'. This recognition finds expression in the fact that with very few exceptions the Christian Churches accept the baptism administered by other Churches as valid.[1]

But the question arises what consequences are to be drawn from this teaching. Most often in church history the Churches have only drawn the negative consequence that they should have no dealings with those outside their membership. The underlying assumption of the ecumenical movement is that each Church has a positive task to fulfil in this realm. That task is to seek fellowship with all those who, while not members of the same visible body, belong together as members of the mystical body. And the ecumenical movement is the place where the search and discovery take place.

This article makes a statement about the belief held by those Churches which are actually in the World Council; and for my part I rejoice greatly that they are seeking the unity which Christ wills and I am convinced that they seek it sincerely and humbly, and I would not do anything to lessen their zeal or to make their effort less appreciated. At the same time I am sure that what is said in this article could not be accepted, as it is worded, by the Roman Catholic Church, nor by the Orthodox. My reservations would run along these lines.

(a) I should like further definition of the term 'Church Universal'. What is the Church Universal? How do the member Churches understand it? Presumably, in accordance with the refusal 'to prejudge the ecclesiological problem' and the resolve to remain 'neutral' with regard to the concept of an invisible Church, of (5) above, each Church may hold that it alone is the Church Universal upon earth. But the wording

---

[1] The Baptists generally deny the validity of infant baptism, and the Orthodox hold that all sacraments outside the Orthodox Church are *per se* invalid, though they can be held valid through the 'economy'.

of this article (3) seems to distinguish between the Church Universal and 'their own Church', and this is incompatible with the conviction of both Roman Catholics and the Orthodox that their own Church is the Universal Church. This may perhaps be only a matter of wording, but as it reads the article is certainly not clear, and introduces complex questions about the relationship of the Church militant and the Church triumphant.

(b) 'Membership in the Church Universal' and 'members of the mystical body': although it is common Catholic teaching that all men of good will, and not only Christians, may belong to the Church 'in some way', by 'an unrealized wish and desire', nevertheless the Encyclical on the Mystical Body says: 'Only those are to be accounted really (*reapse*) members of the Church who have been regenerated in the waters of Baptism and profess the true faith, and have not cut themselves off from the structure of the Body by their own unhappy act or been severed therefrom, for very grave crimes, by legitimate authority.'[1] Therefore according to the teaching either of the Roman Catholic faith or of the Orthodox, as they have often declared, those who do not profess the true faith are not 'really' or 'in fact' members of the Church. The suggestion that all are 'members of the mystical body' or of the 'Church Universal' is not acceptable to the Roman Catholic Church. In the ordinary sense a 'member' has all the normal rights and obligations which other members have; but in fact non-Catholics neither claim the rights of membership in the Roman Catholic Church nor admit the obligations. Only on the hypothesis that the 'Church Universal' is constituted by invisible bonds can the explanation given be justified; and then the invisible Church, like Banquo's ghost, keeps re-entering and shaking gory locks at us. The Roman Catholic Church, like the Orthodox, claims that it alone is the 'Church Universal' and the 'mystical body'.

(c) The expression 'belong together as members of the mystical body' is not clear. What does 'belong together' mean? I think it means merely that the Churches ought to discuss their differences together, principally on the ground of their

[1] English translation, London, Catholic Truth Society, 1943, no. 21, p. 16.

common acknowledgement of Christ and of their common baptism; and, *granted the presupposition existing among non-Roman Churches*, this is reasonable enough and praiseworthy. On the other hand the expression that they 'belong together as members of the mystical body' carries a suggestion that there is a ground of equality which all must admit and that this ground is the basis for 'getting together'. This suggestion is rebutted in the previous article (5) about no prejudgement of the ecclesiological problem. It is not at first sight clear how (5) and (3) are to be reconciled.

(*d*) The distinction between 'the Church of Christ' and 'their own Church body' is not acceptable to the Roman Catholic Church, nor to the Orthodox. Both claim an identity between the Church of Christ and their own church body, whatever may be said regarding *vestigia*, or elements, of the Church outside their own church body.

Would not this article be better worded: 'The member Churches generally recognize the validity of one another's baptism, and all confess the Lordship of Christ. Therefore they seek to enter into living contact with one another.' The explanation about 'membership in the Church Universal', and about being 'members of the mystical body' is a needless complication, introduces difficult and controversial questions and does not seem easily reconcilable with other statements in this document.

4. The member Churches of the World Council consider the relationship of other Churches to the Holy Catholic Church which the Creeds profess as a subject for mutual consideration. Nevertheless membership does not imply that each Church must regard the other member Churches as Churches in the true and full sense of the word.

There is a place on the World Council both for those Churches which recognize other Churches as Churches in the full and true sense, and for those which do not. But these divided Churches, even if they cannot yet accept each other as true and pure Churches, believe that they should not remain in isolation from each other, and consequently they have associated themselves in the World Council of Churches.

They know that differences of faith and order exist, but they recognize one another as serving the One Lord, and they wish to explore their differences in mutual respect, trusting that they may thus be led by the Holy Spirit to manifest their unity in Christ.

The words in the explanation '*cannot yet* accept each other as true and pure Churches' carries the suggestion that possibly there will come a time when they can 'accept each other as true and pure Churches'. This if taken literally contradicts the assertion (3) that the ecclesiological problem is not prejudged. Presumably many 'Churches' look forward to the time when there will no longer be 'Churches' but only one Church and this has been said often by leaders of the movement. Here is latent the 'federation' idea as distinct from the 'organic unity' idea, and the wording of the explanation seems to favour a 'federation' since Churches may in the future be recognized by one another as true and pure Churches; if so, how are the denominations to die? The word 'yet' might well be omitted from line 4 of the explanation.

5. The member Churches of the World Council recognize in other Churches elements of the true Church. They consider that this mutual recognition obliges them to enter into serious conversation with each other in the hope that these elements of truth will lead to the recognition of the full truth and to unity based upon the full truth.

There may, of course, be different understandings of the meaning of these 'elements of the true Church', of the nature of the obligation which such mutual recognition implies, and of the meaning of 'a serious conversation'. The Roman Catholic Church certainly does not consider that there is any obligation to join the World Council or to accept 'conversations' on equal terms whenever suggested; on the other hand clear encouragement has been given to the Unitas Association, many Catholics have written books about the movement, and the Instruction of 1949 says the 'Bishops whom the Holy Ghost has placed to rule the Church of God ought to make a special object of their care and attention this work of "reunion" which is a particular charge and duty of the Church.'

Nevertheless taken in the whole context I do not think that this article (5) implies that no member Church may hold that it has the full truth and full unity.

6. The member Churches of the Council are willing to consult together in seeking to learn of the Lord Jesus Christ what witness He would have them bear to the world in His name.

The explanation is that the Churches ought to take every possible opportunity of speaking and acting together, in order that 'the world may believe.'

7. A further practical implication of common membership is that member Churches should recognize their solidarity with each other, render assistance to each other in case of need, and refrain from such actions as are incompatible with brotherly relationships.

Within the Council the Churches seek to deal with each other with a brotherly concern. This does not exclude frank speaking to each other, in which within the Council the Churches ask each other searching questions and face their differences. But this is to be done for the building up of the Body of Christ. This excludes a purely negative attitude of one Church to another. The positive affirmation of each Church's faith is to be welcomed, but actions incompatible with brotherly relationships towards other member Churches defeat the very purpose for which the Council has been created. On the contrary, these Churches should help each other in removing all obstacles to the free exercise of the Church's normal functions. And whenever a Church is in need or under persecution, it should be able to count on the help of the other Churches through the Council.

It is clear that this very general statement covers a number of possible particular cases in which there might be differences of view; but it is also clear that 'Inter-Church Aid' has been given in many cases generously and without regard to denominational divisions. The questions involved in defining 'proselytism' and 'persecution' are thorny and prickly in many respects, and the factors involved are not always purely re-

ligious, but are very often intermingled with national aspirations and social attitudes. Real persecution, however, certainly
is going on in many parts of the world.

**8. The member Churches enter into spiritual re-
lationship through which they seek to learn from
each other and to give help to each other in order
that the Body of Christ may be built up and that the
life of the Churches may be renewed.**

In the explanation it is said: 'the life of the Church, as it
expresses itself in its witness to its own members and to the
world, needs constant renewal. The Churches can and should
help each other in this realm by mutual exchange of thought
and of experience. This is the significance of the steady work
of the World Council and of many other of its activities. There
is no intention to impose any particular pattern of thought or
life upon the Churches. But whatever insight has been received by one or more Churches is to be made available to all
the Churches for the sake of the "building up of the Body of
Christ"'.

Here the recurring paradox of 'the Church' and 'the
Churches' shows itself again.

Conclusion

None of these positive assumptions, implied in the existence of
the World Council, is in conflict with the teachings of the member
Churches. We believe therefore that no Church need fear that by
entering the World Council it is in danger of denying its heritage.

As the conversation between the Churches develops and as the
Churches enter into closer contact with each other, they will no
doubt have to face new decisions and problems. For the Council
exists to break the deadlock between the Churches. But in no case
will a Church be pressed to take a decision against its own conviction or desire. The Churches remain wholly free in the action
which on the basis of their convictions and in the light of their
ecumenical contacts, they will or will not take.

I make three general observations:

1. This 'statement' was 'commended for study and comment

in the Churches.' The Rev Dr J. Robert Nelson very kindly
informs me that

> there has never been published a list of member churches of the
> World Council which accepted the Toronto statement. I can
> tell you however that this Statement was discussed and approved
> by the Church of England, the Protestant Episcopal Church in
> the U.S.A., the United Church of Canada, the Methodist Church,
> U.S.A., the Swiss Protestant Church Federation, the Moravian
> Church, and several of the Landeskirchen of Germany. In ad-
> dition there has been a considerable amount of discussion and
> writing on the Toronto Statement, but without official eccle-
> siastical decision.

2. The brief remarks I have made, chiefly upon the explanations given after the main affirmations printed in heavy
type, are purely from a Roman Catholic point of view and are
merely my own reflections.

3. Although in Part I (5) and Part II (3) reference is made
to the Roman Catholic Church, the document need not be
taken as if the Roman Catholic Church were principally
envisaged. The World Council includes over 170 Churches, and
references in some of the affirmations and explanations may be
implicitly made to them or to objections or questions they have
raised. The position of many, if not most, of these Churches is
very different from that of the Roman Catholic Church, and it
would be a grave mistake to imagine as addressed to us words
which may possibly be mainly intended to suggest considerations to particular Churches in Africa, India, Indonesia,
Mexico, the United States or elsewhere.

The statement as a whole, however, tends to determine the
nature of the Council as a purely consultative body. Some
Churches might not accept every phrase of the wording and
might feel that there were unexpressed and unacceptable
assumptions; nevertheless, reasons urged against formal participation in the work of the Council ought in future to take
account of this careful effort at clarification.

APPENDIX VI

In April 1957 was published *Relations Between Anglican and Presbyterian Churches, Being a Joint Report by Representatives of*
  The Church of England
  The Church of Scotland
  The Episcopal Church in Scotland
  The Presbyterian Church of England.[1]

The Report is divided into four sections: 1. A New Approach; 2. Theological Considerations; 3. The Modification of Church Polities; and 4. The Goal and the First Steps. The Appendix prints several relevant declarations from the participating Churches which bear upon the present conferences, and an illuminating account of the position of the 'elder' in the Church of Scotland.

Part I, 'A New Approach', gives some of the reasons why those participating in the conferences were convinced of the paramount need of unity: that unity is not a contingent feature of the Church's life, but is of the essence of it; that 'division in the Church distorts its witness, frustrates its mission, and contradicts its own nature'; that discussions of Church unity must take as their basis the unity of Christ and the doctrine of the Holy Spirit; and lastly, that other Churches of differing traditions, such as the Church of South India, have already found a way to organic unity in recent years.

With these presuppositions, and refusing to discuss the errors and faults of the past, the Report confines itself to this central question:

> The New Testament teaching about the nature of the Church being what it is; the Episcopalian and Presbyterian 'Churches' being what, in the course of history, they have come to be, neither of them claiming in its separatedness to exhibit the whole truth and wealth of the One Church of Christ, yet each claiming to possess gifts from the Head of the Church which it cannot in conscience deny or resign, and each being desirous of respecting

[1] Obtainable at The Saint Andrew Press, 121, George Street, Edinburgh, Scotland.

the conscience of the other as it is bound to obey its own—this being the historic situation, are there conceivable modifications and mutual adaptations of the two Church systems whereby they may be reconciled in such a plenitude of faith and order as will conserve the fullness of their traditions?

The authors of the Report, however, do not expect immediate acceptance of their proposals; but they plead for serious consideration of them and for some wider extension of intercommunion.

Part II, 'Theological considerations', includes the following 'five Biblical and doctrinal considerations concerning the Church and its ministry' which are here given in summary form:

1. The whole Church as the Body of Christ participates in His threefold ministry as Prophet, Priest and King, by serving Him as Lord. Sent from God, it is rightly described as apostolic not only in its faith, doctrine, and mission but also in its order.

2 (a) All ministry in the Church is to be interpreted as a ministry of Christ to the Church, that is from the Head to the Body as a whole.

(b) All ministry in the Church is to be exercised within the corporate priesthood of the whole Church.

3. Within this wider exercise of ministry there is a specific Ministry of the Word and Sacraments to which by ordination some are set apart.

4. The unity and continuity of the Church includes the following points:
- (a) The unity and continuity of the whole Body as baptismally incorporated into the royal priesthood of Christ.
- (b) The unity and continuity therein of the ministration of the Word and Sacraments as means of grace in the Church.

5 Among the functions of the ordained ministry is that of exercising 'episcopé' or oversight in the Church. Such 'episcopé', far from being exclusively concerned with administration, can be considered under five aspects:
- (a) Apostolic mission and authority.
- (b) The pastoral office.
- (c) The continuance of the Ministry of Word and Sacraments through ordination.

(*d*) Guardianship of truth and exclusion of error.

(*e*) Representation of the Church in its unity and universality.

There was agreement between the Anglicans and Presbyterians concerning all the above points, except about the manner in which 'episcopé' was to be exercised. In particular it was agreed that 'the continuity of ministerial succession is one element in the unity of the Church through time.'

The divergence is as follows:

In the Presbyterian Churches the ministers of the Word and Sacraments exercise a corporate episcopate, collectively through the Presbytery, along with the lay elders associated with them. 'Episcopé' is thus exercised partly through Presbytery, and partly by the minister himself in his own pastoral charge, assisted in certain functions by the elders and under the jurisdiction of the Presbytery. Ordination is by the Presbytery by prayer and imposition of hands 'by those preaching presbyters to whom it doth belong' (Westminster Form of Church Government). The Presbytery, subordinate to the Synod and General Assembly, exercises authority in worship, doctrine, and discipline; as a sacral court, it carefully preserves continuity of ordination and jurisdiction within the context of the sacramental and corporate life of the whole Church. Presbytery, Synod and General Assembly represent the Church Universal to the local congregation.

In the Anglican Churches there is the distinctive office of the Bishop. The essence of this lies in the coalescence of certain functions in a single person. These functions are: to be the chief minister of the Word and Sacraments; to be the proper minister for the ordination of men to the ministry of the Word and Sacraments; to be the chief pastor of clergy and laity alike; to represent the whole Church to the diocese and the diocese to the whole Church; to have authority in matters of doctrine—vested in the collective episcopate, but exercised in connection with the Church as a whole. These functions together make up the office of a Bishop, as Father-in-God, with succession in his see and succession of consecration, within the continuity of the body of the whole Church.

These divergences, however, did not seem insurmountable, and the concept of a presiding 'Bishop in Presbytery' 'with authority given to him by consecration at the hands of Bishops as well as with the authority of the collective Presbytery, appeared to be a possible modification of the Presbyterian polity'. On the other hand, the concept of Episcopacy, as held by Anglicans, did not seem to exclude something in the nature of a corporate functioning of 'episcopé' through development of 'sacral courts of the Church as found within the Presbyterian order.'

Part III, entitled 'The Modification of Church Polities', has the following preamble:

> In this new approach toward unity through mutual adaptation, the Conference agreed that the appropriate changes in each Church are not to be regarded as accommodations in alternative forms of Church government but as the spiritual and doctrinal requirements in order and practice to which the Churches must give heed if they are to move forward into fuller participation in the true wholeness of the one Church in Christ. In modifications of this kind each Church must fully respect the conscience of the other, while seeking at the same time to urge the acceptance of all that it regards as essential in the form of the order and practice of the Church it has itself received. Moreover each Church must allow the other a measure of freedom in interpreting the changes proposed and seek itself to interpret them not in accordance with the *status quo ante* in its own tradition but in accordance with the plenitude of order and practice in the enriched Church of the future.

The substance, then, of the proposed modifications is given as the acceptance of Bishops by the Presbyterians and the acceptance of 'elders' by the Anglicans. Diverse modifications would accompany this mutual acceptance: on the part of the Presbyterians, the Bishops chosen by each Presbytery 'would initially be consecrated by prayer with the laying on of hands by Bishops from one or more of the Episcopal Churches and by the Presbytery acting through appointed representatives. . . . Each Bishop would be the President of the Presbytery and would act as its principal minister in every ordination and in the consecration of other Bishops. He would exercise pastoral oversight over his fellow-ministers in the Presbytery, and act as its spokesman to the community. . . . Some modification of the number and size of Presbyteries would be necessary, so that each should be large enough to give the Bishop an adequate sphere, and small enough for him not to be over-burdened in his spiritual and pastoral functions.

It is envisaged that the rite of admission to full membership or confirmation would still be administered by each parochial minister, but the rite might come to be shared by the Bishop and parish minister acting together.

There would be a permanent Bishop-in-Presbytery to take the place of the Moderator, who changes every year. Bishops would be members of the Assembly, and 'decisions on doctrinal and constitutional matters might well have to require their consent.'

The Anglicans expressed some anxiety about safeguarding the collective voice of the Bishops as necessary in matters of doctrine and about the general administration of the rite of Confirmation by the Bishop.

On the part of the Anglicans the following changes seemed to be appropriate:

Lay persons would be solemnly 'set apart' for some measure of pastoral responsibility toward their fellow-Christians, in an office akin to the Presbyterian eldership. Lay people would be given appropriate participation in the government of the Church at all levels: parochial, diocesan, provincial, and national. The integration of such lay persons with the Bishop and presbyters in diocesan synods would greatly strengthen their authority and importance, by fulfilling the doctrinal requirement that decisions of the Church must be made by the whole Church, by the Body of Christ in its entirety. This could perhaps be done by assimilating the functions of the existing Diocesan Conferences more closely to those of a diocesan synod. The close cohesion of the Bishop and his presbyters with the laity in the corporate responsibility of the synod, and the closer association of the parish priest with the laity of the parish in parochial affairs, and the greater use of synodical methods would deliver both the Bishop and the parish priest from being too much alone in their cares and decisions.

The suggestion is made of a House of Laity in each Convocation and for a revision of the relationship between the

Convocations and the Church Assembly viewed as a National Synod.

The Presbyterians said that 'they would like to be sure that the laity and the presbyterate were fully linked with the Bishop in the doctrinal and spiritual decisions of the Church, and that the Church had such independence in spiritual things as, for example, to be able to reform its liturgy, or to have its Bishops appointed on the recommendation of the Church, including lay representation.' They desired, too, that greater stress be laid on the prophetic office of preaching the Word; and that the Bishoprics be divided into smaller units, so that the pastoral office of the Bishop might be better fulfilled.

This section ends with the following significant statement:

The whole Conference recognizes that besides such modifications as these in polity and structure, other and not less fundamental changes will or should come about in all the Churches concerned, changes which will involve a revaluation of the place of the Word and Sacraments in the whole life, ministry, and government of the Church. But these can only come about as the Churches grow in spiritual fellowship together, and in understanding of one another's discipline. It is of the nature of Christian truth that deeper understanding can only follow upon faithful obedience. All the parties to these proposals recognize that there are many truths which we shall only appreciate after we have taken together the steps of faith which will set us free to enjoy gifts of God to His Church which we had previously undervalued or of which we had even been unaware.

Part IV suggests that no immediate action be taken on the Report but that it be commended to careful study and examination by the Churches according to their constitutional procedure. Five factors have contributed to the fruitfulness of the present Conversations, and hope is expressed that these factors will be encouraged and extended:

1. Most important, the growing volume of prayer for the reunion of Christendom, in which our Churches take part.
2. Growth in knowledge of, and respect for, the traditions of other Churches and a deeper understanding of the issues which divide us.

3. Visits of official representatives of the four Churches to the meetings of the governing bodies of the others.

4. Interchange of visits of teachers and students among the theological colleges.

5. Meeting in conference of ministers and representative lay members of Episcopal and Presbyterian Churches.

The Report ends with the suggestions that each of the four Churches should call upon their members and ministers to pray and work for unity; should appoint one Sunday in each year as a special Day of Prayer for the furtherance of unity among their Churches and as a day of instruction about the issues involved; the Episcopalian Churches should sanction a wider interchange of preaching by respective ministers, and should extend somewhat, under due safeguards, the occasional reception of Holy Communion by Presbyterians in Anglican Churches.

BIBLIOGRAPHY

The following list of books is by no means complete[1]. It lists some, though not all, books and articles which I have found useful and which may prove useful to others.[2]

GENERAL

BELL, G. K. A., ed., *Documents on Christian Unity*, vol. I, 1920–4, London, 1924; vol. II, second series, London, 1930; vol. III, 1930–48, London, 1948; vol. IV, 1948–57, London, 1958

BRANDRETH, H. R. T., *Unity and Reunion, A Bibliography*, second ed. with supplement, London, 1948

CRIVELLI, C., *Piccolo Dizionario delle Sette Protestanti*, Roma, 1945

LATOURETTE, K. S., *A History of the Expansion of Christianity*, especially vol. 4, London, 1941, and vol. 7, London, 1945

SPERRY, W. J., *Religion in America*, Cambridge, 1945

Official or Semi-official Ecumenical Works

BATE, H. N., ed., *Faith and Order, Proceedings of the World Conference, Lausanne, August 3 to 21*, 1927, New York, 1928

HODGSON, L., ed. *The Second World Conference on Faith and Order held at Edinburgh, August 3 to 18, 1937*, London, 1938

---

1 'Ecumenism' is a subject which ramifies into all aspects of Christianity, and, when one considers the missions, into all aspects of religion in general. It touches upon the philosophy of religion and upon every Christian doctrine, though especially doctrine about the Church, upon the history, organization and administration of 'Churches', their relation to non-Christians, and consequently the history and nature of the 'culture' of all the races and nations of mankind. A complete bibliography is obviously impossible.

2 Only after the manuscript of this book was complete did I see Fr Gustave Weigel's 'A Catholic Primer on the Ecumenical Movement', in *The Thomist Reader*, Washington, D.C., 1957, which was reprinted as *A Catholic Primer on Ecumenism*, Westminster, Maryland, 1958, a most valuable survey, the more so as Fr Weigel was an unofficial observer at the meeting of the Faith and Order Commission at Oberlin, Ohio, in 1957. Fr Weigel's account of the membership in the World Council sharpens the point of the difficulty in defining what is a 'Church': 'The Anglican communion, for instance, has many units in the Council: Australia and Tasmania, Canada, Japan, New Zealand, South Africa, England, Ireland, Scotland, Wales, the Protestant Episcopal Church of America, India, West Africa and the West Indies. Consequently, the *Anglican Church* (italics mine) has many blocs of votes in the Assembly. The Lutherans enjoy a parallel situation. Without counting the many Lutheran Churches of Germany and the Continent, from the United States alone there are five Lutheran Churches with membership in the Council.' P. 25. Fr Weigel suggests an intensely interesting theoretical question: on the unlikely hypothesis of the Roman Catholic Church being in the Council, how would it be represented? As one Church, or by nations, or by 'Rites'? This is another instance of Roman Catholic aloofness saving embarrassment to the World Council.

VISSER 'T HOOFT, W. A., ed., *The First Assembly of the World Council of Churches, held at Amsterdam, August 22 to September 4, 1948*, London, 1949
 The Evanston Report: The Second Assembly of the World Council of Churches, 1954, London, 1955
Evanston Speaks: Reports from the Second Assembly of the World Council of Churches, August 15 to 31, 1954, London, 1954
TOMKINS, O. S., ed., *The Third World Conference on Faith and Order held at Lund August 15 to 28, 1952*, London, 1953
BAILLIE, D. and MARSH, J., ed., *Intercommunion: The Report of the Theological Commission appointed by the Continuation Committee of the World Conference on Faith and Order together with a Selection from the Material presented to the Commission*, London, 1952
EDWALL, P., HAYMAN, E., MAXWELL, W. D., ed., *Ways of Worship, the Report of a Theological Commission of Faith and Order*, London, 1951
FLEW, R. N., ed., *The Nature of the Church, Papers presented to the Theological Commission appointed by the Continuation Committee of the World Conference on Faith and Order*, London, 1952
Social and Cultural Factors in Church Divisions, by C. H. Dodd, G. R. Craig, Jacques Ellul, Preface by Oliver Tomkins, and *Report* of a Conference at Bossey in November, 1951, Faith and Order Commission Papers, no. 10
Ecumenical Surveys
 Our Oneness in Christ and our Divisions as Churches, Commission Papers, no. 18, New York, 1954
 Intergroup Relations—the Church amid Racial and Ethnic Tensions, New York, 1954
 Evangelism—the Mission of the Church to those Outside her Life, New York, 1954
 The Laity—the Christian in his Vocation, New York, 1954
Commission on Faith and Order, Minutes, Evanston and Chicago, 1954, Commission Papers, no. 21
 Minutes of the Working Committee, July, 1956, Herrenalb, Germany, Commission Papers, no. 23
 Minutes of the Working Committee, July, 1958, Geneva, Switzerland, Commission Paper no. 26
The Ecclesiological Significance of the World Council of Churches, a statement received by the Central Committee at its meeting in Toronto in July, 1950, London, no date
'Report of the Executive Committee 1955–1956, and Report of the General Secretary', *Ecumenical Review*, ix, no. 1, October, 1956, pp. 33–47
Provisional Report on 'Christian Witness, Proselytism and Religious Liberty in the Setting of the World Council of Churches', *Ecumenical Review*, ix, no. 1, October, 1956, pp. 48–56
PAYNE, E. A. and MOSES, D. G., *Why Integration? An explanation of the proposals before the World Council of Churches and the International Missionary Council*, London, December, 1957

BOEGNER, M., (A President of the World Council), 'An Appraisal of the World Council of Churches', *Ecumenical Review*, vi, no. 4, July, 1954, pp. 361–70

NELSON, J. R., 'Survey of Church Union Negotiations', *Ecumenical Review*, viii, no. 1, October, 1955, pp. 76–93; and ix, no. 3, April, 1957
'Many Images of the One Church,' *ibid.* ix, no. 2, January, 1957, pp. 105–13

OEBERMÜLLER, R., *Evangelism in Latin America, An Ecumenical Survey*, published for the World Council of Churches, London, 1957

ORCHARD, R. K., ed., *The Ghana Assembly of the International Missionary Council 28 December, 1957 to 8 January, 1958*, London, 1958

ROUSE, R., and NEILL, S. C., ed., *A History of the Ecumenical Movement 1517–1948*, London, 1954

TOMKINS, O. S., 'The Church, the Churches and the Council', *Ecumenical Review*, iv, no. 3, April, 1952, pp. 259–68

VAN DER LINDE, H., 'The Nature and Significance of the World Council of Churches', *Ecumenical Review*, iii, no. 2, April, 1951, pp. 238–47

VISSER 'T HOOFT, W. A., 'Various Meanings of Unity and the Unity which the World Council of Churches seeks to promote', *Ecumenical Review*, viii, no. 1, October, 1955, pp. 18–29
'The Super-Church and the Ecumenical Movement', *Ecumenical Review*, x, July, 1958, pp. 365–85

The Ecumenical Review, obtainable in England from the World Council of Churches, 39, Doughty St, London, W.C.1

The International Review of Missions, obtainable from Edinburgh House, 2, Eaton Gate, London, S.W.1

Conference of Missionary Societies in Gt. Britain and Ireland, (in Association with *The British Council of Churches*), Report *1957–58*, London, 1958

ROMAN CATHOLIC

PIUS XI, *True Religious Unity* (*Mortalium Animos*), with an *Introduction* by H. E. Cardinal Bourne, London, 1928

PIUS XII, *Selected Letters and Addresses*, issued in 1949 by the Catholic Truth Society, London; containing *The Mystical Body of Christ* (*Mystici Corporis*), 1943; *Biblical Studies* (*Divino Afflante Spiritu*), 1943; *Rome and the Eastern Churches* (*Orientalis Ecclesiae Decus*), 1944; *Christian Worship* (*Mediator Dei*), 1947; and some other Messages, Addresses and Broadcasts up to 1949
The Sacred Heart (Encyclical *Haurietis Aquas*), London, 1956

ADAM, K., *One and Holy*, English translation by Cecily Hastings, London, 1954

ALGERMISSEN, K., *Christian Denominations*, English Translation by J. W. Grunder, St Louis and London, 1946

AUBERT, R., *Le Saint Siège et l'union des églises*, Bruxelles, 1946
Problèmes de l'unité chrétienne, Chevetogne, Belgium, 1952

BAUM, G., *That They May be One: A study of Papal Doctrine (Leo XIII—Pius XII)*, London, 1958

BECK, G. A., ed., *The English Catholics 1850–1950*, London, 1950

BÉVENOT, M., 'The World Conference at Edinburgh', 'I. Aims and Spirit'; 'II. The Official Attitude of the Church'; 'III. An Observer's Conclusions', *The Tablet*, August 7, 14, and 21, 1937
    'Church Relations in England,' *The Month* cxci, no. 1003, March, 1951, pp. 174–9
    'Church and State, the Report of an Anglican Commission', *The Month* cxciii, no. 1018, June, 1952, pp. 358–67
    'Membership of the Church', *The Month*, cxxxix, no. 994, June, 1950, pp. 420–31
    'La conception de l'Église dans le programme de travail de la Commission "Foi et Constitution" (Bossey, 11–19 août 1953)', *Istina*, 1954, no. 2, avril-juin

BOYER, C., *Unus Pastor, Per la riunione alla Chiesa di Roma dei cristiani separati*, Roma, 1950. (English translation, *One Shepherd*, New York, 1952)
    'Sur la théologie du conseil oecuménique', *Gregorianum*, Roma, xxxv, 4, 1954, pp. 590–607
    'Are We Making Progress towards Unity?' *Unitas*, vii, no. 1, Spring, 1955, pp. 2–5
    'Protestantism and Catholicism' A Comparison by Protestants', *Unitas*, vii, no. 2, Summer, 1955, pp. 65–71
    'Dr W. A. Visser 't Hooft's Concept of Unity', *Unitas*, viii, no. 1, Spring, 1956, pp. 2–7
    'The Evanston Assembly—an Evaluation', *Unitas*, vi, no. 4, Winter, 1954, pp. 225–9
    'The Evanston Assembly in Retrospect', *Unitas*, vii, no. 4, Winter, 1955, pp. 195–208
    '*Vestigia Ecclesiae*—Elements of the Church', *Unitas*, viii, no. 2, pp. 67–71

CARY-ELWES, C., *The Sheepfold and the Shepherd*, London, 1956

CONGAR, Y. M. J., *Divided Christendom, a Catholic Study of the Problem of Reunion*, London, 1939. (A translation by M. A. Bousfield of *Chrétiens désunis*, with some changes)

CONWAY, W., 'The Recent Instruction of the Holy Office on Religious Unity', *Irish Ecclesiastical Record*, lxxiii, 1950, pp. 360–5

CULLMANN, O., *Catholiques et Protestants*, Paris, 1958

DAMBORIENA, P., 'Trends of the Ecumenical Movement in American Protestantism', *Unitas*, viii, no. 2 and 3, Summer and Autumn, 1956, pp. 79–92, pp. 146–61

DAVIS, C., 'Notes on Recent Work in Dogmatic Theology', *Clergy Review* xl, no. 3, March, 1955, pp. 158–70. (Contains comment on E. Gilson's *Les Metamorphoses de la Cité de Dieu*, Paris, 1955; P. Simon's *The Human Element in the Church of God*, Cork, 1955; E. L. Mascall's *Corpus Christi, the Church and the Eucharist*, London, 1955; and K. Adam's *One and*

Holy, iam cit. Fr Davis's comments on the last are of special interest.)
    'Faith and Dissident Christians', *ibid.* xliv, no. 4, April, 1959
DUFF, E., *The Social Thought of the World Council of Churches*, London, 1956
DUMONT, C. J., *Approaches to Christian Unity*, London and Baltimore, 1959,
    which appeared while the present work was in the press
FLEW, R. N., 'The Church of Rome', in *The Nature of the Church*, London,
    1951, pp. 17–42
GANNON, D., *Father Paul of Graymoor*, New York, 5th printing, 1952
GILL, J., 'Reflections on "the Conversion of England"', *Unitas*, vi, no. 4,
    Winter, 1954, pp. 232–40
    'The Reformation in England', *Unitas*, vii, no. 1, Spring, 1955,
    pp. 8–17
GWYNN, D., *A Hundred Years of Catholic Emancipation, 1829–1929*, London,
    1929
HAMER, J., 'Mission de l'oecuménisme Catholique', *Lumière et Vie*, no. 19,
    Janvier, 1955, pp. 65–79
    'Tension au sein de l'Anglicanisme', *Nouvelle Revue Théologique*,
    1948, pp. 67–79
HANAHOE, E. F., *Catholic Ecumenism*, Washington, 1953
HEENAN, J. C., 'The Holy See and "Reunion",' *Catholic Gazette*, April, 1950
JAKI, S., *Les tendances nouvelles de Ecclésiologie*, Roma, 1957
JOURNET, C., *L'union des Églises et le christianisme*, Paris, 1927
    The Church of the Word Incarnate, English translation by A. H. C.
    Downes, vol. 1, 'The Apostolic Hierarchy', London, 1955, cf. 'Catholic
    Ecumenism', pp. 40–5
JUNG, E. M., 'Roman Catholic Impressions of the Evanston Assembly',
    Ecumenical Review, vii, no. 2, 1955, pp. 117–26
KINDER, E., 'Protestant-Roman Catholic Encounter an Ecumenical Neces-
    sity', *Ecumenical Review*, vii, no. 4, July, 1955, pp. 338–45
LAROS, M., *Schoepferischer Friede der Confessionen*, Recklinghausen, 1950
LEEMING, B., 'The Assumption and the Christian Pattern', *The Month*,
    March, 1951, pp. 142–51
LUBAC, H. DE, *The Splendour of the Church*, English translation by Michael
    Mason, London, 1956
MCNABB, V., *The Church and Reunion*, London, 1937
MATTHEW, D., *Catholicism in England, 1535–1935*, London, 1929
MENN, W. G., 'Roman Catholic Voices on the Lund Conference', *Ecume-
    nical Review*, v, no. 3, April, 1953, pp. 294–8
MAYNARD, T., *The Story of American Catholicism*, New York, 1941
MESSENGER, E. C., *Rome and Reunion: A Collection of Papal Documents*, London,
    1934
OESTERLE, 'Notae Historicae ad Instructionem S. Congregationis S. Officii
    "De motione oecumenica",' *Miscellanea Comillas*, Santander, 1951,
    pp. 203–38
PALMER, P. F., 'Mary in Protestant Theology and Worship', *Theological
    Studies*, (Woodstock, Maryland), xv, 1954, pp. 519–40

PHILIPS, G., *Le rôle du laïcat dans l'église*, Tournai, 1954

ST JOHN, H., *Essays in Christian Unity 1928–1954*, London, 1955

'The Catholic Apostolate of Unity', *Life of the Spirit*, xi, no. 2, January, 1957, pp. 294–301, reprinted from *Unitas*, vii, no. 2, Summer, 1955, under title 'The Chair of Unity and Protestants', pp. 71–6

SKYDSGAARD, K. E., *One in Christ, Protestant and Catholic, where they agree, where they differ*, Philadelphia, 1957

TAVARD, G., *The Catholic Approach to Protestantism*, New York, 1955

THILS, G., *Histoire doctrinale du mouvement oecuménique*, Louvain, 1955

TODD, J. M., *Catholicism and the Ecumenical Movement*, London, 1956

'Vanishing Divisions', *Downside Review*, no. 239, January, 1957, pp. 24–37

TOMKINS, O. S., 'The Roman Catholic Church and the Ecumenical Move-Movement 1910–1948', in *The History of the Ecumenical Movement*, ed. Rouse and Neill, pp. 677–94

VAN DE POL, W. H., *The Christian Dilemma, Catholic Church—Reformation*, London, 1952

'Ecumenical Standpoints', *Unitas*, vi, no. 3, Autumn, 1953, pp. 157–68

VILLAIN, M., *L'Abbé Paul Couturier, Apôtre de l'Unité Chrétienne, Souvenirs et Documents*, Tournai-Paris, 1957

Introduction à l'Oecuménisme, Tournai-Paris, 1958

VISSER 'T HOOFT, W. A., 'Notes on Roman Catholic Writings concerning Ecumenism', *Ecumenical Review*, viii, no. 2, January, 1956, pp. 191–7

VITTE, E., ed. '*A la mémoire de l'Abbé Couturier, témoinages*, Lyon, 1954

VOLLERT, C., '*Humani Generis* and the Limits of Theology', *Theological Studies*, xii, 1951, pp. 3–23

WALKER, L. J., *The Problem of Reunion*, London, 1920

WEIGEL, G., 'The Historical Background of the Encyclical *Humani Generis*' *Theological Studies*, xii, 1951, pp. 208–31

'Protestant Theological Positions Today', *ibid.* xi, 1950, pp. 547–66

'A Catholic Primer on the Ecumenical Movement', *The Thomist Reader*, 1957, Washington, 1957

WHITE, V., *God the Unknown*, London, 1956

WHITTON, T., *The Necessity for Catholic Reunion*, London, 1933

Many periodicals contain most valuable matter, v.g. *The Eastern Churches Quarterly*, Ramsgate, England; *Irénikon*, Belgium; *Vers l'unité chrétienne*, France; *Una Sancta*, Germany; and *Blackfriars*, *The Downside Review*, *The Month*, *The Clergy Review*, often carry interesting articles

THE EASTERN ORTHODOX CHURCHES

ALIVISATOS, H. S., 'Orthodoxy, Protestantism and the World Council of Churches', *Ecumenical Review*, vi, no. 3, April, 1954, pp. 277–86

BEAUDUIN, L., Festschrift for, *L'Église et les Églises*, 2 vols., Chevetogne (Belgium), 1955

BULGAKOV, S., *The Orthodox Church*, London, 1935

DIBELIUS, Bishop Otto, 'Letter to the Patriarch of Moscow, August 5, 1955', *Ecumenical Review* viii, no. 1, October, 1955, pp. 64–6

'Reply of the Moscow Patriarchate to the Central Committee of the World Council of Churches, 30 December, 1955', *Ecumenical Review*, viii, no. 3, April, 1956, pp. 325–7

DULLES, A. R., 'The Orthodox Churches and the Ecumenical Movement', *Downside Review*, lxxv, no. 239, January, 1957, pp. 38–54

FLOROVSKY, G., 'The Orthodox Churches and the Ecumenical Movement prior to 1910', Rouse and Neill, ed., *History of the Ecumenical Movement*, pp. 171–209

GEORGIADIS, H., 'An Orthodox Comment on Ecumenical Encounters', citation from *Sobornost* in *Unitas*, vii, no. 4, Winter, 1955, pp. 231–2
    'Orthodoxy, Rome and Ecumenism', *Eastern Churches Quarterly*, xi, no. 8, Winter 1956–7, pp. 345–61

GERMANOS, Archbishop, (Metropolitan of Thyateira and Exarch of Western and Northern Europe) 'The Eastern Orthodox Church' in Marchant, *The Reunion of Christendom*, pp. 39–61

KARTACHOFF, A., 'Orthodox Theology and the Ecumenical Movement', *Ecumenical Review*, viii, no. 1, October, 1955, pp. 30–6

KIDD, B. J., *The Churches of Eastern Christendom*, London, 1927

KONSTANTINIDIS, C., 'Impressions of the Evanston Assembly', *Ecumenical Review*, vii, no. 1, October, 1954, pp. 14–20

JUHANON MAR THOMA, 'Faith and Order—Our Oneness in Christ and Our Disunity as Churches', *Ecumenical Review*, vii, no. 1, October, 1954, pp. 25–9

ZANDER, L. A., *Vision and Action: the Problem of Ecumenism*, London, 1952

ZERNOV, N., 'The Eastern Churches and the Ecumenical Movement in the Twentieth Century', in Rouse and Neill, *History of the Ecumenical Movement*, pp. 645–74

ANGLICAN

The Five Lambeth Conferences, 1867, 1878, 1888, 1897, 1908, London, 1920

Conference of Bishops of the Anglican Communion holden at Lambeth Palace July 6 to August 7, 1920, Encyclical Letters of the Bishops with Resolutions and Reports, London, 1920

Lambeth Conference, 1930, Encyclical Letter of the Bishops with the Resolutions and Reports, London (no date)

The Lambeth Conference 1948, The Encyclical Letter from the Bishops together with Resolutions and Reports, London, 1948

Idem. 1958

Church Relations in England, being the Report of Conversations between Representatives of the Archbishop of Canterbury and Representatives of the Evangelical Free Churches in England, London, 1950

DOUGLAS, J. A., *The Relations of the Anglican Churches with the Eastern Orthodox*, London, 1921

Report of the Joint Doctrinal Commission appointed by the Oecumenical Patriarch and the Archbishop of Canterbury for Consultation on the Points of Agreement and Difference between the Anglican and the Eastern Orthodox Churches, London, 1932.

Conversations between The Church of England and The Methodist Church, An Interim Statement, London, 1958

The Church of England and the Free Churches, A Report of the Theological and Liturgical Committee of the Church Union, Adopted 6 June, 1951, London, no date

Notes on an Evanston Report,[1] *Church Quarterly Review,* clviii, no. 326, January-March, 1957, pp. 76–83

ADDLESHAW, A. W. O., *The High Church Tradition,* London, 1941

BELL, G. K. A., *Christian Unity, the Anglican Position,* London, 1948
    Randall Davidson, Archbishop of Canterbury, 2 vols., London, 1935

BRILIOTH, Y., *The Anglican Revival,* London, 1925

BRUCE, M., ed., *Barriers to Unity,* London, 1959

GARBETT, C., *The Claim of the Church of England,* London, 1947
    Church and State in England, London, 1950

GOUDGE, H. L., *The Church of England and Reunion,* London, 1938

HARDY, E. R., 'American Letter: Evanston Revisited', *Theology,* lx, no. 434, August, 1956, pp. 325–9

HEBERT, A. G., *Intercommunion, a Study of Christian Unity,* London, 1932
    'The Church which is His Body', *Ecumenical Review,* ix, no. 2, January, 1957, pp. 114–21

HEADLAM, A. C., *The Doctrine of the Church of England and Christian Reunion,* London, 1920

HODGES, H. A., *Anglicanism and Orthodoxy, a Study in Dialectical Churchmanship,* London, 1955

IREMONGER, F. J., *William Temple, Archbishop of Canterbury,* London, 1948

JOHNSON, H. J. T., *Anglicanism in Transition,* London, 1938

KNOX, W. L., *The Catholic Movement in the Church of England,* London, 1923

LACEY, T. A., *Unity and Schism,* London, 1917

LOCKHART, J. G., *Cosmo Gordon Lang,* London, 1950

MASCALL, E. L., ed. *The Church of God, an Anglo-Russian Symposium,* London, 1934

MASCALL, E. L., *The Recovery of Unity,* London, 1957
    Lambeth 1958 and Christian Unity, London, 1959

MARCHANT, J., ed., *The Reunion of Christendom. A Survey of the Present Position,* London, 1929

MAYFIELD, G., *The Church of England, Its Members and Its Business,* London, 1958

MOZLEY, J. K., *Some Tendencies in British Theology, from the publication of Lux Mundi to the present day,* London, 1951

[1] The Council for Ecumenical Co-operation, acting on behalf of the Church Assembly, called together a representative group under the Chairmanship of the Bishop of Chelmsford to study the report and comment upon it.

PAIGE-COX, W. L., ed., *Anglican Essays*, London, 1923

RAWLINSON, A. E. W., *The Church of England and the Church of Christ*, London, 1930

    The Problem of Reunion, London, 1951

SPENCER JONES, *England and the Holy See. An Essay towards Reunion*, London, 1932

TEMPLE, W., *Christian Unity and Church Reunion*, London, 1943

WAND, J. W. C., *A History of the Modern Church from 1500 to the present Day*, London, 1949

WEBB, C. C. J., *A Century of Anglican Theology*, Oxford, 1923

    A Study of Religious Thought in England from 1850, Oxford, 1932

WOODS, F. T., 'The Church of England' in Marchant's *Reunion of Christendom*.

Catholicity, A Study in the Conflict of Christian Traditions in the West, (by a group of Anglican theologians of the 'Catholic' school of thought), London, 1947

The Fulness of Christ, London, 1950. (By a group of 'Evangelical' theologians)

The Church of England and the Free Churches. A Report of the Theological and Liturgical Committee of the Church Union, London, 1951

Doctrine in the Church of England, the Report of the Doctrinal Commission appointed in 1922, London, 1938

Report of the Sixth Anglo-Catholic Congress. Subject The Church, London, 1948

PRESBYTERIAN

MÜLLER, E. F. K., *Die Bekenntnisschriften der Reformierten Kirche*, Lipsiae, 1903

The Confession of Faith; the Larger and Shorter Catechisms with the Scripture-Proofs at Large, etc., Edinburgh, 1894

KIDD, B. J., *Documents illustrative of the Continental Reformation*, part 2, Reformed, Oxford, 1911

AINSLIE, J. L., *The Doctrine of Ministerial Order in the Reformed Churches of the Sixteenth and Seventeenth Centuries*, Edinburgh, 1940

BLACK, C. S., *The Scottish Church*, Glasgow, 1952

CLARK, G. H., *What Presbyterians Believe, An exposition of the Westminster Confession*, Philadelphia, 1956

COX, J. T., *Practice and Procedure in the Church of Scotland*, Edinburgh, 1948

FLEMING, J. R., *A History of the Church in Scotland*, vol. 1, 1843–74, vol. 2, 1875–1929, Edinburgh, 1927 and 1933

    The Story of Church Union in Scotland, its Origins and Progress 1560–1929, Edinburgh, 1929

HENDERSON, G. D., *The Claims of the Church of Scotland*, London, 1951

    Presbyterianism, Aberdeen, 1954

JENKINS, C. AND MACKENZIE, K. D., ed., *Episcopacy Ancient and Modern*, London, 1930

MACLEOD, J., 'Theology in our Era', *The Hibbert Journal* xlix, July, 1951, pp. 354–61

MARTIN, A., 'Church Union in Scotland', in Marchant, *The Reunion of Christendom*, pp. 171–90

MOFFAT, J., *The Presbyterian Churches*, London, 1928

SIMPSON, P. CARNEGIE, *Church Principles*, London, 1923
    The Evangelical Church Catholic, London, 1934

TORRANCE, T. F., *Conflict and Agreement in the Church*, vol. 1. *Order and Disorder*, London, 1959

WARR, C. L., *Presbyterian Tradition, A Scottish Layman's Handbook*, London, 1933

Anon., *Presbyterianism Vindicated: Why We Oppose the Recent Conference with the Anglicans*, published by The National Church Association, no date, but about 1932 or 1933

Many articles of value appear in the *Scottish Journal of Theology*, some of which have been noted in the text.

THE FREE CHURCHES

BROWN, W. A., 'The Other [than the Protestant Episcopal] Churches of the United States', in Marchant, *The Reunion of Christendom*, pp. 211–32

CARTER, H., *The Methodist Heritage*, London, 1951

CHURCH, L. F., *The Early Methodist People*, London, 1947
    More about the Early Methodist People, London, 1949

CLARK, H. W., *History of English Non-Conformity*, 2 vols, London, 1911 and 1912

COCKS, H. F. L., *The Nonconformist Conscience*, London, 1944

COOK, H., *What Baptists Stand For*, 2nd ed., London, 1953

CRAGG, G. R., *Puritanism in the Period of the Great Persecution*, 1660–88, Cambridge, 1957

DRUMMOND, A. L., *Story of American Protestantism*, Edinburgh, 1950

FLEW, R. N. and DAVIES, R. E., *The Catholicity of Protestantism*, London, 1950

GARVIE, A. E., *The Holy Catholic Church from the Congregational Point of View*, London, 1920
    'The Free Churches in England', in Marchant, *The Reunion of Christendom*, pp. 129–148

GILMORE, A., ed., *Christian Baptism*, London, 1959

GOODALL, N. and ORCHARD, R. K., *Church and Mission, a Discussion of the Relation of the London Missionary Society to the Congregational Unions*, London, 1950

GOODALL, N., *Congregationalism Plus*, London, 1953

GRANT, J. W., *Free Churchmanship in England 1870–1940, with special reference to Congregationalism* (Very ample bibliography), London, no date, but about 1951

HANSON, P. P. C., *The Summons to Unity*, London, 1954

HORTON, D. C., *Study in Church Polity*, London, 1955

HORTON, W. M., *Contemporary Continental Theology, An Interpretation for Anglo-Saxons*, London, 1938

JENKINS, D., *Congregationalism. A Restatement*, London, 1948

LANGTON, E., *History of the Moravian Church*, London, 1956

LIDGETT, J. SCOTT, 'The Wesleyan Methodist Church', in Marchant, *The Reunion of the Churches*, pp. 151–69

LITTELL, F. H., *The Anabaptist View of the Church*. ed. 2, U.S.A., 1957

MARLOWE, J., *The Puritan Tradition in English Life*, London, 1956

MATTHEWS, B., *John R. Mott, World Citizen*, London, 1934

MICKLEM, N., *What Is the Faith?*, London, 1936
   Congregationalism and the Church Catholic, London, 1943
   Congregationalism and Episcopacy, London, no date

NELSON, J. R., *The Realm of Redemption, Studies in the Doctrine of the Nature of the Church in Contemporary Protestant Theology*, London, 2nd ed., 1953. (Very ample bibliography.)

NUTTALL, G. F., *The Holy Spirit in Puritan Faith and Experience*, Oxford, 1946

OMAN, J., *The Church and the Divine Order*, London, 1911

OUTLER, A. C., *The Christian Tradition and the Unity We Seek*, London, 1958

PEEL, A., ed., *Essays Congregational and Catholic*, London, 1931

PIETTE, M., *John Wesley and the Evolution of Protestantism*, London, 1937

ROBINSON, H. W., *The Life and Faith of the Baptists*, London, 1927

RUPP, E. G., *Studies in the Making of the English Protestant Tradition*, Cambridge, 1947

SELBIE, W. B., *The Freedom of the Free Churches*, London, 1928
   Congregationalism, London, 1926

TILLICH, P., *The Protestant Era*, Chicago, 1948

TOWNSEND, *The Claims of the Free Churches*, London, 1949

UNDERWOOD, A. C., *A History of the English Baptists*, London, 1947

WAKEFIELD, G. S., *Puritan Devotion, Its Place in the Development of Christian Piety*, London, 1957

WHALE, J. S., *The Protestant Tradition*, Cambridge, 1956

WOOD, A. S., *Thomas Haweis, 1734–1820*, London, 1957

WOODHOUSE, A. S. P., *Puritanism and Liberty*, London, 1938

ANON., *The Nature of the Christian Church according to the Teaching of the Methodists, Statement approved by the Methodist Conference, Bradford, July, 1937*
   London Missionary Society, The One Hundred and Sixty Third Annual Report, 1957–1958, London, 1959

THE CHURCH OF SOUTH INDIA

The Constitution of the Church of South India, with amendments up to 31st December 1951, together with the Basis of Union as adopted by the Governing Bodies of the Uniting Churches in India and elsewhere, The Christian Literature Society for India, Madras, 1952

The Service of The Lord's Supper or the Holy Eucharist, authorized by the Synod of the Church of South India, Oxford, 1952

The South India Scheme, being the Report of a Committee of Theologians appointed by the Archbishop of Canterbury to consider the proposed Basis of Union and Constitution of the future Church of South India, Westminster, no date. Often called 'The Rawlinson Report.'

Report on South India, being the Report of the Delegation to the Church of South India with certain recommendations and theological comments, Episcopal Church, Joint Commission on Ecumenical Relations, New York, 1957

AZARIAH, V., 'The Anglican Church in India', in Marchant, *Reunion of Christendom*, pp. 251–66

BEAUPÈRE, R., 'Les luthériens et l'Eglise de l'Inde du Sud', *Istina*, 1957, no. 2, pp. 175–226

BILHEIMER, M. R. S., 'International Church Assistance and Rapid Social Change', *Ecumenical Review*, July, 1957, pp. 402–9.

BOUYER, L., 'A Roman Catholic View of South India', *Theology*, lix, no. 427, January, 1956, pp. 3–11.

BRUCE, M., 'The Church of England and South India, the Convocations' Decisions', *Ecumenical Review*, viii, no. 1, October 1955, pp. 42–54

BURN-MURDOCH, H., 'Episcopacy Misunderstood', *Theology*, lvi, no. 343, March, 1955, pp. 98–104

GRISBROOKE, W., 'The Constitution and Liturgy of the Church of South India', *Eastern Churches Quarterly*, 1956, (1), pp. 218–31

LE GUILLOU, M. J., 'Les Jeunes Eglises et leur influence sur le mouvement oecuménique depuis Evanston', *Eglise Vivante*, November-December. 1957, pp. 437–47

MACKIE, R. C., 'Impressions of the Church of South India', *Ecumenical Review* ix, no. 1, October 1956, pp. 27–33

MARAT, D. H., 'Oecuménisme anglican et l'Inde du Sud', *Irénikon*, 30, 1957, pp. 266–88

MASCALL, E. L., *The Convocations and South India, What did the Convocations decide and how does their decision affect the Catholicity of the Church of England?*, London, 1955

NEWBIGIN, J. E. L., *The Reunion of the Churches, a Defence of the South India Scheme*, London, 1937

A South India Diary, London, 1951

The Household of God, London, 1953

The Ministry of the Church, Ordained and Unordained, Paid and Unpaid, London, 1954

PAUL, R. D., *The First Decade, An Account of the Church of South India*, Madras, 1958

REA, D., *The Church of South India and the Church*, London, 1956 (and cf. the review by Rev. Francis Clark, in *Unitas*, viii, no. 4, Winter, 1956.)

RAWLINSON, A. E. J., *The Church of South India*, London, 1951

SUNKLER, B., *The Church of South India: the Movement towards Union, 1900–1947*, London, 1954

ST. JOHN, H., 'A Papalist and the Church of South India', *Eastern Churches Quarterly*, Autumn 1950, pp. 299–364

WARD, A. M., *The Pilgrim Church. An Account of the first five years in the Church of South India*, London, 1953

Unitas, viii, no. 3, Autumn, 1956, pp. 171–2, published an unfavourable judgement on the Church of South India by the Anglican Society for Promoting Catholic Unity, under the title 'An Anglo-Catholic Stand on Dogmatic Agreement'; and another to the same effect, vii, no. 1, Spring, 1955, pp. 47–8

The South India Churchman, a monthly published at Bangalore, gives much information, and the Ten Years Anniversary number, September, 1957, is of special interest. I understand that Bishop Lesslie Newbigin is at present engaged on an accurate survey.

Plan of Church Union in North India and Pakistan, third revised edition 1957, Madras, 1959

INDEX